EUROPE IN 1715
AFTER THE TREATIES OF
UTRECHT, RASTATT AND BADEN

SCALE OF MILES

0 50 100 150 200 250 300

Spanish Territory acquired by Austria

Spanish Territory acquired by Savoy

(Savoy's acquisitions in D. of Milan too small to be shown here.)

Spanish Posessions acquired by England

K.=Kingdom   Elec.=Electorate
D.=Duchy   Grd.D.=Grand Duchy
Rep.=Republic   Pcy.=Principality

THE ERA OF THE
FRENCH REVOLUTION
(1715–1815)

BY

LOUIS R. GOTTSCHALK

Professor of Modern History
University of Chicago

HOUGHTON MIFFLIN COMPANY

The Riverside Press Cambridge

The Riverside Press
CAMBRIDGE · MASSACHUSETTS
PRINTED IN THE U.S.A.

TO

THE MEMORY OF

MY MOTHER

ANNA KRYSTALL GOTTSCHALK

AND

MY BROTHER

JULIUS ABRAHAM GOTTSCHALK

PREFACE

THIS book is intended as a general introduction to the study of European history preceding and during the period of the French Revolution and Napoleon. As such, it has little pretension to being anything more than a presentation of the latest interpretations of that era. The study of the Ancient Régime is based very largely upon the works of Sée and Marion; of the French Revolution to 1795 on Mathiez and Sagnac; of the Napoleonic Period on Pariset, Rose, and Driault. Other works have, of course, been used, though the author makes no claim to having read carefully every one of the books included in the bibliography at the close of this volume. In some matters, indeed, the author has, on the basis of his own study of the original sources, ventured to disagree with the chief secondary authorities. If this present study, however, has any merit at all, it is not in any new interpretations or hypotheses that it sets forth but in its adaptation for American readers of the findings of the best European scholarship.

To a number of American students, the author is likewise greatly indebted. Among the several earlier studies of the field in one-volume compass, he owes much to the works of Professor H. E. Bourne, of Western Reserve University, Dean Shailer Mathews, of the University of Chicago, and the late Professor H. M. Stephens, of the University of California. He has ventured to disagree with them quite frequently in the interpretation of men, motives, and movements, in the organization of materials, and sometimes even upon the facts; but he has always found their volumes helpful and suggestive. To his former teacher, Professor Carl Becker, of Cornell University, the author owes not only his interest in the study of the French Revolution but much of whatever his philosophy of history may be.

Five scholars have examined this work in manuscript.

each criticizing one of the five books. Professor M. B.
Garrett, of the University of North Carolina, looked over
Book I ("The Ancient Régime"); Professor G. G. Andrews,
of the University of Iowa, Book II ("The Fall of the Monarchy"); Professor W. B. Kerr, of the University of Buffalo,
Book III ("The First French Republic"); Professor F. L.
Nussbaum of the University of Wyoming, Book IV ("The
Rise of Napoleon Bonaparte"); and Professor C. P. Higby,
of the University of Wisconsin, Book V ("Defeat and Reaction"). Each of these scholars has made so many correc-
tions and suggestions that if they had been added as footnotes to the text, there would be few pages free of footnotes
and it might have been said of this work, as of a recent outline of universal history, that the footnotes were the most
interesting part of it. To each of these gentlemen the
author wishes to acknowledge his great indebtedness.

Several historical atlases have been drawn upon for the
maps in this volume. The maps of France in 1789 are
based upon similar ones in Schrader's *Atlas de géographie
historique*, the English place-names, the figures for the
salt tax, and other minor details having been adapted from
Shepherd's *Historical Atlas*. Among the other atlases that
have been used are Dow's *Atlas of European History*, *The
Cambridge Modern History Atlas*, Putnam's *Historical Atlas*
and Putzger's *Historischer Schul-Atlas*. The author's
thanks are gratefully given to the editors, publishers, and
printers of these and other atlases from which geographical
data have been borrowed.

This book is based upon the six booklets covering the
same field of history that were published by the author between 1923 and 1925. Much has been added and much has
been revised, however, so that, while parts of it have been
taken wholly from those booklets, the present volume is
largely a new offering.

To Misses Lydia Caldwell, Augusta Schoening, Sara
Landau, Maxine Adelman, and Esther Aphelin, who aided
in the preparation of the manuscript for the press; to his colleagues, Professor Avery O. Craven, who read the sections

dealing with America and helped in the reading of the galley proofs, and Professor Carl F. Huth, who also read part of the galley proof; to Miss Catherine Young, Mr. Ernest L. Hettich, and Dr. Leo Gershoy, who made several helpful suggestions at various stages of the book's progress; and to Mr. C. E. Edgerton, who read the whole of the page proof, the author wishes likewise to express his gratitude.

L. R. G.

CONTENTS

PART I

DISSATISFACTION AND REFORM

Book I. The Ancient Régime

Book II. The Fall of the Monarchy

Book III. The First French Republic

PART II

STABILIZATION AND REACTION

Book I. The Rise of Napoleon Bonaparte

Book II. Defeat and Reaction

MAPS AND CHARTS

THE ERA OF THE FRENCH REVOLUTION
. .
.

PART I
DISSATISFACTION AND REFORM

THE ERA OF
THE FRENCH REVOLUTION

BOOK I

THE ANCIENT RÉGIME

INTRODUCTION

FUNDAMENTALLY revolution means change. The Latin phrase was *novae res* (new things). The French Revolution means, not the popular picture of massacre and guillotine, war and terror, but a series of alterations — social, economic, political — in the European scene. The blood and thunder are perhaps more interesting and (alas!) easier to describe and easier to remember. But they are only the tools of the revolution, changing it, shaping it, cutting out its course; they are not the revolution itself. The *novae res* are to be sought in the differences, spiritual and material, that are discernible in 1815, when (and only for a moment) the Revolution came to a halt, as compared to the state of Europe before 1789 when, roughly speaking, the Revolution began.

This period before 1789 has become generally known as the Ancient or Old Régime (*Ancien Régime*), an era when even contemporaries realized what historians can now more easily perceive — that a change was necessary and more or less inevitable. It is easy to exaggerate the chaos and horror of the Ancient Régime, to say that things were so bad that they could not possibly have become worse and had to become better. It must be remembered, however, that our principal sources of information on the evils of the period are the writings of reformers who depicted with biased pens the viciousness of a system that they detested, and petitions to the King (*cahiers*) that, because of their very nature, listed only the worst features of society and government. From such sources, only a distorted picture can be derived. But it is the distortion that interests us most, for it was the distortion that overcame inertia and brought about revolution. That the inertia was overcome, that an entire nation was moved to depths of popular feeling and bursts of popular action almost unprecedented, make it possible to argue, with Shelley, that misrule and superstition were fetters that ate "with poisonous rust into the soul." Things were very, very bad indeed, even if they were not so bad that they could not possibly have been worse. That was true of all of Europe to a varying degree and not of France alone. If England was better off than France, the Germanies, in some respects, were worse off still. But it was in France, and for reasons that will appear later, that the Revolution began. And it is for the institutions of France during the Ancient Régime that we possess the most complete studies and information.

It has been said that few peoples take as keen delight in intellectual controversy as the French; and few subjects present as much room for controversy as the French Revolution. Hence it is that Aulard and Mathiez disagree today on the relative merits of Danton and Robespierre; that Aulard and Caron once waged, in newspaper articles and books, a fervid disputation upon the value of Taine as a historian; and that Faguet and Roustan, at the dawn of this century, championed the seventeenth and eighteenth centuries respectively and antagonistically. To controversies like these we owe much, both in literature and information; and it is to be hoped that they will continue. At present there seems to be no danger of their abatement. The French Revolution is still a vital issue in France and elsewhere. The correct interpretation of events, the just portrayal of character, the last word cannot be determined yet, if ever at all.

However, in the controversy between Faguet and Roustan, between the age of Louis XIV and the age of Louis XV, scholars to-day seem universally inclined toward the eighteenth century — not perhaps as superior to the earlier era, as Roustan would have had it, but as the immediate and productive cause of the French Revolution. To be sure, there was "a revolutionary spirit before the French Revolution," as Rocquain has made clear; and, to be sure, the reforms to which the Revolution gave birth were conceived and even brought to the point of fruition at an earlier day. But to-day is the result of yesterday; the causes of the French Revolution are to be sought (and can more easily be found) in the years immediately preceding it rather than in remoter times.

CHAPTER I

GOVERNMENT UNDER THE ANCIENT RÉGIME

THERE was no diabolical cunning that had devised the tyrannical, confused government of the French monarchy of the eighteenth century, in order to exploit the peasant and to enable a few privileged aristocrats to live in unproductive luxury. In the course of several eras of development, France had gradually evolved, by the seventeenth century, from medieval anarchy and papal domination into a strongly centralized nation. In this struggle for existence the chief contenders against the younger and more vigorous spirit of Nationalism were the centrifugal forces of feudalism that tended to make of each county and duchy in the realm a separate and sovereign entity, and the centripetal force of the Church that tended to make of all of Europe a holy empire dominated by spiritual princes. By a series of conquests, marriages, treaties, and bequests, the Capetian Kings of France, originally the actual rulers of only the tiny Ile de France with but nominal claims to suzerainty over the lands of the lesser nobility, had subdued the barons and increased their holdings until Louis XV was able to hand down to his successor a realm with boundaries such as France boasts to-day, save for Savoy and Nice and a few anomalous enclaves that still managed to survive under foreign rule. Proportionately, the once independent aristocracy had lost their power and had been subordinated to the point where now they regarded it as the highest honor to act as valets of the Grand Monarch in his glorious palace at Versailles. The Church, too, though still looking to Rome for guidance, had in certain respects become a national organization.

The achievement of these results had required not only internecine strife with Church and barony, but also strong men and, frequently, Machiavellian cunning. The Valois

Louis XI and Francis I, the Bourbon Henry IV and Louis XIII had conquered, stolen, and bought land and allegiance until their more illustrious scion Louis XIV would have been able to say, if he did not actually say, "I am the State!" He was the State. Protestants were made to feel it by the revocation of the toleration that they had thus far enjoyed by the Edict of Nantes, as well as Catholics who, in definite cases, were obliged to recognize the superiority of the State over the Church; peasants who paid heavy taxes and quaked at his august name were made to feel it, as well as nobles who attended his levées and fawned upon him at court. Political feudalism was dead, but its executioner had been forced to devise means and to use weapons that had concentrated its power in his hands; and such power was strength to do evil no less than strength to do good. Feudalism was dead! Long live absolutism!

The nobility had not stood by idly watching the King batten upon their losses. Long and bitter had been the struggle, as the fifteenth century came to an end, before the last stronghold of feudal aristocracy was razed by the defeat of Charles of Burgundy at the hands of Louis XI. The barons tried again and again, by religious wars in the next century, by popular uprisings in the century following (the Fronde), by conspiracies at the dawn of the eighteenth century, to regain their ascendancy over France and France's rulers. But each successive defeat resulted only in the greater glory of the monarch, until not only the sun-king Louis XIV, but even his less brilliant successor, Louis XV, reflecting his splendor, identified himself with the State: "My people are one only with me. National rights and national interests are necessarily combined with my own and rest in my hands alone." But after all, the King was still, in a sense, but the chief of the nobles. One was not born a Montmorency or a Rohan, or of any of the other of the proudest families in France, only to hand him his robe as he stepped from his bath, or to amuse his mistresses' pets. Blue blood was still more worthy than ordinary red blood. Society that was society counted ancestors; and it helped to have sixteen quarterings upon one's coat of arms when army commissions were being distributed, when a lucrative ecclesiastical living was to be awarded, or a governmental sinecure had to be filled. If other things were equal, a noble would receive preferential consideration even when the most responsible ministerial and diplomatic posts were to be filled. But very frequently other things were not equal, and some bourgeois lawyer or low-born financier might take precedence over a descendant of the most renowned line in France when merits and ability entered into consideration. Though important offices were still filled by nobles, who frequently were not the best qualified incumbents for their positions, it had ceased to be true that the nobility alone might serve close to the King. Colbert had sat on the right hand of Louis XIV; Turgot and Necker were to give opinions that were practically orders to Louis XVI.

Tradition demanded, however, that one kind of political office the King must still regard as the preëmpted field of the nobility. From the princes of the blood, dukes, peers, and highest personages of the realm the King still chose the governors-general, lieutenants-general, and lieutenants of the King in the forty provinces of France. These provinces had at one time been practically or entirely independent of the King of France. In the course of hectic centuries they had become incorporated with the French nation, sometimes voluntarily, sometimes involuntarily, but almost always with certain conditions and guarantees expressly stipulated in treaties or charters. These conditions, together with local patriotism and tradition, had served to keep the boundaries between the various provinces distinctly marked. Frenchmen were not exclusively Frenchmen; they were Gascons, Normans, Bretons, as well, and proud of their provincialisms. As their governors, the King needs must, if not by written obligation, at least out of respect for provincial feelings, choose a member of an illustrious family high in the local peerage. Officially the provinces were now known as *gouvernements* (governments), though

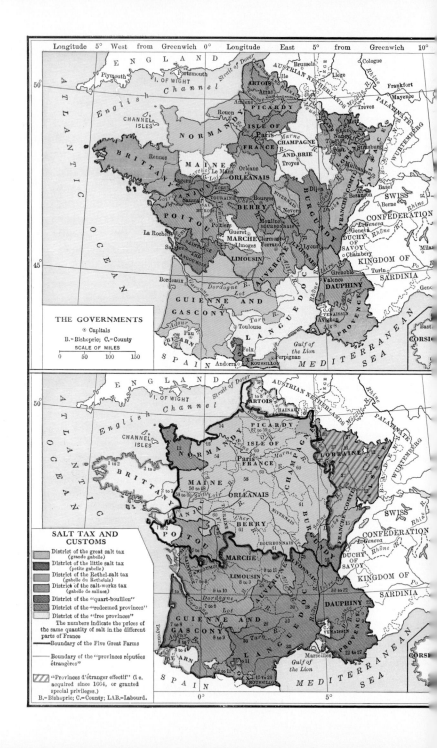

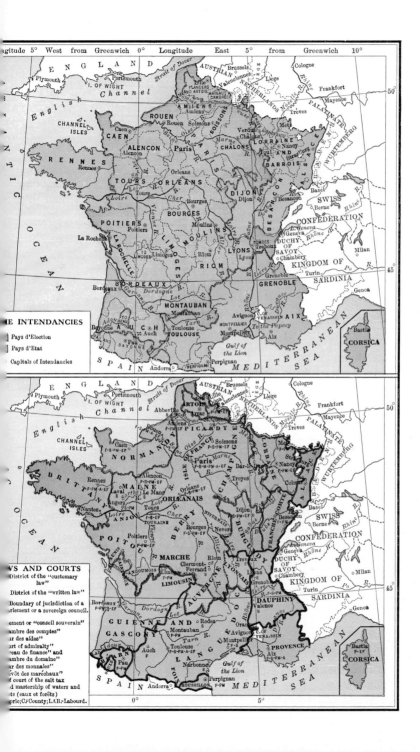

the old names (Artois, Burgundy, Dauphiny, Touraine, Brittany, etc.) still clung. And in the course of time, as step by step the nobility had lost their power and provincialism had become merged with nationalism, the governors-general and their subordinates had become little more than figure-heads. All that now remained to them of the absolutism that had once marred or adorned the annals of Dukes of Normandy, Burgundy, Languedoc were the privileges merely of civil representatives of the army, responsible for the militia, conscription, and administration of the army in their respective jurisdictions.

For all other purposes of administration, Cardinal Richelieu, the man whose work in the seventeenth century had made absolutism in eighteenth-century France possible, had developed a new scheme of local government. Ever since 1542 the Kings of France had appointed certain officers to perform specified duties over definitely assigned territories. These officials were called intendants, and the territories over which they had jurisdiction were called intendancies. Richelieu found a number of intendancies already in existence, ruled over by intendants chosen from the middle class and having boundaries that did frequent violence to the boundary lines of the older provinces. He recognized in the intendants a means of reducing the powers of the governors, and in the intendancies, a weapon against the local prestige of the province. To the intendancies already in existence, he added several new ones and gave to the intendants greater powers than they had hitherto had. His successors followed the precedent thus established.

Except where local pride rendered tampering unwise, the intention of the innovators had been to destroy the integrity of the provinces. In some cases, two provinces or a part of one government and a part of another were joined to make one intendancy. In others, a large province was broken up into more than one intendancy. Geographical considerations were uppermost but since the intendancy was fundamentally an economic division for purposes of taxation, the boundaries were frequently drawn so as to include one metropolis within each intendancy. It was after these large cities that the intendancies were named (Amiens, Bordeaux et Bayonne, Caen, Dijon, Lyons, Paris, etc.). The old boundaries and the traditional names thus were destroyed. Richelieu had met with severe opposition from all the local authorities (Parlements as well as nobles), and civil war under his successor Mazarin for a time checked the development of these intendancies. But, in 1789, all France was divided among thirty-two intendants ruling over thirty-four intendancies (universally, though inaccurately, also called generalities). These thirty-two royal delegates, with some notable exceptions such as the later minister D'Argenson, were almost exclusively chosen from the middle class — practically always from the body of lawyers in the King's Council known as Masters of Petitions (*Maîtres des Requêtes*).

The forebodings of the nobles, who had fought bitterly against the institution of the generalities, proved to have been well grounded. By 1789, the once proud prerogatives of the feudal governors had passed into the hands of the bourgeois intendants. Local affairs were entirely under their control. On occasion, their jurisdiction might overlap the governor's or the local assembly's and conflict might arise that would require a higher authority to settle. D'Argenson spoke scathingly on occasion of the Governor of Hainaut with whom he had to contend. But inside his intendancy the intendant generally was supreme. He might decide whether to assume the responsibility of a decision himself or to send his problems on to Versailles for solution, but every activity, whether it was as trivial as the patching of a church roof or as important as the building of a new highway, was submitted for his approval; and it may be assumed that the ministers at the capital were none too censorious if he acted without disturbing them too frequently. "The Thirty Tyrants" they were called; and the slight arithmetical error may easily be overlooked in view of the appositeness of the phrase.

In each generality were a number of sub-intendants, or sub-delegates, appointed by the King through the intendant. Sometimes the sub-delegate ruled over a subdivision of the generality, but most frequently he was simply an agent of the intendant, with power to perform only the tasks assigned to him by his master. In the larger towns (except Paris and Lyons) there were mayors, chosen by the King or some powerful noble or by the notables of the municipality. In Paris and Lyons the chief municipal officer was a Prevost of the Merchants (*Prévôt des Marchands*), chosen, in Lyons, directly by the King; in Paris, on the 16th of August of every other year, regularly designated notables of the city would gather at the City Hall for the purpose of electing a prevost. They would listen to a letter from the King and then cast their ballots. Almost invariably it would be found that the gentleman elected was one carefully named in the King's letter. Then, as the populace was admitted to watch, the notables sat themselves down to a grand repast. In the country districts, the old town assemblies still continued to meet.[1] In the large cities, too, the guilds, though reduced in number and stripped of the power that, at one time, had made them the commercial, social, and political arbiters of municipal affairs, yet retained important prerogatives in the regulation of trade. Furthermore, some of the provinces still had their local legislatures or estates. Intendants and sub-intendants were thus the representatives of the King, newly created allies in the struggle against feudal aristocracy; governors, guilds, town councils, syndics, local estates, and frequently mayors were survivals of a more remote age when barons were sovereigns and cities were newly chartered corporations. The representatives of the new order frequently clashed with the representatives of the old order, and since their respective jurisdictions were not clearly marked, the struggles were sometimes difficult to

---

[1] For purposes of administration and taxation, they elected a syndic, though frequently syndics might be chosen in other ways. A syndic might also be elected by other municipalities and corporations.

adjust. Always, however, there was the King's Council to appeal to, and the intendants were the appointees of the King — that is to say, of the King's Council. The absolutism of the King thus prevented a deadlock in the conflicting machinery of the State, and was frequently a blessing, though in almost impenetrable disguise.

The King himself might, if he wished, manage all the affairs of State. Louis XIV had taken the business of kingship seriously; Louis XVI would have liked to emulate his example. But the Louis who reigned between them found himself too busily engaged in the more interesting things of life to devote too much attention to governmental matters. Consequently, during his reign, it was only when he became sufficiently concerned for personal or other motives that he took an active part in the deliberations of ministers and councils. In that way, though at any time the King might veto their decisions or take any action contrary to their advice, though he might dismiss or even imprison them singly or collectively, the King's Council had become the actual rulers of France. But nothing could be done without the sanction of the monarch; on less important affairs, the King generally followed the recommendations of the Council, and on more important subjects, the Council generally was careful to agree with the King.

This Royal Council or King's Council (*Conseil du Roi* or *Conseil d'État*) was a body, varying in size from time to time, appointed by the King from among any of his subjects. Once it had had certain judicial powers, but at the end of the fifteenth century, Charles VIII had created a Grand Council (*Grand Conseil*) which, ever since, had taken over these judicial prerogatives. Now the King's Council was the highest administrative body in the State, subject only to the King himself. It was made up of five special Councils.[1] The functions of the various councils were not

---

[1] The Council of State (*Conseil d'État* or, to distinguish it from the King's Council, *Conseil d'en Haut*) was especially entrusted with the conduct of foreign affairs, though it sometimes decided upon internal policies, too. The Council of Despatches (*Conseil des Dépêches*), under the guidance of the Controller-General of Finances, concerned itself primarily with internal ad-

all distinct or carefully defined, and were left very largely to chance. In general, they legislated and administered in the King's name. The Privy Council, besides, seems to have been a training school for the other Councils. All of them gave advice. In addition to the Royal Councils, there was a Committee or Council of War, created in 1787, and a number of *bureaux*, whose business it was to prepare information for the Councillors and to settle matters that might be considered too trivial to refer to the Councils. Thus a meticulous intendant might submit an unimportant question, which had in turn been submitted to him by a cautious sub-intendant, to the authorities at Versailles, where it might be settled by some *bureau* or some Councilor of State, or come up before some Council[1] or eventually be submitted to the King himself.

A good king like Henry IV, who was really interested in state affairs, or a fatuous king like Louis XIV, who loved to meddle in governmental matters, might thus give most of his days to politics. Even Louis XV managed to spare enough time from his mistresses and amusements to attend the meetings of at least three councils quite regularly. Actually, however, it had become the practice for the Controller-General of Finances (since money was the prime necessity of the State) to act as the chief executive authority, taking precedence even over the Chancellor. He was a member of four councils and the Chancellor of only three. It thus devolved upon him to assure a certain degree of uniformity in governmental policy and to keep the various departments from entangling each other hopelessly in bureaucratic red-tape. When entanglements did

ministration. The Council of Finance (*Conseil des Finances*) and the Council of Commerce (*Conseil de Commerce*) acted under the Chancellor and the Controller-General as the chief financial and commercial authorities of the State. The largest Council, made up in 1789 of forty-two so-called Councillors of State, several intendants of finances, and eighty lawyers known as *Maîtres des Requêtes* (Masters of Petitions), assisted by a host of lawyers and minor officials, was called the Privy Council or Council of Parties (*Conseil Privé* or *Conseil des Parties*). Its duties were chiefly judicial.

[1] If it was the Privy Council, the intendant might himself be present, since intendants were always chosen from among the *maîtres des requêtes*.

occur, there was always the absolute power of the King to cut the knots. The administrative branch of the government of France thus revealed the weaknesses of its growth. New office after new office had been created to weaken the old, but the weakened old ones remained as the vigorous new ones multiplied, and the increasing absolutism of the King, which was the result of the weakening of the one and the vigor of the other, sufficed to keep them all working, well enough, at least, to prevent atrophy.

What was true of the administration of France was likewise true of the judicial department. Here, too, there was a jumbled disorganization saved from utter bewilderment only by the arbitrary power of the King. The various organizations within the State that had now become subjugated to the royal authority still retained some vestiges of their once sovereign judicial powers. The Church, which once had claimed the right to try all clergymen, widows, and orphans, and all cases committed on church lands or involving sin, still tried cases of a specified nature, limited now, however, almost exclusively to the offenses of the higher clergy. Blasphemy and sacrilege still were severely punished by lay judges. In 1766, because he had refused to remove his hat and had shouted insultingly at a passing church procession, a lad named La Barre was sentenced to have his tongue torn out, to be hanged, and his body to be burned. The feudal aristocracy likewise retained their manorial courts, trying their serfs and the neighboring peasantry, generally only for minor offenses. The seigneurial judges frequently tended to be partial in the interest of the lords who paid them and were not above accepting bribes openly; and since court procedure was irregular and changing, justice was a variable quantity.

Then there was a galaxy of royal courts — in all, eighteen courts of extraordinary jurisdiction and five of regular jurisdiction.[1] At the head of all these courts, empowered

---

[1] There were military and admiralty courts with jurisdiction over the army and navy. There were courts which took cognizance only of certain taxes — e.g., the *tribunal des élections*, the *cour des aides*, the chief court of the salt tax, the grand mastership of waters and forests. There was also a fairly centralized

to hear appeals from lower benches and to act as the supreme judicial authority of the realm, were the *parlements*. The Parlement of Paris was the most important of these, having in central France appellate jurisdiction over a greater territory than any other and enjoying the prestige that a more illustrious personnel (the Peers of France were members) and a more illustrious tradition lent. For the rest of France there were twelve other parlements, in theory equal in authority with the Parlement of Paris, situated approximately in the twelve largest provincial cities. The Grand Council was sometimes empowered to try cases in which it was feared the parlements would be partial. In all of the courts of the realm torture was considered one of the most effective ways of securing testimony, until it was abolished by a decree of Louis XVI.

Through this labyrinth of legal mazes, there was one power that held out a hope of exit. Justice, like administrative authority, emanated from the King. He could decide any case in any manner he wished, imprison whom he wished, pardon whom he wished. In the last two centuries of the monarchy the practice had grown up of arbitrary arrest by sealed letters (*lettres de cachet*). These letters might order the police to arrest and imprison any subject of the King. In origin, a *lettre de cachet* or *lettre close* was a secret order for the welfare of the realm. They had remained secret, but now, very frequently, the personal interest of the ruler or of one who was close to the ruler's ear was substituted for the welfare of the realm. Political opponents of the King's favorites, writers who had attacked the Church, Bretons who had been too importunate in their petitions, members of a recalcitrant parlement — any one who in any way had incurred the royal disfavor directly or indirectly might at any time find himself, without trial, in the Bastille, or Vincennes, or the Conciergerie, or any of the

system of police courts, presided over in the provinces by royal agents, generally called bailiffs (*baillis*) in the north and seneschals (*sénéchaux*) in the south, who at one time had had considerable powers that were now reduced to minor matters, including the privilege of hearing lesser cases at law. In Paris, the police powers were vested in a formidable court known as the Châtelet.

old fortresses now used as prisons, for any reason or for no reason at all, without knowing why, on whose accusation, or for how long. Altogether too frequently the *lettre de cachet* was an instrument of the private hate of the King or the King's favorite or the King's favorite's favorite. Yet often the ones imprisoned were rightfully restrained by a speedier process than the overlapping system of courts would have permitted; and while horrible stories of what went on behind the stone walls and iron bars were current and a certain Latude became the hero of France because he told a highly imaginative story about his long confinement in the Bastille, nevertheless, the prisons of France were reflective of an age rather than a system — an age during which, even in enlightened England, petty theft was punished with death, hangings were gala spectacles, prisons were meant for cruel punishment rather than for detention and reform, and strong men died of broken backs or broken hearts in galleys. A *lettre de cachet* sent Voltaire to jail for a street brawl, Diderot for political radicalism, Mirabeau at his father's instigation to keep him out of mischief. Quite often, as in the latter case, the *lettre de cachet* was used as a means of preserving the honor of a highly respected family. Prisoners by *lettre de cachet* were almost always better treated than others, being permitted sometimes to bring in their servants and even, by special arrangement, to have their meals out. Nevertheless, they were not free men or women. Thus, the *lettre de cachet*, together with the full power of pardon, gave the King complete control over the criminal proceedings of France's courts.

He likewise held in his hands the power to quash any litigations going on at any time, whether civil or criminal. By the right of *committimus*, not only the King, but a number of notables throughout the realm might demand that civil trials begun in one court be transferred to any other court they preferred. In civil cases the writ of *committimus* was thus of frequent advantage to the wealthy and aristocratic. At any rate, the gentleman with influence at court could always carry his case to the Grand Council or the

Royal Council or the King, since the King was the court of last resort in the realm. But if Justice faltered because ultimately entrusted to a single human being who often was more than frail, it must be remembered that the court system of France was not the devilish invention of tyrants. Like the administrative system of France it had grown up gradually, in the course of centuries. The absolutism of the King was not only a weapon against the centrifugal tendencies of feudal and clerical courts and of thirteen parlements, it was likewise the only means of keeping some kind of order in a conflicting, anarchic hierarchy. It was not without significance that when the nobles rose up against Mazarin and Anne of Austria in the War of the Fronde (1648), one of their demands was for the grant of greater power to the parlements.

Anarchy in the judicial organization of France was intensely aggravated by an archaic system of law and legislation. For the peasant of France, daily behavior, which consisted principally in fulfilling prescribed obligations to a seigneur, was regulated by a series of traditions and contracts. These feudal obligations, whenever they did not depend upon the whimsical interpretation of what was and what was not the custom, were written down in a series of agreements (*aveux*) and more or less carefully filed away in the manorial rolls (*terriers*). Some of them were so ancient that they called for payments in kind that no longer was produced in the neighborhood or for rentals on types of capital that no longer existed. But they had been legal obligations entered into by the peasant's forbears or by the peasant himself; they were renewed periodically (generally every twenty years) and they were still the law. The interpretation of them was left to the manorial court, held at the château, frequently under the eye of the lord himself or the lord's bailiff; and the lawyer who specialized in their expounding (*commissaire à terrier*) was generally the paid henchman of the seigneur. The *aveux* differed in various parts of the country. Custom required certain payments in one region that would be regarded as extraordinary in another. This was an additional respect in which France was not yet a unit.

The same held true even for the common law. The two chief systems of law in France reflected the history of the national development of the country. Southern France had been the first to be conquered by the Romans; there they had entrenched themselves most steadfastly and there Roman influence remained predominant even after the Roman world had crumbled. Southern France (the *Midi*) accepted as its law the survivals, revivals, and perversions which still passed as the Roman codes. But in the north, where the Franks had first penetrated and where the Gallo-Roman element of the population had most effectively been subjugated, customary law, the law of the primitive Germans, amalgamated with the laws of an age of feudalism and an age of chivalry, and tempered with current practices and customs, had become the common code. Thus it was conceivable that a malpractice in one quarter of France might be unknown to the law in another; what was a crime in Limoges might be considered as no offense at all in Poitiers, about seventy-five miles away. Voltaire complained that a man traveling in France changed his laws almost as often as he changed his post-horses and that there were twenty-six differing commentaries on the customs of Paris alone.

Once more the intricacies and complications that migh, have resulted from badly demarcated and sadly overlappin₊ jurisdictions were obviated by the omnipotent royal prerogative. The abracadabra of French legislative prestidigitation that made all things go was: *cy veult le roy, cy veult la loi.* The King's wish was law. The principle was founded in fact and philosophy. Jean Bodin, who in the sixteenth century had assigned to the sovereign "the supreme power over citizens and subjects, unrestrained by the laws," had likewise assigned to sovereignty, as its chief function, the creation of the laws of the State; and Bishop Bossuet, advisor of Louis XIV and preceptor of Louis XV, had added to all of this magnificence the majesty of divine inspiration and sacrosanctity: "Kings should be regarded as holy things." If new laws were needed, if new taxes had to be levied, if an army was to be raised, if some new menace to morality or religion required legislation, if treaties were to be made or war declared, the King issued a royal decree, more or less to the point, and immediately it became the law of the land — part of the only body of law that was registered in all the parlements of the State and observed in all parts of France. Once upon a time, in the forgotten centuries between the reign of the Fair Philip and the regency of the unfair Marie de Medici, there had been a body representing the people of France. Since it met by estates (clergy, nobility, commoners), it was called the Estates General. It had advised the King and assisted, as far as he would permit, in legislation. In cases where the kings were not too self-willed, it had sometimes succeeded in getting its advice accepted. But in February, 1615, Marie de Medici decided that the hall in which the Estates of 1614 met was needed for a dance; and so they were dismissed, not to be convened again for almost one hundred and seventy-five years. During those one hundred and seventy-five years came Richelieu, Louis XIV, and Louis XV, who managed quite well without them; and Louis XVI lived to regret the day that he decided to revive them.

In the interval between 1614 and 1789, though there remained no power with which the King had to share his legislative authority, it nevertheless did not go uncontested. The line that separates judicial procedure from legislation is a very thin one at best. In France during the eighteenth century, when Montesquieu's and Bolingbroke's tripartite division of government into legislative, judicial, and executive was still novel and strange, it hardly existed at all. But even in earlier times, the parlements had had to know what the law was, what the King's latest decrees enjoined. Sometimes they found that the King's decree of yesterday contravened a decree of the day or the year before. It was necessary to inform His Majesty and to receive new instructions. In the course of time, along with information

there began to go words of petition or advice. Eventually the parlements took the stand that unless a royal decree was registered with them, it was not law within their jurisdictions; and in the seventeenth and eighteenth centuries, in the course of several popular struggles against the King, the Parlement of Paris had even found the courage to refuse to register certain unpopular decrees. Had it succeeded in its championing of the democratic cause, it might eventually have established its right to veto the King's ordinances. But the kings found a way to abash them. They held what were known as *lits de justice* (beds of justice), punctilious sessions of the court, at which the King himself presided, surrounded by the most illustrious personages of the nation, all meticulously dressed and posed in accordance with a traditional ritual. There, in august tones, His Majesty, as the fount of all justice, ordered the enregisterment of his decrees, and generally the parlement acquiesced. An unbending resistance on the part of the judges might occasion the King to yield, but was more likely to lead to the exile or imprisonment of the members of parlement by *lettres de cachet*, and the appointment of more amenable substitutes. Opposition to the King's decrees was thus not often effective; whenever it was, it was because the people, looking upon the parlement as their champions against the tyranny of the King, were sufficiently roused to make it inadvisable for the King to be too insistent. It must be said, however, that occasionally parlement, jealous of its prerogatives, refused to register decrees, such as some of Turgot's, that were of definite benefit to the people; in such cases the *lits de justice* were the instruments of democracy. But sometimes, out of pure inertia, sometimes out of consideration for the expense involved, the refusal of the parlement to register was permitted by an indifferent king to remain unanswered. Thus, the Parlement of Paris (and sometimes the provincial parlements) had acquired the power to veto the decrees of a none the less absolute monarch. In the end, the Kings of France were to find that government — even absolute government — rests upon the consent of the governed if the governed ever become agitated enough to act.

One way of rousing public dissatisfaction that all the Kings of France had been careful to avoid was to abolish local privileges and provincial institutions such as were had by the more recently acquired territories when they became part of France. Just as the governors were allowed to remain, though their powers were gradually taken away from them, so in the newly added provinces of France the provincial estates were permitted to remain and to dwindle away to insignificance. Local estates that had once had the right to pass upon all legislation within their provinces now preserved only the right to share in the apportionment and collection of their quotas of the direct taxes and to petition the crown — not altogether empty privileges in a day when direct taxes were apportioned on the principle of all-the-traffic-will-bear and when a peevish king might throw into the Bastille a too insistent petitioner. The provinces that still retained their provincial estates were known as *pays d'état*. In theory they could not be taxed, but, like the clergy, gave "free gifts" to the crown. There were only eleven of them, situated (like Artois, Brittany, Provence) in the outlying quarters of France farthest away from the capital.[1] Though the provincial estates were frequently centers of inefficiency and strongholds of privilege, they were regarded as favored institutions. An effort was made, shortly before the Revolution broke out, to destroy this obvious inequality among the provinces by granting to each an assembly vested with significant powers. In 1787 several such assemblies actually were created. But it was too late. The Revolution, with its insistence upon *equality*, was to level out the differences in the various sections of France much more thoroughly.

[1] The other provinces, centering around Paris, were known as *pays d'élection*, for within their boundaries the functions of government had once been carried on entirely through appointees (*élus*) of the King. The office of *élu*, or special deputy of the King, had been suppressed in 1625, but the courts over which they had presided (*tribunaux d'élection*) still survived and the provinces in which these courts existed and in which the intendant was the absolute financial authority received the name of *pays d'élection*.

Even a bad government can maintain itself if it has prestige, age, and wealth to support it. But not even a good government can maintain itself, despite its age and its prestige, if it does not have money. The government of France in the eighteenth century was not only not a good government, but it was becoming poverty-stricken. This was partially due (as we shall soon see) to the recklessness with which it spent its revenue, but it was also due to the stupid ways in which it raised its money. The pocket nerve of the eighteenth-century Frenchman was no more sensitive than that of others. The system of taxation which he had to endure, however, affected not only that delicate instrument, but also equally quick spots. Class privilege, local tradition, family pride, individual honor were likewise sorely exposed in a society which had come to look upon taxation as a sort of penalty for the offense of having been born in the wrong caste or in the wrong locality. Though in more modern times, additional and sometimes more burdensome taxes have been devised, the method of impost employed in the eighteenth-century France was not only a greater drain upon the budget of the individuals and a greater barrier to the free development of the businesses that could least afford such drains and barriers, but was generally regarded as a social stigma besides.

Taxes are of two kinds — direct and indirect. Direct taxes are taxes paid as such on specified articles. France in the Ancient Régime paid several direct taxes. There was a property tax, known as the *taille*. For the land tax (*taille réelle*), land was divided into two classes, noble land and common land. Noble land paid no taxes; common land, even though now owned by a noble, paid the *taille réelle*. Thus the burden of the land tax fell upon the class that could least afford it — the poor peasant landowner who had just enough to support himself and no more. There was also a *taille personnelle*, levied on the ability of the tax-payer to pay, arbitrarily estimated by the tax collector. Here, too, there were a great number of privileged classes and individuals exempted from the obligation to pay. In

addition, there was a tax on incomes, known as the *vingtième,* originally a twentieth of the subject's income, but now more nearly eleven per cent.[1] Again the upper classes secured the privilege of exemption, but it was the bourgeois rather than the peasant who paid it, since his income was larger. Then there was a poll tax (*capitation*), paid by every individual just for being. Here the nobility were not altogether immune, for all French society was divided into twenty-two classes, theoretically according to their ability to pay; and among these classes were to be found several ranks of the nobility. In theory, the Church could not be taxed at all inside of France. At times the clergy would decide to give to the King what they chose to call a free gift (*don gratuit*), though the sum was fixed by the King's officers; but it almost always made him pay for it by some concession or other, whether it was the suppression of some obnoxious book or the imprisonment of some troublesome reformer. It sometimes happened, too, that a grateful king might give to the Church a sum of money in return that was larger than he had received. *Taille, vingtième,* and *capitation* varied not only among classes, but even in districts, and sometimes, though called by the same name, were assessed upon different values.

Furthermore, there were tariff duties (*traites* or *douanes*) of various kinds. Not only were imports taxed, but certain exports had likewise to pay duty before they might leave the country. Certain articles, indeed, were not allowed to be sent to England at all until more favorable trade arrangements were made in 1786 by the commercial treaty of Eden. Even more burdensome than the restrictions upon international trade, however, were the tariffs upon goods crossing the boundaries between provinces or entering city walls (*octrois*). The *octroi* was especially onerous since it raised the price of agricultural products without bringing any greater profits to the producer or the merchant

---

[1] Originally it had been a *dixième* (a tenth); now, though it was considerably lower, there were sometimes as many as three *vingtièmes* collected at the same time.

and at the same time made it more difficult for the poor city-dweller to buy his food. Finally, there still survived a tax payable in labor. The Government demanded of the peasant the royal *corvée*. (There was also a *corvée* due the seigneur that we shall consider later.) Introduced in the eighteenth century, this personal obligation to do the bidding of the Government, generally for twelve days of the year, consisted in practice of only two tasks. The peasant might be called upon to work upon the public highways or he might be asked to help transport soldiers. For such labors he received considerably less than the current wages and frequently much abuse from the overseers or the soldiers, who were themselves perhaps unfortunate peasant lads who had "volunteered" after an all night carouse or, if in the militia, had been drafted.

Means of avoiding some of these taxes were easily devised. The peasants sometimes permitted their lands and houses to appear dilapidated and impoverished in order to reduce the assessment. Rousseau, forced one day to request food at a peasant's hut, was given only dry bread and skimmed milk, until his host, assured that he was not a tax spy, produced eggs, ham, and wine. But what one peasant saved in taxes, another had to pay. For the quotas were fixed and had to be raised even if a garrison (generally one brutal dragoon) had to be quartered upon the peasant to collect it. To get around the *traites* and *octrois*, smuggling was resorted to and often scientifically perfected. Children, trained by their parents, were the best for internal smuggling, but illicit traffic in and out of France was a man's job. Penalties were very severe, and the prisons and galleys were not allowed to remain empty even of children.

Various attempts to effect some reform in the system of taxation had been made by the few reforming ministers that France had had — Sully, Richelieu, Mazarin, and Colbert. Of these the most successful was the last. He had found the provinces nearest Paris, which profited more by free trade with the metropolis than by the right to tax goods coming from it, united in a sort of tariff union. This union he now named the Five Great Farms (*Cinq Grosses Fermes*) from the fact that a working agreement, continued in the tariff of 1664, was reached for this *zollverein* with regard to five important taxes or farms. But Colbert was able to get only twelve of the centrally located provinces to join his tariff-union.[1] In the end, Colbert succeeded only in alienating the affections of his fellow subjects and in making matters more complicated. Further reforms had to await Turgot, Necker, and the Revolution.

In the mean time, crude methods of collecting the direct taxes continued to be employed. The *corvée* was demanded as needed. The tariff duties were levied as goods actually passed the boundaries. But the manner of collecting the *capitation, vingtième,* and *taille* was even more vicious than the taxes themselves. Generally (although this was particularly true of the *taille*) the sum to be raised for the nation was fixed by the King's Council and distributed — not necessarily proportionally, for the *pays d'état* always took advantage of their privilege to assist in determining their quotas — among all of the generalities. The intendants in charge of the generalities distributed their quotas among the city and rural parishes. In the parishes, the syndic was responsible for collecting the parish quota. He generally had, to help him, a committee of collectors chosen by the village or parish. These collectors and the syndic were made personally responsible for their community's share of the taxes. Until the reforms of Turgot, if they failed to acquire the requisite amount, they could be obliged to make good the deficit themselves or go to prison. Sometimes local magnates were ruined in this way, but sometimes, too, they ended richer than they had begun, because they were permitted to collect a surplus for their labors wherever they could. A syndic with influence at court might, moreover, get the quota for his town reduced at the expense of

---

[1] Those that remained outside had to be considered practically foreign and were so called (*provinces réputées étrangères*), and provinces that had been acquired since 1664 were actually foreign (*provinces d'étranger effectif*) as far as the tariff of 1664 was concerned.

some less fortunate parish and thereby decrease his own risk and increase his profits. But as a general rule, what one subject saved in direct taxes another subject had to pay; and the collectors, fearful of their own pockets and freedom, would squeeze the peasants dry if necessary.

In addition to the direct taxes, there were a number of indirect taxes, by which the French Government raised its revenue. An indirect tax is a tax paid upon a given commodity by the consumer as part of its price. There were several such indirect taxes levied in France during the Ancient Régime.[1] They were a great inconvenience, since they raised the prices of the taxable products and interfered unreasonably in their traffic. But the most burdensome of them was the tax on salt. In the time of Louis XIV France had been divided quite arbitrarily into three distinct districts for the purpose of collecting the salt tax (gabelle).[1] Other divisions had been made since that time, so that in 1789 there were seven distinct regions for which different regulations with regard to the salt tax prevailed. Thus in one district of France, say Brittany, the purchaser would pay only what the salt was actually worth, while in another, perhaps contiguous to it, say Anjou or Maine or Normandy, he might have to pay fifty or sixty times as much. The law required that every man, woman, and child over seven must buy seven pounds of salt a year, which was a reasonable amount for districts where the price was reasonable (the average Frenchman to-day, who is notoriously sparing in his use of salt, uses nine pounds a year), but was exorbitant for the districts where high taxation would have urged economy. The gabelle soon became, next to the taille, the most profitable tax to the Government. Smuggling from the free-salt districts into the high salt-tax districts was very profitable and, despite the danger of detection, quite prevalent.

[1] Most of these were on Government monopolies, such as salt (gabelle), tobacco and snuff (tabac), wines and ciders (aides).

[1] There was the pays de franc-salé, where no salt tax was collected at all; the pays de petites gabelles, where the salt tax was comparatively little; and the pays de grandes gabelles, where the salt tax was excessively large.

The indirect taxes, if systematically collected, would have been a source of tremendous wealth for an impecunious government. But the Government sold the right to collect such taxes for a lump sum to the highest bidder.[1] The individuals who received the contract became known as Farmers-General.[2]

Corruption, venality, greed, extravagance, dishonesty, even among the highest officials, was rampant. Louis XIV had Fouquet, Minister of Finances, arrested for embezzlement; Turgot and Necker, in turn, tried various reforms. But even the power of the King, absolute here as elsewhere and exercised at times through very capable and patriotic Controllers-General of Finances, accomplished no important changes. New taxes were invented and old ones repealed. New syndics, intendants, and ministers replaced the old. Remedies were attempted and, at too rare intervals, economy practiced. But until the Revolution the system remained practically intact, to rouse the people against the Government and to impoverish the Government to the point where it had to yield to the people. Despite the edifice of absolutism that they had inherited, Louis XV by his indifference, Louis XVI by his weakness had permitted the strength of the central power to wane. Though, in appearance, there was an all-powerful will imposing itself upon every phase of the Government and every square foot of the land, upon closer examination, France is found on the eve of the Revolution to be in danger of anarchy, for the administration has developed through the concentration of powers in the hands

[1] There were five great "farms" of indirect taxes, including the *traites* (tariff duties) and the *domaines* (rents and dues from the royal lands), which were actually direct taxes; and there were a number of smaller "farms." Farms were restricted not only in the kind of tax collected, but also in geographical extent. There were sixty of them until the time of Necker, who reduced their number to forty. Each farm was contracted for by bid every six years.

[2] Some of France's leading citizens, such as the famous chemist Lavoisier, held such office. But in the eyes of the taxpayers, publicans were classed with sinners. For, having paid a handsome price for the right to farm the taxes, the farmers set about to regain not only that handsome price, but a handsome profit besides. In general, they collected as much as they could, employing the majesty of the King's name and the good right arms of the King's police whenever necessary. They thus became, at the same time, the most influential and the most hated of the French moneyed classes.

of strong men, and now the powers remain concentrated though the strong men have disappeared. And in the mean time, the middle class clamors for a greater share in the government, while the lower classes cry for an improvement in their lot. An alliance of the monarch with these classes had subdued the Church and subjected the nobles. It remained to be seen whether the King could now keep himself at the head of that alliance.

CHAPTER II

SOCIETY UNDER THE ANCIENT RÉGIME

THE consummation of absolutism in France during the seventeenth and eighteenth centuries had dealt a deathblow to political feudalism. The nobility now were royal servants in governmental matters, distinctly subordinate to the King, and no longer able to take refuge in inland castles and the loyalty of local swains. But feudalism was a hydra-like monster; the lopping-off of the head that had typified political feudalism meant the rapid and vigorous growth of another that typified economic feudalism. There still were hundreds of peasants in various stages of servitude upon the estates of the nobles of France. These owed to their landlords a number of obligations which had some money or labor value; and these obligations were the basis of a kind of feudalism which, though in earlier centuries it had its importance, now, with the disappearance of the local independence of the nobility, had come to occupy a more conspicuous part in the social structure of the country.

That it was more conspicuous now both in the minds of the lord and the peasant, the reformer and the conservative, it is easy to agree. Whether, however, there was an increasing burden upon the peasants, whether the lords were more aggressive in their demands than ever before — these are moot points. In general the best authorities agree that during the eighteenth century there was a "feudal reaction." Their argument is that during the course of the eighteenth century there had been considerable progress in the agricultural sciences. This was particularly true of England, where, to aggravate the situation, there was also the conversion of large tracts of land from food-growing to wool-raising, from farm to sheep pasture. But it was true of land everywhere that it was becoming more profitable and hence more in demand. To the landlords, then, it seemed only fair that their rents should yield a larger sum than ever before. Hence they revived old dues that had long been forgotten, hunted among crackling parchments in dusty manor rolls for old titles that had long been in abeyance, neglected no right and no contract that in former generations had been permitted to stand as dead-letters, demanded more frequent acknowledgments of obligations from their tenants and the more exact fulfillment of each of them, and put enclosures around their estates as rapidly as they could.

The opponents of this theory of "feudal reaction" (Professor Aulard is a conspicuous example) point to the number of peasants who were beginning to buy their own lands and become proprietors. This number increased steadily during the eighteenth century in France, which seems to indicate that instead of a reaction toward economic feudalism there was a constant movement away from it in France. This school does not deny that there was a growing dissatisfaction with feudal privilege during this period, but they attribute it not to the increased harshness of the system but to greater class consciousness on the part of the peasants, nursed by the constant agitation of political writers, especially the group known as "Economists." The only definite answer to the problem that can be made (and it is answer enough for our purposes) is that, whether they were actually being treated better or worse than peasants in previous generations, the peasants of the Ancient Régime found their lot more irksome than their predecessors. Even if better off than his ancestors had been, the French peasant, as a general rule, was not content. English travelers in France, like Arthur Young, a leading agricultural expert of his time, were shocked at the misery they saw in some sections of the country, and French travelers in England were impressed with the atmosphere of comparative prosperity. But if the lot of the French peasant was worse than that of the yeoman of England, there were corners of the Holy Roman Empire, Poland, and Russia, where French and English travelers seldom went, where the serfs might have envied the happiness of their French fellows. On the Continent, at least, it is probable that the French peasants were better off — at any rate, until the reforms of enlightened rulers made their Prussian and Austrian brothers equally prosperous.

For one thing, serfdom was a disappearing institution in France during the eighteenth century. Once upon a time, the words "peasant" and "serf" had been practically synonymous. All farmers were serfs, working for their masters a certain number of days (generally three) of the week and receiving as wages the usufruct of a piece of land which they were permitted to work for themselves the rest of the week. Fundamentally serfdom was a sound economic institution for an agricultural society that did not know the use of money on a large scale and the possibilities of credit. The work that the peasant did for his lord might be regarded as a sort of rent that he paid for his land, or the usufruct of the land that he received might be regarded as a sort of wage for the work he did for his lord. In either case, the land would have been almost valueless without the labor that the serf contributed and the serf would have starved to death without the land that the lord contributed. The serf, then, was not a slave. He was in a sense a paid laborer, though his work was prescribed and though he had certain obligations for which he received no pay in land or otherwise. Furthermore, there was nothing personal in the relationship of serf to master; the serf was bound to the land and not to his lord. To have taken him away from his land would have meant that the land would have remained idle and that he himself would have had no means of livelihood. Hence, every time the land changed owners the serf went along with it. He was an essential part of the soil and the soil of him. Subject to certain obligations and restrictions, understood or written down in the manor records, varying for various regions and even for individual serfs on the same estate, he was free to do as he pleased with the time that was his own and to move about freely. He might even cease to be a serf by going away to a free city and staying for a stipulated length of time, generally a year and a day; and it would be only in times of great demand for agricultural labor that vigorous efforts would be made to bring him back. In the eighteenth century, the courts were usually on his side in such a case.

A great many serfs secured their freedom thus, simply by running away from serfdom. But serfdom in modern times was declining more rapidly for another reason. New economic methods — cash, banking, credit — had come into existence. Landlords found it desirable to pay wages in money rather than in land; tenants found it desirable to pay rents in money rather than in kind or labor; a great many of them found it possible to purchase their freedom and lands. In general in fertile regions, it was found more profitable for the lord to free his serfs and then to hire them as laborers. But in the less fertile regions, where the laborer had to remain bound to the soil if he were to stay, serfdom still survived. The number of serfs there were in France in the last century before the Revolution is doubtful. Contemporary estimates varied from as few as 140,000 to as many as 1,500,000; and historians disagree by an equal margin. The most expert opinion, however, seems to be in favor of the lower figures. Marion says 140,000; Sée, 1,000,000; and Aulard contents himself with "thousands and thousands." These serfs were known as *mainmortables*, because the bond of *mainmorte* (mortmain) was still their severest obligation: they could leave their property only to their children living with them. In general the *mainmortables* were the least enterprising as well as the most unfortunate of the peasants. But there is some truth in the remark that whether a man was a serf or a free peasant was of more consequence to his heirs than to himself.

Among the serfs who had won or bought or been granted their freedom, there was little tendency to drift toward the cities. For the most part, they stayed at home, working the same lands that they or their ancestors before them had worked as serfs. Many of them, by the eighteenth century, had become free agricultural laborers, employed, like our farm-hands, all of the time by a master and receiving wages in cash. Others had become free tenants, renting a piece of land from a lord, working upon it all of the week and paying for it in money rents or in kind. Most of them had become *métayers*, who, like our share-croppers, farmed a piece of land for a stipulated portion (generally half) of the harvest. According to Arthur Young's probably excessive estimate, seven eighths of the tillable land of France was under *métayers*. Some, and their numbers seem to have increased steadily during the eighteenth century, had become proprietors, owning their own pieces of land, though the *franc-alleu*, free from every feudal obligation to the neighboring lord, was very, very rare ("does not really exist in France," said Bosquet) among those whose ancestors had once been serfs; and even these freeholders had certain obligations to observe toward the lord at the manor house. The preponderance of *métayers* was regarded by contemporaries as the cause of most of France's agricultural ills; it encouraged shiftlessness among the peasantry, particularly in the less fertile regions, since they knew that the lord, rather than allow his land to go fallow, would take care of them.

Though the tendency in France was for the peasantry to acquire greater and greater personal liberty, the old feudal obligations of the peasantry to the seigneur survived, and with the increasing value of the land, were now being more severely enforced than had hitherto been customary. Every peasant, except the lucky *franc-alleu*, whether *mainmortable* serf or one of the various kinds of freemen, had to pay some feudal due or other to a lord. The nature and number of these dues varied according to the custom of the region, the good-will of the seigneur, and the status of the peasant. What each owed was set down in writing in a declaration known as an *aveu*. These *aveux* were renewed periodically, or whenever the land changed hands, or whenever a flaw was found in them. The peasant paid the expenses of the renewal, while the seigneur reaped the benefit, since the lawyers who attended to such matters (*commissaires à terrier*) were generally henchmen of the lord. The

aveux were kept in the château archives or manor rolls
(*terriers*).   Both *terriers* and their *commissaires* were bitterly hated by the peasants, and when they received an opportunity to complain about their grievances in the *cahiers*
(memorials) of 1789, many of them did so in unmistakable
terms.

   This ill-feeling can easily be understood.   In the *terriers*
were *aveux* that sometimes spelled personal humiliation,
financial embarrassment, and burdensome obligation to
most of them.   Originally the principal due that a serf
owed to his lord had been labor.   Those who were still
mainmortables continued to perform such labor a given
number of days a week on the manorial estate, but even
peasants who had received a certain degree of liberty were
liable to the *corvée*, not only to the King, but also to their
feudal suzerains.   This generally meant twelve days a year
of difficult physical exertion, though in some districts it
might be more, and in others only a nominal obligation.
But in the eighteenth century the most general seigneurial
right was the *cens*, an annual rental that had become so
typical of the agricultural system of France that *censitaire*
and peasant were considered identical.   The land in which
a lord had the right to collect the *cens* was known as *censive*.
The various kinds of *cens* were not high or burdensome, but
the tax in itself was the characteristic mark of peasant land
— an indication, therefore, of other dues owed by the
censitaire to his seigneur.   Generally, too, the *censitaire*
had to pay a rental in the form of a specified share of the
crop.   This due was called by a number of names in different parts of France, the most general being *champart*.
With the decreasing value of money and the increasing
value of agricultural products, the *champart* rapidly became
a more burdensome obligation than the *cens*, and wherever
they could, the peasantry endeavored to convert payments
in kind to payments in money.   These rentals were collected even in some cases where the land had been bought
outright by the peasant.

   Nor were they the only dues that the *censitaire* was

obliged to pay to the noble who had once held a hereditary title to his land.   There was the payment known as *lods et ventes*, a portion of the selling price (differing in various parts of France) that the peasant had to pay to his lord whenever he sold his land.   The lord likewise had the right, known as *retrait* or *prélation*, to be consulted before such sale became effective, and might, at any time within thirty years after the sale had actually been made, refuse his assent to it.   In such instances, he generally could be bought off by an additional payment.   There are complaints on record against lords who, having once consented to the sale of a piece of peasant land and collected their *lods et ventes*, then refused to sanction the exchange and had to be paid off once more.   And there were peasants who for twenty-nine years had come to regard a stretch of land as theirs, only to find in the thirtieth year that the hereditary lord of the region refused to sanction a sale made over a generation before, and had to be dealt with substantially or yielded to.   Though the practice was not quite universal in France and though the peasant was always reimbursed if he lost his land, the *cahiers* of the peasants were vehement in their denunication of *retrait* or *prélation*.   In addition to the *lods et ventes*, there was a tax known as the *quint*, which was collected, like the *lods et ventes*, on the sale of lands and, as the name indicates, was generally a fifth of the selling price.   Sometimes there was likewise collected a *requint*, or tax upon the *quint*.   The purchaser of a piece of land selling at 100,000 livres then would have to pay a *quint* of 20,000 livres and a *requint* of 4000 livres.   If he had to pay the *lods et ventes* also, his piece of land would come to him very dearly. But frequently in the eighteenth century, where the *lods et ventes* were collected, the *quint* was reduced in amount. The *quint* and *requint* were collected by the lord not only on sales but also upon the inheritance of peasant fiefs.   In cases where a piece of *censive* soil passed to an heir not in the direct line, the lord, by the right known as *rachat* or *relief*, was entitled to the first year's income from that land. *Lods et ventes, retrait* or *prélation, quint* and *requint, rachat*

or *relief*, and a number of other similar dues that the lord
had the right to collect were sources of deep grievance to
the peasants and the most profitable possessions of the
seigneurs; and in the eighteenth century, even if the lords
were not under the influence of a "feudal reaction," the
peasantry was nevertheless more resentful of their feudal
obligations than their ancestors in previous centuries had
been.

All of these dues were survivals of the time when the lord
had controlled the land and were more or less in the nature
of land rents.   There were other dues which could be explained only as payments for the use of capital.   Among
these were the *banalités*.   Once *banalités* had been paid for
services actually rendered — a part of the flour ground at
the lord's mill or of the bread baked in the lord's oven or of
the wine pressed by the lord's press.   The peasants had
been glad enough to pay these *banalités* when the lord alone
possessed the required utensils.   But now there were other
ovens or mills in the neighborhood and the peasant might
own a press himself.   But the *banalités* still had to be paid.
Indeed, the lord might no longer own a mill, but part of all
the flour ground by peasants on his estate still was due him.
In this manner, the *banalités* came to represent nothing more
than fees for the right not to use that which did not exist.

Burdensome as some of these dues were, the bitterest
resentment of the peasant was reserved for the exclusive
hunting and fishing privileges of the nobility.   These rights
were a survival of the days when a falcon on the wrist was
a mark of gentility and the chase was a rite that only the
holders of fiefs could afford to participate in.   Now there
were dovecotes (*colombiers*) scattered through the realm,
where the nobles raised pigeons and doves for the sole purpose of hunting them; and there were large royal game
preserves (*capitaineries*) reserved for the King and his
guests.   Poaching was punishable by dire penalties and
was a very inclusive offense.   Shooting pigeons that swal-
lowed the peasant's seed or rabbits that ate his young plants
or foxes that killed his fowl was hunting, and hunting was

a seigneurial privilege denied to the peasant and therefore equivalent to poaching. Even the peasant's dogs had to be chained to keep them from chasing game. In some parts of France, he might not even weed or mow in breeding time lest he disturb the partridge's eggs. And in any part of France, after a hard spring of plowing and sowing, he had to be prepared to see his fields ridden over by a hunting party and his crops trampled under hoof. Though some lords were more considerate than others and though in some regions the chase was a rare event, the *cahiers* of the peasants were uniformly resentful of it and universally vehement in demanding reform.

These were not all of the obligations that the French agricultural classes owed to the feudal aristocracy, but they were the most important. In addition to these, however, the peasantry owed certain obligations to the Church. In order to support the local church and parish priest and to contribute his mite to the poor, the peasant had to surrender a tithe (*dîme*), theoretically a tenth, but in the eighteenth century varying anywhere from a sixteenth to a fifth, and averaging about a thirteenth, of his farm and dairy produce. Had the tithe been used for the purposes for which it was collected, there would have been little remonstrance against it, but some of it had become the personal property of a few wealthy ecclesiastics or had passed entirely from the Church into the hands of lay owners (the so-called infeudated tithes); and most of the remainder found its way into the hands of the upper clergy, leaving the poor curés largely dependent upon their own little gardens and upon charity for subsistence. The parish priest might sometimes charge a fee or receive an offering for the performance of certain of the sacraments, such as the marriage ceremonies, but these were part of his ordinary tasks as servant of the Lord and were administered whether paid for or not What fees were thus collected sometimes found their way into the hands of the upper clergy likewise. The tithe alone was estimated at about one-eighteenth of the gross product of the soil of France.

The peasant also paid his share of the government taxes. The direct taxes (*taille*, *vingtième*, and *capitation*) weighed particularly heavily upon the peasantry, for they were allowed no exemptions and could ill afford the amounts demanded out of their small earnings. It was for this reason that they allowed their farms to go to ruin and made no improvements, or if they made them, tried to hide them from the eyes of the inquisitive. For each sign of prosperity meant an increased assessment and larger taxes. The dire poverty which contemporary observers reported in certain sections of France may thus have been rather apparent than real in certain cases, though there is not lacking — and sometimes in the accounts of the same observers — evidence of more prosperous and well-kept peasant holdings. Of the indirect taxes, the *corvée* (enforced labor on the roads or in transporting troops) was the most burdensome to the peasant, because it was a tax that no other class of society was called upon to pay.

A final obligation that the peasant owed to the Government was military duty. The militia was a small body, called together only for drill in times of peace and used as a home guard in times of war. Its ranks were filled by draft; service, though not arduous, was for six years. Since it was very easy to claim or to buy exemption, the conscription was chiefly from among the young men of the poorer peasantry and city artisans. The regular army was made up of volunteers, except in cases of national crises, when conscription might be decreed by the King. Volunteering frequently was honestly conducted on all sides, but as the Government employed recruiting officers to keep the ranks of the army filled and paid them a handsome commission on each recruit they brought into camp, sometimes the "volunteering" was the result of swindle, alcohol, and none too gentle persuasion. Once in the service, the "volunteer" was likely to be whipped literally into shape. The period of service in the regular army was eight years; and after eight years of eighteenth-century army life, though various decrees in the time of Louis XVI softened its rigors somewhat, a soldier was generally unfit for anything other than eight years more of it. The volunteers were mostly young men from the farms or from the working-class families of the cities.

Figures differ regarding the amount of his income that the peasant had to pay in feudal dues and government taxes. Taine is about the only authority who has been bold enough to set down a specific amount. Others have disagreed with him, invariably estimating a lower sum. Yet it is not amiss to cite his numbers. According to him, eighty-one per cent of the rural worker's income went to others. In his *Ancien Régime* he puts into the mouth of an imaginary peasant a speech which presents a good summary of the grievances of the farming classes:

> I am miserable because they take too much from me. They take too much from me because they do not take enough from the privileged classes. Not only do the privileged classes make me pay in their stead, but they also levy upon me their ecclesiastical and feudal dues. When, from an income of a hundred francs, I have given fifty-three francs and more to the tax collector, I still have to give fourteen to my seignior and fourteen more for my tithe and out of the eighteen or nineteen francs I have left, I have yet to satisfy the excise-officer and the salt-tax-farmer. Poor wretch that I am, alone I pay two governments — the one, obsolete, local, which to-day is remote, useless, inconvenient, humiliating, and makes itself felt only through its constraints, its injustices, its taxes; the other, new, centralized, ubiquitous, which alone takes charge of every service, has enormous needs and pounces upon my weak shoulders with all its great weight.

Needless to say, Taine's figures are high. Otherwise the poor peasant could have bought nothing whatsoever and would have starved. Yet Taine's intuition was undoubtedly correct; the French peasant must have been saying exactly such words to himself. It made small difference to him that the German peasant was worse off than he. Nor did he mind much that the English peasant was better off. He knew he was miserable, and he would have known it even if Voltaire, Rousseau, and the rest had never lived.

Few peasants could read and the political philosophy of the eighteenth century did not come to them directly. But it did filter down to them through indirect channels, not to create a radical sentiment among them, but to strengthen an already eager desire for reform and to create the hope that the sight of their wretchedness had affected their betters. Arthur Young, the intrepid and observant English traveler of these days, tells of meeting near Metz, one day in July, 1789 (the Revolution had already begun), a poor woman who told him that "something was to be done by some great folks for such poor ones as she, though she did not know who nor how."

The great majority of the population of France in the eighteenth century lived in the country. Cities were not very numerous and not very large. Paris was the largest city in all Europe, and Paris had a population of only 500,-000. Next in size, in France, came Lyons with about 135,-000. No other city in France could boast of more than 100,000 inhabitants — neither Marseilles nor Bordeaux nor Nantes nor Rouen, which came next in size. In all, the urban population of France was approximately 2,000,000, or only about one twelfth of the total. The rapid development of cities came only in the nineteenth century and was due to the introduction of the factory system.

Before the eighteenth century there was no working class that would correspond to our modern city proletariat. Factories became familiar eyesores only in that century in England,[1] but in France they were still rare. Those that existed were almost exclusively in the cities of the northwestern provinces where agriculture was not so remunerative as elsewhere and the influence of England was immediate. Such manufacturing as was done was carried on either by the old domestic system, in the home of the master workman and with the aid of a few helpers (journeymen, apprentices, and members of his family), or by the newer system of rural industry. In the latter case, some wealthy

[1] See the interesting illustrations in Turberville, *English Men and Manners in the Eighteenth Century*, pp. 148, 157, and 159.

entrepreneur, generally called *fabricant*, would lay in a supply of raw materials and of such primitive machinery as was available and would lend or rent these out to the poorer villagers. The farm laborer or the poor tenant's womenfolk would use their spare time and periods of drought to make this raw material into finished products with the borrowed machinery. The finished product was taken by the *fabricant* and marketed. The greater share of the profits went, of course, to the entrepreneur, but needy families were enabled in this way to add appreciably to the incomes that they could eke out of their gardens and their wages as laborers. This system of rural industry was used especially in the manufacture of textiles. It was a transient stage between the old domestic system, still widely prevalent, and the nascent factory system. It was characteristic of the villages of France and was to be found even in cities as large as Lyons as late as 1830.

In the cities there were a few factories and large shops, worked on the domestic system but on a larger scale, that employed workers by the hundreds. There were also a number of establishments approaching the factory, such as breweries, sugar refineries, tanneries, dyeworks, that gave work to great numbers of employees. But on the whole, the city proletariat was made up of artisans who worked alone or with one or two helpers. These were master cobblers, weavers, apothecaries, printers, carpenters, tailors, soap-makers, butchers, bakers, candlestick-makers, and their assistants (*compagnons*) and apprentices. They were organized into guilds (*corporations*) of which there were two kinds — the free trades (*métiers libres*), in which rules of apprenticeship and relations among master-workmen were not fixed, and the organized trades (*jurandes*) in which there was a definite guild administration (*juré*) that regulated the activity of all members. In most communities the guilds were classified according to their social and economic importance. In Paris, the aristocrats of the guilds were the *Six Corps* (drapers, grocers, mercers, furriers, hosiers, and jewelers). The tendency in the guilds was toward greater restriction and concentration of powers; the free guilds, though still in the majority, were gradually giving way before the *jurandes*. They interfered with the freedom of commerce that a number of reformers were demanding and, though Turgot was to try to carry out these demands when he came to power and many of the *cahiers* mentioned the guilds resentfully, they were not abolished until the Revolution. In the mean time, the tendency toward aristocracy within the guilds had caused the journeymen and *compagnons* to form societies (*compagnonnages*) by themselves that were largely social, though they often were the means of carrying on collective bargaining with the masters and of conducting strikes.

In the days before moving pictures, street-cars, and automobiles, when there were few well-paved streets or well-lighted roads and the church was still the chief social center for all classes, it is not difficult to imagine how monotonous and uneventful the life of the city dweller must have been. In Paris, with its handsome residences and palaces, its spacious parks and squares, its monuments and public buildings, its fashionable society and its slums, existence was not so drab as in the provincial towns. Few laborers could read, though those who could surprised contemporary observers by their avidity; even when they could, they were barely class-conscious and there was little in the writing of the day that dealt with their particular problems. But there was fermentation in the cities, nevertheless. On quays and street-corners, there were excited gatherings engaged in heated political discussions. Those who could not read Rousseau or get some one to read him for them, knew some one who had read him. Everybody was in a position, therefore, to pass judgment and to express an opinion. When the time came, the workers in the city were to become one of the most active elements in the Revolution.

It was to the upper classes of the city, however — to the prosperous bourgeoisie — that the unholy trinity of Montesquieu, Rousseau, and Voltaire made their greatest appeal. Wealthy merchants, bankers, Farmers-General, owners of shops and whatever industrial houses that existed, and professional men as they were, they could afford to become educated and to buy books. They could afford to mingle in society, to attend the fashionable salons, and to join clubs, where they discussed the latest radical literature, aired their grievances, and propounded their panaceas. And their grievances were many! True, they did not have to pay feudal dues like the peasants, but then the rascally peasant refused to pay his taxes and the burden fell on them. True, also, they could afford to buy magisterial offices and titles of nobility from a generous and impecunious government, but then the highest honors were reserved for the true nobility, and furthermore, no matter how well-mannered they tried to be, the blue-bloods always treated them as parvenus. Occasionally a chevalier with eight or sixteen quarterings on his coat of arms might consent to marry a banker's daughter, but then, in referring to the alliance, he had an unpleasant way of talking significantly about "the manuring of his land." And, besides, they wanted the right to vote. As members of the guilds, they could vote for a few petty officers, but they wanted a national representative body made up of commoners and elected by commoners. England had such a body. France herself had once had one. Why could not France have a similar one again? Such a body, and a ministry responsible to it, would enable the bourgeoisie to take its rightful position in politics alongside of the nobility and the clergy, and would protect their business interests from the abuses of unstable government and the evils of improvisation in the fiscal system.

With regard to the state of business prosperity, the middle class had no cause for complaint. According to one set of the variable trade statistics of the day, in 1748 France had exported 192,000,000 francs' worth of goods; in 1776 the total exports had gone up to 309,000,000 francs' worth. The few new factories that had recently been established were doing very well. In 1788 France manufactured about a billion francs' worth of goods and, if we may trust one estimate among the unreliable figures of contemporaries, sent 133,000,000 francs' worth to foreign countries. The highly favorable trade agreement recently drawn up with England's ambassador Eden (1786) made it possible for the year 1789 to be a year of record-breaking prosperity with 1,153,000,000 francs' worth of goods imported and exported. Though the Eden Treaty was not very popular in France, fifty more years were to pass before that record was to be beaten. The middle class had, indeed, a great deal to be thankful for. They were growing wealthier, and along with their wealth went the opportunity to acquire knowledge and education. But that they had wealth and education, that they could buy titles of nobility and secure magistracies and intendancies, that they could occasionally marry into the oldest and finest houses of gentility, only made it the more difficult to bear their social inferiority, their exclusion from some of the most important offices, the instability of the government, the unnecessary restrictions upon business, and the burden of taxation that they had to bear. It was not sheer accident that fashioned some of the most active leaders of the reform movement before the Revolution — Voltaire, Rousseau, Diderot — and of the radical movement during the Revolution — Robespierre, Roland, Danton — out of the sons of middle-class families.

The peasantry, the city working class, and the bourgeoisie included all but about 300,000 of the population of France. Regardless of the fact that they had very little in common, they were all grouped together for political purposes and were known as the Third Estate. The other two orders of society — the clergy and the nobility — were known as the First and Second Estates respectively. There were approximately one hundred and thirty thousand in the one and one hundred and fifty thousand in the other. But despite the fact that at the utmost both comprised together only one per cent of the population (Sieyès in his famous speech on June 17, 1789, was willing to allow them four per cent), their influence far exceeded their numbers

The clergy, however, like the other orders of society were

divided into classes.   There was first of all the separation into regular and secular clergy, common throughout the Catholic Church.   The regular clergy lived in convents and monasteries according to a rule (Latin, *regula*) laid down by some founder and accepted by the Pope.   Among the older orders were the Benedictines, Augustinians, Franciscans, Dominicans, and Jesuits.   The seventeenth century witnessed a revival of monasticism; the old orders were inspired with new vigor and some new orders were created. Among these were the Trappists, the Oratorians, the Capuchins, the Carmelites, the Lazarites, and the Sisters of Charity.   These regular clerics devoted themselves to the salvation of their own souls.   For the most part they withdrew from society and gave themselves up to contemplation and prayer.   This was less true of the mendicant orders, like the Franciscans or Dominicans, that lived by preaching and begging, or the Jesuits, that regarded themselves as particular servants of the Pope, than it was of the Benedictines or the Trappists.   But the chief distinction between them and the secular clergy was that they did not associate intimately with the laity.

On the whole, the regular clergy in France were, in the eighteenth century, in a period of decadence.   There were about a thousand monasteries and convents in France in 1789 and in almost all of them the number of monks or nuns had fallen off considerably.   Not only had the old vow of poverty been neglected by the orders, so that some of the religious houses could boast of huge estates and profitable dues, but even individual monks and nuns in the monasteries had forgotten their vows of poverty and chastity. Of many of the abbots it was true that they lived luxurious and unholy lives.   Frequently the King would make some powerful ecclesiastic an abbot in commendation (*en commande*), whereby the income of his monastery would become the commendatory abbot's personal property.   Indeed, it did not have to be a cleric who was thus favored.   Sometimes it might even be a child, though practically never a woman.   Such an abbot left his monastic duties to a prior elected by the monks, and remained free of any duties incumbent upon his office.

Among the convents, while absentee abbesses were rare, there was another sign of yielding to the temptations of the world without. Some of them had been secularized, the inmates freed from the vow of poverty and of the obligation to wear their vestments. Ladies of noble birth got them to these nunneries in great number, until some of them became highly exclusive establishments. The chapter of Remiremont in Lorraine required nine generations of noble descent on both sides of the family of all entrants. The chapter house became more of a fashionable resort than a religious institution. Monasteries and convents alike neglected their charitable and holy work. Hospitals and poorhouses were beginning to decrease in number; and the State now was obliged to take over the work of grace that had once been the tasks of the richer abbeys.

Abbeys in commendation were, in the regular clergy, analogous to an equally vicious practice in the secular clergy — the bishops *in partibus infidelium*. These bishops, once appointed to carry the Gospel to the lands of the heathen, remained in France and had no duties to perform there. But they collected the emoluments and the honors due to the holders of the episcopal rank. Besides the eleven bishops *in partibus infidelium*, there were eighteen archbishops and one hundred and twenty-one bishops in France before the Revolution. These archbishops and bishops, together with the priors, abbots, archdeacons, and cardinals, made up the higher clergy. Many of them were wealthy, some made so by the profits of their offices, others even before they had become clerics. Almost always they were of noble descent. An episcopal see was a highly coveted holding for the younger son (*cadet*) of an influential noble who could not hope to succeed to his father's estate. Many a young blood who knew more about the rules of dueling than the rule of the Benedictine Order became an abbot, while his comrade who had spent more time with the cups than with the chalice became a bishop. Age was no obstacle; one might become a chaplain at seven. Lack of training was no obstacle; the King by the Concordat of 1516 might name any one he pleased to a bishopric, the Pope reserving only the right of veto, which he seldom employed. There were always enough poor but able clergymen whom one could hire for a small remuneration to attend to one's duties.

Of course, being a member of the higher clergy had its disadvantages. One could not openly have a wife. One could not pass on one's property to one's heirs. A certain amount of sobriety was expected of one. But the standard of morality of the eighteenth century was not what it was to become in a later age. Even clergymen were then immune from public censure for acts that might now create enough gossip to keep the suburban commuter busily engrossed in his newspaper for the duration of his trip. Only the rashness of a Cardinal de Rohan, who bought a diamond necklace for a million and a half livres for Marie Antoinette, created a public scandal. Otherwise, the keeping of mistresses, the expenditure of huge sums of money, the neglect of duties for the sake of extravagances in Paris were circumstances too ordinary to excite the notice of the blasé and too remote to attract the attention of the unsophisticated.

These clergymen were to be seen at court, playing a share in the social and political life of their country that even some of the nobles might have envied. The Abbé Fénelon and the Bishop Bossuet sat close to the ear of King Louis XIV; Cardinal Fleury was Minister to Louis XV; and the Archbishop Loménie de Brienne to Louis XVI, though he had failed to become Archbishop of Paris because Louis XVI believed the holder of that office ought, at least, to believe in God. Ecclesiastics were entrusted with the highest executive, judicial, and diplomatic undertakings, while as courtiers and social leaders they yielded not at all to the proudest of the nobility. In wealth, social position, political power, they were to be counted along with the nobles, whose blood-brothers, indeed, they often were.

There were abbots and bishops who took their work seriously and performed their duties faithfully. Hundreds of dutiful prelates are lost to view in focusing attention on the many fewer profligates. But contemporaries committed the same error. It was the sinecures, the immorality, the ignorance of the upper clergy that called forth the vehemence of Voltaire, the ridicule of Montesquieu, the attacks of reformers and *philosophes* upon religion in general and the Catholic Church in particular.

But even the bitterest opponents of the Church spoke favorably for the most part of the curés. Although the curés (the parish priests) were also included in the First Estate, they were distinguished from the higher ranks of clerics by the appellation of "lower clergy." The distinction was necessary not alone on account of rank, but also because of the difference in the *Weltanschauung* of the two classes of clergy. The curé lived with his flock, wrote and read their letters for them, acted as adviser in domestic and spiritual difficulties, baptized them, married them, buried them. Like them, he was poor, subsisting on his meager share of the tithe and the produce of a small farm. While, therefore, for political purposes, they were considered members of the First Estate, the curés and vicars actually were more in sympathy with the Third Estate than with their fellow clergymen of the higher ranks. Among the lower clergy were also to be counted the monks and nuns of the regular orders and the canons of the cathedral chapters, who, since they did not come into contact with the outside world as much as their secular brothers, were therefore less likely than the parish priests to disagree with their superiors.

The clergy, whether lower or upper, regular or secular, were grouped together politically to constitute the First Estate, taking precedence over all other classes of society in France. This prestige was a survival of the medieval tradition of the superiority of the Catholic Church over the State, of the Pope over the Emperor. This tradition had suffered considerably in the course of a few centuries and now was called into dispute even in the most devoutly Catholic of countries. In France ever since the Pragmatic Sanction of Bourges in 1438 the Kings of France had with growing insistence demanded the independence of the French Church. By the Concordat of 1516, Francis I had acquired the right to appoint the bishops of the French Church, nominally with the approval of the Pope. In 1682 Louis XIV reduced the dependence upon Rome to a mere thread by a declaration of the liberties of the Gallican Church, which recapitulated the gains made by the national church in France since the struggle for independence began. These Gallican liberties reaffirmed that the King is subject to no ecclesiastical power in temporal matters, but that the Holy See is subject in spiritual matters to the decision of Œcumenical Councils; that the exercise of Apostolic power ought to be regulated according to universally accepted canons (and therefore invalid in France if exercised contrary to the accepted rules and constitutions of the Fathers of the French Church); that the decision of the Pope in matters of faith is infallible only after having received the sanction of the Church. These decrees made of the French clergy a body of ecclesiastics who, in spiritual affairs, could accept or reject any decision or demand emanating from Rome and who, in political affairs, were becoming more securely bound to Paris.

Yet the tradition that the Church was independent of and even superior to the State — a state within the State — managed to survive. The Church, for example, had its own government. It not only tried its own subjects — clerics of any rank or length of service — in its own courts, but insisted (though with diminishing vehemence in more recent times) upon jurisdiction in all cases involving contract, church property, and the special wards of the Church — widows and orphans. It also had its own legislative body — the Ecclesiastical Assemblies. Ordinary Assemblies met every ten years, and in the decade intervals, one or more Petty Assemblies might convene. To the Ordinary Assemblies each of sixteen archbishops in France sent four representatives, two from the upper clergy and two from the lower clergy, with instructions called *cahiers*. To the Petty Assemblies they sent one from each rank. These Assemblies were empowered to handle the secular and financial affairs of the Church, but in late years their principal function had come to be the appropriation of Free Gifts (*dons gratuits*) to the King, and the apportionment among themselves of the *décimes*, a self-imposed tax to meet the debts and obligations of the Church.

The *dons gratuits* were but another survival of the tradition that the Church was independent of the State. In theory the Church could not be taxed. As an actual rule, the ecclesiastics did not pay the *vingtième* (income tax) or *capitation* (poll tax) and church lands did not pay the *taille* (land tax). But the Church did make frequent Free Gifts to the Royal Treasury, which, since they often were granted in return for specific redress — such as punishment of some anti-clerical writer or the burning of some book, were not free, and since they were frequently made in the realization that if these sums were not gratuitously forthcoming they would none the less be collected, were not gifts. Between 1715 and 1788 the Church made twenty-two such Free Gifts, totaling 268,050,000 livres, an average of less than 4,000,000 per year.[1] It sent almost that much yearly in the form of annates and other taxes to Rome. Considering that the property and persons of the clergy, if taxed, would have yielded an annual revenue greatly in excess of this sum and that sometimes the King made valuable concessions in return for these Free Gifts, the independence of the Church really was something more than empty legend.

Although there were never more than 130,000 clerics of all ranks and kinds in France, and at the end of the Ancient Régime this number was considerably reduced, the dominant position of the clergy, not alone in society and in politics, but also in the financial organization of the govern-

---

[1] See, *Economic and Social Conditions in France during the Eighteenth Century*, p. 62, puts the annual average figure at 5,400,000 livres, but see Marion, *Dictionnaire des institutions de la France aux XVII et XVIII siècles*, p. 105.

ment, was far in excess of their numbers. While they comprised less than one per cent of the population of France, they controlled about five per cent of the land and an annual income from the tithe of 123,000,000 livres to say nothing of smaller sums derived from other sources. This wealth was not evenly distributed, even among the higher clergy. Certain bishops, particularly in the southeast, gleaned but meager incomes of a few thousand livres from their dioceses, but in the north, bishoprics might yield incomes running into the hundred thousands. The Archbishopric of Strassburg, the richest of all, produced 400,-000 livres. They were "a motley crew," the eighteenth-century French churchmen, rich and poor, high and low, regular and secular, literate and illiterate, honest and scurvy, some of them having only the pretensions of their class and the pride of its high and independent tradition, many of them arrogant and undeserving, all probably no worse than 130,000 other men in the same circumstances might have been. Some reform of the clergy was undertaken even in the Ancient Régime, but the only important changes effected were a reduction in the number of monks and congregations and a greater activity of the State in eleemosynary work. Patronage, laxity of behavior, incompetence in the higher ranks, and abuse of authority continued to make ordinary men wonder and wise men protest.

Strip the French upper clergy of the Ancient Régime of their cassocks, surplices, scapularies, their robes, frocks, and palls, their bishops' mitres or cardinals' hats and all their ecclesiastical vestments; put upon them the sword, spurs, and jaunty costumes of the nobility, and you have the upper class of the Second Estate, the court nobility. Almost, but not quite, to the same extent as the clergy, the nobility were exempt from taxes. Unlike the clergy, they had to pay the income tax (*vingtième*), but generally managed to secure at least a partial exemption through their influence at court; they were also included in the twenty-two classes arranged for the purposes of the poll tax (*capitation*), but did not pay in proportion to their ability, if they paid at all.   In fact, it was regarded a dishonor to pay taxes, and as often as they could, the nobility refused to do so.   Their duty, they felt, was not to be bled, but to bleed for their country.   The army and navy were their chosen fields; and all the higher ranks in the armed forces of France were monopolized by them.   It had once been possible for a common soldier to work his way from the ranks, but in 1781, at a time when France was aiding the American democracies to achieve their independence of England, Louis XVI's Minister of War, Ségur, had decreed that no one could acquire the commission of second lieutenant unless he could prove four paternal generations of nobility.   Furthermore, although it was still possible for a bourgeois like Colbert, Turgot, or Necker to hold important positions in the King's Council and all the intendants were generally chosen from the ranks of the upper middle class, nevertheless the most coveted posts even in civil departments were held by the aristocracy.

But if the clergy was divided against itself, the nobility was even more so.   Theirs was also a fourfold division, although the categories were not entirely distinct.   The more blue-blooded of the nobility were those already described, the so-called "nobility of the sword," descended directly from the ancient feudal nobles who had been granted their fiefs in return for military service.   The rise of a standing army had done away with the ancient forms of feudal payment, but since no other occupation befitted a gentleman, they still regarded the army as their exclusive preserve.   Sometimes the scions of an ancient house were to be found among the ranks of magistrates and parliamentarians.   But most of this "nobility of the robe" were *nouveaux riches*, like Montesquieu, whose ancestors had bought some judicial office carrying with it a title of nobility and the right to wear a pompous gown.   There were perhaps fifty thousand such offices owned by wealthy bourgeois families.   But they were no more welcome in the society of the nobility of the sword than parvenus have ever been among the ranks of the élite. Sometimes a high ministerial dignitary was admitted to court and became one of the nobility who surrounded the King, living on the royal bounty when his own means of income were deficient. The "court nobility," however, was made up largely of nobility of the sword, the wealthier nobles who could afford to leave their estates in the hands of others, abandoning their peasants to all the horrors of absentee landlordism and depending upon their stewards and *baillis* to provide them with enough to meet the demands of life at court. The poorer nobility, together with an occasional patrician too proud to fawn at court, remained upon their lands, to become known as the "country nobility." How poor some of them were was revealed in 1789 when they met with the rest of the nobles of their bailiwicks to elect the representatives of their Estate to the first of the Revolutionary Assemblies. The minutes of the electoral assembly of the Poitou nobility tell us that "seven gentlemen were present at the assembly dressed like peasants. None of them had a sword at his side. The commissioners appointed by the order of the nobility procured arms for them and paid their bills at the hotel. When questioned, these gentlemen said that their daughters worked in the farmyard, made the bread, and kept sheep in the fields."

Such, then, were the three estates of French society — clergy, nobility, and commoners. None of them was a homogeneous group. The clergy were divided longitudinally into regular and secular, and latitudinally into upper and lower clergy. The nobility, almost in the same way, were divided into sword and robe, court and country nobility. And the commoners consisted of a number of classes of different and sometimes conflicting interests — merchants, professional men, capitalists, peasants, artisans, etc. But the members of the Third Estate had this in common — that they all opposed the Ancient Régime and longed for a new era; and the upper orders had not even a common dissatisfaction to unite them. For the over- whelming majority of the upper clergy and the court

nobility were well satisfied with the world, while the lower
clergy and the nobility of the robe and of the country were
not so complacent. Even among the higher clergy (particularly the regulars) and the court nobility, there were a
number of liberals. Many an abbé had read his Rousseau and
Montesquieu and had been impressed with the wickedness
of the aristocracy, and many a vicomte had read Voltaire
and resolved that the Church was an instrument of reaction
and oppression. There were some among them — Duport,
Mirabeau, Lafayette, Sieyès, Grégoire, Gobel, Talleyrand
— who were as outspoken reformers as the most outspoken
country lawyer pleading the cause of Franklin's lightning
rod as the cause of progress against superstition (Robespierre) or the most unabashed physician espousing the
rights of the poor to a livelihood (Marat). It was a foregone conclusion that the reform party would win if ever the
question of reform were to be permitted a fair and open
discussion.

In the society thus constructed, standards of social behavior were not the same as they have since become, or
even as they were then in a more austere England. Restraint of emotion has never been a pronounced Latin
characteristic. In the eighteenth century, ostentatious
indulgence in deep feeling was even the mode. Fashionable
men and women wept copiously in public, loudly swore
love and friendship to each other, boasted in written and
oral confessions of their conquests. Ladies entertained
their gentlemen callers in their boudoirs or while their maids
got them ready for receptions and balls. It was no unusual
thing for a man who could afford it to have a mistress;
Louis XV had set the style. Together with the Papal
Nuncio and the Grand Almoner of France, Louis XV once
called upon Madame Du Barry before the royal mistress had
got dressed for the day, and the holy men were said not
to have been displeased. Education for the noblest sons
and daughters of France consisted chiefly in dancing and
etiquette. In high society the art of seduction was sedu-
ously studied and practiced. The wealthiest churchman

in France even considered the Queen of France fair quarry. Cardinal de Rohan had long been in the disfavor of Marie Antoinette, and hoping to regain her confidence, he had permitted himself to be duped by a clever gang of crooks into buying a diamond necklace worth a million and a half livres for the Queen, because he was led by forged letters and skillful impersonations to believe she wished him to do so. The crooks made way with the necklace, and when the jewelers began to ask for their money, it came out that the Queen knew nothing of the entire transaction. The scandal resulted in the arrest of Rohan in the midst of a cathedral ceremony; and in many quarters he was considered less deserving of such humiliation than the Queen.

Marie Antoinette, herself an Austrian, was under the influence of current French philosophical ideas. Under Rousseau's "back-to-nature" influence, she turned the Trianon Palace near the larger palace at Versailles into a sublimated farm and played at dairy maid with her retinue. And yet, amidst this affected simplicity, when she fell ill of the measles, she had four noblemen to attend her. Rousseau, who excoriated the wickedness of civilization and praised the simplicity of nature, was himself the paramour of several, and abandoned at a foundling hospital the children that he had by Thérèse Levasseur, who came nearest of all his mistresses to being his wife. Voltaire lived with Madame du Châtelet, and when Châtelet and he opened her locket upon her death to see whose resemblance she had carried about with her, they found the picture of a third man. It was, then, not altogether without precedent or cause that the behavior of a later period — society under the Directory — was to become what a more severe generation has seen fit to call shameless.

It is easy, however, to exaggerate the looseness and lasciviousness of such an age. These incidents that shock the austere mind are gathered from memoirs and confessions written at a time when it was not bad taste to reveal intimacies. Casanova's *Memoirs* and Rousseau's *Confessions* are good examples. A distorted picture of actual social behavior is bound to arise from reading only the scandal of an age. Probably there have been periods before and since that have been equally immoral, though it would be difficult to find in recent times, if we except Restoration England, a period when laxity was so much the social fashion. It was hardly due to mere irreligion. The eighteenth century was not without religion. The lower classes in France, excepting a small percentage of Protestants who were half-heartedly permitted a clandestine existence, until Louis XVI granted them complete toleration, were still devoutly Catholic. To be sure, the Baron d'Holbach could inform David Hume (when the latter had protested at dinner one day that he had never seen an atheist) that Hume had indeed been unfortunate, but that right then he was sitting at table with seventeen of them; but the upper classes of France were, for the most part, deistic or pantheistic rather than atheistic. Social profligacy was due rather to the fashion set by the rulers — the Regent and Louis XV, followed by their courtiers, and aped by all else who could afford the luxury of escape from regular living. If statistics could be found for such matters, it would probably be discovered that the very great majority of the French populace lived in a manner that even a post-Victorian age could not have censured.

CHAPTER III

THE POLITICAL PHILOSOPHY OF THE EIGHTEENTH CENTURY

LOMBROSO, the Italian sociologist, has estimated that during the Middle Ages there were seven thousand two hundred and twenty-four revolts and that between the years 1791 and 1880 alone there were eight hundred and thirty-six. It is comparatively easy to define a revolt in the sense in which he used it; any act of throwing off allegiance is a revolt. A revolution is not so simple a matter, and for that reason one can probably count the important revolutions of the world's history without using more than two digits. Extent and success enter into the distinction, but an essential factor without which any revolt, no matter how widespread and how successful, would still be a revolt and with which any revolution, no matter how limited in scope, would still be a revolution is the question of its philosophy. *Revolution* means *change* and *novae res*, and generally a change that is in the minds of the leaders, no matter how vaguely, when it begins. Success or failure measures only the speed with which the changes are wrought. Extent determines only the regions affected.

That *novae res* were necessary in France in the Ancient Régime was evident to all but the most blindly conservative. It needed no Voltaire to point out the abuses of the Church to an intelligent bourgeoisie or to the lower clergy who every day experienced the consequences of those abuses. It needed no Montesquieu to analyze governments for liberal nobles and officials who were endeavoring to their utmost to bring a moss-backed court to see their point of view. It needed no Rousseau to point out inequalities in the distribution of property or in the control of the government to peasants who annually saw the greater part of their hard-earned incomes going into the coffers of

privileged ecclesiastics or noble seigneurs.   The philosophers did not create the dissatisfaction with the Ancient
Régime; they did not even give voice to it completely, for
there is little that concerns the peasant in eighteenth-century philosophy.   But they did lead the thoughts of their
educated readers in the direction of reform.   Without them,
the peasant, driven to desperation, might have attacked
their lords; they might even, if successful enough, have
brought about a revolution in their status.   As a matter of
fact, that is practically what we shall see did happen in the
July and August revolts of 1789.   A social revolution was
possible because the peasant had his own simple program
of reform.   But to change the entire political structure of a
kingdom such as France, something more than simply a
destruction of the old régime was necessary.   There had to
be plans for a new régime.   And these plans the so-called
philosophers (we should now call them political scientists)
provided.

It is not difficult to pick out for different eras catch-
words that will describe their dominant intellectual at-
titudes.   There are the Ages of Faith, of Renascence, of Rationalism, of Progress.   Scholasticism is the guidepost of the
first; classical knowledge of the second; nature of the third;
and evolution of the fourth.   The eighteenth century was the
age of rationalism and Nature was its God.   Just as we now
talk in terms of progress and attribute every development
to evolution, just as medieval man talked in terms of the
Bible and attributed every development to God, so the
intellectuals of the eighteenth century talked of Nature and
natural developments, natural law, natural religion, natural
government, natural man.

By "natural man," "man in the state of nature," they
did not quite mean the savage brute.   Though sometimes
it is hard to distinguish "natural man" from primitive man,
though sometimes the *philosophes* themselves seem to treat
the two terms as synonymous, they generally, by "man in
the state of nature" meant a civilized man without all the
folderol, ceremonies, and conventions of civilization, but

with the advantages that the increased knowledge and learning of civilization are supposed to give. Forgetting or choosing to forget that the conventions are a historical development as well as civilization itself, they tried to conceive of a person without any inhibitions and restrictions upon his actions and thoughts save those put upon him by his own good will. Such a man was "natural man," very often near to primitive man; and the government, the law, the religion that such a man would choose for himself would be natural law, natural government, natural religion. The only problem was to find out what such a man would choose.

That problem did not present any too great difficulties, because the eighteenth-century philosopher thought that by the use of his own mind and common sense he could discover all such truths. Descartes, in the middle of the seventeenth century, had maintained that scientific method was geometric, that it consisted of logical deductions from clear and simple ideas accepted as axioms. The theories of Descartes soon acquired an enviable popularity. They found ready listeners even in the salons of the ladies of polite society, and Molière satirized the *Wise Ladies* who spoke so knowingly and casually of Cartesian principles. To this work of vulgarizing scientific theories, Newton, at the end of the seventeenth century and the beginning of the eighteenth, lent a hand. Newton taught that the universe was controlled by very definite and often ascertainable natural laws. It was no longer necessary to assign all inexplicable phenomena to God; Nature did just as well. To be sure, Newton himself was not interested in replacing God by Nature and simply wished to discover certain scientific truths. It is not probable that Newton was readily digested by the general reader of the eighteenth century. But Newton met a fate that later scientists, Darwin and Einstein, were to encounter. Like them, he was interested only in scientific propositions; few people could understand his works and fewer read them. Yet more people bought his books than opened them; and almost everybody with any claim to modernism scanned some popularization of his work or attended some lecture upon it. Newton's *Principia* ran into forty English, seventeen French, eleven Latin, three German, one Portuguese, and one Italian edition. There were numerous adaptations and popularizations, including an Italian *Newtonianism for Ladies*, which itself was translated into French. Before long, everybody but Newton knew that he had proved that to explain the physical world all that was necessary was to discover the immutable laws of Nature, leaving God in his heavens alone.

But was it just as true in the matter of human relationships that there was a Natural Universal Order? Descartes implied this, but it remained for a compatriot and contemporary of Newton to answer the questions more definitely. The human mind, said John Locke in his *Essay Concerning Human Understanding*, is a blank upon birth; innate ideas do not exist. Mind is simply the accumulation of experiences, and experience is the result of impressions received from the external world — that is, sensations. In other words, man's mind is a direct product of his natural environment; therefore Man himself is part of Nature and can very easily determine in human relationships what is and what is not according to the laws of Nature. Locke's *Essay Concerning Human Understanding* is not very entrancing reading; Andrew Lang once asked, "How did the dreary devil stagger like Crockett to a 26th edition?" And the answer has been made:

> Locke, more perhaps than any one else, made it possible for the eighteenth century to believe what it wanted to believe: namely that in the world of human relations as well as in the physical world, it was possible for men to "correspond with the general harmony of Nature"; that since man, and the mind of man, were integral parts of the work of God, it was possible for man, by the use of his mind, to bring his thought and conduct, and hence the institutions by which he lived into a perfect harmony with the Universal Natural Order.[1]

[1] From *The Declaration of Independence*, by Carl Becker. Copyright, 1922, by Harcourt, Brace and Company, Inc. See also Teggart, *Theory of History*, 84–85.

The influence of Descartes, Newton, and Locke together, then, conspired to establish in this Age of Rationalism a conception of a Universal Natural Order. Eighteenth-century thought made more than one attempt to set forth the "Code of Nature" in detail. For the System of Nature was accepted as teleological throughout and the Laws of Nature were as specific and as purposeful as the laws of any human legislator. Montesquieu and Voltaire and a few uncanny Scotch philosophers (Hume, Ferguson) might laughingly or satirically question the existence of an ideal "natural man," but even they had to a certain degree to concede to current philosophical conceptions. In this respect, at any rate, Rousseau, inconsistent and eccentric though he was, reflected the dogma of his age much better than they. It is to Locke particularly that is due the belief in "the Laws of Nature and Nature's God" postulated in the American Declaration of Independence, and in the "natural, inalienable and sacred rights of man" prefixed to the French Constitution of 1791. Jefferson and Mirabeau were both lineal spiritual descendants of the English philosopher. But Jefferson was a direct descendant; he went right to Locke in his search for self-evident truths. Mirabeau was one generation of French philosophers removed.

The longest-lived of that generation of French philosophers, and a contemporary of all the others, was François Marie Arouet. His pen name is said to have been an anagram of the letters in the family name — AROUET — and the initials L and J, taken from the French words *le jeune*. These, if spelled with the classical equivalents of U and J, might be arranged to give VOLTAIRE. By this assumed name, at any rate, he has best been known to contemporaries and to posterity. Voltaire was born at Paris in 1694 of a family of tradesmen. His father was a notary, who wished his son likewise to study law. But the young man chose the career of letters, which brought him lifelong trouble and enduring fame. Until his twenty-fourth year, he had done nothing to win a reputation. In that year he was sent to the Bastille, perhaps unjustly, for two libels against the Regent.   There he revised a play, *Œdipe*, that he had previously written, and began an epic on Henry IV, *La Henriade*, which is still considered one of the great poems of French literature.   After eleven months of imprisonment, he came out of the Bastille, thenceforth to be known only as Voltaire.   The *Œdipe* was a great dramatic success at the Théâtre Français, but his other plays were not as warmly welcomed, and Voltaire now had to live on the bequest of his father, who had recently died, and a pension which he received from the Regent for petty diplomatic missions.   *La Henriade*, in the mean time, was completed, but won no immediate renown.

Voltaire might have spent a long lifetime thus, as a petty office-holder with a knack for poetry, were it not for a fortunate episode at this time.   He quarreled with the Chevalier de Rohan, perhaps over a lady.   In the course of the quarrel, Voltaire, who had been snubbed by the Chevalier, reminded this cadet of one of France's proudest families that while he himself did not carry about a great name, he at least won respect for the name he had.   The Chevalier had Voltaire beaten by his hirelings some time later, and then, to avoid a duel, had Voltaire for a second time thrown into the Bastille.   There Voltaire stayed for about a fortnight, and then, on his own request, was exiled to England.

It was in the year 1726, at the age of thirty-three, that Voltaire first came under the influence of English men of letters.   He made the acquaintance of the Walpoles, Bolingbroke, Pope, Dr. Samuel Clarke, a leading Newtonian, and other great insular literati.   Through them he learned of Newton, Locke, and the political institutions of the British.   For three years, broken by surreptitious visits to France, he lived in an English environment.   In 1729 he was permitted to return to France, having acquired an Anglophile background that was to color all his future political compositions.   Except for some plays, his first important product, when he was once again legally on French soil, was his *Lettres Philosophiques sur les Anglais*

(1733). It was a double-edged criticism of French government and religious institutions, holding up the English state
and church for praise while ridiculing the French. The
Parlement of Paris condemned it to be burned (1734) and
the author was obliged to seek refuge with his "respectable
Emily" at the Châtelet establishment at Cirey. For
fifteen years, not altogether idyllic, he lived at Cirey, producing dramas, writing history, dabbling in mathematics,
engaging in business enterprises, and even enjoying the favor
of Louis XV, whose royal historiographer he became in 1745

Upon the death of Madame de Châtelet, Voltaire accepted the oft-tendered invitation of Frederick the Great
who was himself the author of some mediocre political
writings and some bad poems, to live at the palace of Sans
Souci at Potsdam. But these two great men, who could,
both before and after this visit, be friendly and cordial to
each other by correspondence, did not make good intimate
friends. Although Voltaire loyally praised and corrected
his patron's French verses, although Frederick gave him
honor and an important post in his service, three years of
mutual misunderstanding led to Voltaire's flight from
Prussia, and the temporary arrest of Voltaire and his niece,
on Frederick's orders, at Frankfort. After a short sojourn
in Switzerland, Voltaire finally took up his abode at Ferney,
inside France, but near enough to the border to offer refuge.
There he lived and continued to write and to manage his
estate for almost twenty years. In the last year of his life,
he was permitted by Louis XVI to return to Paris, where he
was fêted and lionized by the people, the theater-goers, the
Academy, and other celebrities. In 1778, at the age of
eighty-four, after living long enough to deny several premature reports of his death (he had always been sickly and
hypochondriac), he finally died. Burial in consecrated
ground was secured for him only with the greatest difficulty,
but in 1791 his remains were Pantheonized — the greatest
honor that Revolutionary France had it in its power to
bestow. Recently, when his grave at the Pantheon was
opened, it was found that his body had disappeared.

Until his exile to England, Voltaire was known chiefly as the writer of *La Henriade*. But after 1726 he wrote not only poetry, but dramas, critical essays, philosophy, polemics of various kinds, stories, novels, scientific treatises, histories, and volumes of correspondence. The first post-humous edition of his complete works fills seventy large volumes. It would be hard to name his *magnum opus*, there is so much of supreme significance. Yet, for political importance, it is possible to narrow the discussion down to the *Lettres Philosophiques sur les Anglais* (1733), *Essais sur les Mœurs* (1756), *Traité sur la Tolérance* (1763), and the *Dictionnaire Philosophique* (1764). In this connection, also, his *Éléments de la Philosophie de Newton*, and his poems *On the Nature of Pleasure*, *On the Nature of Man*, *On Natural Law*, *On Natural Religion*, and a group of others of the same kind, are to be mentioned as illustrative of his foundations in the naturalistic philosophy of his time.

It is hard to name Voltaire's *magnum opus* for the simple reason that it was through no particular work that he exerted his greatest political influence. It was as a person-ality that he made his genius felt. He corresponded with everybody of any importance — Frederick the Great, Catherine the Great, Necker, Turgot, Diderot, Rousseau, and a host of others. Was the Protestant family Calas persecuted unjustly? They found a champion in Voltaire, who not only defended them personally, but wrote one of his famous *Essays on Tolerance* in their behalf. Was the former governor of India, Lally-Tollendal, unjustly accused of treason? Voltaire devoted himself to clearing his name also. Did some young philosopher — Rousseau, Holbach, Marat — allow his enthusiasm to run off with his good judgment? Voltaire swooped down upon him with that irony and wit and malicious good sense in which he was so eminently proficient. And always there was his extraordi-nary activity, calling the attention of the world in a play or a poem or an essay to some abuse that ought to be removed, urging some reform upon a ruler, giving advice on all sub-jects to all seekers. This astonishing activity was carried on despite his great fear, tantamount to moral cowardice, of getting into difficulties, and his cautious, even hypocritical, desire to retain a bourgeois respectability, which caused him to deny some of his best works, to fawn upon people in authority, to quarrel with his fellow philosophers, particularly Montesquieu and Rousseau, for their radicalism (among other reasons, not excluding sheer jealousy).

Nothing was too insignificant, nothing too complex, to receive the consideration of his almost universal genius; his *Dictionnaire Philosophique* was a little encyclopedia of philosophical, religious, and literary questions. But one phase of his work stands out more salient than the rest — his attack upon intolerance. Voltaire was himself a deist, who believed in a pantheistic god to be worshiped without ceremony and sectarianism; the relation of God to the individual was for him purely a personal matter. That was the "natural religion" he spoke of in his *Dictionnaire Philosophique* (articles *Dieu* and *Théisme*) and in his poetry. One sometimes feels that the old rascal was an atheist, but too fearful of public opinion to admit it. Hence his chapel at Ferney with its ambiguous inscription *Deo erexit Voltaire* (*Voltaire has erected this to God!*); hence his haste to protest against Holbach's materialistic *System of Nature*; hence, if the story is true, his anxious return to the Vatican one day when he had forgotten to kiss the Pope's toe; hence his entire deistic philosophy. But whether deist or atheist, Voltaire had no use for sects — for Roman Catholicism less than any other. In his history of civilization, made up of the *Essais sur les Mœurs* (in which he pleaded for what would now be called the "new" history), the *Siècle de Louis XIV*, and the *Précis du Regne de Louis XV*, he tried to show how natural, simple religion, customs and art were still impossible in the complex society of France, because the superstitions, fanaticism, and ceremony of the Catholic Church still prevented the introduction of reason into religion; the progress of civilization was but a struggle between fanaticism and reason. His *Treatise on Toleration*, his articles in the *Dictionnaire Philosophique* (*Dieu, Dogme,*

Fanatisme, Théisme, Théiste, Torture) take up the same attack, not alone upon sectarian intolerance, but upon all
other kinds of intolerance as well.   Hear his prayer to God:

> Thou hast not given a heart for us to hate and hands for us
> to kill.   Make us help each other to carry the burden of a pain-
> ful and passing life.   Let not the small differences between the
> clothes that cover our feeble bodies, between all our inadequate
> languages, between all our ridiculous customs, between all our
> imperfect laws, between all our silly opinions, . . . let not all
> these nuances which distinguish the atoms called men be
> signals for hatred and persecution.[1]

Historical analogies are odious and easily abused.   Yet,
bearing in mind the caution, the intelligence, the encyclopedic knowledge, the fear of revolutionary outbreaks, and
the none the less powerful propagandizing influence of both
men, it is not altogether inappropriate to call Voltaire the
Erasmus of the French Revolution.   We shall find the
names of Rousseau and Montesquieu more often on the
lips of the orators of the Revolution, for Voltaire's was a
personal influence not so easy to quote by chapter and
verse, and his attack was on no one phase of his times, but
upon the whole system he saw around him; *Écrasez l'infame!   (Crush the infamous!)* was his slogan, regardless of
whether *l'infame* was religious, political, economic, or
social.   If Luther could not have done his work without
Erasmus, the Father of the Humanists, having prepared the
way, no more could the religious reform and therefore an
essential part of the political and economic reform of the
French Revolution have been possible without Voltaire, the
Father of the Philosophers.

Born before Voltaire (1689) and already author of a
bitter satire on French institutions, *The Persian Letters*
(1721), when Voltaire was still an obscure poet, Montesquieu
comes the nearest of all of that generation of philosophers
to Voltaire in universality of genius.   The two might very
easily, had they also been artists, have traveled in the
company of Leonardo da Vinci and Michelangelo.   Montes-

---

[1] *Traité sur Tolérance,* chap. xxii.

quieu's family was of a good, though not ancient house. He was Baron de la Brède in his own right and Baron de Montesquieu by inheritance from an uncle.   At the age of twenty-seven, he became *président à mortier* of Bordeaux by the same bequest.   His early interest in science and the wit of his *Lettres Persanes* won him a seat in the Academy (1728).   Having sold his magistracy in 1726, he devoted the rest of his life to a study of governments, traveling extensively for five years and reflecting on his subject for seventeen more.   In 1734 he published his *Considerations on the Causes of the Greatness of the Romans and of their Decadence*, a sort of preliminary study for his main work. Fourteen years later (1748) came his *chef d'œuvre*.   He called it a *prolem sine matre creatam* (*an offspring born without a mother*), by which he probably meant to imply his sole responsibility for it, since his friends had tried to dissuade him from publishing it because they feared it was either too radical or, as in the case of Helvétius, too moderate.   It is this *Spirit of the Laws* which interests us most of all the writings of Montesquieu.

In a way, the two earlier works had been a preparation for it.   The *Persian Letters* was a series of fictitious correspondence between two Persian nobles named Rica and Usbek, who travel in France, and their friends back in Persia.   It was really the first book in the *philosophe* movement.   Written in a pleasantly amused style, it, nevertheless, chagrined those at whom it poked fun or who respected the traditions and institutions that so entertained these unusually intelligent Orientals, who smiled that the King of France had more statues in his palace than subjects in a large city, and found that the corps of lackeys was more respectable in France than elsewhere because it was a seminary for great lords, and told of the Utopia of the Troglodytes.   The book went through four editions in one year, but was as much condemned in certain quarters as commended in others.   Cardinal Fleury's displeasure with it caused some delay in the election of Montesquieu to the Academy

It was partially in order to live down the reputation for being merely a satirist, but also to prepare the way for his work on the philosophy of law, that Montesquieu wrote his history of the Romans, which those of his critics who preferred the mere satirist referred to as the *Grandeur et Décadence de Montesquieu.* Perhaps the ideas of his Italian contemporary Vico had no influence upon Montesquieu, though their theories were similar, but at any rate, both of them were indebted for their philosophy of history to their sixteenth century predecessor, Jean Bodin. In his *Causes of the Grandeur and Decadence of the Romans*, Montesquieu adopted Bodin's theory that natural environment predetermines the character of a people and conditions their government; the violation of this fundamental character under the Empire caused the downfall of the Romans. It was a naturalistic philosophy that, after considerable delay, he finally ventured to set forth as a philosophy of law.

The full title of the work in which he did this reveals its argument. It was called *The Spirit of the Laws; or of the Relation that Laws ought to have with the Constitution of each Government, Manners, Climate, Religion, Commerce, etc.* Through an encyclopedic mass of facts, sometimes uncorrelated and gratuitous, there is evidence of a continuous line of thought. This is that natural conditions, such as climate, topography, fertility of soil, location, etc., determine the character of a people; the character, in turn, determines whether their government should be a despotism, a monarchy, an aristocracy, or a republic; and the form of government determines what kind of laws the people should have. In each form of government there is a fundamental characteristic, or "virtue," as Montesquieu called it, of the people upon which it depends and change of which necessitates change in government. Despotisms flourish on a sense of fear. Their institutions, their manners, their education, their political structures, and therefore all their laws ought to be shaped with the purpose of inculcating this fundamental "virtue." Hence Montesquieu finds that

slavery, polygamy, and Mohammedanism are best suited
for despotisms, which flourish in extremes of climate, huge
extents of territory, and Oriental atmospheres.   The fundamental virtue of monarchy is honor, by which Montesquieu meant not so much the sense of honor as the desire
for distinction; and laws in a monarchy are based upon this
principle.   Privileged classes, sale of offices, restriction of
commerce to the middle class find their explanation in the
necessity for nourishing this virtue.   Countries of fair size,
Catholic religion, and temperate climate are best suited for
monarchy.   Aristocracy depends upon the virtue of moderation.   Hence no excesses of authority, wealth, honor,
size, or behavior must be permitted by law.   And finally
"political virtue" is the fundamental principle in democracies.   Lest there be any dispute as to what he meant by
"political virtue" and any displeasure that he might seem
to exclude virtue from monarchies, Montesquieu hastened
to define his meaning more clearly (II, III):

> What I call virtue in the republic is the love of country, that
> is to say the love of equality. . . . There is honor in republics,
> although political virtue is their source, and political virtue in
> monarchy, although honor is its source.

This peculiar kind of patriotism that included a passion for
equality, then, was the principle that republican governments and institutions must try to inspire by law, learning,
and tradition.   Hence they must be small enough to
enable each citizen to represent himself in government
affairs; there must be no privileged or wealthy classes, there
must be frequent rotation in office, there must be checks
and balances upon all powers.
  The chief criticism that is to be made of Montesquieu's
work is obvious.   Despite an objectivity of tone, despite
his unwillingness to wed himself to an ideal, despite his
anxiety to point out the inevitability of certain kinds of
institutions under certain conditions, he nevertheless explains the *ought* by the *is*.   Though he criticizes certain
institutions of his time. his method is essentially conserva-

tive. He looks about him, discovers China and Russia are despotisms, France a monarchy, Geneva a republic, and explains why this must be. Actually he is rationalizing existing institutions and situations rather than attempting to theorize about an ideal or to draw any general law of cycles in government. In this regard, he was not in accord with his century, which considered logic a better means of arriving at fact than observation, and philosophic specula- tion more true than historical development. Because Hume and Vico and Montesquieu did not have great faith in natural man, however, the eighteenth century did not lose faith in him. Logically he could be inferred and a career traced for him; if actual study of the past showed there was no such being, an age which was brought up to respect logical deduction more than historical fact simply disregarded history. Montesquieu's theory of the spirit of laws, therefore, bore greater fruit in a future century that produced Savigny and Buckle than in his own.

Montesquieu's analysis of the actual workings of govern- ment made a more immediate impression. Even he, despite his objective tone, did not hide his preferences. For states of large size, it was quite clear that he preferred the monar- chical form of government; and for states of small size, the republican form. His feeling was that such governments are best fit for liberty. But liberty can exist only when power is not abused. It is therefore necessary, in moderate governments, that all powers be so checked as to prevent any danger of abuse. The various phases of government must be strictly defined, and distinct groups of persons, for- bidden to join their powers, entrusted with the functions of the separate phases. Before Montesquieu, Locke in his *Two Treatises upon Civil Government* (Bk. II, ch. 22, secs. 143–45) had divided government into three branches — the legislative to have control of the laws, the federative to have charge of foreign affairs, and the executive to enforce the public law. Montesquieu welded Locke's federative and executive bodies together into one body which he called the executive, and provided a new group that he called the judiciary, which was to dispense justice and interpret the law. This tripartite division of government he borrowed, as Locke had before him and the Fathers of the American Constitution were to do after him, from the English Constitution.

To the admiring eyes of the French bourgeoisie, Montesquieu, as Voltaire also, held up England as a model of government. With as much enthusiasm as his monotonous style would allow, he spoke of its jury system, its lower house representing the people, its upper house representing the aristocracy, its king held in check by the legislature's control of finances, the veto power granted to the king, and its cabinet appointed by him and responsible to him (The eyes of a contemporary could not discern that the King of England in George II's time was fast becoming a figurehead.) He spoke of its *Habeas Corpus* Act, its procedure in criminal cases, its Bill of Rights. In some respects, to be sure, he went even beyond English institutions, advocating religious toleration, a criminal code in which penalties would be proportionate to the crimes committed, and a careful limitation upon the laws of *lèse majesté* and treason. But his general respect for England's government shows that Montesquieu believed that for a country of the extent and climate of France and England, Nature had intended a limited monarchical constitution with a powerful nobility to act as a defender of the law. He has been severely censured as an apologist for the *parlements*.

Montesquieu's book was immediately seized by the educated public, so that for the first twenty months of its existence in print an average of a new edition each month was necessary, and translations of it were already rendered in numerous languages. It was put on the Index in 1750 and attacked by both Catholics and Jansenists. On the other hand, Catherine the Great and Frederick the Great both admitted its influence upon them and we find it quoted in *The Federalist* by Madison and Hamilton. In the early years of the French Revolution the influence of Montesquieu was paramount, though it waned as the influence of Rousseau became greater. "Yet," it has been said, "if one should wish to write a single name upon the work of the Constitution of 1791, that name is Montesquieu." [1] In 1755, while, like Voltaire twenty-three years later, he was on a visit to Paris, he died. He was buried in the Church of Saint-Sulpice. The Revolution, which Pantheonized the other two of the triumvirate of *belles-lettres* to which he belonged, destroyed all trace of his remains.

In Voltaire we have the active cynic, in Montesquieu the detached observer; Rousseau was the personification of the sincere reformer. He comes as near to being the simple man in nature as any the eighteenth century, with all its seeking after Nature, was able to produce. Embarrassed in company, unencumbered by any ironclad moral code, committing blunders and intensely remorseful afterwards, making his *Confessions* without restraint to the world at large, devoid of historical sense and even historical knowledge, refusing royal gifts and pensions and preferring to live in poverty all his life, making enemies constantly because he feared to make friends, he is the simple, primitive, natural soul that he always had in mind. His philosophy is therefore to a large extent subjective and introspective, based upon his own experience, and inconsistent, varying with his mood. His influence, too, is not alone political, but, because of his *Émile*, has expressed itself in the endeavor to make education a process of self-expression, and because of his *Nouvelle Héloïse*, as well as his *Confessions* and his own personal example, has had its effect upon the Romantic movement in the literature of the nineteenth century.

"Rousseau," says Amiel, "had been badly brought up, or rather had not been brought up at all." [2] His mother died at his birth; his father did nothing more than to give him a lasting knowledge of Plutarch. After a youth spent at several different trades, he went to live with Madame

[1] Redslob: *Staatstheorien der Französischen Nationalversammlung*, 214-15.
[2] Amiel: *Jean Jacques Rousseau*, trans. by Brooks, 27.

de Warens for ten or twelve years. The variability of Madame de Warens' affections, however, eventually induced him to make his way to Paris. There he lived an obscure life as a musician and musical critic and as a private secretary, unable to support and therefore abandoning at a foundling hospital the five children he had by an ignorant servant girl, Thérèse Levasseur, who, nevertheless, remained faithful to him after many of his friends had been alienated by his queerness.

Until he was thirty-eight years old, he was known only to a very limited circle of intellectuals in whose retinue he maintained himself. If we are to believe his own account, in 1749 came his Vision of Damascus, a sudden inspiration for an essay to submit for the prize offered by the Academy of Dijon on the question: Whether the Progress of the Arts and Sciences has tended to corrupt or to improve Morals. He tells us in his *Confessions* that one day, when on his way to visit Diderot, who was in prison for one of his writings, he stopped under a tree to rest. When he awoke, his eye fell on an announcement of the Academy of Dijon's prize offer, and suddenly, by an inspiration that manifested itself in unmistakable physical reactions, the entire scheme of his essay presented itself to him. Diderot tells a different story. He claims to have advised Rousseau, who was very anxious to take the side of civilization as an improver of morals, that the other side would be the more likely to win the prize. But the discrepancy is interesting rather than important. The resulting First Discourse, however it was suggested, won the prize and enrolled Rousseau among the ranks of distinguished men of letters. Man, he maintains, is naturally happy and good, but civilization has accustomed him to ease and luxury and has created immorality. Nature is good but Civilization corrupts. This idea is developed further in the essay on "The Origin of Inequality among Men and Whether it is authorized by Natural Law," which he submitted the next year (1753) when the Academy of Dijon offered another prize. He first presented an idyllic picture of primitive life in which every man is the equal of every other. Then some one fences in a piece of land, declares "This is mine!" and begins the institution of private property. Inequality between rich and poor is born at that moment and grows as agriculture and industry increase wealth and poverty. Society and government are then organized to protect the rights of the wealthy, and natural equality disappears forever. Not only did Rousseau not win the prize for which this essay was intended, but after it had been published and he sent a copy of it to Voltaire, the old cynic replied that the book made him "feel like going on all fours," but "it is more than sixty years since I lost the habit. . . . Nor can I take ship to go out and join the savages in Canada; first because the diseases which bear me down oblige me to stay near the greatest physician in Europe; . . . second, because . . . the example of our nations has made the savages almost as cruel as we are."

There followed for Rousseau a period of amours with Madame d'Épinay and Madame d'Houdetot and of quarrels with other philosophers, during which no important political work issued from Rousseau's pen. In quick succession, however, in the years 1761–62, came his three most influential books — *Julie ou la Nouvelle Héloïse*, *Le Contrat Social*, and *Émile*. The first was a novel in which the author, immoral though he would be accounted by our present standards, showed conjugal fidelity triumphant over illicit love. The last, which may likewise be considered a novel, is important because it gives Rousseau's ideas on education; it narrates the story of the bringing up, in accordance with the Laws of Nature, of the young Émile from the time of his birth until his marriage to a girl, who, being only a girl, had received a distinctly inferior training. Rousseau, having showed in his First and Second Discourses how civilization corrupts, felt called upon in this work to show that it was possible to educate children in such a way as to eliminate the inhibiting, unnatural, warping influences of civilization. He teaches his hypothetical young student by experience rather than by books, by observation rather than precept, the practical rather than the ornamental, and permits him very little association with other people.   Step by step, as Émile grows older, more information and more complex problems are set before him. These, under careful and sometimes restrictive mentorship, he masters for himself.   In the end, Émile is a young man, fully prepared to marry his Sophie and equipped with the knowledge that civilization has accumulated without suffering any of the spoiling effects that civilization brings. Nevertheless, in a sequel novel, Rousseau wrecks the ideal marriage of *Émile et Sophie* and sends them out in quest of new adventures.   The *Émile* was not Rousseau's only work on education.   There were replies to the critics of *Émile*, in which Rousseau expatiated on some of his educational theories.   There were letters to a fond German prince-father on the education of his daughter.   There were provisions for public education in Rousseau's scheme for the reorganization of unhappy Poland — *Considérations sur le gouvernement de Pologne*.   But the *Émile* is generally supposed to have had a greater effect upon educational theories since his time than any of these.   Since Rousseau's generation, and largely because of his teachings, educators have emphasized education by observation rather than by rote, learning of the useful rather than the ceremonious or ornamental, and personal contact between the mentor and the student.   The theory of public education in the work on Poland has since met with general application in most Occidental countries.

The fourth part of the *Émile*, setting forth the deistic religion that Émile learned, is entitled the *Profession de Foi du Vicaire Savoyard*.   It is this fragment of the work that won it its greatest condemnation and notoriety.   The eighteenth century is generally referred to as deistic in religion, and contemporaries described themselves as deists. In philosophical deism — the belief that God, having created the world and man, then withdrew to transcendental heavens to allow his creations to work out their own destiny — there was something too cold, too impersonal to be adopted generally by an age that believed so devoutly in Nature and in emotional display. Even among the intellectuals, there was need for a more intimate God, for a Supreme Creator who, without resorting to miracles and thaumaturgy, yet played his part in human affairs, was approachable and robust. As rationalists and students of the sciences they could not accept any conception of an anthropomorphic God or the God of the Bible. Hence they resorted to a sort of pantheism. God was Nature; he manifested himself through natural phenomena; he was to be worshiped as natural man might worship him, not in magnificent temples with flattering rituals and unctuous sacraments, but humbly and simply, whenever and wherever His comfort and aid were needed. This was the religion of which the Savoyard Vicar told Émile; and it was the religion that the so-called deistic eighteenth-century intellectuals for the most part professed. It was this phase of the *Émile* that led to an extensive controversy between Rousseau and the Archbishop of Paris and the Council of Geneva, to which we owe Rousseau's *Lettre à M. de Beaumont* and *Lettres de la Montagne*. In 1762 the *Émile* was ordered burned by Parlement and Rousseau himself was outlawed.

Before he fled, however, he published the *Contrat Social*. It is the *Contrat Social* that is Rousseau's most significant contribution to the political philosophy of the eighteenth century. Like Montesquieu he is deeply indebted to Locke, who in his treatise *On Civil Government* had set forth the theory that, somewhere in the past, independent and equal individuals had entered into an agreement to form a society and a government, and on the ground that James II had violated that original compact, had tried to justify the English "Glorious Revolution" of 1688. The contract theory was not original even with Locke. To go no farther into the past, Calvinists in Holland, Huguenots in France, and Jesuits in England had used it in their appeal to force against their rulers in the sixteenth century. Rousseau likewise assumes that "man is born free" and that since he is now "everywhere in chains" and since governments do now exist, they must have come about originally by a covenant which guaranteed to each his rights of liberty, equality, and property. The individuals taken together are therefore the sovereign; taken separately the subjects. The government cannot be sovereign, since it is only a device for keeping order more easily. Whether the government is a monarchy, an aristocracy, or a democracy (and he borrows Montesquieu's ideas regarding the determination by Nature of the forms of governments), the people ought to keep close watch on the government to see that it carries out the General Will. For the sovereignty of the monarch, therefore, Rousseau substituted the sovereignty of the people whose General Will is expressed by a majority vote. Unless corrupted, this General Will is always right, since each individual votes not according to his own interests but according to what he believes the General Will may be. The majority may coerce any individual to act according to the General Will, for to do so "means nothing more than that they force him to be free." The idea of a social compact gave rise to the feeling that constitutions existed even before governments and that by those constitutions all men were equal. We shall find the Frenchman of the eighteenth century preferring equality to liberty, even when he does not confuse the two.

After Rousseau's *Émile* was condemned to be burned and Rousseau himself outlawed, he fled from place to place, welcomed neither in Berne, nor Geneva, nor England, nor Normandy, nor Paris, whither he was permitted to return in 1769. He spent his last years writing his *Confessions* (a sort of *apologia pro sua vita*), his *Dialogues*, and the *Reveries du promeneur solitaire*. Hallucinations, inconsistencies of thought, quarrels with his best friends mark his closing years even more than his earlier ones. Some of his contemporaries called him insane; more lenient critics since have called him paranoiac. Perhaps he was neither, but certainly he was not an ordinary, normal person. His *Confessions* strip bare his own soul in the merciless manner of Russian novelists with others', and perhaps serve as his best defense, if, indeed, he needs a defense; he used himself merely as a means through which to observe the relations of man and nature. In 1778, the same year as his enemy Voltaire, he died at the home of a friendly Marquis de Girardin at Ermenonville. Like Voltaire, he was Pantheonized during the Revolution. Voltaire had made possible the Civil Constitution of the Clergy; Montesquieu had made possible the Constitution of 1791; Rousseau was the voice crying in the wilderness for the Declaration of Rights. If it were possible to sum up a man's work in one word, the word for Voltaire would be Tolerance, for Montesquieu Liberty, for Rousseau Equality. To Rousseau, also, must be ascribed the Back-to-Nature movement that had its effect on Marie Antoinette and has recurred in succeeding generations. Byron called him "the self-torturing sophist, . . . the apostle of affliction," who "knew how to make madness beautiful."

The greatest intellectual triumph of the eighteenth century, however, was not the work of any one man. It was the *Encyclopédie*, edited and largely written by the *littérateur* Diderot and the mathematician D'Alembert, but contributed to by many others, among whom were Voltaire, Montesquieu, Rousseau, Holbach, Morellet, Quesnay, Turgot, Condorcet, and perhaps the great naturalist Buffon. Originally undertaken as the French translation of Chambers's *Encyclopedia*, it immediately broke away from any existing model and became an ambitious endeavor (in the words of Condorcet) to "bring together all that had been discovered in science, what was known of the productions of the globe, the details of the arts which men have invented, the principles of morals, those of legislation, the laws which govern society, the metaphysics of language and the rules of grammar, the analysis of our faculties, and even the history of our opinions." Its first volume appeared in 1751; the thirty-fourth and thirty-fifth, its indices, not until twenty-nine years later (1780). In that same year, Panckoucke undertook the *Encyclopédie méthodique*, originally intended as a new and enlarged edition of the *Ency-clopédie* but arranged as a system of separate dictionaries of one volume each, on Mathematics, Physics, Medicine, etc. The Revolution interrupted this project, and it was not completed until 1832.

Diderot's *Encyclopédie* was twice suppressed by the Council, and without the editor's knowledge, the publisher mutilated the manuscripts in order to make them less objectionable to the authorities. D'Alembert had, before this episode, withdrawn from the work, afraid to continue, but under Diderot's editorship and largely by the products of his own pen, and with the connivance of some who officially censored it, it nevertheless progressed and finally reached completion. There was "much paste" among the "fine diamonds," Voltaire found. But the work was a brave monument to eighteenth-century knowledge and philosophy. It not only summarized, as far as was possible in that day, practically all the available information that scholars had at their disposal, but it also contained much in the way of polemical attacks and constructive political philosophy. "On every page was inscribed the watchword of the age: Reason." [1] Articles like those on Authority (*Autorité*), Faith (*Foi*), People (*Peuple*), Privileges (*Privilèges*), Taxes (*Impôts*), and the famous article on *Geneva* by D'Alembert, which caused a temporary suppression in 1759, were more often political tracts than learned treatises, attacking the abuses of the Government and the Church. Despite the fact that among its four thousand subscribers were many men and women of wealth and power and that it was dedicated to the King and to D'Argenson, one of the King's ministers, and that it received the support of Madame de Pompadour and the reticent admiration even of the King, the editor was persecuted and the work delayed. Clandestinely and, at the close, alone, Diderot persevered. In the end, however, more than any other means, the *Encyclopédie* served as a medium for propagandizing the ideas of the *philosophes*. It was an encyclopedia that

[1] Abry, Audic, and Crouzet: *Histoire illustrée de la littérature française,* 385

was used for more than library decoration; it was discussed in the salons and even in the palace, where an astute king, once at least, defended it against its detractors.   Diderot himself wrote 1139 articles, totaling about 4132 quarto pages.   He wrote much else — plays, other political tracts, philosophical letters, even essays on physiology, but this editorial work on the *Encyclopédie* is his *monumentum aere perennius*.   It may even be said, with certain limitations, that the *philosophe* movement of the eighteenth century is embodied in the *Encyclopédie*, that the words *philosophe* and *encyclopédist* are synonymous.   Only less than Vol-taire's was Diderot's personality the guiding influence of intellectual France in the Age of Enlightenment.   "He who only knows Diderot in his writings," said Marmontel, "does not know him at all."   His conversation was the delight of the Holbachians, as Rousseau, who despised their atheistic bent, called the group that dined and descanted at the salon of Baron d'Holbach's wife.   He was the friend of Grimm, the guest of Catherine the Great.   In July, 1784, having outlived the greatest of his contemporaries, he brought a magnificent life to a close.

There were a number of minor philosophers who must be mentioned before the story of the *Aufklärung*, as the Germans call this age, can be regarded as complete.   There were Mably and Morelly, who may be regarded as pre-cursors of the Utopian Socialists of the nineteenth century. There was Helvétius, whose book *De l'Esprit*, a materialistic study attempting to reduce all human motives to utili-tarianism and destined to be the inspiration of the future Benthamites, precipitated a crisis in 1758, when it was itself condemned to the fire and helped to bring about the suppression of the *Encyclopédie*.   There was the Baron d'Holbach, whose *System of Nature*, which tried to reduce all things to physical actions and reactions, is a good example of the philosophers' attempts to make government, religion and society conform to Nature, although he went further in the direction of atheism than most of them were prepared to follow.   There was the Italian Beccaria, whose

Traité des Délits et des Peines did much to bring about an agitation for the reform of existing criminal codes. There was Raynal, perhaps the greatest of this minor group, whose *Histoire philosophique et politique des Établissements et du Commerce des Européens dans les deux Indes* (parts of which were written by Diderot) showed the beauty and happiness of primitive society and, by contrast, brought into disrepute almost every institution in France. There was the dramatist Beaumarchais, whose *Mariage de Figaro* popularized the philosophers' arraignment of society. There was the Marquis d'Argenson, who stood for democracy long before Rousseau and for local self-government. There was a host of lesser lights — French Boswells to French Johnsons — Fontenelle, Marmontel, Madame du Deffand, Duclos, La Harpe, and others — whose writings, important in themselves, are more interesting for their reminiscences of greater contemporaries.

And finally there were the Physiocrats, fathered by Quesnay and Gournay, boasting as one of their followers the finest practical reformer of the age, Turgot, proudly able to claim the English economist Adam Smith, author of the *Wealth of Nations*, as their disciple. They maintained that by Nature the only source of wealth was land and agriculture, and that industry and commerce ought therefore to be let alone (*laisser faire*) and all taxes be levied only on land. The ranks of the Physiocrats were recruited from among noble and bourgeois landowners — the elder Mirabeau, La Rivière, Dupont de Nemours — who ran their farms on the latest principles of scientific agriculture. Since the corn laws and other internal tariff duties were a great obstacle for them in marketing their produce, there was something more than mere theory behind their opposition to mercantilism. But whether their motives were intellectual or materialistic, they must nevertheless be considered the founders of modern political economy. Their importance in the age of enlightenment is that they were the only group among the philosophers who, in more than a general way, were interested in the peasant and his problems, though their politics was essentially plutocratic. They looked to enlightened despotism as the form of government best fitted to carry out their policies. The others, excepting possibly Rousseau and Voltaire, were altogether bourgeois both in spirit and in appeal. The peasant cared little about inequality, social contracts, or even, since he was a good Catholic, religious intolerance. The land, which was the problem of the Physiocrat, was his problem too.

It was the educated merchants, lawyers, and bankers who read the philosophers and agreed with them; and it was the liberal nobles and clergy (particularly the abbés) who were the most impressed. These intellectuals and dilettantes spent their evenings at the homes of wealthy ladies in engaging and sometimes exciting discussions of philosophical questions. There were "Tuesdays" at the salon of Madame de Helvétius, where they might encounter the renowned and gentle Franklin. There were "Thursdays" and "Sundays" at Madame d'Holbach's where, like as not, one might hear atheism and materialism discussed. At Madame de Necker's a more pious tone prevailed. Madame du Deffand's yellow upholstery and red ribbons attracted D'Alembert and Grimm as well as Luxembourgs and Broglies, or Humes and Walpoles, though Bolingbroke and Chesterfield were said to be found more readily at Madame de Tencin's when they were in Paris. At the salon of Madame de Geoffrin, who contributed two hundred thousand livres to the *Encyclopédie*, the *philosophe* clique could count on a powerful influence to be used (discreetly) in their favor. Thus did polite society help the triumph of new ideas.

Younger and poorer folk with ideas and a desire to be heard had, however, to make up their own societies and clubs. Many of them joined the Masonic order, at the head of which, in France, was the First Prince of the Blood, the Duke of Orléans. In their lodges they could and did talk to their hearts' content of Rousseau and Voltaire, and propound their panaceas. There were Masonic lodges in every good-sized town in France, and where there were not, or even where there were, there was some less formal organization in which the young serious thinker might air his views and debate the most recent political tracts. The Illuminati, who were supposed to be the most aggressively reforming as well as the most perniciously secretive of the ritualistic lodges of the eighteenth century, were not so strong in France as they were in the Germanies and elsewhere in Europe. These and other liberal and radical clubs were the cradles of oratory and parliamentary law for the Robespierres, Brissots, Marats of the days before the Revolution. And these young men were not alone content to talk of Rousseau and Mably, Raynal and Montesquieu; they needs must write like them too. Saint Just, Brissot, Marat, Robespierre had already contributed their attacks on social injustice and political abuse to the current of philosophical literature before the Revolution.

The peasant, to be sure, did not read, but neither was he without his notion of what greater folk than he were thinking and saying of his plight. The curés' sermons were one means of spreading the new ideas among the peasantry, but even where the curé was cautious, the peasant might hear and be fired by the traveling troupes that visited the countryside. Stock characters they were — Harlequin, Columbine, Pierrot, Scaramouche — and their impromptu dialogues and plays were no less stock, but in them the rural spectator might sometimes behold his own misfortunes portrayed, his own grievances put into words, and might perhaps take a vicarious revenge upon his persecutors. In the villages, the country lawyers championed the new order, and many a time the old régime was put on trial along with some abused offender. In the cities, the *Mariage de Figaro* of Beaumarchais played to large audiences at the Théâtre Français and elsewhere, and nightly the artisans and middle-class theater-goer might applaud Figaro's stealthy thrusts at his noble master and sympathize with Figaro's bitterness. But in the city it was the street corner, the quay, and the cafés that served as the school for politicians and citizens. Here one might overhear some Stentor reading from the

Social Contract or from some article in *Le Mercure*; or at least, might engage in an argument with a neighbor whc did not quite agree with one. Paris was thus a large debating club even in times of peace. When there were disturbances — anti-Jesuit demonstrations, pro-Parlement riots, or funerals of the illustrious — Paris (and only to a lesser extent the smaller cities) was more than ever "the café of Europe," as Holbach's salon was called.

One was not likely to hear Plutarch cited or Livy quoted in a Parisian café; and yet the classics were a very definite factor in the *philosophe* movement of eighteenth-century France. Montesquieu's *Considerations on the Romans* reveals his debt more clearly than the more concealed influence that the Latins and Greeks played upon his confrères discovers them as debtors. But a younger generation then growing up, which was to play the lead in the next era, freely avowed Plutarch as an intellectual progenitor. Charlotte Corday, and Manon Phlipon, soon to become Madame Roland, suffered with the heroes of the *Parallel Lives* as much as equally sentimental ladies of the same time suffered with the *Nouvelle Héloïse*; and Manon "wept that she had not been born a Spartan." Marat quoted Livy and Tacitus to show how tyrants had always welded *Chains of Slavery*. Louvet, Vergniaud, and other future Girondin orators were now learning the speeches of Brutus and Cato that were to stud their Convention addresses, and Babeuf was now acquiring that love for the Roman tribune which in later years was to induce him to change his good Christian name of François Noël to Gracchus. The Battle of the Ancients and the Moderns at the end of the seventeenth century had been won by the Moderns, and as standards of literary art, the classics were now somewhat in disrepute. But Plutarch survived, and though dead for over fifteen hundred years, was spiritually to be enrolled in the ranks of the *philosophes*.

Unwittingly marching in these ranks were also to be found the Fathers of the American Revolution. The French Government had long hesitated to join forces with the Americans, not alone because it was inexpedient at a time when a policy of economy was being assiduously urged by a practical Ministry under the banker Necker, but also because a large part of the population, including *cérébraux* like Madame du Deffand as well as conservative nobles, doubted the wisdom of interference on behalf of rebels and radicals.   But that very opposition created an increased enthusiasm for the American cause in other circles.   Mirabeau, Beaumarchais, Orléans, Lafayette, Dekalb — all wrote on behalf of the colonies or offered their services. The venerable Franklin, sent as envoy to the court at Versailles, was fêted everywhere, eulogized in poems, addressed on public occasions, lionized by polite society, elected to the Academy, made the leader of one of the most influential chapters of the Masonic Order (the Lodge of the Neuf Sœurs, to which Voltaire, Condorcet, Bailly, Brissot, and Danton also belonged now or later), coyly courted by ladies of high birth, invited to experimental demonstrations by Marat, and begged to accept dedications by Robespierre in a letter that even allowances for the conventions of polite correspondence do not save completely from obsequiousness.   Vergennes, while pretending to demur, secretly aided the American cause by sending French officers, money, and supplies, and subvening American propagandists.   Finally the Battle of Saratoga induced Vergennes to come out openly for an alliance with the new confederation, and until the peace of 1783 the newest republic and one of the oldest monarchies in the world fought side by side.

The fraternal bond thus created increased the interest in the New World, which had always been great in France. Travelers in America, actual or vicarious, had written many volumes for an avid French audience before the Alliance of 1778.   None achieved the vogue of Raynal's *Two Indies*, but all won a large public.   And now French officers, returning from American campaigns flushed with success, added to the accumulating literature on the younger world. Filson's, Carver's, Ramsay's, Barnaby's accounts of various regions in America, translated into French, enjoyed as many readers as the originals or more. Chastellux's book on *Travels in America* was soon followed by Crevecœur's *Letters of an American Farmer* and Brissot's *Voyage in America*; and these were but a few of the number that were quickly gobbled up by an eager public. The Declaration of Independence, the Articles of Confederation, the Constitutions of the new States had been translated and published in numerous editions. The *philosophes* and their followers were at last able to point to nations in which the eighteenth-century ideas of tolerance, liberty, equality, the rights of man, and social contract were set down in writing. And when the Convention at Philadelphia drew up the Constitution of 1787, the heat of the discussions in France regarding its merits and demerits was second only to that in New York and Virginia, and was joined in by Raynal, Mirabeau, Condorcet, Mably, Turgot, who all welcomed it, though they found certain details to criticize, and by Jefferson, who, having succeeded Franklin as American representative at Versailles, felt called upon to defend it. The problems of the two countries were not the same. In the one there was the question of an obsolete feudal aristocracy, in the other of a nascent nationalism. The problems of Church, serfdom, privileged nobility, overtaxation barely entered into the discussion of American institutions, even when carried on by Frenchmen. But the spectacle of simplicity rewarded, virtue triumphant, Reason prevailing, Nature enthroned which *philosophes* and French intellectuals sought and managed to find in the American republic was a source of great comfort and increased fluency to them. Small wonder that Jefferson and Gouverneur Morris were expected to take part in the French Revolution when they were in Paris, that Franklin and Washington were given honors by the National Assembly that few natives enjoyed, that Thomas Paine actually became a member of the National Convention. Without really having added much to eighteenth-century French political thought, they had become part of the *philosophes'* stock in trade.

Perhaps now we can understand what Chateaubriand

meant when he said that the French Revolution "was accomplished before it occurred."   The average man is an inert being.   He is not interested in any radical philosophy, unless it touches upon some actual tyranny and grievance against which he is already embittered.   When his dissatisfaction has been roused to sufficient height, he accepts the philosophy nearest at hand which conforms to his demands, not because the philosopher is a genius who leads him to better things that he has never dreamed of, but because the philosopher gives him a program for which he has already been groping.   Two things, therefore, are essential before a revolution becomes a possibility — dissatisfaction and a political philosophy promising immediate redress of grievances.   When these two have taken hold of men's minds, a revolution is already accomplished even though it has not yet occurred, particularly, as in this case, when the powers-that-be have already acknowledged the weaknesses of the old régime and have hesitatingly begun to make a number of reforms of their own.   Only an immediate cause is then lacking for the final rupture, and that is but a question of time and chance.

CHAPTER IV

STAVING OFF THE REVOLUTION

THE immediate cause of the French Revolution was that the French monarchy found itself faced with financial bankruptcy. The storm had been gathering for almost seventy-five years before 1789, when it actually broke. The close of the reign of Louis XIV (1715) found France in a sorry financial plight. Four wars in quick succession, the last (the War of the Spanish Succession) involving every nation of importance in Europe and fought on four continents, had proved disastrous to the strong nation that had gradually risen from feudal anarchy through the efforts of Henry IV, Richelieu, and Mazarin. In none of these wars was the self-styled *roi soleil* decisively defeated; indeed, he might have claimed the first three as victories. But in each, France had fought alone or practically alone against powers allied at least in sympathy and, in the last two conflicts, allied in fact. The splendid army built up by Vauban and Louvois had been depleted; the wealth painfully accumulated by Colbert had been squandered. Despite the huge palace built on a swamp at Versailles, which was shoddily imitated by lesser monarchs, despite the sycophant obedience of powerful nobles to the King, despite the predominance of French literature, language, style, and manners among foreign peoples, observant men knew that the state of France was unhealthy and unsound. It would be one of the most ironical, if it were not also one of the most pathetic tableaux in history to behold Louis XIV, the Grand Monarch and Sun King, upon his deathbed, confessing his failure to his grandson's infant son:

> My child, you will soon be sovereign of a great kingdom. Do not forget your obligations to God; remember that it is to Him that you owe all that you are. Endeavor to live at peace with your neighbors; do not imitate me in my fondness for war,

nor in the exorbitant expenditure which I have incurred. Take council in all your actions. Endeavor to relieve the people at the earliest possible moment, and thus to accomplish what, unfortunately, I am unable to do myself.

France rejoiced when death closed the reign of the king who had sat upon his throne longer than any other ruler in modern times. But this joy was premature. The new king was but a child of five, and his profligate grand-uncle, the Duke of Orléans, ruled in his name. Peace was never secure during the Regency and a war with Spain (1719–20), to teach the Bourbon ruler of that country that the Treaty of Utrecht (1713) was to be taken in earnest when it prohibited the union of both France and Spain under the same crown, resulted in no remuneration for the ill-spared expenditure of French blood and money it entailed, though it ended in victory and brightened a dimming prestige.

The anxiety to wipe out the public debt in one miraculous swoop led to the support of a Scotch adventurer named John Law and his Mississippi Scheme. Law was not altogether incompetent. Quite the contrary, his financial enterprises on earlier occasions had been successful and no more shady than similar ventures of now illustrious financiers, like his older contemporary Paterson, of the Bank of England. While he was still Controller-General of Finances, he created a stock company — the Compagnie d'Occident — for the exploitation of the Louisiana territory in America. Owing to the fact that the Controller-General did not himself draw a careful distinction between his stock company and the Royal Bank that he had founded under government auspices, confusion rapidly took possession of the popular mind. It was generally thought that the Compagnie d'Occident had been launched with state support, and its stocks rose very rapidly. Hundreds of investors, aching for a market for surplus capital that lay idle in vaults and stockings because of the scarcity of banks and reasonable investment projects, now eagerly bought up shares in Law's company. As the price of the stocks rocketed skyward, only a few of the more prudent investors, of whom Law was not one, sold their shares. The bubble broke, and a number of curious and pathetic changes were found to have taken place in the economic structure of France. Valets had become millionaires, millionaires had to become valets. Law was obliged to flee the country, though his personal responsibility was neither premeditated nor unique. The Bank failed along with the Compagnie, and part of the national debt had to be repudiated. Even so, it had increased by 20,000,000 francs, although the interest was considerably reduced. Other half-hearted attempts at reform were made, but the only really lasting change that was effected in France by the Regent was that he converted the example of austerity that Louis XIV had set for his subjects in his last years into one of frank and unashamed license. Almost the one bright spot in the eight years of the administration of the Duke of Orléans was the appearance of Montesquieu's *Persian Letters*.

The reign of Louis XV aggravated an already intolerable situation. For over fifty years after the death of the Regent, Louis XV continued to reign, counseled in the first twenty by the ignorant Duke of Bourbon and the senescent Cardinal Fleury. In that half-century France fought, with small profit, three wars of world dimensions. By the War of the Polish Election (1733–38), Lorraine was acquired, indirectly and after a lapse of time; but in the War of the Austrian Succession (1740–48) and the Seven Years' War (1756–63), France lost to England all her vast possessions in the Western Hemisphere save a few islands and French Guiana, yielded to England her commercial supremacy in India, and surrendered to that country, likewise, whatever footholds she had in Africa. Louis XV magnanimously presented what later became the Louisiana Territory to Spain to indemnify his ally for her losses in coming to his assistance. But at home taxes increased, the national debt increased, court splendor (what with the feminine wiles of Madame de Pompadour and Madame du Barry, the two most important of the royal mistresses) increased, and dissatisfaction grew apace.

When Louis XV first came to the throne of France, he was called by his subjects, and by none more loudly than the *philosophes*, Louis the Well-Beloved (*le bien-aimé*). Nor was it mere mockery. A handsome child the new king was, and quiet, unassuming, precocious. The tenderness of his youth, compared to the crabbed old age of his predecessor, appealed to his subjects, as did also the precariousness of his state of health. All France sang *Te Deums* when the King recovered from his chronic illnesses and when he married his Polish princess Maria Leczinska; and at no time was anxiety more critical or France more desolate than when he fell ill at Metz in 1744, during the War of the Austrian Succession, when his armies were fighting those of Maria Theresa and George II in an effort to divide the territory of the Hapsburgs and to secure control of India and America. France was happy once more only when the King passed from danger.

But thereafter his popularity began to wane. It was not alone that Louis commenced to be weary of the king business and lusted more and more after pleasures, nor that his conduct lost its earlier purity and became an open scandal, nor that Louis XV, no more than Louis XIV, could actually win wars and, more than Louis XIV, did squander the nation's wealth. It was due also to the fact that there was now beginning to arise a new spirit of restlessness, an outcry from popular sources that had once come from nobles and clerics, against the royal prerogative. The rise of the periodical and the journal, the increase in the number of pamphlets and broadsides, the greater frequency of public gatherings and open discussions had now created a force in politics which, while not new, was now more to be reckoned with than ever before. Public Opinion was rapidly attaining maturity.

Three times during the reign of Louis XV crises occurred which, if they did not shake the security of the throne, at least indicated that, somewhere in the future, revolution lurked. The issue in all three cases was one of freedom of thought. Since the days of Louis XIII a sect called the

Jansenists, after Jansenius, the Dutch theologian, had flourished in France at Port Royal. The Jesuits found that they believed in predestination and other heresies, and after a prolonged controversy during the reign of Louis XIV, had had them condemned by the papal bull *Unigenitus* (1713) and had succeeded in making the bull part of the national law. The law, however, was a dead letter until the ministry of the ecclesiastic Fleury, who in 1730 tried to make all the clergy accept it. The high-handed attitude of the Government created much opposition, which found its champion in the Parlement of Paris. It became necessary to exile some of the members of the parlement and to decrease its powers; and in 1742 a royal decree made it a criminal offense to own a book "injurious to good morals." Public opinion was at fever heat, and the unsuccessful prosecution of the War of the Austrian Succession increased the popular bitterness. Anti-conscription riots occurred and revolution seemed certain.

On the occasion of this first crisis, however, Louis XV was still the *Bien-Aimé*. The love his people bore him and his own good sense, in which he was never altogether lacking, served to meet the emergency. Louis XV yielded for the moment, granted a certain degree of freedom to the press, and called to the ministry the Marquis d'Argenson, a champion of tolerance, to whom the *Encyclopédie* was later to be dedicated. Voltaire was appointed royal historiographer and in 1746 received the King's authorization to present himself to the French Academy. The glorious victory over the English at Fontenoy in 1745, coming shortly after the King's remarkable recovery from his illness at Metz, added to the general good will.

But the war continued, and the ultramontane Jesuits only increased their activities against the Jansenists. The censorship was soon renewed against objectionable books Peace, when it finally was declared in 1748, was considered a humiliation, for France, though she lost nothing, had nothing to show for her pains. Taxation, despite the protests of the parlements, continued to grow more burdensome.

Finally the Archbishop of Paris ordered that no one who could not show a certificate of confession signed by a priest adhering to the bull *Unigenitus* should be permitted to take part in the mass. Popular demonstrations took place when priests refused to perform the last sacraments for dying impenitents. Feeling ran especially high against Madame de Pompadour, whose influence was popularly, and not altogether justly, supposed to have perverted the King's goodness of heart and soundness of spirit. In 1752 several notable demonstrations took place in Paris and the provinces. The Parlement of Paris would have punished the offending priests but for the interference of the King. On the night of May 8, certain members of the Parlement of Paris were exiled by *lettres de cachet.* The others, however, declared that they sympathized with their colleagues and were immediately transferred to Pontoise and later to Soissons. Feeling was intense throughout France against the King and the bishops. D'Argenson tells us in his *Journal* that he looked at any moment for a massacre of priests. On Christmas Day of 1753 Lord Chesterfield, confirmed letter-writer and arbiter-extraordinary of English manners, wrote that "all the symptoms which he had ever met in History, previous to great changes and Revolutions in government, now exist and daily increase in France." But again Louis XV, now openly execrated by the very ones who, when he lay ill at Metz, had been the most disconsolate, thought it advisable to surrender. He recalled the parlement, exiled the Archbishop of Paris, and gave the parlement a free hand in dealing with the lesser clerics. The crisis of 1752–54 thus came to a peaceful conclusion.

Then the Seven Years' War broke out (1756). France now, by a diplomatic revolution brought about largely by Chancellor Kaunitz of Austria and Madame de Pompadour, went to the aid of her formerly inveterate enemy Austria against a newer and more ominous foe, her erstwhile ally Prussia, which received the aid of England, but yesterday the friend of Austria. New taxes once more were levied and a reaction soon set in. Louis XV, on December 13, 1756, forced the parlement by a *lit de justice* to register three decrees limiting its own powers over religious questions and obliging it to accept the bull *Unigenitus*. The quarrel burst forth again with renewed fury, and an attempt was made upon the life of Louis XV himself. The brilliant victory of Frederick the Great over French arms at Rossbach heightened the resentment of the people against the Government. Furthermore, the King began to demand free gifts from every town in the realm in addition to the regular taxes. Quebec fell to the English in 1759, and Louis asked for more taxes. But peace brought another reaction. The parlement, appealed to in a lawsuit against a leading Jesuit, had already been able to limit the activity of the Society and finally, on August 6, 1762, to dissolve it altogether. This act was confirmed by the King in 1764. It would seem that the forces of liberalism, represented in the parlements, had triumphed over the forces of reaction, represented by the Jesuits.

But the struggle between the two forces continued unabated. In fact, in 1762, the same year as the suppression of the Society of Jesus, more books were officially condemned than in any other year between 1715 and 1789. The works of the *philosophes* came forward in increasing numbers, nevertheless. The growing sentiment for democracy made the old king fearful. In April, 1770, he inadvisedly opposed the parlement in its trial of the Duc d'Aiguillon, the King's Governor of Brittany, on the charge of having perverted justice in the disorders accompanying the quarrel between the King and the parlement. The parlement objected to the King's interference, and under the influence of his Chancellor Maupeou, Louis issued an edict preventing the parlements of the realm either from corresponding with each other or from resisting him by resigning in a body, both recent practices that had given them a unity and coherence that made them a formidable group. The parlement refused to register this decree even after a *lit de justice*. The controversy raged back and forth, until on January 19–21, 1771, the parlement was exiled and the Grand Council (the so-called Maupeou Parlement) took its place as the highest court in the land. Paris was in an uproar. "I declare," wrote Regnaut, a contemporary witness of events, "that if at that critical moment there had been found a leader, the Revolution would have been most terrible." The provincial parlements protested vigorously. The lower courts joined with them. People began to talk of calling the Estates General, a suggestion which, though it had been voiced even in the reign of Louis XIV, was still considered a counsel of desperation. But the King returned to the attack. In 1771 the provincial parlements likewise were suppressed. Exiled priests and Jesuits were allowed to return. Louis threatened to execute within twenty-four hours any one, were it even his own brother, who mentioned the Estates General to him. And Madame du Barry placed before him Van Dyke's portrait of Charles I of England. For the remaining three years of Louis XV's reign the parlements did not exist and ever imminent bankruptcy was postponed by new taxes.

Three times the Revolution had threatened and three times it had failed to come. Some have an explanation for this in the fact that the philosophers were not yet well known. This is only partially true, for while Montesquieu alone was famous in 1743, by the time of the crisis of 1771, the entire group had written and published their most valuable works. There is also a partial explanation in the fact that the parlements were not so much interested during the struggle in the question of the people's rights as they were in preserving their own privileges. But more important than either of these reasons is this: the fundamental issue at stake in 1743, 1752–54, and 1771 was one of religious toleration, only slightly confused with that of defeatism and taxation. On the question of religious freedom France could reach a high point of excitement, but it required the more personal motives of opposition to increased taxation and the desire for further control of the Government to rouse even an emotional people like the French to the point of revolution.

On May 10, 1774, Louis XV died, defiantly asserting that

he "owed an account of his conduct to God alone." His reign had done much to create a radical spirit. Grimm, who knew everybody of importance in the literary world of France, wrote in August, 1774, "To-day there is hardly a young man, on leaving college, who does not form a scheme to establish a new system of government, hardly an author who does not believe himself obliged to teach the powers of the earth the best way to rule their states." Louis XV is supposed to have replied, when his advisers told him that his treasury was running low, that things would last as long as he, and after him the deluge! (*Après moi, le déluge!*) Again tradition has been more epigrammatic than the actual words would warrant, but the thought was Louis' own. How truly he spoke his successor was soon to discover.

At the accession of Louis XVI, an honest, plodding soul, who much preferred hunting and tinkering with machinery to piloting the ship of state, France believed that a new era had dawned. The young king was not averse to playing the part of the enlightened monarch that so well fitted his con- temporaries — Frederick of Prussia, Catherine of Russia, Joseph of Austria, and Charles of Spain. One of his first acts was to exile Maupeou, to recall the parlements, and to reëstablish them with all their former prestige. Under the delightful and not incapable Maurepas as Prime Minister, he created a ministry of talents. For Controller-General of Finances he chose Anne Robert Jacques Turgot, a leader among the Physiocrats and one who had already effected important reforms as intendant in the Generality of Li- moges. Among the earliest measures of Turgot was the re- moval of all restrictions on the grain trade in order to cope with the direful situation that a bad harvest in 1775 had created. Thus he lived up to the physiocratic principle of *laissez faire* in commerce. But by abolishing internal reve- nues on one of the products that had hitherto been most profitable for provincial and municipal customs officers, he created a resentment that was soon to make itself felt. There followed a series of decrees, abolishing the govern- mental *corvée*, restricting the powers of the ancient guilds, curtailing the expenditures from the royal treasury. Turgot even had the temerity to try once more to create a royal bank, a project which John Law earlier in the century had so completely rendered hateful. In 1776, Turgot established the Caisse d'Escompte (Bank of Discount), which he tried as nearly as possible to divorce from the State. The next year, though Turgot had himself, in the mean time, been cast into the discard, the Caisse d'Escompte began to circulate banknotes, and by 1783 it had an unquestioned and stable circulation of 40,000,000 livres. Thereafter, as the successors of Turgot began to make excessive demands upon the Caisse d'Escompte, it had to weather several stormy crises. But it not only survived, it managed also to tide over the Government during the period of severely straitened financial circumstances that came immediately before and after the convocation of the Estates General in 1789.

Other reforms were under consideration by Turgot, for he was in haste; "in my family," he said, "we die of the gout at fifty." At the same time, his colleagues Saint Germain in the War Department and Malesherbes, Minister of the King's Household, were undertaking certain reforms in their departments. The privileged classes became apprehensive, and this time, the parlement, as one of the privileged bodies, was on their side. The people also mistrusted Turgot, for somehow they held his reforms responsible for the current food shortage. As if this combination of forces were not enough for him, the Queen, Marie Antoinette, incensed by his having demanded the recall of her friend, the Comte de Guines, as ambassador to London, influenced the King against him. Malesherbes, who as a parlementarian, had been in the van of Louis XV's opponents and who was, at a future time, to plead in vain for the life of Louis XVI before unfriendly judges, was the first to resign. Turgot, who cared as little for the King's good will as for the unpopularity he had everywhere accumulated, wrote the troubled Louis, who would have liked to retain him (for, he said, "Only Turgot and I love the people"), a strongly worded lecture on the necessity for steadfastness. Twelve days later (May 12, 1776) Turgot was obliged to resign, and Saint Germain followed suit the next year.

For an insignificant period of five months, a decrepit old reactionary named Clugny filled Turgot's place and brought bankruptcy just so much nearer. To meet the crisis, the King chose, on Clugny's death, a successful Genevese banker, Necker, who was named Director-General of Finances, since, as a Protestant, he could not take the higher title of Minister. Expectations ran higher than Necker's accomplishments warranted. He found huge sums of money going to favorites as gifts and pensions; the expenses for the royal table alone were six millions a year; and every time the King's household moved from the city to the country in the summer, another six millions had to be expended. Necker tried drastic measures of economy, at the same time that he made huge loans to postpone bankruptcy. Some of Turgot's most important reforms he kept and improved upon, and, in addition, brought about certain reforms of his own. In 1779, the King was induced to abolish all serfdom on his own estates, setting a precedent that a few nobles followed, and thus enormously decreasing by a single step the percentage of serfs in the kingdom. The number of farmers-general of the taxes was reduced and other financial measures contemplated. Necker planned to establish provincial estates for every province in France. Finally in 1781 he published his *Compte Rendu*, which, quickly printed and spread throughout the length and breadth of the country, revealed, not without deliberate inaccuracies that were meant to bolster up credit, the state of the receipts and expenditures of the royal treasury and the financial abuses of the Government. For the first time in the history of France, the people were enabled to see, in so far as Necker was willing to let them see, how much money they paid in taxes, how much was paid out, and to whom. Sometimes the information thus acquired was astounding. But all to no avail! In 1778, because of the desire to regain at least commercial, if not territorial supremacy in America,

and on the insistent demands of a great number of the liberal
intelligentsia, France went to the aid of the American colonies fighting for their independence of England.   The
French navy, for a time, swept the seas; the army to which
Cornwallis surrendered was made up mostly of French
soldiers.   French military honor was redeemed, but at the
expense of the French treasury.   All Necker's efforts to save
money were nullified.   They had resulted only in rousing
against him the factions opposed to reform and the courtiers whose pensions he had diminished and financial secrets
published.   In May, 1781, failing in his request to be included in the Ministry, he resigned, leaving a larger treasury
deficit than he had found.

Joly de Fleury, the succeeding administrator of finances,
allowed the taxes to be increased to meet the costs of the
war in America, but when the war came to a close, the King
announced his intention to lower the taxes and dismissed
Joly de Fleury.   A young man named D'Ormesson then became Controller-General.   His good intentions were not
sufficient to make up for his lack of ability and in a few
months he made way for Calonne, an obliging fellow whom
certain courtiers had influenced the King to name.   Calonne tried to put a bold face upon the entire matter, spent
money lavishly, floated loans, and promoted lotteries to acquire more.   For a time (what with successful crops and
a successful war) he was able to make things take on an air
of prosperity.   But loans became increasingly hard to float
and again an increase of taxes was proposed.   But the
parlement refused to register the tax decrees, and Calonne
hit upon a new scheme: the King must call the Assembly of
Notables!

The Assembly of Notables, a body of the leading personages of the realm, had not met since 1626.   The idea of
suddenly calling upon this *deus ex machina* for aid struck
many as ludicrous.   Their thrusts were justified by the
events.   The Assembly, consisting, in Carlyle's phrase, of
a "round Gross" of princes of the blood and other celebrities, organized in seven bureaus, each under one of the

princes of the blood, might have done something effective
by permitting the upper classes, which they represented, to
be taxed.   But self-sacrifice did not appeal to them so much
as finding a scapegoat.   After all, as a contemporary caricature portraying Calonne as a farmer and the Notables as
the barnyard fowl revealed, the question in his opinion was
not whether they were to be cooked at all, but in what
sauce they were to be cooked.   Naturally the Notables
demurred.   The national debt was somewhere between
three and four billion livres, but Calonne would or could
give the Notables no exact information about it.   He even
deliberately understated the budget deficit, putting it at
eighty millions, though he later admitted it was fifty per cent
higher.   A struggle resulted between the Assembly and the
Minister; the Queen joined forces against Calonne; and
Calonne went the way of Turgot and Necker, — farther,
indeed, for in disgust he exiled himself from France.
Loménie de Brienne, Archbishop of Toulouse, who had led
the opposition to him, was appointed in his place.   A little
over a month longer the Notables lingered on and, on May
25, adjourned.   In his Six Propositions, Calonne had suggested a few minor reforms that had been mentioned elsewhere before (particularly by Turgot), such as the suppression of the *corvée* and the corn laws and the creation of
provincial estates.   And one of the Notables, the young
Marquis de Lafayette, recently returned from America
with radical ideas, had even dared to mention the convocation of the Estates General.   But, on the whole, the
Council of Notables had accomplished nothing.

Loménie de Brienne showed no particular ability to cope
with the rising deluge that Louis XV had ironically forecast.   He, too, tried to meet the impending bankruptcy by
new taxes, devised by Calonne.   But again the parlement
refused to register them, even after a *lit de justice*, and
demanded that the people be consulted through the
Estates General.   Paris was in a ferment.   What had begun
as a controversy between the Minister and the parlement
seemed likely to become a war between the King and his

subjects. Feeling ran particularly high against the Queen,
who, since the Diamond Necklace Affair, was suspected by
the people and whose extravagance was now regarded as
the chief cause of difficulty. Finally, in August, 1787,
Louis XVI, who had begun his reign by reëstablishing the
parlements that his grandfather had abolished, now followed the precedent of his predecessor and exiled the parlement to Troyes. That did not end the trouble, however.
The lower courts supported the parlement. The provincial
parlements also refused to register the decrees. In certain
provinces, particularly Dauphiny and Franche Comté, the
Government was openly defied. In Dauphiny, under the
leadership of a young Grenoble lawyer named Mounier, the
people of the province had created for themselves a local
assembly. Hoping to offset the example thus given and to
undermine the influence of the revolutionary principles
that were daily being enunciated in this Assembly of
Vizille, Brienne secured for Dauphiny the right to elect a
new assembly that would have the royal sanction. But the
people chose for the new and legal body practically all the
members of the old and insurgent one, which continued to
voice its support of the parlements as loudly and to give out
as radical opinions as before. In the mean time, at Troyes,
the exiled parlementarians had become the lions of the
crowds. The Government, faced with the danger of war
with England and Prussia over a political squabble in Holland, whose stadholder, brother-in-law of Frederick William
II of Prussia, had been driven out by the democratic faction
that had had French support, deemed it advisable to yield.
With wild rejoicing the people of Paris welcomed back
their parlement.

The words "Estates General" were on everybody's lips.
The King delayed as long as he dared, in the mean time
endeavoring to reduce the power of the parlement. In a
lit de justice on May 8, 1788, he ordered the parlement to
register a series of decrees by which the lower courts were
to be reformed and systematized and a new high court, the
cour plénière, was to be created and to take over many of

the functions of the parlements.   It was a much-needed
reform that, had it come earlier, would have been welcomed by the liberal opinion of the time, but was now
looked upon simply as a *coup d'état* intended to undermine
the position of the parlementary champions of the popular
cause.   At the same time, however, the King promised to
call the Estates General.   But still he did nothing definite
in that regard.   Rabid pamphlets appeared; crowds dis-
played ill-temper; even the soldiers were jostled.   Brienne
had hoped for a large gift from the clergy which would have
enabled the Government to hold out longer, but again he
was disappointed.   Finally on July 5, 1788, a decree was issued calling upon all organizations and individuals in France
to investigate the history of the Estates General, which had
not met for a century and three quarters, and to send the
results of their researches to the Keeper of the Seals.   And
on August 8, the King decided that the Estates General
would meet in May, 1789.   France once more was happy.

Brienne, in an endeavor to calm the incipient revolts in
the provinces, did not get the support of the King that he
wished, and resigned.   Necker, the idol of the French populace and the only minister in whom the bourgeoisie had any
confidence, was now recalled.   France had in the mean time
been flooded with literature telling what the Estates General were and ought to be.[1]   The most notorious of the
pamphlets among this literature were by the young Grenoble leader Mounier and by a member of the upper clergy,
the Abbé Sieyès.   Abbé Sieyès' *Qu'est-ce que c'est le Tiers
État?   (What is the Third Estate?)* is still the best known.
Of the many persons, says Lowell,[2] who in our own time
have wondered how to pronounce his name, all are aware
that he asked and answered the following questions:

[1] The general estimate of the number of these pamphlets runs into the
thousands.   Professor Garrett, however, in the *Howard College Bulletin* of
June, 1927, p. 40, studying *The Pamphlet Crisis in France in 1788*, says: "I am
inclined to believe that less than five hundred pamphlets written by individuals
were published between July 5 and December 27, 1788.   After a diligent
search in the libraries of Paris and elsewhere, I have not been able to find as
many as three hundred."

[2] Lowell: *The Eve of the French Revolution*, 336.

(1) What is the Third Estate? Everything.
(2) What has it been hitherto in the political Order? **Nothing.**
(3) What does it ask? To become something.

There were many other pamphlets, by men, who, like Marat and Rabaut Saint-Étienne, already had or were soon to acquire considerable reputations, and by a great number of lesser writers. But they were all of much the same tenor: the Third Estate really is the entire nation; hitherto the influence of the small percentage of the population in the two higher Estates had reduced its power to a cipher; but, in the future, steps must be taken to give it its proper position in the political structure of France. In general, the advocates of the *Tiers* considered it a sufficient guarantee of the importance of the Third Estate that it be allowed as many representatives as the other two orders combined and that voting should be by head, each representative having one vote, instead of by order, as hitherto, each estate having one vote determined by its majority.

As the King had announced in the previous July, he took seriously under consideration the suggestions made in these pamphlet studies he had instigated. In November, a second Council of Notables was assembled to consider the composition of the Estates General. More conservative than the King himself, the Notables were unwilling to give to the Third Estate half of the representation in the Estates General. The King dismissed them, after they had been in session only about a month, and Necker now presented his "New Year's gift" to the French nation. By the *Résultat du Conseil* of December 27, 1788, it was decreed that the Third Estate — the Commoners — should have as many representatives as the other two orders combined. Privilege was fast crumbling. But on the matter of vote by head or vote by order, Necker was not so definite, and this question was allowed to hang fire. A distinct program of reform was likewise announced. The nation's purse-strings were to be put in the hands of the Estates General by giving to them the control of taxation, the civil list, and the annual budget.   Censorship of the press was to be abolished, and *lettres de cachet* were no longer to be granted. With regard to the privileges of the upper classes, Necker was by no means equally radical.   He expressed the hope that they would themselves surrender their exemption from taxation, but added that the seigneurial honors and prerogatives were personal private property and no Frenchman would consider, nor would the King permit the slightest infringement of them.   It was an altogether sober plan of reform the Government thus outlined, falling far short of the expectations of many even among the privileged classes.   But so popular were both the King and Necker at this moment, so often did even their most vehement future enemies call down blessings now upon their heads, so enthusiastic were the most rabid of the pamphleteers on the best of ministers and the greatest of kings that, if the King's Government had stood forth unwaveringly for it, they might have succeeded in carrying it in its entirety.

The method of electing the representatives to the Estates General was set forth in the Royal Letters of January 24, 1789.   Suffrage was granted to every male (and some women were also allowed to vote) over twenty-five years of age who were on the tax rolls.   In Paris, where this latter qualification might have been too generous, suffrage was restricted to those who paid six livres in taxes or who held university degrees or letters of mastership in the crafts or an official title.   Following the precedent of the Estates General of 1614 as closely as it could be determined, the district of the *bailliage* or the *sénéchaussée* was used as the electoral unit.   On a given day, the *bailli* was to call the clergy of his *bailliage* or bailiwick together.   Each clergyman, including the parish priests, was to represent himself in person or by proxy and to be eligible to the Estates General, save that cathedral chapters were represented on the basis of one representative for each ten canons and monasteries might each be represented by only one delegate of their choice.   The number of curés that thus took part in the elections accounts for their control of the first Estate when it met in the following May. On the same day, the *bailli* was to call the nobility together, and they likewise, by direct representation, were to choose their deputies to the Estates General. But the Third Estate chose its deputies by two and sometimes by three separate steps. In the country districts, the villages elected their deputies to the bailiwick assemblies, while in the cities the guilds, and in the larger cities, the districts, especially delimited for this purpose, chose representatives to the municipal electoral assembly that, in turn, sent representatives to the bailiwick assembly; and there only did the bailiwick assembly elect its deputies to the Third Estate. Paris and four other large cities were given direct representation, except that they were divided into electoral districts. These sectional and municipal electoral bodies remained as they were originally instituted, to play a very significant part in the early stages of the Revolution. Each body of electors was required to send with its candidates a *cahier de doléances* (list of grievances) stating the reforms it wished to have made in its community. Though the tone of the royal letters was somewhat of a disappointment to the attentive reader because of its emphasis upon the financial needs of His Majesty's treasury and its comparative indifference to the other defects of the times, there was every reason to believe that the King meant to do more than to prepare simply for a financial crisis.

The French rejoiced universally. As early as 1787, Mirabeau had said that "France was ripe for the Revolution." People began to dream of a Constitution and to feel that a new era was dawning. And so it was. But had they been able to foresee the cost in blood, the waste of money, the sacrifice of happiness, the degradation of passions, the heights of selfishness, the failures and the triumphs of the next generation, how much less joyous they would have been! There was in England at the end of that next generation a young man and poet who had studied and watched these events with the intuitive insight that youth and genius impart. This was Shelley. No finer words than those he wrote in his preface to his *Revolt of Islam* need be given in explanation of the glory and the horror of that generation:

> Such a degree of unmingled good was expected as it was impossible to realize. If the Revolution had been in every respect prosperous, then misrule and superstition would lose half their claims to our abhorrence, as fetters which the captive can unlock with the slightest motion of his fingers, and which do not eat with poisonous rust into the soul.

Fénelon in the age of Louis XIV and Boulainvilliers in the time of the Regent had suggested that the Estates General be revived. More than three generations had passed since their time, two powerful rulers had fought against the demand, becoming ever more persistent, and now at last France had arrived at the point where it was to elect its representatives to the Estates General. As some gloomily feared, as others cheerily hoped, that Estates General was to transform itself into a constitutional convention and thoroughly reform the institutions of France. Opposition to these reforms was to lead to measures even more thoroughgoing to offset the opposition. Civil war, foreign invasion, wholesale executions, popular massacres, conquest and empire were to result. When the smoke cleared away, it was to be found that along with the destruction much had been done that was enduring and commendable. But of these there was little that had not already made some small beginning, had not already sent out some tender roots into the soil of the Ancient Régime. The limitation of the power of the Church, the division of the land among the peasantry, the organization of the judicial hierarchy, the centralization of local government, the codification of the laws, the national system of banking, the newly acquired prerogatives of the middle class — all these were to be found in incipient stages somewhere in the eighteenth century. Not even so thorough a reversal as the French Revolution can escape from the inexorable law of continuity in history.

Of the monarchs of the Age of Enlightenment, Louis XVI was not the only one who felt called upon to take the nation

EUROPE

IN 1789

SCALE OF MILES
0   50 100 150 200 250 300

ATLANTIC OCEAN

NORTH SEA

HEBRIDES

ORKNEY IS.

Inverness
SCOTLAND
Aberdeen
Perth
Kirk
Edinburgh
Prestonpans
Belfast
Carlisle
Solway
Newcastle

IRELAND
Dublin
Limerick
Wexford
Cork

Preston
Chester
K. OF
YORK

GREAT
ENGLAND
BRITAIN

Birmingham
Bristol
Severn
Thames
London
Plymouth
Portsmouth
Dover

Bergen
Konigsberg
Arendal
Christiansand

NORWAY
DENMARK

Aarhus
Tönning
Lubeck
Bremen
Hanover
Munster
Cassel

UNITED
Amsterdam
Utrecht
NETHERLANDS
Brussels
Liege
Cologne
Mainz Frankfurt
Würzburg
Ansbach
Stuttgart

THE

English Channel

Cherbourg
Havre
Rouen
Reims
Verdun
Metz
TOUL
LOR-
RAINE
Mühlhausen
Strassburg
Ulm
Constance
Zurich
Basel
SWITZERLAND
Geneva
Bern
Neuchâtel

Caen
Versailles
Paris
Chartres
Fontainebleau
Orleans
Brest
Rennes
Angers
Nantes
Loire
Tours
Nevers
Dijon (To Spain)
Besançon
Montbeliard

K. OF FRANCE
Montpellier
SAVOY
Lyons
Grenoble
Turin
PIEDMONT
Milan
MILAN

Pompadour
Bordeaux
Garonne
Agen
Pau
Toulouse
Narbonne
Valence
Avignon
Marseilles
Nice
Toulon

Coruna
Oviedo
Pontevedra
Leon
Braga
Oporto
Duero
Coimbra
Ciudad Rodrigo
Bayonne
Pamplona

Burgos
Saragossa
Cardona
Lerida
Gerona
Barcelona

Tortosa

K. OF PORTUGAL

Madrid
K. OF SPAIN
Lisbon
Tagus
Alcantara
Toledo
Olivenza
Guadiana
Badajoz
Valencia
MINORCA
(To Gr. Britain)
Port Mahon
Palma
MAJORCA

Lagos
Seville
Guadalquivir
Cordova
La Carolina
Alicante
Murcia
IVIZA

Sagres
Malaga
Granada
Cadiz
Cartagena

MEDITE

Tangier
Gibraltar
(To Gr. Britain)
Ceuta
(To Spain)
Melilla
(To Spain)
Oran
(To Spain)
Algiers
Tunis

CORSICA
(To France, 1768)
Ajaccio
Bastia

SARDINIA
Sassari
Cagliari

Florence
Genoa
Duchy
Parma
Modena

A   F   R   I   C   A

Longitude   5°   West   0°   5°   Longitude   10°

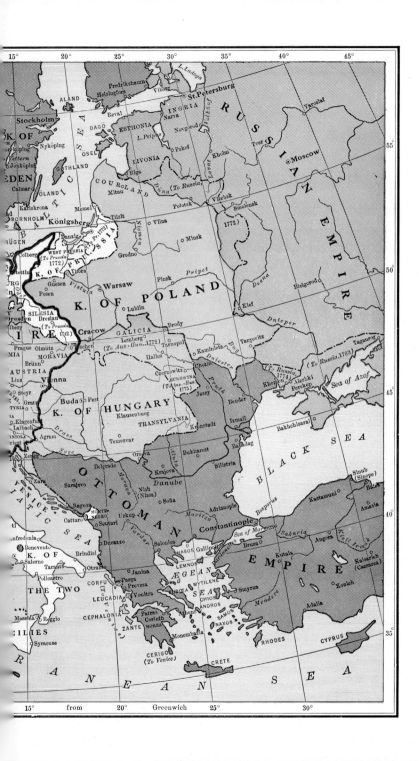

into this confidence and ask for suggestions upon general reform. Of the Enlightened Despots of the eighteenth century, none was more despotic and only one perhaps (Frederick the Great) more enlightened than Catherine of Russia. Catherine kept up a steady correspondence with Voltaire and exchanged Christmas presents with him. Diderot for a time came to live at her palace. La Harpe, disciple of Rousseau and somewhat of a *philosophe* in his own right, and Monsieur de Boudry, brother of a fairly well-known scientist soon to be known as Marat, the Friend of the People, were the tutors of her children, legitimate and illegitimate. It was characteristic of this lady, who had risen from an obscure principality in Germany to the position of Czarina by intrigue and murder, that she read Machiavelli and Montesquieu impartially. In fact, from Montesquieu she borrowed almost entirely the ideas contained in her famous Nakaz, instructions that she prepared for the Constitutional Convention, called from all the classes and regions of her vast empire to St. Petersburg, to draw up new provisions for the government of Russia. The Convention did not meet with striking success, except that it was a remarkable achievement in itself to have brought such a motley throng together. Catherine got no marked response upon any of her suggestions for reform except when she spoke of the freedom of the peasants, to which the noble landowners showed a very marked negative reaction. The Convention adjourned without having done anything substantial. Other enterprises of Catherine were much more successful. She turned St. Petersburg from a collection of wooden hovels into a city of brick and stone; she reorganized the system of taxation and found money with which to pay long-standing arrears to the army; she encouraged business enterprise by abolishing the government monopolies, reforming the currency and introducing paper money; she built hospitals and schools and, by offering herself as the first victim, introduced vaccination against smallpox into Russia. How far Catherine was motivated by a genuine reform spirit and a lively interest in the condition of her poorer subjects is an open question, as it is, indeed, for all of the Enlightened Despots. There certainly was no intense democratic fervor in the way in which she cannonaded miners on strike and peasants in revolt into submission, or in the severe strictures she passed upon the French after they had had the audacity to oppose their rulers openly. But that she was conversant with the latest political theories and played at the game of benevolence expertly must at least be granted her.

Catherine disliked her Austrian sister Maria Theresa thoroughly and admired Frederick of Prussia the more because he likewise shared her contempt for that pietistic lady. Maria Theresa had succeeded, in two wars (the War of the Austrian Succession and the Seven Years' War) in keeping her territories intact, save for Silesia which she reluctantly had to surrender to Frederick. In the intervals of peace she too found the opportunity to follow the fashion set for Enlightened Despots. She did not have so much to do with the *philosophes* personally as her contemporaries, but she did undertake certain reforms within her realms, which, if they did not suggest, they at least would have approved. With the aid and advice of Haugwitz as Chancellor and Kaunitz as Minister of Foreign Affairs, she tried to make, out of a collection of territories having their own privileges, traditions, languages, and racial distinctions, a united empire of Austria. She reduced the power of the provincial assemblies by demanding fixed contributions to the national treasury and centralized control of the army. Following the example of the intendants of France, she placed local authority in the hands of royal appointees, though her *Gubernium* consisted of a group of autocrats rather than a single royal agent. Local supreme courts (*Hofräthe*) were established in some of the provinces; and *Kammers* (chambers of finance) and *Kanzlei* (chanceries of administration) took care of financial and executive matters for the central government. The Ministry was reorganized and a Privy Council created. The army was increased and revised. Internal tariff duties, exemptions of the nobles from taxation, and other financial abuses were partially eliminated. The severity of feudal dues upon the peasants were mitigated and an opportunity given them to buy their lands. A state system of education was begun by the establishment of a close affiliation between the University of Vienna and the Government. It was a very ambitious program of reform for her Austrian possessions that the Empress thus carried out. When one considers, too, that it was done in a state where there were not only Germans, but Hungarians, Czechs, Slovenes, Slovaks, Italians, Flemings, Walloons, Croats, and into which there was soon to be introduced a huge Polish and Ruthenian element; where there were provinces and kingdoms jealously guarding what remained to them of their independence, and a nobility and a Diet that only begrudgingly surrendered any of their privileges, and where the ruler was likewise interested, as Empress, in an even vaster and perhaps more complicated congeries of principalities in the Holy Roman Empire, one can perhaps, while sharing Catherine's contempt for some of Maria Theresa's ways, still feel great admiration for her achievements.

Maria Theresa's work was carried on by her co-ruler and (after 1780) successor, her son Joseph II, who once declared that he had "made Philosophy the legislator of his Empire." Joseph undertook an even more thorough policy of reform than his mother. In a great many of his enterprises he failed pathetically, largely because he undertook too much in the face of too deeply rooted opposition. But some of his endeavors yielded splendid results. He divided the most important of his Austrian possessions into thirteen governments for military and judicial purposes. Each of these governments was given two law courts — one for the nobles and one for the commoners. At the head of this judicial hierarchy was placed a Supreme Court at Vienna, with the right of final appeal. The power of local diets was reduced by a policy of neglect, and their functions turned over to the governments. By insisting upon nominating Austrian bishops, by abolishing a number of bishoprics, monasteries, and convents, by placing church schools under the State and making education free and compulsory, by granting religious freedom, by taxing the lands of the Church, Joseph went far beyond any of his Catholic contemporaries in subordinating the Church to the State. The German ecclesiastic who wrote under the name of Febronius had recently preached the subordination of the Church to the State. So thoroughly did Joseph II follow his precepts that *Josephism* was now used where the word *Febronianism* had been the fashion to describe this policy.

Nor were the nobility allowed to remain untouched; they were likewise required to pay a land tax and a number of their feudal dues were abolished or reduced in value. The lower classes were frequently the recipients of this benefaction, since a free school system was opened to them, they were permitted to buy and sell their lands, they were allowed to transform their labor dues into money payments. But even despots, no matter how enlightened, must not move too fast. Hungarian nobles constantly threatened revolt in defense of their Church and their privileges; and in the Austrian Netherlands, a revolt, in which Austrian troops were consistently worsted, darkened the last years of the life of a ruler who would gladly have exchanged them for Bavaria, had the jealous policy of Frederick of Prussia and his successor, Frederick William II, permitted. In February, 1790, Joseph II died, laconically asking that on his tombstone should be cut the epitaph: "Here lies a prince, whose intentions were pure but who had the misfortune to see all his plans miscarry." But a grateful people put upon his statue instead: "*Josepho Secundo, arduis nato, magnis perfuncto, majoribus praecepto, qui saluti publicae vixit non diu, sed totus.*" (To Joseph II, born for the arduous, performer of great things, planner of greater, who lived for the welfare of his country, not long but wholly.)

Squabbling with Catherine, Maria Theresa, and Joseph, and always wryly laughing at them even when he coöperated with them in some Machiavellian undertaking, Frederick II of Prussia dominated the German, if not the entire European scene.   His father, Frederick William I, skinflint and termagant, had nevertheless consolidated Prussia's possessions, organized her industry and agriculture, saved a huge sum of money and built a magnificent army, of which the most famous corps was his darling regiment of six-foot Potsdam Guards.   Though he had made the young Frederick's life miserable by beatings and unpleasant chores so that the young man tried to run away from home, his work really made possible the greatness of Frederick. Even when the oversensitive lad, who wrote poetry, played the flute, and composed an *Anti-Machiavel* as a plea for paternalism in monarchical government, had grown into one of the most crafty and unscrupulous rulers of his day, he never quite forgot his poetry, flute, and opposition to Machiavelli.   He gathered about him, at his palace Sans Souci at Potsdam, scores of the best-known literary men of his generation from all over the world; and among his best friends, when they were not actually fighting each other, was to be counted his literary counterpart Voltaire. His first act, upon ascending his throne, was to violate his father's sacred oath to the Pragmatic Sanction, according to which Maria Theresa was to be allowed to succeed to all of the Hapsburg possessions intact, by occupying Silesia. Since France and Bavaria soon joined him to do their share in breaking up the Austrian Empire, he was rapidly able to establish himself firmly there.   Three times during this war of the Austrian Succession (1740–48), he deserted his allies, only to enter hostilities again if Silesia became endangered.   When peace was declared at Aix-la-Chapelle, the only gainer thereby was Frederick, who was confirmed in his possession of Silesia.   In the scramble for new alliances in anticipation of the next war, Frederick won the support of England, formerly allied with Austria, and when the Seven Years' War (1756–63) broke out, he entered the lists against France and Austria on the Continent, while the elder Pitt concentrated the English forces upon America and India.   This time he received only small support from his ally, while Saxony, Sweden, Russia, and Spain joined Austria and France against him. Only a brilliant series of victories at Rossbach and Leuthen (1757) and Liegnitz and Torgau (1760) and the death of his enemy Elizabeth of Russia (1762), to make way for his admirers Peter and Catherine, saved him from complete collapse. In the Peace of Hubertsburg, he was permitted once more to retain Silesia, while in the synchronous Peace of Paris, his ally, England, received a vast domain in America from the French and established control over India.

Prussia had become a world-power and stood forth clearly as the rival of Austria for predominance in the Germanies. When, upon the death of Maximilian Joseph, Elector of Bavaria (1777), there broke out, in accordance with the best eighteenth-century dynastic practice, a scramble for the territory of the deceased, Frederick was able to organize a League of German Princes to prevent Joseph II from exchanging Belgium for Bavaria. And when, on the initiative of his good friend Catherine, it was decided to divide parts of Poland among them, since that country's overdemocratic institutions [1] kept the country in a constant disorderly state, Frederick permitted Catherine to have the lion's share, while he himself was content with West Prussia, having a largely German population and linking his Duchy of East Prussia directly with his Brandenburg possessions. Maria Theresa felt deeply moved by the sorry fate of the Poles; but both Catherine and Frederick remarked that while she wept, she nevertheless was prevailed upon to accept a fairly large slice of Poland including Galicia and the city of Cracow. The Cardinal de Rohan, of Diamond Necklace fame, at this time French Ambassador to Vienna, described Maria Theresa's attitude less pithily but more subtly than her two accomplices: "I have seen Marie-Thérèse weep over the misfortunes of oppressed Poland; but this princess, practiced in the art of not allowing herself to be seen through, appears to

---

[1] The election of her ruler and the *liberum veto*, by which, only by unanimous vote of the Diet, could any important legislation be passed.

have sobs at her command. In one hand she holds a handkerchief to wipe away her tears, while with the other she seizes the sword to complete the partition."   Add to these episodes two wars of Russia with Turkey,[1] in the second of which Joseph of Austria joined Russia, and the salient features of the foreign policy of the three leading Enlightened Despots are outlined. Throughout it all, as long as he lived (d. 1786), Frederick played the central rôle — a sort of Mephistopheles to Joseph's Faust.

But it was a benignant Mephistopheles withal. Perhaps it was only because he realized that it is a contented subject who makes the best soldier (which is a motive clearly to be assigned to the other rulers of the *Aufklärung* as well), perhaps it was because he had not forgotten his paternalistic plea in his youthful *Anti-Machiavel*, perhaps it was because in the Germany of the age of Leibniz, Wolf, Klopstock, Kant, and Goethe, who were, to a greater or less degree, spreading French philosophical notions in German-speaking lands, there was an atmosphere of reform, or perhaps it was simply to be in fashion — at any rate, Frederick, like Catherine, earned the title of *the Great* as a reformer.   Out of the royal treasury he set to work to rebuild the ravages of his wars. He remitted taxes here and distributed seed and cattle there.   He encouraged, even to the extent of resorting to publicity agents, the immigration of workers and farmers into Prussia.   He drained swamps, dredged rivers, built roads, subsidized mines, protected home industries, and, of course, improved the army. Along political lines, Frederick followed strictly the program begun by his father, who had abolished feudal tenure of noble land, reduced the obligations of peasants to certain fixed dues, permitted religious dissent, founded schools, and coordinated various conflicting branches of the civil government.   Frederick's chief innovation in these matters was

[1] The first (1768–1774) went on while the Partition of Poland was in process and ended in the Treaty of Kutchuk Kainarji, by which Catherine increased her possessions by a very significant strip of the Black Sea coast. The second broke out in 1787 and ended with the Treaty of Jassy in 1792, by which Russia extended her boundary to the Dniester.

his heroic undertaking to codify Prussian law and reform the judicial hierarchy. When he died, despite the fact that his country had been invaded by French, Austrians, Swedes, and Russians at various times, and that Berlin itself had three times been captured by the Russians, he left a more prosperous country than he had found.

To complete the roll-call of the school of Enlightened Despots, it is necessary at least to name Charles III of Spain and Gustavus III of Sweden. Even George III of England, of odious reputation in America, where he is remembered more for his despotism than his enlightenment, may, in a sense, be included. As a pupil of Bolingbroke, he honestly tried to play the *Patriot King*, and his Minister, the younger Pitt, after the War of American Independence, actually contrived to bring about a number of significant reforms and might have achieved more but for the reaction that followed the outbreak of the French Revolution. But Charles III, founder of the Spanish Academy, acquisitor of Louisiana, proponent of the power of the State against overweening Spanish Jesuits and Inquisitors, and Gustavus III, dramatist and historian, restorer of the power of the Swedish throne (just in time to prevent his uncle Frederick of Prussia and Catherine of Russia from partitioning Sweden as they had Poland), who abolished torture and granted freedom to the press, deserve a conspicuous place in that august company. The passion of his Minister Struensee for reform might even cause the inclusion of the insane Christian VII of Denmark. Nor must Joseph of Portugal, whose energetic Minister Pombal was the first to expel the Jesuits and in twenty-seven years of active administration carried out a number of important changes, be left out of the illustrious list.

Enlightened Despotism, however, was but an inadequate answer to the problems of the eighteenth century. The rise of public opinion, the increasing demands of the middle classes, the propagation of rationalistic literature, the slow amelioration of the lot of the humblest peasants, the gradual transformation of methods of agriculture, the beginnings of a factory system — all these meant a new spirit that must be met by no half-measures patronizingly granted from above.   Such measures could and did only postpone the eventual conflict.   They staved off the revolution, but not indefinitely.   When the conflagration began in France, despite and because of the enlightened despotism of Louis XVI, the enlightenment of the reign of Frederick in Prussia, Maria Theresa in Austria, Charles in Spain, Gustavus in Sweden — even of George in insular England or of Catherine in remote and frozen Russia — proved inadequate as fireproofing.   It is not, after all, in the most benighted countries that revolutions happen.   A little antecedent reform may act as an effective revolutionary leaven.

BOOK II
THE FALL OF THE MONARCHY
CHAPTER I
THE ESTATES GENERAL BECOME THE NATIONAL ASSEMBLY

THE month of May in the year 1789 opened in Paris with pleasant spring weather. Ever since the end of April, the people in the streets had beheld a number of strangers — noblemen, clergymen, attorneys, merchants, an occasional peasant — arriving from the provinces with the air of dignity and concern that betokened importance. They were the representatives of the people of France, called together by King Louis XVI, to help in an overwhelming financial crisis. For a hundred and seventy-five years the Estates General of the representatives of the people had not been consulted by the autocrat of France, and now, because he could not borrow money and had encountered too great opposition in levying new taxes, he was willing to allow them at least a momentary existence. To be sure, he had intimated that he would be prepared to hearken to their grievances and to make an effort to reform them. But to him the important part of the work to which the Estates General was to devote its attention was not political or social reform but the ever-present deficiency in the royal treasury.

Part of the deputies of the daily increasing body of the Estates General that came crowding into Versailles, so rapidly that the King had to regulate rents to keep them from being mulcted, were in full accord with the King on that question. These included practically all the nobility, save a few liberals like Lafayette and Clermont-Tonnerre, and practically all of the upper clergy. In their estimation, the Estates General were to do little more than to provide for a more efficient means of acquiring national revenue. They could not entirely disregard the demands for a constitution that had grown so insistent in the last few months, but they felt that that constitution ought to be nothing more than a confirmation in black and white of the institutions and customs that already existed. France, they felt, had a constitution; it merely needed definition. Political parties, in the modern sense, did not yet exist, but this group was united by a common conservative point of view.

The members of the Third Estate, who represented the twenty-four millions (more or less) of the French people who were neither nobles nor clergy, did not share this feeling in any way. These deputies could likewise count upon the active sympathy of a small faction of liberal noblemen and the mass of the lower clergy. It was not in vain that they had been reading Voltaire, Montesquieu, Rousseau, and their company. It was not in vain that they had read, if indeed they had not written, the thousands of pamphlets that agitated for a rehabilitation and an increase in the power of the Third Estate and for a reform of the abuses in the government and society of France. It was not in vain that they had taken part in the enthusiasm and excitement of the election of the deputies to the Estates General. And now, secure somewhere on their persons, they had brought with them the *cahiers* which the King's edicts regulating the procedure of the elections had required the various electoral bodies to draw up. There was no doubt that these cahiers, these memoranda of grievances, instructed them to demand redress. No! France had no constitution, and they had come to see that one was drawn up. Had they had a tradition of political institutions behind them, they would undoubtedly have been organized as a reform party. Their organization, however, was yet to be effected. They did not even know each other's names. But they anticipated no unsurmountable difficulties, and many of them expected to be returning home shortly.

What these reformers wanted was all in the cahiers. There had been thousands and thousands of these cahiers composed in the early months of 1789. The nobles had drawn up theirs, the clergy had drawn up theirs, but the great majority of them had originated in the electoral bodies of the Third Estate. Many of these cahiers were but repetitions of each other, based upon model cahiers that liberal writers had published throughout the country, or copied by one electoral assembly from that of another, or introduced by some near-by Masonic lodge into a rural electoral assembly. But on the whole, they were truly representative of real grievances. There was nothing startlingly radical about them. The French loved their good King Louis too much for that. There was no demand whatsoever for a subversion of the monarchy; had not the *philosophes* taught that republics were suited only to small nations, and was not Louis XVI the best of kings? France must be an hereditary monarchy, that was conclusive.

But there must be no more of the tyranny of the past. The people must have a voice in their own government through some sort of national representative body. There was some difference of opinion as to how this body was to be elected, but all agreed that the right of suffrage should be liberal. The constitution must also grant to the people of France the ordinary civil liberties. There must be an abolition, or at least a modification in the use, of *lettres de cachet*, so that no man could thenceforth be deprived of his freedom without trial (save, as some cahiers were willing to concede, when the State could best be protected by his speedy detention). There must be no more persecution of religious sects by the Government, although the cahiers of the clergy were by no means unanimous on that score. There must be freedom of speech, of thought, of the press. And the privileges of the various orders must be abolished; the nobility and the clergy must bear their just share of taxation, must surrender their exclusive hunting rights, and must allow some concessions with regard to their feudal dues.

All cahiers were unanimous in deploring the humiliation of the peasant classes, but the cahiers of the nobility were unwilling to go as far as those of the Third Estate demanded.

All things considered, the demands of the peasants were reasonable. They were willing to allow the nobles compensation for the financial losses that the abolition of their feudal dues would mean. Only a very few of the cahiers drawn up by the village electoral assemblies demanded complete confiscation without any compensation whatsoever. The cahiers demanded, with a fair degree of unanimity, a complete revision of local government in order to do away with the conflicts between guilds and mayors, intendants and governors, feudal courts and royal courts and church courts, customary law and Roman law. They also urged the King to abolish the internal tariff duties, and to reform the injustices in the collection of indirect taxes.

One of the vital questions that all the deputies were interested in and that ought to have been decided before they met, was how they were going to vote on the measures that were to come before them. The conservative elements answered that question by consulting the past. Since France, in their eyes, already had a constitution and since in previous meetings of the Estates General voting had most often been taken "by order," each of the three Estates having one vote determined by its majority, they maintained that now, too, in the rejuvenation of the Estates General, vote should be by order. But the reform element thought differently. By the *Résultat du Conseil* of December 27, 1788, the King, through Necker's influence, had allowed the Third Estate to have as many representatives as the other two Estates combined. If voting was to be by order, it would make small difference how many deputies an Estate was permitted to have; in any case, its vote would be one. The clergy and the nobility had in the past been accustomed to acting together, thereby defeating the vote of the Third Estate by two to one; and there was no reason to believe that the clergy and the nobility had changed during the interim of one hundred and seventy-five years in which the Estates General had been in abeyance. In voting taxes particularly, but also in most other instances, it had, indeed, become necessary, before 1614.

for all three orders to be in agreement; thus the new Third
Estate did not have to fear being outvoted, so much as,
what was perhaps worse, disagreement and consequent
inaction at a time when action was what they most desired.
Should each order receive but one vote, as of old, even
though the six hundred representatives of the Third Estate
represented all but a small portion of the French People,
while the three hundred each of the First and Second Estates
represented together but one per cent of the population, the
conservative policy of the two higher orders would either
prevail over or negative the reform policy of the Third
Estate and a new constitution would become an impossi-
bility. But if vote were to be by head, that is to say, if all
three orders were to meet together and each deputy receive
one vote, then the Third Estate, having half the representation of the entire Estates General and reasonably expecting
some support from the lower clergy and the liberal nobles,
would be able to carry their policy of establishing a new
constitution. It was a most critical problem, and as the
representatives of the people met in the spring of 1789, no
solution of it had yet been proposed.

The early days of May were spent in ceremonies. On
May 2, the King officially received the representatives of
his subjects. The conservatism of the Court was made apparent by an otherwise insignificant episode. The clergy,
or the First Estate, were received first in the King's private
room (*cabinet du roi*) with all doors thrown wide open and no
restrictions upon their intercourse with His Majesty. Afterwards, the nobility were received, in the same room, but
with the panels between the King's room and the others half
closed. The Third Estate, however, received last, were
introduced into the huge Hall of Mirrors (Salle de Louis
XIV) rather stiffly and formally. Some of the deputies,
Mirabeau asserted, wished there and then to protest this
initial discrimination among the deputies of the nation, but
it was allowed to pass without comment. On May 4, a
procession of all the deputies, the royal family, and the
ministers wended its pompous way from the Church of

Notre Dame in Versailles to the Church of Saint Louis.
The behavior of the populace, as they watched them parade
by, indicated their attitude toward the separate orders.
The Third Estate came first, dressed in the drab black that
the tradition of 1614 required.   They were enthusiastically
applauded, though only Mounier, Bailly, Mirabeau, Sieyès,
and one or two others of them were at all well known.
Then came the nobility, led by the Duke of Orléans, who
seemed anxious to march as close to the Third Estate as
possible.   The Duke was given a warm reception, but his
colleagues, clothed in the gaudy ceremonials of their class,
were allowed to pass in silence.   Next came the clergy,
some in the colorful robes of the upper clergy, many in the
somber cassocks of curés; and again there was no demonstration by the spectators.   Last came the King and the Queen.
The King received a rousing ovation, silence for the Queen.
At the Church of Saint Louis mass was said and the Bishop
of Nancy delivered the sermon.   It was a long, uninspired
address, but at one time, when the preacher referred to the
"just and wise monarch," the assembly, despite the holiness
of their surroundings and the code of etiquette that forbade
applause before the King, broke out into enthusiastic ap-
probation.   The Third Estate, throughout the entire performance, was placed in the rear of the church, behind the
clergy and the nobility, despite outspoken protests by some
of them.

The opening session of the Estates General was held on
May 5.   The hall in which they met was called the Salle
des Menus Plaisirs.   It no longer exists.   Here the deputies
waited for four hours for the royal family, in the mean time
calling the roll of the Estates, the monotony broken only
by the applause for the Bishop of Nancy as he came into
the room.   About noon, the King, the Queen, and the royal
ministers entered.   At last Louis' policy would be announced and the question of vote by head or vote by body
would be decided.   France could then know whether it was
to have a new constitution or simply the old one put down
in writing.   But no one in the royal *entourage*, not even

Necker, seemed to realize the significance of the moment. The King was everywhere regarded as a popular idol. Had he taken the lead in the policy of reform, the people and their representatives would have followed him unquestioningly. But that the Court had no comprehensive plan of reform, that it would reluctantly consent only to a few sops in return for substantial supply, was soon evident.

Louis XVI made a short speech in which he recommended coöperation. It was received with lively approval, but had promised little and had decided less. Barentin, the Keeper of the Seals, followed him with a more explicit statement of reform: the Court would consider changes in the criminal code, a redistribution of taxes, a grant of liberty to the press; and he urged the Estates to avoid all dangerous innovations. Barentin implied that the Government was not opposed to the vote by head in financial matters, but on political problems it favored the vote by order as a more effective check upon hasty action. Barentin's speech was disappointing to the majority of the representatives, even though they applauded. But, contrary to the precedent of 1614, there was still another speaker. That was Necker, and Necker understood! He would outline a comprehensive policy which the Estates could complete within a few weeks and then go home with the satisfaction of knowing that they had established liberty inside of France forever. But Necker delivered a speech three hours in length and talked almost all the time about finances. There was no danger of bankruptcy, he insisted. He placed the deficit at only fifty-six million livres, whereas actually it was about three times as large. But, he went on, it was necessary for the Estates General to approve a loan of eighty million livres. On the question of the vote, he took no definite stand. He implied, however, that in certain cases it might be desirable to vote by order; the honor of sacrificing their pecuniary privileges would then not be taken from the clergy and the nobility.

The policy of the Government stood revealed. It was chiefly interested in the financial problem, but was willing,

in return for pecuniary aid, to grant a few much-needed reforms. It sympathized, on the whole, with the conservative faction of the Estates General and wished the votes of
the three Estates to be taken by order. The compromise
that the Court seemed to advocate of vote by head on some
matters and vote by body on others did not meet with
sympathetic response in the Third Estate. In a letter to his
constituents, Mirabeau said, "Since these two methods are
diametrically opposed, if one is essentially good, it follows
necessarily that the other is essentially bad." The victory
of the Third Estate in obtaining six hundred members to
the three hundred of each of the other two would be an
empty victory indeed, unless a staunch resistance was put
forth against the court policy.

On May 6, the three bodies met in separate rooms of the
Hôtel des Menus Plaisirs. The clergy and the nobility
immediately proceeded to verify credentials, but the Third
Estate realized that to do so would be to sanction the vote
by order, and refused to organize. The first step the Third
Estate took to gain its point was to send an invitation to the
other orders to join with them for the purpose of verifying
credentials. The clergy rejected this invitation by a narrow margin (133 to 114) and the nobility by a larger one
(188 to 47). It was clear, however, that even in the ranks
of the Second Estate there were those who sympathized
with the commoners' point of view and were willing to
yield to it. The First Estate, controlled by the members
of the lower clergy, was obliged to adopt a mediatory policy.
On May 7, it suggested that committees from each body be
named to confer upon the matter of organization. Such
a commission was elected by the clergy between May 9 and
11. The nobility accepted the suggestion on May 13 and
the Third Estate not until May 14. The tardiness of the
Third Estate was due in part to their lack of formal organization, which they refused to complete until the problem of
verification of credentials was settled, but it was likewise
due to a rising unwillingness to compromise the vote-by-
head position in any degree. The election of the joint com-

missions was completed on May 20, and on May 23 they began their meetings. The chasm between the positions of the Third Estate and the nobility became clear; one would make no concessions to the other, although the clergy, almost equally divided between curés and bishops, would have welcomed compromise. The First Estate even resorted to ruse. The harvest of 1788 had been so meager that, though certain sections of France had plenty, they hoarded it so as not to raise prices in their communities, while other sections starved. The clergy, some of them no doubt sincerely, determined to send a committee to the Third Estate to urge upon them the necessity for completing the organization of the Estates General that they might the more quickly consider remedial famine measures. The Third Estate replied, however, with a summons to the upper orders to join them in the consideration of such matters. Thus the ruse failed. The joint conferences of the commissions, meanwhile, got nowhere. They lasted until June 9 without arriving at any acceptable decision. Even the intervention of the King, who, on May 28, sent Barentin to attend these conferences, could effect no compromise between the nobility and the commoners.

In the mean time, the Third Estate had adopted another line of tactics. On May 27, on the proposal of the Abbé Sieyès, author of *Qu'est-ce que c'est le Tiers État?* and a member of the Third Estate despite his ecclesiastical rank, the Third Estate had summoned the clergy "in the name of the God of Peace and of the national interest" to join with them. This was clearly an effort to take advantage of the curés' support of the Third Estate to divide the upper two orders against each other. The curés were willing to comply, but the bishops prevented any action. On June 3, the Third Estate organized so far as to name Bailly, well-known astronomer and member of the Academy of Sciences, president, and Camus, another of the Paris delegation, secretary of their body. Finally, on June 10, Sieyès moved that a committee be appointed to summon the clergy and the nobility to meet with the Third Estate and that, whether

they accepted or not, the verification of credentials be made
of all deputies from all of the bailiwicks. The roll-call of
the members began on June 12, without any of the upper
two orders being present, and was continued the next morning, when three curés joined the commoners. They were
loudly acclaimed. It was a small victory, but it augured
well. Practically every day thereafter an additional group
of clergy came to the meeting-place of the Third Estate,
until by June 16 there were nineteen of them.

Not satisfied with thus constituting itself the general
assembly of all three orders, on June 17, again on the motion
of the Abbé Sieyès, the Third Estate, with its handful of
clerical adherents, declared itself the National Assembly.
A number of other titles had been suggested by Mirabeau
and others, but they were all too long or too nondescript.
"National Assembly" had in the distant past been the name
given to the Estates General, when, at the King's command,
they met as a single body for a given purpose. Adopting it
as a permanent name was a bold stroke, tantamount to
declaring the power of the other two orders null and to defying the express wishes of the King. In the next days the National Assembly proceeded to pass laws as if it were in fact
the only truly representative body of France. The most
important of these, putting the wealth of the kingdom under their control, declared that no tax that had not received
its consent would thereafter be valid.

But the reform party was not thus to have its own way
unmolested. Already a group of the King's ministers, led
by the Keeper of the Seals, Barentin, had taken a stand of
opposition to Necker, the Controller-General of Finances,
who sympathized with the Third Estate. The Queen, too,
and the King's brothers, the Duke of Provence and the
Count of Artois, sided with the nobility and hated the idea
of what they considered excessive reform. When news of
the high-handed action of the Third Estate came to Marly,
where the royal family had retired after the death of the
Dauphin (June 4), the King, influenced by Barentin and the
Count of Artois, the younger of his brothers, and unmindful

of the advice of Necker, decided (June 19) to call a specia. meeting of the Estates General for June 22, there to lay down the law regarding the method of voting and the reforms that the Court would entertain.   In the mean time, the room in which the Third Estate met was to be closed to allow for preparations for the royal session.

The King had not been careful to inform Bailly, the President of the National Assembly, about his intentions in time for Bailly to notify his colleagues that there would be no meeting until June 22.   Bailly learned of the King's decision only on the morning of June 20 through letters sent him by the Duke de Brézé, the Royal Master of Ceremonies.   On June 20, therefore, at the usual hour the deputies gathered before the Salle des Menus Plaisirs, only to find soldiers guarding the doors and carpenters working on the interior.   It seemed to be a ruse to frustrate their efforts, much too obvious to succeed.   Bailly, Camus, and a handful of other deputies were permitted to enter and went through the formalities of opening and closing a meeting before they were obliged to retire.   Near by was an indoor tennis court, and there it was suggested the representatives betake themselves.   When they arrived, they found only one chair and one table.   In the excitement and confusion that prevailed, Mounier proposed that the members of the National Assembly take an oath "never to separate and to reassemble wherever circumstances demand until the constitution of the realm be established and affirmed upon a solid basis."   Bailly, standing upon the only table in the room, solemnly took the oath first, followed by all the others but one insignificant attorney, whom Bailly with difficulty saved from physical harm.   The National Assembly had resolved, as Benjamin Franklin said of the Continental Congress, to hang together in order not to hang separately.   This "Tennis Court Oath," containing the declaration that wherever the representatives of the nation were met together, there was the National Assembly, thereby denied the King's right to dismiss them at his pleasure, and pledged this indissoluble body to draw up a new constitution.   The Third Estate had gone far in the direction of revolt since May 5.

The meeting of June 22 (the 21st had been a Sunday) was held at the chapel of the Church of Saint Louis.   There the National Assembly was joined by a deputation of perhaps one hundred and fifty clerics and two noblemen.   The spokesmen of both of these delegations were very explicit in their declarations that they had come only for the verification of credentials, and Bailly, in his replies, was equally careful to avoid any assumption that the union thus effected was permanent.   But, from their general behavior, it was clear that these deputations, at any rate, were prepared to accept the National Assembly as a *fait accompli*.   Before this meeting of June 22 was over, it was understood that, on the next day, right after the royal session, which in the mean time, because of the King's vacillation, had again been postponed to June 23, the National Assembly would meet again.

The boldness of the Third Estate was gradually winning support from the upper two orders.   But there was still grave apprehension as to what the King's attitude might be on the morrow.   The King's ministry was more hopelessly divided than ever before.   All of the astuteness of the Count of Artois, who with his brother was unprecedentedly admitted to ministerial meetings, and all of the persuasive powers of the Queen were needed to keep the Necker faction from prevailing.   On account of the difficulty the King found in making up his mind, the royal session that had originally been called for June 22 was postponed until June 23.   Before the King's arrival at the Hôtel des Menus Plaisirs on that day, the Third Estate was obliged to wait until the guards were ready to admit them.   De Brézé apologized to Bailly for the delay on the grounds that the sudden death of one of the King's clerks inside the building had created great confusion.   When they entered, however, they found the clergy and the nobility already seated.   The King delivered a long speech, really made up of three separate documents. in which he annulled the resolutions of June 17, and ordered the three Estates to meet separately thereafter except in a few specified cases. He demanded that all feudal and ecclesiastical property be respected. He evinced a willingness to grant certain of the ordinary rights of citizens, to abolish several feudal and fiscal abuses, indicated a desire to give important financial powers to the Estates General, though he refused to consider any change in the army.

Save for the attitude on the vote by order, it was by no means a reactionary stand that the King now took. Had Louis XVI been as definite at the opening session of the Estates General on May 5, it is very likely that his program would have been carried out with only little opposition. But, even assuming that the King's proposals would actually be carried out (of which there was some doubt), the intentions of the Third Estate had already gone far beyond the point where the King wished them to stop. They were bound together to-day by an oath to draw up a new constitution for France. And now, when Louis closed his speech with a threat that, if the three Estates would refuse to coöperate with him, he would carry out his own program alone, and with an order to the assembled deputies "to separate immediately and to go to-morrow morning, each to the chamber allotted to your Order in order to take up again your sessions," only the nobility and the clergy followed him as he left. The Third Estate and a small group of others remained behind. "Gentlemen," cried the Grand Master of Ceremonies De Brézé, "you know the King's wishes." And up spoke fat, ugly, pock-marked Mirabeau, a noble from Aix representing, nevertheless, the Third Estate, whose brother was a leader of the most conservative faction among the nobility: "Go and tell them that sent you that we are here by the will of the people, and that bayonets alone shall drive us hence!"[1] De Brézé then

[1] Barthou: *Mirabeau*, 185. Mirabeau's exact words are in dispute. The above quotation is based upon Mirabeau's own version of the incident, which was the only immediately contemporaneous source not to ignore the speech entirely. It was somewhat later, after Mirabeau had become very famous, that journals and memoirs magnified its significance. See also Fling: *Source Book of the French Revolution*, 123-48. The exact words of these quotations cannot, of course, be given with absolute certainty.

turned to Bailly, and Bailly, who later said he saw no reason for Mirabeau's reference to bayonets, since no one had said anything about them, mildly replied that the Assembly could not adjourn without having met, and turning to his colleagues said, "I believe that the Nation when assembled cannot take orders?" De Brézé is said to have been so impressed that he went out backwards, in the manner in which he was accustomed to leave the royal presence. He reported what had just happened to the King, whose display of determination had already been too much for him. "Oh, well!" said he, "damn it! let them stay." So they stayed, and, realizing the danger they were in for having resisted the royal authority, they passed resolutions declaring that they still abided by their former decisions, that the person of a member of the National Assembly was inviolable and that any attempt to arrest or detain him was treason. "You are to-day," said Sieyès, who spoke in epigrams whenever an opportunity presented, "what you were yesterday."

The nobility and clergy still continued to meet separately. But on June 24, more than half the clergy again joined the National Assembly. On the 25th came more clerics and forty-seven members of the nobility led by the Duke of Orléans and Clermont-Tonnerre. Lafayette hesitated, because he felt himself bound by his instructions and perhaps also in order to sow discord among the still stubborn nobility. On the 26th more of the upper orders came over. The crowds in the street made life unhappy for those who continued to hold out. Rumor, probably floated in order to make it easier for the upper orders to evacuate their position, related that even the King's life was threatened. The King's position, indeed, was not an enviable one. He was torn between a desire to fulfill the expectations of the mass of his subjects and a loyalty to his class and friends that could brook no usurpation of authority by commoners. Having once made himself the leader of the conservative group, however, by consenting to the measures he proposed at the royal session, he should have had the vigor to force their acceptance or to suffer defeat in the attempt.   Perhaps it was the fear that there might be counter-measures taken by the people of Versailles, who all day of the 23d had made no secret of their attitude and had cheeringly and joyfully escorted Necker to and from the palace when he offered and was persuaded to reconsider his resignation; perhaps it was because he felt that Necker and the Assembly were more in the right after all — whatever the explanation, he made no real effort to use force.   Some of his advisers were made of sterner stuff.   Lafayette, Liancourt, and a few other liberal nobles actually prevented the movement of a small body of troops that day against the Assembly, and the Count of Artois was known to be in favor of a military demonstration.   But the National Assembly remained, for the time being, unmolested.   The King had determined to yield.   On June 27, Louis ordered the clergy and the nobility to unite with the Third Estate.   With a bad grace, the recusants did so and were received with great enthusiasm into the National Assembly.   Even after they had joined the National Assembly, however, both the clergy and the nobility drew up protests to the King; and one proud noble is supposed to have met by himself for some time thereafter, refusing to merge the identity of the Second Estate in the National Assembly.

But the Third Estate had, none the less, won a great victory.   The Estates General had become the National Assembly with the King's consent.   Vote henceforth would be by head; a new constitution would therefore be a foregone conclusion if only the King would remain steadfast in his support.   There were bonfires and joyful celebrations in Versailles and Paris that night.   But those who felt that the victory was complete and final were soon to be disillusioned.

CHAPTER II

THE PEOPLE PREVENT COUNTER-REVOLUTION

THE surrender of the upper orders to the Third Estate made it appear, for the moment, as if the cause of reform were triumphant. The Court had been defeated and seemed to have resolved to accept defeat wholly and gracefully. But the most conservative of the court party were determined not to yield without a struggle. They began to devise means by which to regain control once more. At the home of the Countess of Polignac, devotee of the Queen, leading deputies were entertained and no efforts were spared to win them over. D'Éprémesnil, once one of the warmest advocates of democracy in the Parlement of Paris, in this way was converted into one of its most decided opponents.

But persuasion was not enough. The Count of Artois had decided that "if you want an omelette, you must not be afraid of breaking the eggs." The conservative court party, led by the Queen and the King's brothers, were prepared, if necessary, to put down the upstarts in the National Assembly by force of arms. But where to get the requisite force? The French volunteers in the army were not to be trusted. Revolutionary propaganda was rife throughout the country. An actual count has revealed more than three hundred riots in the spring of 1789. Many of these were due only to hunger and social dissatisfaction, but some were purely the result of revolutionary fervor. And the King's troops were not immune. The French Guards, one of his choicest regiments, were as much affected as any. They were the darlings of the Parisians, to whom it was their duty to give police protection, and one of the King's own guards, in which some privates had qualifications that were later to entitle them to high commissions in the revolutionary army. They nevertheless were to be found, when on leave, at the Palais-Royal, talking politics around café tables like any bourgeois and fervently avowing their faith in revolutionary principles.   Some of them had carried their principles to the point of mutiny and had been imprisoned, first in the barracks and then in the prison of the Abbaye.   Each time, however, they were released by a Paris mob.   It was quite clear that this alliance between the French people and the French soldiers made it impossible to depend upon the native military to preserve a royalist sense of order, let alone to support the King against the Assembly, if the choice should have to be made.

But there were plenty of Swiss and German mercenaries who were still loyal to those that paid them.   The King issued orders for these troops to be brought up to Versailles; and early in July they began to arrive.   The movement of the mercenaries was no secret.   Everybody at Versailles and Paris knew that the King — or some one who got his authority from the King — was gathering an army of Germans in the vicinity of the National Assembly.   On July 8, Mirabeau delivered an impassioned address to the National Assembly on the subject.   Have the advisers of the King ever stopped to consider how revolutions begin, how a moderate people are driven toward excesses?   He proposed two measures — that an address be sent to the King to point out the effect upon the minds of the people and the increased drain upon the already too meager food supply by the concentration of troops, and that a bourgeois guard be established to maintain order.   The National Assembly, on the next day, decided to adopt only the first proposal, and a committee was sent with such an address to the King.   Louis XVI replied that the presence of the troops was a mere precaution against further disorder and the Assembly had no cause for anxiety.   If, however, they were afraid to remain in Versailles with the troops so near, he would gladly consider their removal to some other town.   Was the King really trying to assuage what he considered gratuitous apprehension on the part of the National Assembly?   And if so, was there some other mind at the Court subtly framing this device to get rid of the obnoxious

Assembly? For it had already been noted at Court that it would be easier to control or dissolve the National Assembly in some provincial town than near Paris. But the Assembly decided to stay. The importunities to the King had not been, they proudly replied, out of fear for their own safety, but in order to prevent further tumult.

Their solicitude proved to be well-grounded. The court party had continued to find Minister Necker unmanageable and unwaveringly on the side of the reform faction in the National Assembly. Several of his colleagues supported him. Obviously, since they had failed to get the Assembly to decree its own removal, the next step of the conservatives at Court would have to be to rid themselves of this champion of change in the very sanctum of the King. This was decided at a council meeting at which Necker and his friends were not present. On July 11, emboldened by the sense of security that ten thousand foreign mercenaries lent, the King dismissed Necker and ordered him out of the kingdom. Montmorin and two other ministers, who had supported Necker faithfully, were also dismissed. In their places were appointed Foulon, Breteuil, and De Broglie, well-known standpatters. On July 12, Necker was on his way to Brussels.

He was back at Versailles as the King's minister again within a few days. The people of Paris had been receiving rumors of the Court's counter-revolutionary activity for several days. The numerous disorders of the previous weeks had had good cause, and these rumors furnished better. For the poor, the price of bread was going up; for the rich, there was the ever-present danger of financial panic, which would depreciate the value of their securities. On the news of the dismissal of Necker, the Bourse (Stock Exchange) closed its doors. The people and the financiers had great confidence in Necker and the National Assembly. If let alone, these two might remedy everything, but now the King had dismissed Necker and was threatening to use force against the National Assembly. Banker and pauper were equally outraged.

Paris first learned of the fall of their idol on July 12 through a young journalist, recently come to Paris and frequently to be seen at the Palais-Royal — Camille Desmoulins. At the Palais-Royal, jumping excitedly upon a table, he shouted his tidings. Necker had been dismissed! A Saint Bartholomew of patriots was planned! With leaves plucked from the trees as their symbol, off the crowd went to Curtius, wax artist, for busts of Necker and the Duke of Orléans. Parading with these at their head, they could at least show unmistakably how they felt. There was a brief skirmish that day with some German cavalry at the Tuileries Gardens. Nobody was seriously hurt, but all felt they were in danger. They must arm! The French Guards joined the crowd as it rushed from shop to shop in search of weapons. On the next day, the Assembly again asked the King to dismiss his troops, and again the King replied that they were intended only to preserve order in Paris and Versailles.

But in Paris a miniature revolution was taking place. The electoral assemblies of the sixty districts into which the city was divided, which should have dissolved after electing the representatives of the Third Estate of Paris to the Estates General, had remained organized and active. Now, without any legal authority, they took charge of the city and elected a central committee which went to the Hôtel de Ville (City Hall) to share with the old council in the government of Paris. They chose Flesselles, the Prevost of the Merchants, as their chairman, thus borrowing an air of legality. This *Comité permanent*, in order to preserve some kind of order, created a bourgeois guard, made up of eight hundred members from each of the sixty districts. Together with the French Guards, this citizen guard preserved order all day on the 13th. But the people still feared not only a Saint Bartholomew of patriots but also the activity of the lawless. They searched for arms at the Hôtel de Ville, at the Monastery of the Chartreux, at the Arsenal all that day. The early hours of the 14th found them demanding arms at the old soldiers' home (the Hôtel

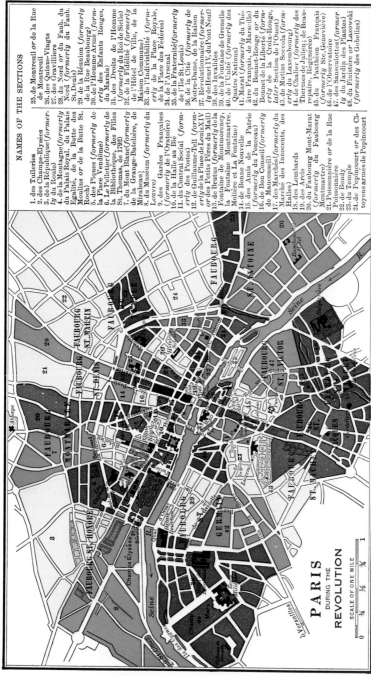

NAMES OF THE SECTIONS

1. des Tuileries
2. des Champs-Elysées
3. de la République (*formerly du Roule*)
4. de la Montagne (*formerly du Palais Royal, du Palais Egalité, de la Butte des Moulins or de la Butte St. Roch*)
5. des Piques (*formerly de la Place Vendôme*)
6. Le Pelletier (*formerly de la Bibliothèque, des Filles St. Thomas, of 1792*)
7. du Mont Blanc (*formerly de la Grange-Batelière, de Mirabeau*)
8. du Museum (*formerly du Louvre*)
9. des Gardes Françaises (*formerly de l'Oratoire*)
10. de la Halle au Blé
11. du Contrat Social (*formerly des Postes*)
12. de Guillaume-Tell (*formerly de la Place de Louis XIV or des Petits Pères du Mail*)
13. de Brutus (*formerly de la Fontaine de Montmorency, la Fontaine Montmartre, la Fontaine de la Fontaine*)
14. de Bonne Nouvelle
15. des Amis de la Patrie (*formerly du Ponceau*)
16. du Bon-Conseil (*formerly de Mauconseil*)
17. des Marchés (*formerly du Marché des Innocents, des Halles*)
18. des Lombards
19. des Arcis
20. du Faubourg Montmartre (*formerly du Faubourg Montmartre*)
21. Poissonnière *or* de la Rue Poissonnière
22. de Bondy
23. du Temple
24. de Popincourt *or* des Citoyens armes de Popincourt

25. de Montreuil *or* de la Rue de Montreuil
26. des Quinze-Vingts
27. des Gravilliers
28. du Nord *or* du Faub. du Nord (*formerly du Faub. St. Denis*)
29. de la Réunion (*formerly de la Rue Beaubourg*)
30. de l'Homme Armé (*formerly des Enfants Rouges, du Marais*)
31. des Droits de l'Homme (*formerly de la Place Royale, de la Place des Fédérés*)
32. de la Fidélité (*formerly de l'Hôtel de Ville, de la Maison Commune*)
33. de l'Indivisibilité (*formerly du Roi de Sicile*)
34. de l'Arsenal
35. de la Fraternité (*formerly de l'Ile St. Louis*)
36. de la Cité (*formerly de Notre-Dame, de la Raison*)
37. Révolutionnaire (*formerly de Henri IV, du Pont Neuf*)
38. des Invalides
39. de la Fontaine de Grenelle
40. de l'Unité (*formerly des Quatre Nations*)
41. Marat (*formerly du Théâtre Français, de Marseille*)
42. du Bonnet-Rouge *or* du Bonnet de la Liberté (*formerly de la Croix-Rouge, later Section de l'Ouest*)
43. de Mutius Scevola (*formerly du Luxembourg*)
44. de Chalier (*formerly des Thermes de Julien; de Beaurepaire, Régénérie*)
45. du Panthéon Français (*formerly Ste. Geneviève*)
46. de l'Observatoire
47. des Sansculottes (*formerly du Jardin des Plantes*)
48. du Finistère *or* Lazowski (*formerly des Gobelins*)

PARIS
DURING THE
REVOLUTION

SCALE OF ONE MILE

des Invalides) and again at the Chartreux. At the Hôtel des Invalides they encountered slight opposition. Some of the crowd were ugly and there were a few cases of disorder. The all-night search had produced a large quantity of arms and powder, but not enough. Most of what had been at the places where they went had been removed by the King's men to the Bastille, an old fortress in the center of Paris, now used as a prison. There the crowd determined to go in its quest for arms.

It is very likely that the Parisians feared the Bastille. It is very likely that they regarded it as a symbol of the much-hated Ancient Régime and of their subjection to the King. It is very likely that horrible stories were current about the terrors of its dungeons and the agonies of its victims. (If so, they were gross exaggerations, for only seven prisoners were found in the old fortress when it was taken on that day, all of whom might have been there in a more advanced era.) But whatever the feeling of Paris about the Bastille, only one motive drew the people toward it on July 14. They were looking for arms and powder. It was only afterwards that the attack upon the Bastille was looked back upon with sentimental patriotism, lords and laborers, ladies and actresses, working side by side to tear it down leisurely but thoroughly, bits of its stones sold at handsome prices to be worn as jewels or kept as sacred relics, its captors regarded as mighty paladins in a holy cause. But on July 14, the attack on the Bastille was no more premeditated than had been the previous attacks on other buildings.

At the Bastille they encountered real opposition, however. De Launay, the governor of the fortress, with a garrison of about a hundred *invalides* and Swiss Guards, was under orders to hold the fort. He refused to allow the crowd to enter. He treated deputations sent to him from the Hôtel de Ville with courtesy, even after the fighting had started, except for one, which having stopped to harangue the crowd, after receiving permission to advance, created the suspicion that it was planning a ruse and was fired upon. De Launay was anxious to be reasonable. Before the firing began, he withdrew his cannon from their menacing position, promised not to fight unless attacked, but refused to let down his drawbridges. The crowd had managed to get into the outer courtyard, which was easily accessible, but the inner court was impregnable. Two men succeeded in climbing upon a near-by building and leaping into the inner court. They cut the chains that held the drawbridge up and the crowd rushed in. There was still another drawbridge.

Then somebody fired. The crowd firmly believed that De Launay had himself let down the outer bridge in order the more easily to make a target of the people as they came within closer range. Who fired the first shot remains a mystery to this day, but it was most likely on De Launay's orders. The fighting thus began at one o'clock. Most of the losses were on the side of the people, exposed in a disadvantageous position. At three o'clock the French Guards came up from the Hôtel de Ville with cannon. De Launay might have held out, but had no food. He wished himself to blow up the place, but his subordinate officers prevented him. On the threat that he would do so, however, the commander of the French Guards allowed him an honorable capitulation. Despite the efforts of the officers of the French Guard, the mob, believing that De Launay had tricked them, made a prisoner of him and later butchered him. Some of his men were similarly treated, though the rest were safely put in prison. Flesselles, who had conscientiously done what he could to preserve order, had given the impression that he opposed the "patriots." Several of the triumphant mob demanded his arrest. Flesselles submitted, perhaps in order to save his colleagues, and while on his way to the Palais-Royal to be tried by a popular tribunal, was assassinated. Within a week (July 22). Foulon and his son-in-law Berthier, Intendant of Paris, who had incurred the people's displeasure by their hostility to the popular cause and were suspected of speculating in foodstuffs, were likewise taken away from the authorities and lynched

Paris spent the night of the 14th in fear of an attack from Versailles, but none came. The story goes that the Duke of Liancourt woke the King at two o'clock in the morning to tell him of the capture of the Bastille. "Why," said Louis, "this is revolt!" "No, sire," replied the Duke, "it is not revolt, it is revolution." The story is probably not true. The King must have known of the fall of the Bastille before two o'clock on the following morning; the National Assembly knew of it on the evening of the 14th, and had determined to remain in session all night. But it is true that the fall of the Bastille was a revolution and not merely a revolt, and the French have good reason for now regarding it as their national holiday. The King, who seems so far to have been but a tool in the hands of his more energetic relatives, wearied of his part. Feeling that the situation required of them that they remain at their posts; perhaps, too, not daring to go home lest they be met by troops with *lettres de cachet*, the deputies of the nation had stayed in the Salle des Menus Plaisirs all night. Early in the morning of the 15th, Louis and his two brothers came to the Assembly and announced that he had ordered his troops to leave Versailles, and promised to recall the dismissed ministers. For the first time, he addressed them by the title of "National Assembly," having up to this point refused to call them anything but "The Estates General." He further promised that he would deal with them in the future directly and not through intermediaries, as he had previously insisted; and he authorized them to send a committee to Paris to tell of his decisions. The reform party had once more won over the King from the conservatives.

The Assembly sent a delegation to Paris, including Bailly and Lafayette. The electors of the Hôtel de Ville named Bailly mayor of Paris and Lafayette, "the hero of two worlds," as the journals were soon to call him derisively, commander-in-chief of the citizen guard formed on July 13. On July 17, Louis bravely decided to go to Paris himself. The city, at first sullen to him, burst into prolonged cries of " *Vive le roi!*" when he appeared upon the balcony of the

Hôtel de Ville wearing on his hat the cockade that had come to signify support of the revolution. For fifteen minutes there was a continuous demonstration of approval. "Henry IV," said Mayor Bailly, "had reconquered his capital; now, the capital has reconquered its King." Louis' journey to Paris was an admission of defeat for the counter-revolution and a sanction of the revolution that had taken place in Paris. Louis, though still loved by his people, was now no longer their leader. Henceforth he would have to follow wherever they chose to lead. Some of the nobility, clergy, and wealthier bourgeoisie, disgusted with the victory of the people and fearful of further disorder, left France. The emigrations, thus begun, by a group in a rather cheerful mood who expected soon to return, were to continue until Napoleon was to take a lenient attitude toward *émigrés* and to permit their repatriation. The Count of Artois soon became recognized as their leader, and his bitterness grew as his exile was prolonged. But at home, people rejoiced that the revolution had been saved and that Necker had been restored.

In the provinces of France, the patience of the peasants, whose hopes of reform had been lifted high by the discussions that had accompanied the elections of their deputies, had now become exhausted. They had seen almost three months go by without producing any measures to relieve them. On July 16, before the news of the fall of the Bastille could have traveled that far, there had already taken place in Franche Comté an insurrection against the local lords who required the payment of the hated feudal dues. In July and August, what with the expectant unrest in which the peasants lived and the slowness with which news traveled, leaving them in constant doubt as to what was happening at the capital and constant fear that foreign countries or rascally landlords or unscrupulous knaves and bandits might take advantage of the difficulties that France was then experiencing, a curious panic seized the countryside. It began in the middle of July in certain districts and did not reach others until August. "Spontaneous anarchy,"

Taine called it, but more sympathetic historians have preferred the less hostile name of the "Great Fear." Cries would go up that "the bandits are coming!" Peasants with scythes, old soldiers with muskets, all able-bodied men with whatever weapons they could find turned out to fight the enemy, and the enemy did not appear or proved to be some innocent traveler who had raised more than the usual amount of dust upon the highway. Since there was no enemy, it was not hard to create one. There were the accursed manor-houses, the local Bastilles; they would attack them! The National Assembly had paid no attention to their cahiers demanding relief from the lords' domination. Very well, then, they would do it themselves. And so the peasants, summoned by the quick, double stroke of the village church bell, the *tocsin*, to fight an imaginary foe, naturally turned against a very real enemy. Most often the insurrections were entirely peaceful. The lord or his representative, called upon to surrender the *terriers* that held the humiliating record of each peasant's obligations, saw the futility of resistance and yielded with a good grace. But in some cases the peasants met with resistance and resorted to violence. Sometimes they massacred the odious stewards and even destroyed the châteaux in their anxiety to destroy the records they contained. The peasant thus went a good deal farther than anybody had wished him to go, farther than he had originally intended to go himself. His demand was henceforth to be for a complete abolition of the claims sanctioned in the manor-rolls that he had just destroyed. He had carried out a more radical economic and social revolution than any head in Versailles had as yet contemplated. If his plans were allowed to materialize, economic feudalism would thenceforth be a thing of the unhappy past.

That the peasant insurrections were influenced by the example set by Paris on July 14 is evident, but, since they began in certain districts before the taking of the Bastille was known and since the Great Fear can only by stretching a point be regarded as having originated in Paris, that influence could not have been as great as has sometimes been supposed. More direct was the influence of the fall of the Bastille upon the larger provincial towns. In Bordeaux, Lyons, Marseilles, and elsewhere, the precedent established by the capital was followed to the letter. The old municipal governments, divided between the intendant and the guilds, were entirely abolished or, at least, supplemented by a new revolutionary council; citizen guards were established; and wherever there were local Bastilles, these were captured, and in the course of time, demolished, as was the Paris prison, or devoted to other purposes. Sometimes the disorders accompanying these petty revolutions were equal to those which had taken place at Paris.

News of what was happening in the villages and cities of the provinces was not slow in reaching the representatives of the people in Versailles. A committee was appointed to investigate the causes of the anarchy and to suggest a remedy. This committee recommended, on August 3, that the National Assembly should decree that, until the proposed constitution was completed, the old laws remained in force and all the customary dues were to continue to be paid. The report was unsatisfactory to some of the deputies, but a new committee on the next day reported to the same effect. To have passed such a law would have meant the creation of an irrevocable schism between the peasantry, who had everything to lose by it, and the conception of the revolution represented by the National Assembly. In fact, a similar suggestion made by Lally-Tollendal on July 20, though rejected by the Assembly, was regarded in some quarters as the explanation of the severity with which the people of Paris treated Foulon and Berthier on July 22. It would undoubtedly have given rise to the feeling that the National Assembly, made up of members of the upper classes, was not interested in the agrarian problem.

But the evening before, at the Breton Club, which was an association originally of only the deputies from Brittany, but by this time including some of their colleagues, the same question had been discussed, and the Duke d'Aiguillon, one of the largest landowners in France, had declared that he would propose at the Assembly on the morrow the confiscation, with an indemnity, of all the feudal rights of the lords. On August 4, after the committee had rendered its report, the Viscount de Noailles, evidently seeking to make a name for himself, rose before the Duke d'Aiguillon to make such a motion. He was seconded by the Duke, by Kerangal, who had been a Breton peasant, and by others of the liberal nobility. They were followed by a group of landowners, who surrendered their hunting rights and their exemption from taxation, and by curés who yielded their tithes and their fees. One after another, with enthusiastic abandon, the privileged rose to vie with each other in sacrificing their privileges. The cities gave up the peculiar advantages which their ancient charters gave to them. The provinces that had enjoyed a favored position surrendered their estates and their control of taxation. At the end of a session lasting all of the night, the Assembly decided to proclaim Louis XVI the Restorer of French Liberty. For a quarter of an hour the deputies hurrahed for the King and embraced each other out of joy that the unity and liberty of the nation had at last been achieved.

The cynical historian has been unwilling to bestow upon the nobility and the clergy who shared in the events of the night of August 4–5 the glory of self-sacrifice that once was ungrudgingly conferred. Buchez and Roux, and Kropotkin have pointed out that they were surrendering that which no longer belonged to them: their châteaux were in ruins, the records of their rights reduced to ashes. Marat, contemporaneously, had the same feeling. Madelin, almost malignantly, declares that Noailles, who started the race of abnegation, owned no land (he was known among his fellows as "John Lackland") and therefore was the lord of no peasants and could command no feudal dues; that it was a clergyman who had moved that the nobility surrender their hunting privileges and a noble who had moved that the clergy give up their tithe. And Aulard shows that if the Duke d'Aiguillon, who inspired the entire session, had been able to carry his original intention, the dues would have been surrendered, to be sure, but made redeemable at a price that would have enriched the seigneurs. The ardor of August 4–5 can thus be interpreted as a coolly calculated effort on the part of former owners to save what they could out of the wreck of their feudal privileges. It is true that there were some saner minds, like the imperturbable Dupont de Nemours and a few of the less sanguine nobles, who yielded only reluctantly to the contagious atmosphere or even erected about themselves a sullen *cordon sanitaire.* Their behavior, however, only emphasizes the sincerity of the others the more. Whatever the materialistic motives behind the enthusiasm may have been, there was probably also some genuine idealism in it all, some earnest desire to create a new era of peace and good will.

Then came the calmer realities of sobriety. The next week was devoted to putting into permanent legal form the general statements made upon August 4–5. The solidification of the municipal revolutions presented no difficulties. On August 10, the National Assembly adopted a resolution creating a National Guard out of the bourgeois guards that had sprung into existence in the insurrections of July, and placing these guards, not under the King, but under the municipalities. But the liquidation of feudalism presented many insurmountable obstacles. It was found that the abolition of the tithe would involve certain very definite financial entanglements, since much of the tithe had been subinfeudated — that is to say, farmed out to the highest bidders — and was now in private hands. Moreover, the nobility might, in some cases, be reduced to penury by the confiscation of their feudal rights, which was all the property a number of them owned. The decrees in their final form were presented to the King for his sanction on August 13. The abolition of the unequal privileges of the two higher orders of society was still the guiding note. The National Assembly boldly declared that it "hereby completely abolishes the feudal system." It forbade all personal servitude, exclusive hunting rights, purchase of office,

class discrimination in governmental service, unearned
pensions, and plurality of benefices. But it also declared
that certain tithes and certain feudal rents were to be redeemed only by money payments and in a manner that
would thereafter be determined by the National Assembly;
until that time, they were to continue to be paid. The
feudal system thus was still permitted to cling tenaciously
to life. And in the country districts, dissatisfaction and
the *jacqueries*[1] remained unabated.

In Paris, at any rate, for several weeks following the
July insurrections, quiet prevailed. This gave the National
Assembly an opportunity to go on with the more sober
work of drawing up a constitution. Feeling was unanimous that there should be a declaration of civil liberties.
There was some question as to whether it should come before or after the body of the constitution. It was decided
that it should come first. Some felt, too, that there ought
to be a declaration of the duties of citizens synchronously
with the declaration of their rights. It was determined
simply to declare the rights of man. The Assembly had
already been divided into bureaux; each bureau was now to
submit its proposal for such a declaration. The suggestions
of the sixth bureau were adopted. It contained contributions from Mounier, Sieyès, and Lafayette — Lafayette,
who had framed the first ten amendments to the American
Constitution in a double frame, leaving the other half va-
cant for the day when he might frame their French equivalent. The Archbishop of Bordeaux, who acted as spokesman for the bureau, acknowledged a generous debt to the
American example. Historians have recently been agitated
over the question of the origins of this Declaration of the
Rights of Man and the Citizen. Jellinek, an Austrian
scholar, has maintained that it derived its inspiration from
the great English charters and the Bills of Rights in the
constitutions of the American States. But French histori-

[1] "Jacques" was a common name among the peasants (cf. The English
"Jack"). The original *jacquerie* was in 1358. Since that time all peasant
uprisings were loosely described by that name.

ans have risen in defense of its Latinity, claiming that it
is directly ascribable to the French philosophers of the
eighteenth century. It has also been pointed out that the
Declaration of Rights has an empirical basis; that the deputies set out, by constitutional statute, to nullify and to
make illegal for all future time abuses such as in the past
they had known and suffered.[1]

In broad, general terms, the Declaration of Rights
granted freedom of the press, freedom from arbitrary
arrest, and trial by jury. Religious freedom and freedom
of thought were granted only conditionally: "No one shall
be disturbed for his opinions, even on religious matters,
provided that their manifestation does not trouble the
public peace established by law." "Every citizen can
freely speak, write, and print, subject to responsibility for
the abuse of this freedom in the cases determined by law."
The Declaration of Rights was severely criticized for these
reservations in the radical press. Yet, if only some machinery could be found to carry out these broad provisions,
the Declaration might nevertheless establish civil liberty.
It granted equality before the law, equality in taxation,
equality of opportunity for public office, equality of franchise. Thus it sought to create civil equality. It stated
that the right of private property was inviolable, that
sovereignty resided in the nation, that there should be a
careful separation of governmental powers, that unlawful
oppression might be resisted. Thus it incorporated the
principal political tenets of eighteenth-century philosophy.
It was a splendid collection of political aphorisms. Even
the King, who refused to sanction them, said they would
make proper regulations for the Assembly to follow in drawing up the constitution. But as the old government of
France was undergoing disintegration and as the new
government was not yet achieved, they were as yet little
more than revolutionary propaganda — prohibitions of
past wrongs rather than the foundations of present rights

Jellinek: *Declaration of the Rights of Man and Citizens*; Boutmy: *Annales des Sciences Politiques*, XVII; Robinson: *Political Science Quarterly*, XIV.

There were now two distinct parties in the National
Assembly. Deputies of sympathetic views had naturally
and gradually acquired the habit of sitting together, and
in the same places at all meetings. The conservative
nobles and clerics sat on the right. They were faced by the
bourgeois reformers and their adherents on the left. It was
rapidly becoming customary to speak of the conservatives
as the Right and of the reformers as the Left. Questions
were now to come up that would divide the Left into two
groups. There was one group, known as the Anglophiles
or Moderates, who wished to create a constitution like that
of England. Their prophet was Montesquieu. There
was another, known as the Patriots, who were unwilling to
give to Louis XVI the power that George III was supposed
to have, or to create a House of Lords. Theirs was a
bourgeois outlook upon life. Their ideal of government was
one in which the King would be a servant of the merchant
class, the aristocracy having little, if any, power. The
leaders of the one group were Mounier and Malouet, of
the other Duport, Barnave, and Alexandre and Charles
Lameth. The first had the powerful support of the best
mind and the most eloquent tongue in the Assembly —
Mirabeau's. The other was able to win temporary support
from the leaders of the extreme Left — Robespierre, Pétion,
and Buzot — and the Paris populace.

The committee to draw up the constitution had been
appointed in July. Its spokesman was Mounier. Its first
task (July 27) had been to make a summary of the political
contents of the cahiers. It found nothing in the cahiers
that would agitate against their plan for a new constitution,
though there were several questions upon which the cahiers
were not agreed. During August and September the
reports of this committee were made and discussed. It
proposed a constitution by which there would be an upper
house and the King would have the right of absolute veto.
Mirabeau himself was opposed to an upper house, but he
did believe in strong monarchy and therefore favored the
Mounier plan as a whole. Despite the eloquence and logic

of Mounier and Mirabeau, two of the most influential figures in the entire body, the National Assembly rejected the Anglophile proposals. The Patriots opposed it because they feared the power it would vest in the King and an aristocracy; and the conservatives opposed it because they believed it was practical and therefore likely to succeed; they hoped, by adopting the alternative, which they considered utterly bad and unworkable, to lead to a reaction that would enable them to recover their lost influence. Against such a combination of radicals and conservatives, the mere liberals could muster but a small minority. On September 10, the Assembly decided in favor of a unicameral legislature, and on the next day it was decreed that the King should be given only a suspensive veto; on September 21, it was decided that a measure passed over the King's veto by the two following legislatures would nevertheless become law. Thus, since each legislative body was to last for two years, his veto would delay a law at least more than two years and possibly as many as six. The King was by no means thereby rendered a *fainéant*. Subsequent measures were to grant to him the right to choose his own ministers, provided they were not taken from the legislative body. Though they were to have the right to appear before the legislature and to take part in its discussions, they were to be entirely responsible to him. He was given the command of the army and permitted to name most of the higher officers. The arbitrary right to declare war or peace was taken from him, the consent of the legislature being required in either case, but the right of preparing for war — which can so easily become synonymous with the making of war — was vested in him. In short, by the measures adopted in September, 1789, and subsequently, while the King was no longer the autocrat he once had been, he was still permitted very important powers that he might use for evil or for good.

Paris had followed the debates on the organization of the legislature and the veto power with unusual interest and anxiety. There had sprung up, during the last few months, a popular press — Prudhomme's and Loustallot's *Révolu-tions de Paris*, Desmoulins' pamphlets, and more recently Marat's *Ami du Peuple* — which kept the people some-times informed and always agitated. And it was not diffi-cult to agitate Paris, chronically in a state of intense excite-ment. Food was constantly going up in price; bread was scarce, because of bad harvests; business was bad and un-employment on the increase because of the unsettled politi-cal situation. Stocks had fallen at the Bourse; runs were being made on some of the banks. People feared the activity of the Count of Artois who was busily engaged in visiting foreign courts. They suspected, also, the inten-tions of certain groups in the Assembly; some of them did not know exactly what the veto was, but many of them felt it was something the King ought not to have. Only on September 20 did he reluctantly appear to accept the August resolutions, and he was now refusing to sanction the Declaration of Rights, the unicameral legislature, and the suspensive veto. In other words, he was vetoing the constitution itself. Mounier and several others, who fa-vored the veto while it was under discussion, had received threatening letters from anonymous sources. On the de-feat of the Anglophile proposal for a constitution, Mounier and his committee had resigned and a new committee had been appointed consisting of men with the bourgeois Patriot point of view — Target, Sieyès, Rabaut Saint-Étienne, and others of that sort. Mounier was now elected President of the National Assembly, but this mark of the confidence of his colleagues in him did not increase his confidence in the way things were going or in the actions of the Paris populace.

The apprehensions of the people in the city were sincere, their panic spontaneous, but certain individuals saw in it an opportunity to further their own ends. The Duke of Orléans, first Prince of the Blood and Grand Master of the Masonic Order, one of the most popular men in France, hoped to be able to overthrow his cousin, Louis XVI, and to establish himself as Lieutenant-General of the realm or as Regent during the minority of Louis XVII. It is even possible that Mirabeau, at this time courting the favor of the Paris populace, had come to some secret understanding with him. The Duke's money passed freely from hand to hand those fine autumn evenings at the Palais-Royal. A young lawyer named Danton (at this time gratuitously signing himself D'Anton), who had made himself the leader of the radical section of the Cordeliers, was said to have received a good share of it.

But it was not the intrigues of any prince of the blood that were to set Paris agog. The King had not learned the moral of the Fourteenth of July. Again he was concentrating foreign troops about him, although now less openly than before. On September 23, the Flanders Regiment entered Versailles and on October 1, at a banquet tendered to their officers by the King's Bodyguards, there were fervent demonstrations of loyalty to the royal family. Toasts were drunk to the King and Queen, and the national cockade of red, white, and blue was trampled under foot. The black cockade of Austria, the Queen's native country, or the white cockade of the Bourbons was substituted for it. On October 3, the ladies of the Court even tried to charm the National Guard of Versailles to the side of the Queen. Vague and terrifying rumors reached Paris. "Marat," said Camille Desmoulins, "sped to Versailles and returned like a streak, making as much noise as four trumpets on the Day of Judgment, crying 'O Dead! Awaken!'" The other journalists joined the din. On October 4, the crowds at the Palais-Royal grew menacing.

The next morning, a mob, made up mostly of women, led by Maillard, a hero of the attack upon the Bastille, who had at first tried to check the impetus of the crowd, started for Versailles. They were hungry and their chief thought was that the King and the Assembly must do something to alleviate the food situation. They were followed by a group who were not only hungry but also determined upon some political move; they felt that the King's presence at Versailles left him at the mercy of designing ministers and nobles who hated the revolution and they wanted to take him away from the court party and bring him to Paris. It rained all the way to Versailles. Mirabeau knew about noon that they were coming, although it was not until half-past four that they arrived. Some of the mob contented themselves with visiting the Salle des Menus Plaisirs, where the Assembly sat, hooting at its enemies, applauding its favorites, shouting for bread, listening to Maillard make speeches, and in general so impeding the work of that body that Mirabeau-Tonneau,[1] the Count's younger brother, and leader of the conservatives, thought it not amiss to flirt with the best-looking of them.

The greater part of the mob went to the palace. The gates had already been carefully closed and the Bodyguards were prepared for any emergency. The King, hastily recalled from the chase, received a deputation from the crowd kindly, promised them his best endeavors to ameliorate the famine, and some of the crowd departed. But most of them stayed on. At eight o'clock the King reluctantly announced to a deputation sent from the National Assembly that he accepted the Declaration of the Rights of Man "purely and simply." An earlier request for the sanction of the decrees passed since August had, that very morning, met with hedging and conditions on the part of His Majesty. But the presence of an angry mob, opposed to the veto and favoring the decrees, was an argument the King could not resist. For a moment he contemplated flight, but Necker and his own disgust at becoming a fugitive dissuaded him. Finally, at midnight, Lafayette arrived with thirty thousand National Guardsmen and volunteers. He had not wanted to come at all — perhaps for fear that the Guards would only aggravate the situation, since they too (most of them being old French Guards) wished to remove the King to Paris. He had finally consented only when his men became unruly, threatening to lynch him or to go without him.

The King was genuinely glad to see him. After Lafay-

[1] That is, "Barrel" Mirabeau, because of his tremendous liquid capacity.

ette had taken none too careful precautions, everybody —
Court, guards, and people — tried to get some rest. At
daybreak the mob managed to break into the palace and
made for Marie Antoinette's chamber. Several were killed
on both sides in the skirmish. Two guards bravely sacrificed themselves in order that the Queen might have time
enough to escape by a secret passage to the King's room.
The National Guard succeeded in driving the mob out and
restoring order. Lafayette's popularity solved the remaining problems. He effected an alliance between the National Guards and the King's Bodyguards. He led the
royal family to the balcony; the crowd shouted, " *Vive le
roi!*" but it made faces at the Queen. Lafayette led her
out a second time alone. Kneeling beside her, he kissed her
hand, and cries of " *Vive le général! Vive la reine!*" went
up. Then came shouts of "The King to Paris! The King
to Paris!" and the Court prepared to go.

It was a tired troop of people that reached the City Hall
of Paris on the evening of October 6. But the populace was
glad; they had brought with them "the Baker, the Baker's
wife, and the Baker's boy." Somehow or other, bread
would be cheaper, the King would be free from the influence
of treacherous nobles whose bad influence had caused so
much trouble at Versailles, and there would be no more
danger of his organizing a counter-revolutionary army.
At ten o'clock the King reached the Tuileries, from which a
host of pensioners had just been dispossessed, which he had
never seen before, but which, until his deposition, was
for the next three years to be his home and practically his
prison, save for one brief, unhappy period of a few days,
when he was able to make his escape. The National Assembly believed it its duty to accompany the King. Upon
his request they had sent some of their number to the palace on October 6; and on October 12, upon the motion of
Mirabeau, they went to take up their residence at the Archbishop's Palace on the Île de la Cité; on November 9, they
moved to the Salle de Manège near the Tuileries. The
National Assembly now, as well as the King, was in a posi-

tion where it could more easily be influenced by any pressure brought to bear by the citizens of Paris.

The period immediately following the insurrection of October 5–6 witnessed a reaction. On October 7, a mob of women of the market-places (Les Halles) demonstrated in favor of the King and Queen in the Tuileries Gardens. The Châtelet, the police court of Paris, was empowered to conduct an investigation to discover the instigators of the uprising. The Châtelet outlawed the journalist Marat and made things so uncomfortable for the Duke of Orléans that he was glad to retire from France to become ambassador to London; but, after a year's investigation, they could find nothing definite or conclusive. Mirabeau, if he ever indeed was in league with the Duke of Orléans, now repudiated him completely. He would not even have the Duke of Orléans for a valet, he said. On October 21, a baker was lynched for hoarding bread. The National Assembly, that same day, on Mirabeau's motion and despite Robespierre's opposition, passed a law permitting the municipalities of France to declare martial law at their own discretion. At this time, too, Mounier, Lally-Tollendal, and a few other moderates, disgusted with the insurrection of October 5–6 and the radicalism of the Assembly in general, retired from the Assembly. Mounier even tried to rouse his province of Dauphiny against the Assembly, but failed and left the country. The insurrection of October 5–6 had thus done two very significant things. It had taken the leadership of the revolution away from the King and the National Assembly; they were now not much better than political agents of the public opinion of Paris. And by depriving them, the Duke of Orléans, Mirabeau, Mounier, and others, of their influence and prestige, and by making it possible for Lafayette to appear the hero of the occasion, it had placed Lafayette in a position almost of dictator of France, which he did not hesitate to occupy. It remained to be seen whether he could prove equal to his opportunities

CHAPTER III

THE TRIUMPH OF THE BOURGEOISIE

WHEN the deputies to the Estates General first came to Versailles, probably not one of them expected that the month of October would find them farther from a completed constitution than they then thought they were. As they now took their places at the Manège, however, the immensity of their task must have been clear to them. By the August decrees, they had hoped to destroy feudalism; by the Declaration of Rights, they had tried to create civil liberty, equality, and toleration; by the September decrees, they had, in part, formed a legislature and determined its relations with the executive. So much of the constitution they had already drawn up, but what there was of it was yet vague and insecure. And there still remained much to do.

The interval between October, 1789, and September, 1791, saw the job completed. It was an interval of intrigue and subterfuge, of plots half-hatched and near-successful, of attempted *coups d'état* and civil war, of mutinies and street brawls, but with no great crises like those of July and October, 1789, to check or to incite the work of the National Assembly, until the flight of the King in June, 1791. Many of the petitions and demonstrations of the Paris Sections, many of the counter-moves by émigrés and clergy were to influence the turn of events at the Manège, but the work of drawing up a constitution went on uninterrupted for almost two years, until the Constitution of 1791 was adopted and put into force. When it was completed, it represented the opinions of the majority of the Assembly, expressed freely and without duress. For while the galleries made themselves heard, while the journals clamored against certain groups of deputies, while petitions of the Sections and letters from individuals sometimes threatened dire consequences to some of the leaders, they were held in check by the guards and spies that Lafayette constantly kept surrounding the hall. It was not until a later date that the people of Paris so far forgot the sacrosanctity of the legislators as to subject them to personal violence.

But the pressure of public opinion was, nevertheless, expressed through several legitimate channels. The various districts of Paris still continued to meet, and at their meeting-places there were frequent and heated discussions of current problems that often resulted in deputations and petitions to the National Assembly. The Breton Club had come to Paris with the deputies that had constituted its original membership. It now made its headquarters at the former monastery of the Jacobin monks and became known as the Jacobin Club, though its formal name, was, first, the *Amis de la Constitution*, and then the *Amis de la Liberté et de l'Égalité* (Friends of Liberty and Equality). Local patriotic societies were rapidly formed in every municipality of any size in France. They soon began to correspond with, and to send representatives to the Jacobin Club at Paris. Thus, within a year, there were several hundred provincial chapters of the Friends of Liberty and Equality looking to the Jacobin Club at Paris as their mother chapter. Membership in these organizations was open to any one who could pay the low dues. These societies were frequently more advanced in their views than even the radicals of the National Assembly. They had no official organ, but could count on the support of the leading radical journalists such as Marat, Loustallot, Prudhomme, Carra, Gorsas, Audouin, and Desmoulins. Inside of Paris there were a number of other popular societies. The Cordeliers Club, under the leadership of Danton and Marat, was even more outspoken than the Jacobins and its dues were lower. The Cercle Social, whose leader, the Abbé Fauchet, edited a socialist newspaper called *Le Bouche de Fer* (The Iron Mouth), stood for a kind of social equality. *Les Amis des Noirs* (The Friends of the Negroes), whose organ was Brissot's *Le Patriote Français*, advocated the freedom and enfranchisement of the black slaves in the French colonies. There were few reforms undertaken by the National Assembly that were not endorsed — indeed anticipated — by some kind of organized public opinion.

There were also clubs of a more conservative tinge, though these were not so numerous and were not affiliated with any provincial chapters. Without officially breaking with the Jacobin Club, a number of its more moderate members had organized themselves as the Club of 1789 and soon came to be called Fayettists, as Lafayette was considered their leader. Condorcet's *Journal de la Société de 1789* was the newspaper that best presented their point of view, though the *Moniteur*, begun in November, 1789, by Panckoucke and soon to become the most competent journal of the revolutionary press, was likewise at their disposal. More conservative than the Fayettists were the monarchists such as Mirabeau, Clermont-Tonnerre, and Malouet, who organized as the *Amis de la Constitution Monarchique* (Friends of the Monarchical Constitution). A group of reactionaries, led by the Abbé Maury and Mirabeau-Tonneau, met at the convent of the Capuchins and later at the Salon Français; their ideas were expounded in the journals of the Abbé Royou (*Ami du Roi*) and Rivarol (*Actes des Apôtres*). These conservative groups grew weaker and weaker as more and more of their number emigrated, while the popular societies increased in the numbers of their chapters and in the membership of each chapter with the spread of the revolutionary fervor. Each of these clubs, with its supporting journals and following, was represented by some element in the National Assembly.

The monetary problem was one of the first to claim the attention of the National Assembly. By declaring (June 19) that the National Assembly alone controlled taxation, by assuming the responsibility of abolishing not only noble and church dues, but also certain national revenues in the decrees of August, the deputies of the nation had already established themselves as the financial dictators of France. Palliative measures were necessary, however, before a complete reorganization of the economic structure could be effected, for it was the danger of bankruptcy that had been the final argument inducing the King to call the Estates together. Necker proposed loans, and in August two loans aggregating 110,000,000 livres were voted. In December 80,000,000 more were granted, and again, in March, 30,000,- 000 more. But the loans were hard to float, and what they produced hardly sufficed for the needs of the Government Besides, very few of the King's subjects were paying their taxes any more. To meet the situation, Necker proposed, in September, 1789, that there be a blanket tax — a *contribution directe* of twenty-five per cent on all incomes. The Assembly accepted his recommendation. But the machinery for collecting taxes was so disorganized and the state of public opinion such that to have collected it systematically would have resulted in disaster. Very little income accrued to the royal treasury by this enormous tax.

More was forthcoming in another way. On September 7, 1789, some Parisian women made a gift to the National Assembly of their jewels in order to help meet the national debt. This established a precedent. As free gifts, many were willing to pay what could not have been collected from them as taxes. Thus the *dons patriotiques* became a source of huge sums granted to the Government. Necker himself gave such a patriotic gift of one hundred thousand livres, which was reported to have been more than one quarter of his income. Men of larger fortunes gave more. The royal family sent their gold and silver to the mint. Gentlemen surrendered the silver buckles from their shoes, ladies their jewels, little boys and girls their trinkets. Cities, corporations, monasteries sent in their gifts. For a number of days in November, 1789, it was part of the usual procedure of the National Assembly for these contributions to be piled on the desk of the President and for an announcement of the principal donations to be made. But the *dons patriotiques* were productive of good feeling rather than wealth. Even the decree of October 7, that all citizens (there were to be no privileged classes henceforth) were to pay their

taxes and each legislature would fix its own budget, did not
increase the amount of taxes collected.   It became necessary to think of means more radical than loans and taxes.

The cahiers of 1789 had spoken of a redistribution of the
lands of the Church, though none of them had dared to
mention confiscation by the State.   But the times moved
fast.   On August 8, La Coste; on September 24, Dupont de
Nemours; on October 10, Talleyrand spoke of the authority
of the State over church property.   It was inevitable that
such talk should be heard.   Church property was easily
worth three billions, which was about the size of the public
debt at this moment.   When, therefore, Mirabeau proposed
a statement that all the goods of the Church belonged to
the nation save what was necessary to maintain worship,
the clergy, and the poor, his motion was not altogether unexpected.   Indeed, in confiscating the tithe by the August
decrees, the National Assembly had already established a
precedent by which it might again put violent hands upon
the property of the Church.   The decree of November 2
was intended at the time to provide only a redistribution
of the church lands in order to put what the Church did
not need for cult purposes at the disposal of the State.
There was as yet no idea of spoliation.   Nevertheless, the
debates were very sharp.   Abbés Montesquiou and Maury,
the Archbishop of Aix, and Camus lined up against Mirabeau, Chapelier, Talleyrand, and Thouret in the struggle
for ecclesiastical integrity.   Their arguments were that land
was already a drug on the market (which was true), that by
confiscating church lands a bad precedent in favor of the
loi agraire (communism) would be established; that the
land was held only in trust by the Church for the performance of certain charitable, educational, and religious work
which the State could not perform equally well.   In reply,
their opponents answered that corporation-owned lands
were inefficiently operated, that small proprietors were the
backbone of the nation, that the Church was not performing
its charitable and educational work adequately.   But their
best argument was necessity.   And when the vote was

taken, chiefly because there appeared no other way out of the financial straits of the Government, the confiscation of the church lands was passed by 568 ayes to 346 noes (November 2, 1789). As yet, however, it was only the theory that the lands of the Church belonged to the State that had thus been approved.

This declaration alone was, nevertheless, a great victory for the cause of reform. A class that hitherto had ranked first in society and politics was now rendered propertyless and hence much reduced in prestige and power. It was a step that might have been forecast long before it actually happened. The nationalization of the French Church had gone on through Pragmatic Sanction, Concordat, and Gallican Liberties too far; the precedent, even in other Catholic countries, had been too striking; Voltaire had been too active to permit any observant person to remain long in doubt as to what the outcome of the debates on the secularization of the church lands would be. Liberals rejoiced when the decision was reached. It meant a victory over privilege, over an anti-national force, over the fount of intolerance, over a body that had frequently had a reactionary influence in French affairs. But there were many who were troubled. Who would take care of the hospitals, the poorhouses, the schools that only slowly had come to be regarded as the charges of the State and that still were almost exclusively in the Church's hands? How could the religious needs of the people be ministered by an impoverished Church? What reply could be made to the devout who would be shocked by the spoliation of the things that were God's? The National Assembly hesitated to proceed along the path that now was inevitable.

It required renewed economic pressure to induce the National Assembly actually to put the church lands on sale. Necker had borrowed most of the money that he had used so far from the Caisse d'Escompte. He now proposed (November 14) that the Caisse be permitted to collect the *dons patriotiques* and the money from the sale of the church lands in return for 170,000,000 livres that were to be borrowed for current expenditures. The proposal did not meet with favor in the National Assembly, but for over a month they could not decide to take the only alternative that then seemed feasible — to issue national paper currency upon the church lands as security. By two decrees adopted on December 19, 1789, this was finally agreed upon.[1] It was hoped that the result of this legislation would be to pay off part of the old debt, prevent any new debts from accumulating, and at the same time distribute the Church's property in more equitable portions among the population.

But the assignats did not prove very popular. The sale of church lands went on only very slowly. It was quite clear that the old claims of the Church were powerful enough to scare off purchasers. What if the Church should renew the fight for its property? What if some old treaty rights were discovered that would have to be respected? What if the Church should return to power? And what if the creditors of the Church should exert some claim to the lands? To allay these fears on the part of prospective buyers, and also to have more lands to put upon the market, the National Assembly decreed upon February 13, 1790, the abolition of monasteries and convents. All monks and nuns who wished to be free of their monastic vows might become so upon declaring their intentions before their municipalities. The monks who wished to remain within their orders were concentrated in a few houses set aside for their use. Monks engaged in public education or charity,

[1] It was provided that the 70,000,000 livres already borrowed from the Caisse d'Escompte be paid back at the rate of 20,000,000 a year and that a new bank, the Caisse de l'Extraordinaire, with the right to collect the patriotic gifts and the money received from the sale of church lands, would issue *assignats* or interest-bearing notes (five per cent) of one thousand livres each with the church lands as security. These assignats were to be exchanged for all interest-bearing debts of the State. Four hundred million livres worth of the land was to be put on sale and that amount of assignats printed. The assignats were to be received — indeed, given preference — in payment for such land, and were to be destroyed at a fixed rate as they returned to the Caisse. One hundred and seventy million livres of such assignats were to be paid the Caisse d'Escompte in return for a cash loan of that amount to pay current governmental expenditures.

however, and all nuns were permitted to occupy their old houses. All religious orders were thenceforth suppressed.

This measure was not enough, however. After almost three months of the existence of the assignats, Necker once again appeared before the National Assembly (March 6). He needed 250,000,000 livres more for current expenses, and wanted a new loan and the right to issue paper money to meet this new loan. The National Assembly hesitated. They felt convinced that the principle of the assignats was fundamentally sound. On March 17, they put the responsibility of selling the lands in the hands of the municipal governments, Paris alone, on her own request, receiving 200,000,000 livres worth, or half the land to be sold. Still the anomalous position of the Church in these transactions made it difficult to dispose of the lands even through the new agents. For another month, the National Assembly delayed and argued. But on April 14, it finally made the State responsible for the debts of the Church, the maintenance of the Church's functions, and the payment of clerical salaries. Thus it was hoped to allay the caution of hesitant buyers who feared the liens of the Church's creditors upon the land. On April 17, the interest on the assignats was reduced to three per cent, accumulating day by day. As fast as they came into the treasury in payment for public lands, they were to be burned in lots of 1,000,000 livres. They were now to be issued not only in 1000 livres denominations, but also in 300 and 200 livre notes. And they were to circulate no longer as promissory notes of the Government, but as paper money valued at face value plus the accrued interest.

For a time, the assignats flourished and their immediate tendency was even to stimulate business. On May 9, in order to increase the amount of salable land, the domain of the King was confiscated. But having despoiled the royal family and the Church of their means of independent income, the National Assembly had to provide for their maintenance. On June 9, when 25,000,000 livres were appropriated for the King's civil list, the liberal press raised an outcry that it was too much; already they suspected it was being used to pay conspirators in the King's employ.

On July 12, the National Assembly provided for the maintenance of the Church. The long series of decrees by which this was done was given the name of "Civil Constitution of the Clergy" — "civil," in order to indicate that the clergy were thenceforth to be a governmental institution, and also to disown any intention on the part of the National Assembly to dictate dogma or theology. France had already (December 14, 1789) been divided into eighty-three departments and the departments into districts and cantons. This had been done partly to weaken the bonds of the local patriotism clinging to the ancient provinces and bailiwicks, and partly, since as little violence to the boundaries of some of the provinces as possible was done, to provide a unit of government small enough to permit intimate contact between the officials and the governed. Each department was now made into an episcopal diocese. The eighty-three dioceses were divided into ten metropolitan districts, each under an archbishop. Affiliation with Rome was reduced to the lowest possible minimum, the clerics, upon being chosen, merely informing the Pontiff of that fact in a polite letter. Salaries, ranging from seven hundred livres for vicars in small places to fifty thousand livres for the Archbishop of Paris, were all to be paid by the National Treasury. What scandalized the clergy most was the democratic way in which they were to be chosen. The curés were to be named by their parishes, and the bishops were to be elected by the departmental electoral assembly. The bishop of the leading city in each metropolitan district was to act as archbishop. Protestants, Jews, and freethinkers might serve among the electorate.

It was a sweeping reform and one calculated to win unrelenting opposition from the clergy and good Catholic laymen. For a time there was a danger that no already ordained bishops would be found willing to pass on the Apostolic Succession. Seven prelates, among whom the best known were Talleyrand, Gobel, Brienne, and Grégoire, were willing, however, to take the oath to the Civil Constitution of the Clergy, and one of them — Talleyrand — proved willing to ordain the new clergy. So great was the dissatisfaction among the old clergy that on November 27, 1790, the National Assembly found it advisable to pass a law requiring all former clerics to take an oath "concerning the Civil Constitution of the Clergy" [1] or forfeit their ecclesiastical positions. Even this threat did not have the desired effect. It merely succeeded in creating a schism in the ranks of the clergy between those who took the oath (*jurors*) and those who refused to take it (*non-jurors*). The opposition was keenest among the lower clergy, despite the fact that their salaries had been considerably bettered by the new legislation. The bishops, not opposed to increased freedom for the Gallican Church, advised the Pope in council to accept the decrees, though they still refused themselves to take the prescribed oath. They kept secret the correspondence with the Pope that they carried on, in the hope that eventually he might be induced to take an attitude more compromising. They even offered to resign in a body to make it easier to replace them. What finally induced the Pope to come out openly and decisively against the Civil Constitution of the Clergy, the confiscation of the church lands, the suppression of the tithe and the annates, and all the work of the Revolution was the failure of the National Assembly to send an armed force to suppress his subjects in Avignon, who were demanding incorporation in France, which surrounded them completely and whose revolution roused their admiration. The most the National Assembly would do was to delay in annexing Avignon until the very end of its career. It was only six months after the Civil Constitution of the Clergy was adopted that the Pope (April 13, 1791) denounced it and declared all the work of

[1] Strictly speaking, the oath was not to abide by the Civil Constitution. It was an oath "to watch with care over the faithful of the diocese or the parish which is confided to them, to be faithful to the Nation, the Law, and the King, and to maintain with all their might the constitution decreed by the National Assembly and accepted by the King."

the Revolution anathema: "Had not God restricted human liberty?"

There had been serious opposition to the old Catholics on the streets of Paris and other cities before. Now it became very much worse. Loyal congregations drove out the new constitutional priests on the one hand, while, on the other, patriotic groups would break up old Catholic processions and services. The National Guard on several occasions had to be called in to preserve order, sometimes too late to prevent the loss of life and the destruction of property. In the South, and particularly in the city of Nîmes, where the Protestant population was very large, the disorders were worst.

The National Assembly was inclined to be tolerant toward the recalcitrants. After all, the Declaration of Rights did grant religious toleration of a sort. The Directory of the Department of Paris, which included Talleyrand and Sieyès, determined to permit non-juring clergy to acquire new property and to conduct their worship unmolested. The constitutional clergy objected vehemently. To permit the old Catholics to carry on their religious activities was very often to deprive the constitutional priests of their parishes, for most of the women were still staunchly Roman, and the men who were patriotic enough to be loyal to the new Church seldom attended services. Despite the opposition of the "patriots" and the constitutional clergy, the National Assembly, on May 7, 1791, adopted the policy of the Paris Directory for all of France. But the problem had ceased to be merely a religious one to be settled by a grant of toleration; it was now one of the foremost political problems of the Revolution, for every non-juring clergyman became a center of counter-revolution. The lower clergy, hitherto the friends of reform, had become more reactionary than the émigrés, and their influence was considerably greater. Despite all that the National Assembly could do, the non-juring clergy remained a problem to be bequeathed to future legislative bodies.

By assuming responsibility for the Church's debts and

for the payment of church and royal household salaries, by
promising to compensate the holders of suppressed titles
and offices, and by shouldering several other similar fiscal
burdens, the National Assembly had succeeded in raising
the national debt from the figure of 3,119,000,000 livres
that it had found, to 4,262,000,000 livres, on which the interest alone was about 262,000,000 livres a year. No means
of coping with a situation, becoming steadily worse, were
devised other than the assignats. Already the assignats
had begun to depreciate. Specie was rapidly disappearing,
since the wages of mercenary troops, debts owed to foreign
bankers, accounts payable to foreign merchants on imports
(which were increasing because of the disintegration of
French industry) were paid in coin as far as possible, and
hoarding rapidly took the rest from circulation. There was
a good deal of speculation in assignats and in the lands they
represented, both at home and abroad; counterfeiting became a regular practice not only of criminals, but on a more
extensive scale, of émigrés, who saw in the financial difficulties of the National Assembly a weapon of offense; the
general practice of banks and other business houses of issuing paper notes of their own tended toward inflation; the
unwillingness or inability of the treasury to burn the assignats, and their reissue in smaller denominations increased
the amount in circulation beyond the legal limitation. By
the end of 1791 they had fallen in some parts of France
twenty or thirty per cent. In the spring of 1792 they were
quoted at about fifty or sixty per cent of their face value
in foreign countries. And the worst was not yet, for a
pound of candles that had cost about eighteen cents in 1790
was to cost eight dollars in assignats in 1795 and forty
dollars in assignats in 1796. In February, 1796, one franc
in gold was to be worth six hundred francs in paper. And
they were shortly afterward to be repudiated entirely by
the Government of the Directory.

But in August, 1790, when the question of paying off
new financial obligations for which the National Assembly
had made the State responsible was under discussion, con-

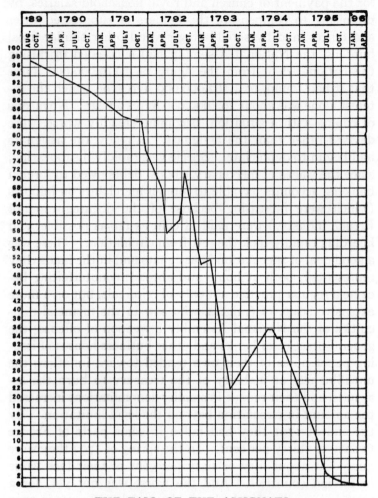

THE FALL OF THE ASSIGNATS

Drawn by Mr. E. S. Palmer of the Graduate School of the University of Chicago. The rise in the value of the assignats in August and September, 1792, may be attributable to the expectations attendant upon the election of the Convention. The more steady rise in 1793–1794 is a concrete justification, from one angle at least, of the Terror.

THE ASSIGNAT AU COURS

VALUE OF 100 LIVRES OF ASSIGNATS IN METAL: [1]

Year	Month	livres		sou		deniers	
1789	August	98					
1790	October	91					
1791	June	85					
..	October	84					
..	November	82					
..	December	77					
1792	April	68					
..	May	58					
..	August	61					
..	September	72					
1793	January	51					
..	May	52					
..	August	22					
1794	May	36					
..	June	36					
..	July	34					
..	August	34					
..	September	31					
..	October	29					
..	November	27					
..	December	24					
1795	January	21					
..	February	19					
..	March	17					
..	April	13					
..	May	10					
..	June	6					
..	July	3	livres	10	sou		
..	August	3	"	5	"		
..	September	2	"	10	"		
..	October	1	"	19	"	3	denier
..	November	0	"	16	"	6	"
..	December	0	"	12	"	6	"
1796	January	0	"	8	"	9	"
..	February	0	"	8	"	9	"
..	March	0	"	7	"	9	"
..	April	0	"	8	"	3	"
..	May	0	"	7	"	0	"
..	June	0	"	3	"	9	"
..	July	0	"	0	"	0	"

[1] Falkner, S. A., *Das Papiergeld der französischen Revolution, 1789-1707*, pp. 47-48.

fidence in the assignats was still strong. They had depreciated a little, but the lands were being bought up, and
the property of a once dreaded corporation was passing
into the hands of the people. Statistics available for the
date of November 1, 1791 (about a year later), show that
already 1,526,000,000 livres worth of the church lands had
been sold. Consequently, when the Committee of Finance
proposed either new five per cent non-circulating notes with
the public domain as security or a new issue of assignats to
meet these new obligations, after a month of deliberation,
the National Assembly (September 29, 1790) determined
upon the latter expedient. A few notes of caution were
interjected by the Physiocrat Dupont de Nemours and by
Camus, but the best financial wizards — Cambon and
Clavière — and the best political minds — Talleyrand and
Mirabeau — were for the assignats. For they had come
to mean not only a financial expedient,[1] but a political
weapon as well. Said Montesquiou, spokesman of the
Finance Committee, "The point is to confirm the constitution, to take all hope away from its enemies, to chain them
to the new order by their own interests." Make every man
a creditor of the new France by paper money and he will
become anxious for the prosperity of the new France. By
decree of September 29, 1790, the amount of 1,200,000,000
livres in assignats was fixed as the permanent limit of their
issue. Immediately they were issued to that sum, and now
in small denominations, so that the lower classes —hitherto
protected because the absence of assignats of a denomina-
tion less than two hundred livres had made it necessary for
them to deal in coinage — were now affected by their steady
inflation. The limit provided by this law was not observed
by future legislatures, nor even by the National Assembly
itself. When the Directory finally suppressed the assignats
without compensation, there were, it has been estimated,

[1] In fact the only one. The *dons patriotiques* had fallen off, and practically all
taxes, direct and indirect, had been abolished by a series of decrees in 1790 and
replaced by four new taxes — a land tax, a personal property tax, tariff duties,
and the *patente* or tax on all industries that were not yet regularly collected.

39,999,945,428 livres in circulation. Other estimates run higher.

But the assignats, despite the increase in the cost of living, the destruction of many private fortunes, the discouragement of thrift and the encouragement of rapid spending and riotous living that they produced, were not an unmitigated evil. For, in a way, they helped to solve the agrarian problems of France. The August decrees had left much to be desired by the peasant, since, though they abolished outright all dues that had their origin in serf obligations, they made all other dues repurchasable in a manner to be determined by the National Assembly. The peasants waited impatiently for the decision of the National Assembly upon this matter. But the Committee of the National Assembly encountered a number of difficulties. They found that in some regions the same dues might, in some cases, have their origin in some servile obligation, while, in others, they might be merely a form of ground rent. They found, too, an increasing unwillingness on the part of some peasants to pay certain dues, no matter what their origin, and an equal unwillingness of some lords to surrender without compensation. In February, 1790, the Jacqueries began again in some parts of France that had been pacific in July and August, 1789, and some authorities say, with greater vehemence than the earlier outbreaks. Finally in March, 1790, the Committee succeeded in passing through the National Assembly its recommendation that all dues be abolished without compensation, save those which represented an actual rent on land or interest on capital actually in use. The law was a radical departure from the decrees of August, but was by no means satisfactory to the land-hungry peasantry, since many of them had paid no dues after the uprisings of July and August and were unwilling to begin again now, and since the burden of proof was made to fall on the peasants; and how could they prove the origin of certain dues when the records for the most part lay charred in the ashes of the châteaux they had themselves burned down?

But passive dissatisfaction became active resistance again only when on May 4, 1790, the National Assembly fixed the prices of the repurchase of dues.[1]   The law was a very reasonable one.   By paying in twelve yearly installments what he would have paid in twenty or twenty-five without acquiring title to his land, the peasant might now become his own landlord, freed from all feudal obligations.   But he had almost for a year so regarded himself.   And furthermore, why should the National Assembly have assumed that annual payments were uniformly only four or five per cent of their total value?   And why include the contingent fees?   The Jacqueries broke forth again.   For about a year they continued, sometimes (since the National Guard was often sympathetic) without any effort of the local authorities to quell them.   The National Assembly in 1791 appealed to the peasants to abide by the law and begged them to see the advantages the Revolution had brought them. But the Jacqueries went on unabated, and few peasants endeavored to meet their old or new obligations, until (as we shall see) the Convention in 1793 abolished feudalism in its entirety.

In the mean time, however, some of the peasants acquired land, absolutely free of feudal restrictions, through the assignats and the sale of church lands.   In large part, the former ecclesiastical property found its way into the hands of speculators, wealthy bourgeoisie and landholders, and even some former nobles.   The alacrity of the well-to-do classes in acquiring these lands was not a measure of their confidence in the Revolution or their willingness to speculate.   It was merely that securing title to part of the public domain, no matter how insecure and no matter how soon depreciated, was a better gamble than holding on to the assignats.   Yet enough of it was distributed among the peasants to have made of France ever since a country containing

---

[1] Those that had been paid in cash were to be redeemable at twenty times their annual value; those that had been paid in kind, at twenty-five times their annual value; contingent dues (such as *lods et ventes, quint* and *requint*) were to be included in determining this price.   The peasant was given twelve years in which to make his purchase by annual payments.

a great number of small farmers, each owning a farm free from seigneurial obligations and just about large enough to subsist upon. This process, begun by the rapid increase in the number of small peasant proprietors before the Revolution, was now completed by the Revolution. It was one of the most permanent and perhaps one of the most desirable changes that the Revolution created. It was also one of the most statesmanlike, for the peasants and others who received a share of the former church lands (to which later were added the lands of the émigrés and convicted counter-revolutionaries) became staunch supporters of the Revolution, fearful that a counter-revolution would deprive them of their newly won possessions.

The financial necessities of the State destroyed the clergy as a class in society. The agrarian reform demanded by the peasantry almost destroyed the nobility as a power. The finishing touch came on June 19, 1790, when all titles and coats of arms were abolished and nobles were henceforth required to use their family names (Capet for the royal family; Mottier for Lafayette; Riquetti for the Mirabeaus; Égalité, by a comic-opera gesture, for the Orléans family). Thereafter, the nobility, obliged to pay taxes, deprived of, or unable to collect their feudal dues, known only by common names, were to enjoy no advantages in the social order save those that came, for some of them, from owning large estates. Even these, many of them were soon to lose.

At the other end of the social ladder were the proletariat of the cities. The working men and poorer artisans had long been excluded from the guilds, which had passed into the hands of the richer masters. The National Assembly, following the best Physiocratic principles and the precedent of Turgot, abolished these guilds. But working men had for some generations now been organized into their own associations, called *compagnonages*. While these were primarily for social and benefit purposes, they had at various times gone out on strike, and in the early part of 1791, as the assignats fell and the price of living rose, they threat-

ened united protest and violence. Pleading the desirability of freedom of trade, on the demand of the employers
of Paris, the National Assembly, on June 14, 1791, passed
the *Loi Chapelier* (christened after its proponent), forbidding all associations of any kind for professional reasons,
and threatening strikes and any violent disturbances on
the part of workmen with the penalties of sedition. One
of the motives of the National Assembly was undoubtedly
to guarantee the freedom of trade. For that reason they
had already (March 2, 1791) abolished all vocation monopolies and declared all crafts, professions, and trades open
to any who cared to learn them. But the severity of the
Chapelier Law is to be explained also by the fact that the
constituency of the National Assembly was chiefly of the
employing class.

The National Assembly had taken from the clergy their
lands and their social prestige and had reduced them to
the status of civil servants. It had taken from the nobility
their titles, most of their feudal dues, their exemption from
taxation, their control of office. Everywhere, as signs
posted in shops and coffee-houses indicated, the democratic
titles of "citizen" and "citizeness" were used for every one.
(*Ici tout est citoyen!*) It had destroyed the power of the
working class by preventing their organization and collective bargaining. It had left the position of the peasantry
unsettled and in ferment. The only aristocracy that remained was an aristocracy of wealth. The measures directed against the nobility and clergy were perhaps inevitable, if the abuses of the old régime were to be remedied.
To maintain that it was the deliberate intention of the
bourgeois majority of the National Assembly to destroy
these formerly privileged classes in order that thenceforth
the destinies of France might rest in bourgeois hands might
be to ascribe to them motives that had only an indefinite
existence, if any at all, and of which they themselves were
not entirely aware.

But not content with negatively establishing the advantages of the middle class by destroying the power of the

hitherto predominant classes, the National Assembly erected the supremacy of the bourgeoisie positively by concentrating in the hands of the richer citizens the rights of franchise and office-holding. Despite the protests of Robespierre within the Assembly, and of Marat and the radical press without, that it was a violation of the Declaration of Rights, the National Assembly created a property qualification for voting and holding office. In other respects, the aphorism in the Declaration of Rights that *all men are born and remain free and equal in rights* was not overlooked.[1] But not even the Rousseauans of the National Assembly were willing to carry this aphorism in the Declaration of Rights to its fullest conclusion. By a series of decrees in October and November, 1789, the National Assembly provided for the eligibility of voters and office-holders. France was divided into two groups of citizens — active and passive. Only active citizens could vote or bear arms (that is, serve in the National Guard). To be an active citizen, one had to "be or have become French," to be over twenty-five years old, to have lived in his canton a year, and to pay a direct tax of the local value of three days' wages, and not to be working as a domestic.[2]

By a carefully arranged hierarchy of property qualifications, political power was concentrated in the hands of a plutocracy. At the principal town of the canton, or in the sections of the cities of over six thousand people, the active citizens gathered for the purpose of choosing electors.

[1] Jews were eventually given all the privileges of citizenship. A strenuous effort, demanded especially by Brissot's club called *Les Amis des Noirs* (The Friends of the Negroes), was made to abolish negro slavery. The interests of the plantation owners actually rendered it impossible to do so in the colonies, though a law (May 15, 1791) giving the right to vote to mulattoes of free parentage who owned some real property was passed, and it was provided that all negroes were to become free as soon as they set foot on French continental soil. The disappointment of the colored population of Haiti led to bloody slave uprisings there that were not ended until the independence of the colony under negro domination was won.

[2] By the census made public on May 28, 1791, out of a population of about 26,000,000 there were only 4,298,360 active citizens in France. About 3,000,-000 adult males were unable to qualify. These active citizens were inscribed upon the records of their cantons, subdivisions of about four square leagues (French) into which each of the eighty-three departments of France was cut up.

There was to be one elector for every one hundred active citizens. To be eligible as an elector, one had to pay the equivalent of ten days' wages in direct taxes. These electors united at the principal town of the department and chose the bishops, deputies, and officers of the departments. The electors might choose only active citizens who paid the equivalent of ten days' wages in direct taxes for any office save that of deputy to the national legislature. To be a deputy, one had to pay the equivalent of a silver mark (about fifty francs) in direct taxes. Thus there were certainly no more than fifty thousand electors (between three hundred and eight hundred per department) and still fewer eligibles to the legislature in all of France. So great was the agitation against the *marc d'argent* in the journals and the popular societies of France that now existed in all parts of France that it had to be repealed.[1]   But the repeal came too late (August 27, 1791) — only after the one election held under the Constitution of 1791 had already taken place.

The National Assembly also arranged local government in such a way as to emphasize the political control of France by the aristocracy of wealth. Each of the departments (eighty-three between 1789 and 1791; the number grew eventually) was divided into districts, more or less arbitrarily, by the National Assembly, and the districts into cantons. The cities, of course, were kept intact, and divided into sections. At the head of each department was a departmental council of thirty-six members, half of whom were chosen each year by the electors (from among ten-day contributors by ten-day contributors). They were not paid; therefore only the wealthier citizens could afford to serve. This council took over the duties of the old intendants. To advise it, the departmental electoral assembly chose a procureur-général-syndic, who held office for four years, was consulted on every question of impor-

[1] But at the same time the qualification of electors was raised to the payment of a direct tax of from one hundred to four hundred days' wages, according to the locality.

tance, but did not have a vote in the council. The councils were represented in the intervals between their sessions by a directory of eight of their members who sat permanently. Each district had like institutions — council, directory, procureur-général-syndic — chosen in the same way. In the cities all active citizens might participate in the election of the mayors, but candidates for the office had to be ten-day contributors. The mayor was aided by a city council of notables and municipal officers.

Each district likewise had its courts, made up of five judges chosen for six years by the departmental electoral assemblies from among ten-day contributors. Below these courts and subject to appeal on the more important cases, were the cantonal courts, each presided over by a justice of the peace, also chosen by ten-day contributors from among ten-day contributors. The district courts, at first, were the courts of last appeal in all but the most important criminal cases, though there might be appeal from one district court to another. On January 20, 1791, the necessity for higher courts to which the district courts might appeal, led to the formation of departmental criminal tribunals, of which the president, named by the departmental electoral assembly, alone was permanent; the other three judges were chosen in rotation from among the judges of the district tribunals.[1] In cases of irregularity in the trial, appeal was permitted to a national court called the Court of Cassation, which was made up of one judge from each of the departments, and could determine only to send back cases to the original courts for retrial. For the trial of impeachments brought by the National Assembly, and for offenses against the nation, a National High Court was created, made up of the judges of the Court of Cassation and of a high-jury drawn from a panel of 166 members, two from each department. There was no supreme court for the interpretation of the constitution or for the trial of

[1] For civil and commercial cases, the departmental council was empowered to create a tribunal of commerce of five judges for the principal cities, to be elected by the business men of that city and resorted to by them at their option. For domestic affairs, the judges of the peace might create *tribunaux de famille.*

disputes between the departments; the Legislature was to
determine all such questions for itself.   In this way, though
there was provided a National Convention for the amending
of the Constitution, it was conceivable that the Constitution might be amended through an unforeseen interpretation by a majority of the National Legislature.   In every
criminal case, there was to be trial by jury, no torture, and
free privilege of attorney, if necessary.   The humanitarian
principles of the Assembly went even so far as to cause it,
for a time, seriously to consider Robespierre's proposal to
abolish capital punishment altogether.

The department was the unit upon which France now
was based.   It was the diocese for religious matters, the
electoral unit of the deputies of the National Legislature,
the administrative unit in all internal affairs — fiscal, judicial, legislative.   Each was administratively independent of
the others and of the National Government.   This was
largely a reaction to the old confusion in local government
— to the conflict of intendants, governors, baillis, and
prévosts, the rivalry of seigneurial, royal, clerical, and
parlementary jurisdictions, the absolutism of the King and
the indifference of the bishop in local affairs.   Now each
department was a carefully organized religious, judicial,
fiscal, and administrative unit.   Parlements, intendants,
baillis, bishops *in partibus infidelium*, guilds, and a host of
other ancient survivals had disappeared.   But there were
many who, although they did not regret their loss, yet
looked with suspicion upon the new aristocracy.   After all,
there had been many more nobles than there were now ten-
day contributors, and the nobles had by no means controlled all the offices of the ancient government.   There
were many who wondered whether the Revolution had yet
been accomplished, whether a new movement might not
be desirable.

Aside from the National Legislature, which represented
the separate departments as distinct units, the only bond
of union provided by the new constitution was the King.
The King, too, was the only effective check provided against

the tyranny of the Legislature.   His veto, to be sure, was
only a suspensive veto.   Moreover, it was not to be exercised in any legislation that was considered of a constitutional nature, or upon any money bills, or in deliberations
involving the responsibility of ministers.   Yet it was not
an empty prerogative.   In fact, because the King was
actually to use his veto power with great effect on several
occasions under the Constitution of 1791, he was considerably to increase his notoriety as a counter-revolutionary.
The King also had the right to make appointments.   He
chose his own ministers, though they might not be chosen
from the Legislature, were subject to interpellation, required
to account for their expenditures, and liable to impeachment before the National High Court.   The number of
ministers was now reduced to six — Finance, Foreign
Affairs, War, Marine, Justice, and the Interior.   The King
also chose most of the lower officers in the army and navy
(the rest being awarded their posts by the right of seniority)
and all of the admirals and marshals.   He still appointed
all of the ambassadors and gave them their instructions,
though, in the conduct of diplomacy, his powers were
greatly reduced, as he was obliged to secure the ratification
of all treaties by the Legislature and was unable to declare
war or peace without their consent.   The King was by no
means a *fainéant*, but since the Legislature now controlled
the civil list and the budget, might annul his treaties and
public declarations, might impeach his appointees and even
himself, and might claim for its members the privilege of
legislative immunity, he did not have an effective power to
check the potential tyranny of the Legislature.   "Under
monarchist appearances," says Mathiez, "France had in
fact become a republic, but it was a bourgeois republic."

Yet there was no reason why a republic, even a bourgeois
republic, should not have succeeded.   The Constitution of
1791 was in itself not an impractical instrument; in some
respects, indeed, it deserved and received universal approval.   If it left much to be desired, it must be remembered that there was much demanded.   It did, after all,

abolish feudalism for the most part, privilege almost entirely, absolutism altogether. It did create a kind of social and political equality and equality before the law, and endeavored to create equality of opportunity. It tried to abolish arbitrary arrest, religious intolerance, restrictions upon free trade. Worse constitutions have met with longer life. The weakness of the Constitution of 1791 was not so much inherent in itself as in the conditions of its birth. The forces aligned against it were too many and too strong, and not always motivated by a sense of the unfitness of the Constitution of 1791.

CHAPTER IV

THE COUNTER-REVOLUTION

THE circumstances in which Louis XVI and Marie Antoinette were placed after their removal to the Tuileries in October, 1789, made it impossible for them to feel any more confident than theretofore about the Revolution. But it also made it desirable that they follow a course quite different from the one they had pursued in July and October. As virtually the prisoners of Paris and Lafayette, they could not appeal to the military, whether openly or secretly, through fear of detection. Their personal influence, however, still counted for something, and it counted for something not only at home but also abroad. At home, there were the leaders of the popular cause who might be bought off in one way or another. Abroad, there was the possibility of persuading rulers — particularly those related to the royal pair, like the Bourbons of Spain and the Hapsburgs of Austria — that it was to their own interest to intervene in the conflict between the French King and his subjects.

Both schemes were tried at practically the same time. The problem of winning over Lafayette was solved by the General himself. Lafayette was not opposed to a strong monarchy. Granted certain democratic features in the government, he would have liked to see the King left with considerable powers in foreign, military, and internal affairs. He was therefore willing to use his great influence to prevent any further diminution of the royal prerogative. To take the utmost advantage of his influence, he felt it was necessary to have the King's complete confidence. In that way, he would become the actual power behind the throne, as well as the hero of the people and the foremost member of the National Assembly. Upon his own request, the King granted him command of all the troops within fifteen French leagues of the capital (October 10, 1789), and, tongue in cheek, expressed certain statements of confidence. **At** the same time, however, Louis began negotiations with the Spanish Bourbons. For a whole year this double game was carried on.

In the mean time, the King had bought off another of the leaders of the Revolution. Mirabeau, if he had ever been in the employ of the Duke of Orléans was left in October, 1789, without employment. His debts, his spendthrift ways, his indulgent nature, and his essentially monarchistic tendencies made it easy for him to pass into the employ of the King. It was well known that he desired to be a minister. It was the fear that he, who had been so very eloquent as a representative, might become too persuasive and influential as both representative and minister that induced the National Assembly to pass the law of November 7, 1789, preventing a deputy in the Legislature from becoming a minister of the King as well. Mirabeau, nevertheless, secretly passed into the employ of the King. The matter was conveniently arranged by a furtive meeting with Marie Antoinette, secured through the mediation of Mercy-Argenteau, the Austrian Ambassador at Paris and confidant of the Queen. But the King and the Queen never considered Mirabeau anything but an adventurer, and looked upon their bargain with him as only a guarantee that he would not agitate against them. They failed to see that while the man was unscrupulous enough to accept money from those whom his opinions might aid, he could not be bribed. "I may be paid," he once said of himself, "but I cannot be bought." Although he received a goodly sum for his services, he was, as Lord Acton put it, "paid to be of his own opinion." [1]

Mirabeau and Lafayette disliked each other and possibly were jealous of each other. In private, the first considered the second incompetent and the second considered the first dishonest. But ostensibly they worked together for a com-

[1] It should be pointed out, however, that at the time of the Favras affair, Mirabeau agreed, for a price of fifty thousand livres, not only to aid the King in matters which he favored, but also to be silent upon matters upon which he was not "convinced." This clause of the contract was later suppressed.

mon cause. One of the first good turns they were able to
do for the royal family was in connection with the Favras
incident. In December, 1789, there had been a conspiracy,
led by a former noble named Favras, very likely with the
connivance of the Count of Provence, to carry off the King
and Queen to Metz, where they might dissolve the Assembly
and convoke a new Estates General. Lafayette discovered
the plan before it could materialize, and Favras, promised
leniency if he would reveal his accomplices, confessed that
he had acted upon the orders of Monsieur and the Queen.
His confession was kept a secret, and he paid the penalty
on the guillotine, nevertheless. Some letters belonging to
the Count of Provence, found on Favras, were restored, un-
opened, by Lafayette; and on Mirabeau's suggestion, Provence went to the City Hall to deny any connection with
the conspiracy and to swear loyalty to the Constitution.
Louis XVI, as if to assure France that he had not been privy
to the plot, visited the Assembly on February 4, 1791, and
declared his attachment to the Constitution. While re-
echoing shouts of "Long live the king!" filled the room,
"Barrel" Mirabeau, in disgust, broke his sword, crying,
"When a king breaks his scepter, his servant may break
his sword." But the King did not live up to his promises;
and it is more than likely that on February 4 he played the
part of the politician, intentionally deceiving, rather than
that of the weakling, subsequently induced to change his
mind.

The first Easter to come under the new régime seemed to
many of the non-juring priests and the royalists a fitting
occasion to unite the faithful in a protest against the new
church and government. In April, 1790, rumbles of civil
war, led by the dispossessed clergy and financed by the
émigrés, were heard in the Midi. The loyalty of the National Guard in the southern cities, however, prevented any
important outbreak. If the King had expected any conso-
lation from that quarter, he had now to admit defeat. On
a letter which Lafayette had written him on April 16, 1790,
outlining his policy, the King wrote:

> I promise M. de Lafayette the most complete confidence upon all matters which may look to the establishment of the constitution, my legitimate authority, as set forth in this note, and the return of public tranquillity.

But secret negotiations with the foreign rulers became no less importunate therefor, and visits by leading émigrés to foreign courts likewise continued.

Spain at this moment was particularly displeased with the turn of affairs that the Revolution in France had brought about. A dispute had arisen between her and England over control of Nootka Sound and the possession of Vancouver Island. Some English settlers were unceremoniously driven from the island by Spanish forces, and Pitt threatened war. It became important to know whether the Family Compact, which bound the Bourbons of France in close alliance with the Bourbons of Spain, would be operative in this instance. The Constituent Assembly spent the entire month of May considering that question in particular and the diplomatic powers of the King in general. Mirabeau wished the alliance to be converted from an understanding between two royal houses into a defensive treaty of alliance between two peoples and tried to achieve the concentration of the treaty-making power and control of the army and navy in the hands of the King; but the National Assembly (we have seen) reduced the treaty-making power of the King to the point where he might merely negotiate, subject to the ratification of the Legislature, and considerably reduced his power over the armed forces of France. Spain gave up the quarrel, Vancouver, and the Family Compact. A vigorous king might have listened gladly to Louis XVI's importunings; but Spain was ruled by Godoy in the same way that Athens was ruled by Themistocles' son: the King was dominated by the Queen, and Godoy was the Queen's paramour. And Godoy had none of the attributes of a Themistocles.

The first anniversary of the Fall of the Bastille approached. The National Assembly, hoping to use the general approval of that event to foster a return of good

feeling, decreed it an occasion of festivity.   Everybody lent
a hand to prepare the Champ de Mars for the ceremony.
On July 14, 1790, contingents from the National Guard of
the eighty-three departments of France — Fédérés, as they
were called — participated in a parade along with the King,
the Queen, Lafayette, and the Assembly in a body.   All
present swore fidelity to the King, the law, and the nation;
and the King swore to maintain the Constitution.   Talleyrand said mass at an *autel de la patrie,* especially erected in
the center of the parade ground, and everybody but the
skeptic bishop himself was impressed.   The hero of the
occasion was Lafayette, but the King and even the Queen
were warmly received.   The entire ceremony of the Federation was marked by an ardor that even heavy rains could
not dampen.   It was a symbol not only of approval of all
that the Fall of the Bastille signified, but of the fraternity of
Frenchmen everywhere.   It was the first public translation
of the Revolution into a national religion.   The fervor lasted
for several days, as Paris danced, and sang the new revolutionary song — *Ça ira, ça ira,* and more and more of the
national troops took the civic oath

The Federation was another step in the dissemination of
revolutionary feeling among the soldiers.   Some regulars
had taken part in the festivity.   There had already been a
mutiny among the sailors at Toulon in 1789, which had been
put down only with some severity.   Now at Nancy, the
garrison, made up largely of the Swiss regiment of Château-
vieux, passed into open revolt.   Accusing their officers of
misusing regimental funds and of harsh treatment, they arrested them or drove them out.   The National Guard and
the people of Nancy were sympathetic, but throughout
France there was great consternation.   The fear that
France, in the throes of a revolution, might be considered
fair prey by unfriendly neighbors was constant and widespread.   If the soldiers were now to mutiny, France would
be helpless indeed.   The Nancy garrison had sent a deputation to the Assembly to present their case.   But the Assembly decided only to send General Malseigne to restore

order. Malseigne acted arbitrarily and inadvisedly, and
was himself obliged to flee to a near-by town. General
Bouillé, staunch supporter of the King, was commander of
the Army of the East. The Nancy garrison fell within his
jurisdiction. With a faithful army and the aid of some
loyal National Guards, he besieged and captured the garrison. He executed some of them and sent the rest of them
to be tried and sentenced to the galleys.

The National Assembly breathed freely once more, and
drew up a resolution of thanks to Bouillé. The King likewise expressed his approval. A few popular leaders sympathized with the regiment, and Marat began an agitation for
the release of the soldiers sent to the galleys that eventually
(April 15, 1792) ended in success. The nation at large,
however, shared the gratitude expressed by the National
Assembly. But the movement was fundamentally a victory
for the King. "Preserve your popularity," he wrote secretly to Bouillé. "It may be very useful to me and the
kingdom. I consider it a safe anchor and look to it to re-
establish order some day." In the panic created by the
Nancy mutiny, the concentration at the Château de Jales
of twenty thousand National Guardsmen of royalist tendencies, bearing the cross as their standard (August 17, 1790),
was almost overlooked. They had organized to protect the
Catholics of Nîmes and its environs against the anti-Catho-
lics who in June had acquired complete domination over the
town. There they remained until, in February, 1791, it
became necessary for the National Assembly to drive them
out by force and to send three commissioners "to purify
the country." Nor did the mutiny of the fleet at Brest in
October rouse the same fear as the Nancy rebellion, and it
subsided upon a few simple concessions.

Necker resigned on September 4, 1790, and left the kingdom, only with difficulty, to spend the rest of his life apolo-
gizing for his administration of finances. The people of
Paris, who had once risen in revolt at his dismissal, viewed
his departure with indifference, except for those who thought
he ought to be retained to answer for his errors. After his

departure, the ministry was considered more royalist than ever before. On October 20, 1790, the forty-eight sections of Paris, led by Danton of the Cordeliers Section, demanded the dismissal of all of them but Montmorin, and the Lameths supported this petition in the Assembly. Reluctantly the King complied and accepted in their places a ministry practically named by Lafayette. The King thenceforth retained no faith whatsoever in the Constitution. It was apparent that even those rights which it supposedly left him, he was not to be allowed to enjoy. He renewed with greater vigor his representations at foreign courts.

The King soon acquired an even more definite reason for taking a strong stand against the Revolution. Hitherto it had simply jeopardized his own position and that of his friends and relatives. That hurt him and rendered him an easy victim to their counter-revolutionary advice. But, upon the passage of the Civil Constitution of the Clergy his resistance became more active. Now, it appeared, the National Assembly was driving France from the Catholic fold, and Louis was intensely religious. He felt that the eternal welfare of his soul was at stake. He had reluctantly sanctioned the Civil Constitution of the Clergy, but as he beheld the disturbances that rent France because of it, his hatred of the Constitution grew. When the Constituent Assembly, in order to suppress the resistance of the non-juring priests demanded an oath to the Constitution, failure to take which would mean dismissal from office,[1] Louis delayed his sanction as long as possible and signed at last (December 26, 1790) only with the secret protest that he "would rather be King in Metz than King of France under such conditions."

Plots to set him free and to take him where he could successfully regain his mastery of France were already afoot. Perhaps Louis himself knew of the dramatic conspiracy to abduct him of the *chevaliers du poignard*. These "gentlemen of the dagger," in February, 1791, taking advantage of

[1] See above, p. 161 ff.

a day when Lafayette and his Guards were off at Vincennes
to defend that venerable fortress against a Paris mob,
perhaps instigated by royalists, gathered at the Tuileries,
about four hundred strong, with daggers in hand, to take
the King from Paris.   But Lafayette learned of their attempted *coup* in time to return and drive out the would-be
rescuers.   The fiasco, if it did nothing more, at any rate
indicated that if the King would not surrender to his unpleasant circumstances, he must look not to the few faithful
who were willing to risk their lives for him inside of Paris.
There was royal sentiment enough throughout France, as
was witnessed by the several royalist clubs and newspapers,
notably the *Ami du roi* of Royou, which, together with the
Ami du peuple of Marat, was to be outlawed by the Legislative Assembly in May, 1792, for being as rabid in one direction as the other was in the other.   But they were disorganized, and their leaders were being constantly lost by
emigrations, particularly after the château of the Duke of
Castries was sacked (November 13, 1790) because he had
wounded Charles Lameth in a duel.   Only an armed
demonstration on the part of some foreign power would
rally them and give them sufficient force to stem the rising
democratic flood.

The King, if not led, at least eagerly seconded by the
Queen, planned to flee this accursed Revolution that had
already destroyed his temporal power and now also endangered his spiritual salvation.   In February, 1791, the King's
two aunts had, after some difficulty and several arrests,
succeeded in leaving France.   The royal family was determined to join them.   As long as Mirabeau was alive, they
proceeded very cautiously, however.   Mirabeau was opposed to the King's putting himself at the head of the
forces pledged against the Revolution.   Such a course, he
foresaw, would be disastrous.   He did think, however, that
it was time to call a halt to the work of the National Assembly and therefore was willing to allow the King to withdraw from Paris, if necessary as far as Metz, where he could
force the National Assembly to terms or call a new one, if

the present one proved recalcitrant.   But there must be no collusion with the émigrés at Worms, Spires, Coblentz, and other German cities near the French border, who were trying to influence the none too reluctant foreign rulers to intervene in French affairs against the Revolution.   Above all, there must be no civil war (although at times he was inclined to believe that even civil war would be inevitable), with the country on the side of the National Assembly and the King supported by his brother monarchs.

But Marie Antoinette had never forgiven Mirabeau for having spoken ungraciously of her on more than one occasion, and the King did not have any greater confidence in him.   The Queen, even while Mirabeau was still alive, tried to induce her brother Leopold, Emperor of the Holy Roman Empire, to come to her aid.   While Mirabeau lived, however, there was no serious effort made by the royal family to flee.   But on April 2, 1791, Mirabeau, worn out by his own excesses and by the tremendous burdens that he had recently had to bear, died after a brief period of suffering. He was mourned by almost the entire nation, though Marat and a few others who were suspicious of his relations with the Court called upon the people to rejoice.

Within a little more than a fortnight (April 18), the King and his family made their first attempt to escape and failed.   On the day before, Louis had been publicly denounced by the Cordeliers Club, one of the most radical of the new democratic societies, for the hearing of mass with a non-juring priest.   On April 18, he tried to go with his family to Saint-Cloud, one of his summer palaces, to hear Easter Mass.   But the Paris populace and the National Guard, warned by Marat and other patriot journalists and led by Danton, gathered in front of the Tuileries and refused to allow his horses to move.   Despite all that Bailly and Lafayette could do, the King was finally obliged to reenter the château after an hour and a half of impatient waiting.   Perhaps the King's intentions had been to go no farther than Saint-Cloud, but the incident of April 18 showed conclusively that if the royal family ever hoped to leave Paris, they could not do so openly. Lafayette suspected that the only purpose of this move on their part had been to convince foreign watchers that such was the case.

In the mean time, the Count of Artois, one of the most active as well as one of the first of the émigrés, presented his brother's difficulties more assiduously to the sympathetic rulers of Europe. On April 23 (so well had Louis learned the game of dissemblance, once entirely foreign to his nature) a circular letter was sent about to all the foreign courts disowning the "Frenchmen who have voluntarily exiled themselves from their country, instead of sharing its glory, and who, if they are not its enemies, have at least abandoned their posts as citizens," and announcing "the intention of His Majesty to maintain [the Constitution] with all his power." But Louis nevertheless kept up his secret correspondence with the rulers of Europe. The King of Prussia was willing to intervene for a territorial compensation, which Louis was unwilling to grant, though he was willing to pay in money. Finally, Leopold of Austria, on May 18, 1791, told Louis' messenger that he would send troops to the border to coöperate with Bouillé in order to secure the freedom of the King and his household, but only on condition that the King left Paris and openly repudiated the Constitution. Louis' next step was thus defined.

About a month later (June 21), Paris woke to find that the royal family had fled. The intervening weeks had been employed in arranging a plan of escape by which the devoted General Bouillé, in command of the loyal Army of the East, was to meet the fugitives near the border. Leopold, true to his promise, had amassed a strong force upon the frontiers. On the night of Monday, June 20, all was in readiness. A passport had been secured for a Baroness de Korff and her household, and a late stroller near the Tuileries might have seen the Baroness (Madame de Tourzel, the governess of the royal children), the Baroness's two children (the Dauphin and his sister), the governess of the children (Marie Antoinette), her valet (Louis XVI), her maid (Madame Elizabeth, the King's sister), three servants (three bodyguards of the

King) and their coachman (the Count of Fersen, a Swedish
noble, who, it was commonly said, loved Marie Antoinette
and was the only man ever truly loved by her) entering the
De Korff coach on their way from the city.   Lafayette
passed by them as these preparations were going on without
perceiving there was anything amiss.   Was it the muse of
comedy or the muse of tragedy that presided over the event?

But a face that has been stamped upon hundreds of assignats and golden coins cannot be disguised even by menial
costumes.   After an all-night ride, the fugitives stopped for
a change of post horses at Sainte-Menehould, where Post-
master Drouet, later a member of the National Convention,
recognized the resemblance of the valet's head to the one
imprinted upon the fresh assignats given him for his services.
All the best-laid schemes went agley; slight mishaps along
the road had put the King's coach several hours behind
schedule, and troops that should have met him had already
been disbanded, their officers believing that "the treasure"
they were ordered to guard would not pass that day.
Drouet, by taking a short cut through the woods, was able
to reach the village of Varennes before the De Korff berlin
and to warn the village authorities.   When the heavy coach
lumbered up, it was stopped by the municipal officers of
Varennes.   Louis at first tried to deny his identity, even
though Drouet proved it by his assignats.   But after he had
been recognized by a local judge who had seen him often at
Paris, he admitted that he was the King of France.

The people of the country roundabout were loyal and devoted to their sovereign.   They showed him every courtesy.
but refused to allow him to continue on his way.   Paris was
notified, and on June 22, the royal family under a heavy
guard retraced its course back to the Tuileries.   On the 23d
they were met by a deputation sent by the National Assembly to take charge of their return.   The journey back
to Paris was more humiliating than the escape from it in
disguise had been.   Hurried from town to town by municipal authorities who dreaded tumult or rescue, jeered by
crowds that all but massacred a sympathizer at one town,

fatigued by five days of anxiety and travel, they finally arrived at Paris on Saturday, June 25. From their coach windows they might have seen the walls of the houses placarded with the proclamation: "Whoever applauds the King will be flogged; whoever insults him will be hanged."

And Paris during those five days? The first reaction on the morning of the 21st in the city had been one of amused hostility to the King. "At bottom," says Madelin, "the people were laughing to keep themselves from weeping." One gay spirit had put up a sign "House to Let" on the gates of the Tuileries, and a market-woman sold her cherries over the Queen's bed. But more serious minds were filled with fear. There could be no doubt as to the King's intentions. Like an eloping lover, he had left a note — one, however, not asking forgiveness, but filled with reproaches: the disorders at Paris were the work of "the factious"; the Constitution made good government impossible; the King was reduced to a figurehead; he had been humiliated on several occasions; he was no longer free even to follow the religion of his fathers; and there followed an apostrophe to all true Frenchmen to return to their king, and an injunction ordering the ministers to sign no documents until further notice. Paris now knew that its king had definitely joined the ranks of the counter-revolutionaries, that he might even return at the head of foreign troops to create civil war.

But France without a king! True, there were some who had spoken vaguely of a republic, but their followers had been few. Even the most radical now thought only of a change in rulers, and the Duke of Orléans made himself conspicuous on the streets of Paris once again. But most of France wanted its old king back. The National Assembly took immediate steps to close and to defend the frontier. To make the situation easier to handle in the event of the return of the King, it manufactured the fiction that the King had been abducted against his will. Nevertheless, they declared him suspended from office temporarily and proceeded to legislate in his absence, causing his seal to be affixed without his consent. When he returned, he was kept more than ever a prisoner at the Tuileries; and, for the time being, France, for all practical purposes, was a republic.

But the radical club of the Cordeliers was not satisfied with Louis' mere suspension. They began a petition in favor of his deposition. Part of the Jacobin Club supported them. Some of its members, like Brissot and Condorcet, were outspokenly republican. But others protested so radical a position. The committee sent by the National Assembly to escort the royal family back to Paris from Varennes had included Barnave and Pétion. These men had been among the leaders in the struggle against the monarchist faction led by Lafayette and Mirabeau. For some time now, the triumvirate — Barnave, Duport, and Alexandre Lameth — had been considering that the reduction of the power of the King had reached the proper limit, and no further diminution of it ought to be permitted. The anti-monarchical spirit that was unmistakably perceptible as the King's coach and its occupants moved steadily along the road from Varennes to Paris, furnished Barnave with the inclination and the opportunity for the formation of a liaison with the royal family that was to provide Louis XVI and Marie Antoinette with advisers who enjoyed a greater confidence than Mirabeau or Lafayette had ever had.

The triumvirate, distinguished for their fight to destroy the power of the King, were now the King's chief bulwark against further depredations. These men and Lafayette, but yesterday the leading rivals in the National Assembly, joined forces at the Jacobins to prevent endorsement of the Cordeliers' republican petition. The more democratic faction of the Jacobins drew up another petition less radical than that of the Cordeliers, but even with this the Fayettists and Lamethists would have nothing to do. They seceded, held their meetings at the Monastery of the Feuillants, and thenceforth became known as the Club of the Feuillants, wedded to the *status quo* as created by the reforms already adopted. They were willing to countenance no further change; if anything, they favored a revision of the Constitution of 1791 in the direction of greater royal authority.

The petition of the Cordeliers was placed upon an altar on the Champ de Mars, where a large number of people flocked to sign it. On July 17, two wretches, probably impelled by nothing more vicious than curiosity, hid under the table. They were discovered, accused of being spies of the Government, and slaughtered. To preserve order and to suppress continued agitation, Bailly and Lafayette read the riot act, in accordance with the law of October 21, 1789, and called upon the crowd to disperse. In the commotion, they were probably not heard and the crowd did not budge. The National Guard was ordered to fire and the mob broke up leaving a number of victims behind. Marat, Danton, Desmoulins, Brissot, and others regarded as responsible for the petition fled from France or went into hiding.

Filled with apprehension by such tumults, the National Assembly, led by the Feuillants, gave itself over to a wave of reaction. To be sure, a series of clauses were added to the Constitution providing that if at any time the King should be guilty of treason against France, he should be regarded as having abdicated. But the period following the massacre of the Champ de Mars is also the time when the King's ministers were permitted to speak on the floor of the Legislative Assembly; when a high tax, the equivalent of one hundred to four hundred days' wages, instead of only ten days' wages as heretofore, was now demanded of candidates for the electoral assemblies, though the payment in direct taxes of a *marc d'argent* as a property qualification of candidates to the Legislative Assembly was repealed; when amending the Constitution was made more difficult; and when the Civil Constitution of the Clergy was declared by the Triumvirate to be simple statute rather than constitutional law. Likewise, as the work of the Constituent Assembly was fast coming to a close and elections were already taking place (with the result that the old qualifications rather than the new determined who should or should not vote), the revulsion of feeling that pervaded France after the massacre of the Champ de Mars effected the election of an overwhelming majority in favor of the Constitution of 1791. Inside of France, then, the flight of the King had had a considerably less radical influence than might have been expected.

But not France alone was interested in what happened to Louis XVI and his family. Neither Leopold nor Frederick William could be depended upon to sit idly by while a crowned head suffered humiliation. If there were any danger that they might forget Louis' plight, Marie Antoinette's still uninterrupted appeals to her brother and the insistence of the émigrés at their courts acted as spurs to their memories. Furthermore, there was the threat that radical ideas might percolate through to their own dominions. Leopold was particularly fearful on that score. The Bishop of Liège had been driven from his principality, and the Austrians had but recently managed to restore themselves in Belgium, from which a revolutionary uprising had driven them likewise in 1790. Foreigners everywhere were joyfully enthusiastic over events in France, and in the Germanies, Kant, Fichte, Humboldt, Klopstock, and other celebrities were among the admirers of the " Neo-Franks."

The Revolution in the Netherlands and the attention required by a war, fought by Austria and Russia for the purpose of partitioning Turkey, had kept Joseph II, Leopold's predecessor, too occupied to intervene actively on behalf of his sister in French affairs. When Joseph II died (February, 1790), and was succeeded by his brother Leopold, who had earned an enviable reputation as an enlightened despot in Tuscany, Leopold came to an understanding with the Prussians at Reichenbach in July, overthrew the revolutionists in Belgium and Liège, and signed the Peace of Sistova with Turkey in August, at about the same time that Russia agreed to preliminaries that led to the Treaty of Jassy in 1792. Leopold was now free to turn his attention to the revolutions in France and in Poland

where an effort was being made by a group of liberals under
General Kosciusko to create a new government that might
give Poland the strength and unity to resist another partition of her territory.

On July 5, soon after Leopold learned of the failure of
the King's flight, he sent around the Padua Circular, urging
the monarchs of Europe to unite in a declaration "which
may cause the leaders of the violent party [in France] to
come to themselves." Only Prussia was willing to act with
Leopold in such a declaration, but on August 27, largely to
put an end to the importunity of the émigrés that they
recognize the Count of Provence as the Regent of France,
the two rulers met in Saxony and issued the Declaration of
Pillnitz. It was couched in mild terms, for Leopold desired
to be known as a diplomat rather than as a soldier; it stated
that if the other sovereigns of Europe would join them,
they would use the necessary force to allow Louis the most
complete liberty "to lay down the basis of a monarchical
government adapted to the rights of sovereigns and the
well-being of the French nation." While the French were
bitterly resentful against the two rulers for their hostile
interference in France's internal affairs, Leopold was quite
satisfied. For he knew that Pitt, Prime Minister of England, who was committed to a policy of non-intervention,
would not act in accordance with the Declaration, and
that, therefore, he himself was not bound to act. Louis XVI
and Marie Antoinette also urged Leopold not to go to war,
since they took heart once more from the reaction following the massacre of the Champ de Mars and feared that
open force might endanger their lives and the lives of their
sympathizers. The National Assembly, furthermore, did
away with every pretext for war by asking Louis XVI once
more to become the King of France by the Constitution of
1791.

Indignation in France very shortly made way for rejoicing. On September 14, the King took his oath to abide
by the Constitution. Louis had hesitated for some time to
do so. It was only after Barnave and Lameth had per-

suaded him to believe that the Civil Constitution of the Clergy would be modified and that his position would undoubtedly be remedied by later assemblies that he was willing to comply.   By his acceptance he now became a constitutional monarch and the stigma of suspension was automatically removed.   On September 30, the National Constitutent Assembly met for the last time.   The King repeated his oath of acceptance of the Constitution, and amidst hurrahs for the King, the nation, and liberty, the Assembly, having lived up to its Oath of the Tennis Court, brought its career to a close.   Save for a minority of radicals and reactionaries, dissatisfied with the Constitution of 1791 because it did not go far enough or because it went too far, all of France was pleased.   The Revolution apparently was now over.   So completely was the old slate to be wiped clean that, on the motion of Robespierre, the National Assembly had decreed that none of its members would be eligible to sit in the new Legislative Assembly; and before it adjourned, it declared a general amnesty for all political offenders, even including the émigrés; France was thereafter to be governed, it was hoped, by the provisions of a highly desirable document and by men who would have no factional quarrels to influence them.   If only the enemies of the Revolution would accept the *fait accompli!*   But the enemies of the Revolution — the radicals, the émigrés, the non-juring priests, the royalists within (led by the King), and the foreign rulers without — were very numerous and very powerful and not very tractable.

CHAPTER V

CONSTITUTIONAL MONARCHY FAILS

To expect that the people who had lost most heavily by the Revolution and those that were in danger of losing equally, in case it spread from France to other countries, would accept their plight without lifting a finger in defense of what they considered their rights was to ask too much of the frailty of human nature. The émigrés in the German principalities near the French frontiers refused to accept the Constitution of 1791 and continued to put forth their best efforts to induce foreign rulers to intervene on their behalf. Foreign princes had begun to adopt an attitude of hostility toward the new developments in France, and the recent Declaration of Pillnitz demonstrated that lack of unanimity among them alone prevented their armed intervention. The King and Queen still dreamed of a restoration of their former munificent autocracy and did not stop at treason to secure it. As events wore on, therefore, the danger of actual hostilities with some foreign power quickly turned into a reality.

Inside of France, too, the Legislative Assembly, which now, in accordance with the Constitution of 1791, succeeded the Constituent Assembly as the National Legislature, found itself heir to several problems that the Constituent Assembly had left unsolved. There was the constant fall in the value of the assignats and the resultant rise in the cost of living to contend with. The non-juring clergy, not allowed to preach and obliged to surrender their benefices, endeavored, in season and out, to raise religious bigotry against the Constitution. In the rural districts, the Jacqueries had not entirely abated, and something had to be done either to satisfy the land-hunger of the peasants or to preserve order, if it was not to be satisfied. In the cities, the various clubs continued to meet and to agitate, even though, by an eleventh-hour decree of the Constituent Assembly (September 29, 1791), there had been decreed several severe penalties vainly intended to limit their activities.

The high cost of living, the non-juring clergy, the Jacqueries, the clubs were the cause of a number of internal disorders. An uprising in the town of Étampes, early in 1792, to procure a fixed price on butter, eggs, wood, coal, and other necessities, resulted in the assassination of Mayor Simoneau. Even the Jacobin Club joined with the Legislative Assembly in praise of him as a martyr in the cause of order. But prices continued to mount, and along with them, dissatisfaction. In the departments, where there were strong royalists and Catholic sentiments, there were still other martyrs. The peasants of the Department of Lozère, early in 1792, having obliged the national troops to evacuate the city of Mende, imprisoned the leading 'patriots,' closed the local club, and forced an indemnity upon the city. There were patriotic reprisals in near-by towns.

Such was the situation about the time the Legislative Assembly began its career. Even a body made up of experienced statesmen might have trembled at such problems. But when the Legislative Assembly, provided by the Constitution of 1791, held its first meeting on October 1, 1791, there was not a man among them who had had any previous experience as a legislator. In a burst of generous but improvident self-sacrifice, the National Assembly had decided that none of its members might sit in the Legislative Assembly. Perhaps the best-known men in the new organization were Condorcet, who had contributed to Diderot's *Encyclopédie* and enjoyed quite a reputation as a *philosophe*, and Brissot, editor of *Le Patriote Français* and the leader of *Les Amis des Noirs*. But there were also some who were soon to become famous — Vergniaud, Carnot, Isnard, and others. These were the leaders of the group, sometimes called the Brissotins, but soon to be known as the Girondins, from the fact that many of them came from the Department of the Gironde. They were a reform party; Brissot and Condorcet were, in a passive manner, republicans, and all of them had remained loyal to the Jacobin Club after the Feuillant secession. On the right sat the Feuillants, pledged to maintain the Constitution. There were two hundred and sixty-four Feuillants and only one hundred and thirty-six Girondins, but the most numerous party, consisting of three hundred and forty-five members, sat in the Center, shifting its support as occasion and popular demand required.

None of these groups were parties in the modern sense of the word. They had no official leaders, no definite organization, no caucuses. But they were drawn together by similarity in point of view, a willingness to follow the direction of certain men, and membership in the same political societies. Those who were inclined to distrust the King and were willing to consider extending the franchise were likely to sit on the Left and become associated with the followers of Brissot and Vergniaud, and were likely to attend the Jacobin Club, where Robespierre, acting as prosecuting attorney (*accusateur public*) for the Paris criminal court, was now the outstanding figure. Those who believed that the provisions of the Constitution of 1791 must be firmly rooted before any further reform be considered were likely to sit on the Right and become associated with the followers of Théodore Lameth, brother of the Constituents, and General Dumas, and were likely to attend the Feuillant Club, where Lafayette and the old Triumvirate were the outstanding figures. Even the Brissotins were not essentially radical, however. It must be remembered that every one of them had had to qualify for his office from among a class of whom there were only about fifty thousand in the whole of France. Their outlook was therefore bound to be bourgeois, even if occasionally ideological. The overwhelming majority of the Legislative Assembly were, therefore, "Constitutionals," anxious to preserve the government that was made possible by the Constitution of 1791. Only a minority of malcontents on the Left, supported by a handful of journalists like Marat and

other radicals scattered throughout France, believed that
the Revolution was yet incomplete.   But the King, though
still beloved throughout France, in his stubborn refusal to
realize that 1791 and 1792 were removed from 1789 by a
pregnant interval, was to play into the hands of the minority, increasing its strength until it controlled the destinies
of France.

The first days of the Legislative Assembly were spent in
organizing and in determining the relations of the Assembly
and the King.   The Legislative Assembly later described
itself in one of its decrees as " eager to devote itself to the
great matters which call for its attention to the consolida-
tion of credit and the system of finances."   But when the
deputies began to consider their most serious problems, it
was the émigrés who first received that attention.   On
October 31, 1791, it decreed that Monsieur the Count of
Provence was to lose his rights to the throne if he failed to
return to France within two months.   On November 9, it
was proposed that all other émigrés must return to France
before January 1, 1792, or suffer their property to be confiscated by the State and themselves to be subject to punishment for treason.   The King was willing to sanction the
decree regarding his brother, but on the advice of his Feuillant confidants, would not consent to the law against the
émigrés.   It appeared too inclusive and too severe.

The Legislative Assembly, nothing daunted by royal
interference, devoted itself to the problem of the recusant
clergy.   The number of disturbances due to their recalcitrance had strikingly increased during 1791 and not always
were the old Catholics involved merely in self-defense.
Religious uprisings in the Vendée had led to the sending of
a commission there to make an investigation.   Upon the
report of the commission, the Assembly decreed (November 29) that non-juring ecclesiastics would thenceforth be
" reputed suspects of revolt against the law and of bad intention against the country," and if involved in disorders,
punishable by removal from their usual places of residence
or imprisonment.   Louis also refused to sanction this de-

cree. At the same time, he and the Queen kept up a secret correspondence, as regular as the circumstances permitted, with the rulers of Austria and Prussia. They hoped for intervention in their behalf, but Frederick William would act only on the promise of an indemnity and Leopold was pacifically inclined. In the meanwhile, the radical press vigorously denounced the royal family for acts that seemed to mark them as defenders and accomplices of rebels and traitors.

As 1792 drew near, the King adopted new tactics. He had begun to believe, amidst all the current war-scare, that a brief war would be altogether to his advantage. If France were defeated (of which he had very little doubt), the new democratic form of government would be regarded as ineffective, and the people would look to him, as former autocrat, to save them. Strangely enough, the King was supported in his schemes by the Brissotins. Filled with the same religious spirit of revolution that always characterizes revolutionaries and urges them to spread their gospel throughout the world, they desired to make war against all tyrants and believed that a war would rally all factions of the country to the single cause of victory, making advocates out of many who were now opponents of the Revolution. At the same time, they believed, a war would reveal the true attitude of the King. If he were actually a supporter of the Revolution, he would end all relations with foreign courts, but if he were really in sympathy with the émigrés, his behavior would then easily discover him and make it possible to treat with him as he deserved. Furthermore, they argued, a foreign war would keep the assignats from depreciating and the cost of living from mounting. They were quite sure that France was prepared for a conflict, for the militaristic Minister of War, Narbonne, and the other generals, feeling that a successful war would restore the prestige of the King and his officers, reported very confidently that the army was equipped, the soldiers loyal, the officers capable, the fortifications secure, and supplies adequate. For entirely different reasons, then, the two elements opposed to allowing the Revolution to stand as it then was, joined forces to bring about a war.

A faction of the Jacobin Club, led by Robespierre and Marat, opposed war, because, not convinced by Narbonne's favorable reports, they believed France unprepared. Robespierre had little or no confidence in the generals. Lafayette was now the most important of them. He had resigned as Commandant of the National Guard and had become a candidate for the mayoralty of Paris. But in the elections of November 16, 1791, so unpopular had his part in the massacre of the Champ de Mars and his Feuillant tendencies rendered him that he received only 3126 to the 6728 votes of the Jacobin Constitutent Pétion. There were 80,000 active citizens in Paris. Evidently the newly acquired rights of citizenship were no more coveted in Paris than they have been in countries where they have been recognized much longer. The King assigned Lafayette to the Army of the North, where he shared command with Generals Rochambeau and Luckner, both quite aged and unable to earn the confidence of Robespierre and his followers. Furthermore, Robespierre maintained that war would only increase the cost of living and therefore the misery of the French people. The efforts of the Legislative Assembly, he held, ought to be devoted to securing the triumphs of the Revolution within France rather than to propagating it abroad. Marat's journal, time and again, warned his readers that the war was the last refuge of scoundrels, an effort to reëstablish the throne and destroy the Constitution. In this struggle over the question of war, the Jacobin Club was once more split into two opposing factions, though, this time, neither the Brissotins nor the Robespierrists seceded. Strangely enough, the only other group in the state that supported the pacifist attitude of the extreme Jacobins were the Feuillant advisers of the King, the Lameths and Barnave, who were anxious for a continuation of the old Austrian alliance as a means of strengthening the monarch's position inside of France.

But sound argument did not overwhelm mere chauvin-

ism. Having decided on war, the Assembly could very
easily choose an enemy. Most of the émigrés were gathered at Coblenz in the Archbishopric of Trèves. Upon
the initiative of the Assembly, the King, on December 24,
announced that he was going to demand that the Archbishop send away the émigrés. A refusal to do so would
mean war. But Leopold, as Emperor of the Holy Roman
Empire and suzerain of the Archbishop, advised him to
yield. At the same time, however, the Emperor ordered
part of his army into Trèves to resist invasion. Resentment
in France now concentrated upon the Emperor. Departing
from the fundamentally peaceable attitude of the Pillnitz
Declaration, he had already protested to the King of France
regarding France's attitude toward Alsace. Alsace had
been turned over to the French King by the Treaty of
Westphalia (1648). But many of the landowners of Alsace
were German princes over whom the Emperor exercised
some overlordship and to whom he owed protection. These
princes of the Empire, Germans opposed to surrendering
their feudal privileges because of French notions of liberty,
protested against the decrees of August, 1789, and March,
1790, by which their feudal payments in Alsace were abolished. The Alsatian question remained a subject for diplomatic controversy from February, 1790, onward. Although the Constituent Assembly had offered to indemnify
the Alsatian princes (which was more than they were willing to do for the French princes), the German lords appealed
to the Imperial Diet for the maintenance of their rights.
The Diet asked the Emperor to press the case of the Alsatian nobles. In December, at about the same time that
Leopold's stand in the Trèves affair became known, there
came from him a strongly worded dispatch on the Alsace
controversy. In reply, on January 21, 1792, he was per-
emptorily required by the Legislative Assembly to explain
his attitude toward France. Leopold, realizing that peace
would now be difficult to preserve, formed an alliance with
Prussia, and on February 19 gave his answer. He did not
intend to make any attempts upon the sovereignty of

France, he said, but the Jacobins were a "pernicious sect" and "disturbers of the peace." The hand of the letter was the hand of Leopold, but the voice was the voice of Kaunitz, who resented the destruction of the Gallo-Austrian alliance he had worked so hard to create.

The Emperor's reply was put before the Assembly on March 1. The first effect of this letter was that Narbonne, too eagerly pressing for war, was dismissed by the King. This incensed the Brissot war party. The Feuillant Minister of Foreign Affairs Delessart was made their scapegoat. Feeling that he had endured Leopold's truculence too meekly, the Independents of the Center were no less indignant than the Girondins. The Girondins not only demanded Delessart's resignation, but succeeded also in starting impeachment proceedings against him before the National High Court. Delessart and his Feuillant colleagues were dismissed and in their places the King reluctantly accepted Girondin sympathizers.[1] Of these Roland, a former inspector of manufactures, sober-minded and methodical, and Dumouriez, a debonair *ci-devant* and soldier with some experience as a diplomatic intriguer, were the best known. This ministry favored war.

On March 1, Leopold died suddenly at Vienna. Stocks rose on the Bourse sixteen per cent in the expectation of peace. But Leopold's son and successor, Francis II, did not have the same pacific tendencies. He listened with approval to the solicitations of his aunt, Marie Antoinette, and her followers, and pressed the case of the Alsatian princes. The émigrés received a sympathetic audience from the new Emperor, who watched with deeper concern than his predecessor the spread of revolutionary ideas among his German subjects. He also complained against the annexation of Avignon (1791), a district entirely surrounded by France, but hitherto belonging to the Pope, which the Constituent Assembly, after long hesitation, had accepted into

[1] Roland as Minister of the Interior, Clavière as Minister of Finances, Dumouriez as Minister of Foreign Affairs, Grave at first and later Servan as Minister of War, Lacoste as Minister of Marine, Duranthon as Minister of Justice.

the French nation shortly before its adjournment. The French decided to take the offensive in the quarrel, and on April 20, 1792, war was declared against Austria. The Assembly, in order to reassure other neighbors who apprehensively watched the military parties of France gaining control, promised "not to undertake any war with a view to making conquests, and never to employ its forces against the liberty of any people," declaring the war with Austria to be for "the just defense of a free people against the unjust aggression of a king." Prussia, in accordance with the terms of their alliance, soon joined Austria. Catherine of Russia, anxious to have her hands free to deal with the new nationalist movement in Poland, but having been completely scared out of her once democratic benignity by the specter of revolution, urged the two allies on; and for a moment Gustavus III of Sweden, forgetting his enlightenment and remembering only his despotism (such as it was), had conferred with the émigrés at Spa, though he took no active steps now to join the alliance.

The French staff determined to take the aggressive and to attack the Austrian Netherlands (Belgium). Unfortunately, many of the émigrés were the finest officers that the French army had had and their places were now filled by inferior and inexperienced soldiers. Furthermore, the volunteers, brave, no doubt, and inspired with an ardent revolutionary fervor, but nevertheless unused to the vicissitudes of long campaigns, made up a large part of the rank and file. The troops conducted themselves well until one of the three advancing columns came within sight of the enemy, when they were seized with panic, fled pell-mell, and murdered their commander, General Dillon, who tried to restore order. Cries of "Treason! Treason!" arose, and there was good cause to suspect that Marie Antoinette had betrayed the French plans to the enemy. Lafayette, commanding the attack, had no choice but to retreat and to take the defensive.

News of the disastrous campaign reached Paris, which was already in ferment. What little was needed to create a crisis the King's tactless conduct could be depended upon to produce. The activity of the non-juring priests had increased constantly and in turn had roused more counter-demonstrations during the early months of 1792. Finally, on May 27, the Legislative Assembly reënacted its former decrees against the non-juring clergy, adding a measure more radical than any previous one: henceforth, should any cleric refuse to abide by the Civil Constitution of the Clergy, he was to be liable to banishment from the country at the request of twenty active citizens and with the consent of the local authorities. But the Legislative Assembly reckoned without its host; the King vetoed the decree. And when (June 8) the Assembly, fearful of an attack upon Paris, voted that a camp for twenty thousand men be established near Paris, the King vetoed that measure like-wise. Even though Louis had sanctioned an earlier decree (May 29, 1792) disbanding his Bodyguard, which the Assembly looked upon as a royalist stronghold, he appeared again to be giving aid and comfort to the enemy.

There was some right on Louis' side. The action against the non-juring clergy was perhaps more severe than cir-cumstances demanded, and there was room for suspicion that the volunteers in the proposed camp might encourage the only too frequent outbreaks in Paris. The King, how-ever, forgot that in exercising his legitimate right to veto, he was dealing with a people that had every cause to mis-trust his intentions. Roland, Minister of the Interior, took the occasion to protest against Louis' acts, and in none too courteous tones. In reply the King angrily dismissed not only Roland, but also those of his colleagues who refused to countersign the King's vetoes. Dumouriez, less incensed than the others by the King's policy, was retained, and by his countersign the King's vetoes became constitutionally valid. But when the Brissotins threatened an investigation of his conduct of foreign affairs, he too resigned. The King now appointed a royalist ministry, and spent large sums out of the civil lists to foster a royalist sentiment in the capital. Duport's paper. *L'Indicateur*, urged the King to dissolve the Assembly and make himself dictator.   The war seemed to be bringing about the result that the royalists had hoped from it.

Again the Paris mob prevented counter-revolution.   The dismissal of the Girondin ministry savored of the dismissal of Necker in July, 1789.   The leaders of some of the sections of the city thought they discerned another attempt to thwart the Revolution.   On June 20, 1792, the third anniversary of the Tennis Court Oath, several delegations, followed by a troop of sympathizers, went to the Manège to celebrate the occasion and to petition the Assembly to protest against the King's policy.   On the way from the Manège, they had to pass the Tuileries.   Nothing was more natural than to adopt the inevitable suggestion that they pay a call upon the King.   The gates were found unguarded and the crowd easily gained access.   Its intentions were peaceful; it meant to do no more than to bring its opinions forcibly to the attention of His Majesty.   Louis behaved admirably.   He met the mob without flinching, listened patiently to the gibes and tirades of the butcher Legendre and the brewer Santerre, who had constituted themselves leaders, heard the insulting remarks of the mob without losing his self-control, put on the red cap of liberty, drank a toast to the nation, urged a National Guard standing near by to feel whether his heart did not beat calmly, but refused to promise to sanction the decrees.   It was a remarkable display of physical and moral courage not unmixed with hypocrisy.   After two hours of the ordeal, Pétion, the popular successor to Bailly as Mayor of Paris, came to the rescue. His delay argues his sympathy with the demonstration, for, as the King insinuated, it did not take two hours for news to travel from the Tuileries to the Hôtel de Ville.   Indeed, if Girondin leaders were not actually the instigators of this demonstration, they at least did not regret it.   The mob, at length, yielded to Pétion's persuasion and left, casting insulting reproaches upon Marie Antoinette and the Dauphin on the way out.   Some among them vowed that they would return.

There was a wave of monarchist reaction to this uprising of Girondin sympathizers. The Château de Jales once more saw a gathering of royalists, two thousand strong; and in Finisterre there was another Bourbonist demonstration. Lafayette left his army and hastened to Paris to assail the Jacobins on the very floor of the Assembly (June 28). He was greeted with applause. His plan was still to rescue the King and set himself up as the power behind the throne. But the Queen feared Lafayette more than she did the Jacobins. Her dislike went to the extent that she revealed to Pétion the General's intention of reviewing the National Guard and rallying his partisans. The review was prevented, and only about one hundred appeared on the Champs Élysées to take part in the gigantic rally. Lafayette returned to his army disgruntled. His behavior in Paris had merely united the forces of the Brissotins and the Robespierrists in the Jacobin Club against him, if only for a moment.

To the émigrés mobilized on the frontier of France, news of the latest humiliation of the King and Queen came as a goad to their already intolerable bitterness. They persuaded the Duke of Brunswick, commander of the Prussian forces, to sign an imprudent manifesto that had been written by one of their number, M. de Limon. If in the future, it said, any further violence were to be committed against the royal family, Paris would be turned over to "military execution and total annihilation." More than Bismarck's famous Ems dispatch the manifesto was to act as "a red flag to the Gallic bull." The people of Paris were in no mood to be ordered what not to do. On July 11, as the invaders stepped upon French soil, the Legislative Assembly had declared *la patrie en danger* (Our country in danger!) and had appealed to the patriotism of every citizen to protect his fatherland from its foes. Bands of radical Fédérés — the Bretons, who had gone farther in the direction of republicanism than Paris, and the Marseillais, who paraded the streets before cheering spectators, singing a song written in a moment of inspiration (perhaps alcoholic)

by the young Lieutenant Rouget de Lisle — heightened the
fervor of the moment and increased the opposition to the
King.   It was at this point that the Brunswick Manifesto
reached Paris.   Robespierre, defying the Minister of Justice, talked boldly of dethronement in addresses to the
Jacobins (July 11 and July 17) and urged the Fédérés not
to take the oath to the King.   The more radical sections of
the city declared themselves to be sitting *en permanance*,
always a sign of trouble.   Revolutionary committees were
organized to deliberate upon plans for an insurrection.
Petitions were sent to the Legislative Assembly asking for
definite action, and threatening that otherwise the people
would act for themselves.

But the Assembly did nothing.   On July 3, Vergniaud
had delivered an impassioned address denouncing the King
for complicity with the émigrés and talking vaguely of
abdication.   The Assembly had ordered the speech to be
printed and circulated throughout the country, which was
the customary manner of showing approval.   On July 7, in
a wave of hysteria, the members of the Legislative Assembly, urged on by the eloquence of Bishop Lamourette,
swore friendship and loyalty to each other and exchanged
embraces.   Before long Parisian wags were describing the
incident as the "kiss of *l'amourette* (the trivial love affair)."
The outspoken insistence of Robespierre, the Fédérés, and
the Paris petitions repelled the Brissotins once more.   The
actual prospect of a republic did not appeal to Brissot, the
theoretical republican.   On July 25, he demanded penal
action against republicans, and the Girondin leaders again
began negotiations with Louis XVI in the hopes that he
would himself consent to a reduction of his own powers,
and thereby prevent insurrection.   To the various petitions
from the sections of Paris and even from departmental
towns, therefore, the Assembly turned a deaf ear.   Some of
these petitions mentioned August 9 as the latest the sections would wait for action.   Two measures that the Assembly now took were bound to make that date a critical one.
On August 8, the demand for the impeachment of Lafayette

was defeated by a large vote in the Assembly. On August 9, Condorcet reported for the Extraordinary Commission of the Assembly that the question of the King's dismissal be postponed. That night the tocsin sounded throughout the city and the radical sections ran to arms.

The 10th of August came. A body made up of representatives from the various sections of Paris took control of the Hôtel de Ville, creating the famous *Commune du Dix Août*. At the Tuileries an attack was momentarily expected. The royalist Mandat, in command of the National Guard, had taken every precaution that unfavorable circumstances would permit. Early in the morning the King reviewed the Swiss mercenaries, the volunteer nobles, and the National Guard that served as his garrison. But as soon as the Revolutionary Commune took charge at the City Hall, they summoned Mandat to appear before them. He was ordered arrested for having taken measures to shoot down his fellow citizens, and on the way to prison was butchered on the steps of the City Hall by the mob outside. Meanwhile the crowd marched on to the Tuileries. Before they arrived, Roederer, the procureur-général-syndic of the Department of Paris, tried to persuade the King and his family to seek refuge with the Legislative Assembly. The Queen at first refused. Perhaps it was out of a mistaken sense of security. The King had spent millions in July and August to buy supporters. Madame Elizabeth, the King's sister, had written the night before: "We are at ease. We can count upon M. Danton." But whether this means that they thought they had bought off Danton (Lafayette says Danton received fifty thousand écus) or were counting on Danton's moderation, they soon yielded to Roederer's urgings. Danton, as a matter of fact, had been at his estate at Arcis-sur-Aube, and had not returned until the eve of the 10th.

When the royal family entered the Manège, Vergniaud, President of the Assembly, made it perfectly clear that his sympathies were with the King and Queen. "Sire," he said, "you may count upon the steadfastness of the

National Assembly; its members have sworn to die maintaining the rights of the people and the constituted authorities." The royal family were assigned to an adjoining room, for the Constitution forbade the Assembly to deliberate in the King's presence. There the phlegmatic Louis indulged his appetite on a fowl that was brought him, while Marie Antoinette in chagrin and mortification ate not at all. Suddenly firing was heard in the direction of the Tuileries. The mob had come up. The National Guard fraternized with them, but the Swiss Guard and the gentlemen of the King would not yield. Again, as in the taking of the Bastille, the people thought they had been tricked, for the Swiss on the staircase indicated a friendly attitude, while those in the upper windows fired as the people drew nearer. The struggle, thus begun, lasted from half-past seven until ten o'clock. The King had earlier sent orders to his guards to cease firing. But the messenger could not (or according to some accounts, would not) make the command reach all of them and the battle continued. At last, overcome by numbers and threatened with exhaustion of their ammunition, some of the Swiss retreated to the Legislative Assembly, where they were made prisoners. A detachment of about sixty of them attempted to march to their barracks, but were captured. Those that remained behind fought until every one of them had fallen. In two and a half hours' fighting, about eight hundred of the King's forces had been killed, while the attackers had less than four hundred in both killed and wounded. The traveler in Lucerne still may behold the Thorwaldsen monument, erected by the Swiss Republic to the Swiss Guards who died in defense of a French king: a wounded lion guards with his life the *fleur de lis*. *Helvetiorum fidei ac virtuti!* But it must be said that they would have been just as loyal and manly if hired to fight on the other side. If some of the accounts of atrocities committed upon the defenders of the Tuileries after its capture are to be given credence, the people wreaked a terrible vengeance for the treachery of which they believed themselves the victims

In the mean time, the Legislative Assembly, understanding that some decisive stand was necessary, having hesitated as long as the fate of the Tuileries was in doubt, now deposed the King, and, in accordance with the Constitution of 1791, called for the election of a National Convention to draw up a new constitution. All men over twenty-one years of age, who were born or had become Frenchmen, were to be permitted to vote for the delegates to this convention. Thus the cause of universal suffrage won a marked victory. To provide for an executive, it replaced the King's royalist ministry by a Provisional Executive Council. In this, the only member who was not a Girondin was Danton, who became Minister of Justice and practically chief of the government. It was hoped that by naming a popular leader of the people, one who had always been spoken of very highly by the *Ami du Peuple* and who had been substitute Procureur of the Paris Commune, there might be arranged some sort of compromise between the Brissotin faction, now in control of the Assembly, and the Robespierre faction, now in control of the sections and the Commune.

The events of August 10, as the Girondins had feared, solidified the opposition of the Bourbonists. Danton later said that the insurrection of August 10 divided France into two parties, the one attached to royalty, the other desiring a republic. There were two petitions circulated in the more fashionable districts of Paris, protesting against the outcome of August 10; and on August 11 the signers of these petitions were excluded by the Commune from the exercise of public functions. There was some grumbling in the army too. For a time, Lafayette tried to induce his army to follow him to Paris in order to restore the King and disperse the Assembly. But they refused to do so, and on August 19 he deserted. He refused to join the émigrés, however, and was kept a prisoner of war until his release in 1797, upon the demands of Napoleon Bonaparte. Lafayette's friend, the Baron de Dietrich, Mayor of Strassburg, tried to rouse Alsace in favor of the King, but likewise failed and deserted. The Executive Council rapidly sent commissioners to the army and to the departments where there was danger of disaffection to crush any royalist manifestations. There were no further disorders, and the results of the August uprising were apparently accepted throughout France. England, however, thereafter refused to recognize Chauvelin, the Ambassador from France, or the Government he represented.

Lafayette's desertion was but one of a series of military reverses that French arms were now encountering. Lille, though in the end it held out bravely, was daily expected to surrender to the Austrians. Longwy surrendered to the Prussians. And on September 2, Verdun fell, the Commandant Beaurepaire, forced to admit his defeat, having blown out his brains. On the morning of September 2, Paris could not have known that Verdun had actually fallen, though Danton might have. But the surrender of the fortress was expected at any moment. Panic seized the city in fear that when Verdun succumbed, there would be nothing left to stop Brunswick's victorious march upon Paris and the fulfillment of his dread manifesto. Danton delivered his plea for coöperation before the Assembly: "Daring, more daring, and still more daring, and France is saved." Marat kept calling for extreme measures against the counter-revolutionaries in prison and out. Both had their effect. The volunteers came, eager to be led against the invaders of their country, but resolved not to leave any traitors behind. Rumor had it that there was a plot among the royalists in the prisons to break out. The volunteers felt they could not go to the front, leaving their dear ones behind, a prey to the horrors of a white terror.

There had grown up a feeling that August 10 had been a conspiracy on the part of the King to rouse the city so that it might be caught between two fires, the attack of the defenders of the King within and of the enemies of France without. Soon people were talking of the *Conspiration du 10 Août*, as if it had been the work of the King and his henchmen alone. On August 11, upon popular demand, a revolutionary tribunal had been established by the Legislative Assembly to deal with the conspirators, but it acquitted a number of defendants who were regarded as cryingly tainted with royalism. The radicals lost all confidence in the new tribunal. On September 2, constituting themselves committees of judgment and execution, groups visited L'Abbaye, La Force, and other prisons of Paris. The ubiquitous Maillard was conspicuous among them. The Committee of Surveillance and Police of the Commune of Paris had in some cases already had the petty offenders segregated from the counter-revolutionaries. The self-appointed judges gave hasty trials to the latter and turned over those whom they considered guilty to the crowd. Estimates of the number "executed" in Paris between September 2 and 6 vary from nine hundred and sixty-six to somewhere near sixteen hundred, but the most likely figure is that given in the report of the Committee of Police and Surveillance — ten hundred and seventy-nine. On September 3, this committee sent a circular letter to the departments approving the massacres and urging them to follow the example set by Paris. In several towns outside of Paris this was done, although nowhere except at Versailles were there more than ten victims.

So near is explanation to justification that the historian runs the danger, in trying to make things understood, of also condoning them. It would be futile to underestimate the horror, the savagery, the uncalled-for brutality of those September days. Nevertheless, despite all that has been written to attach responsibility to one body or another, to one individual or another, the fact remains that the movement was spontaneous, an inevitable result of the panic arising from the fear of foreign invasion and internal conspiracy. The Committee of Surveillance, made up of staunch Jacobins like Marat, Panis, Sargent, actually issued orders for the arrest of Roland, Brissot, and Duport, which Danton quashed. But from the Committee's point of view, these men were guilty of friendly relations with the monarch. It was their business to arrest suspects: and they

certainly made no effort to have these three massacred.
Panis and Sargent issued instructions to the "executioners"
to "try" all the prisoners at the Abbaye except the Abbé
Lenfant.   But Lenfant was the brother of one of the members of the Committee; might not the address have been
intended only to shield the Abbé?   For the massacres had
already begun in other prisons.   The Committee also paid
some of the "executioners," but only after their work was
done and some of the sections had demanded it.   The
Committee of Police and Surveillance, at worst, is guilty of
directing the massacres after they had begun; it cannot be
considered the instigator of them.   Marat, in particular,
was accused of having started the massacres — during his
lifetime, by his enemies; after his death, by men who, while
he was alive, were regarded as equally guilty.   Marat himself claimed to have been taken as much unawares as any
other by the outbreak and to have exerted his efforts to
save the petty delinquents.   He approved of the massacres
— in fact, was chiefly responsible for the appeal of September 3 to the departments to do likewise.   But Panis said
of him that his influence at the Committee of Police and Surveillance was no greater than that of other members; and
Marat's last demand in his journal for the execution of the
conspirators of August 10 had been on August 19.   Obviously, then, he cannot be regarded as the immediate instigator either of the Committee or of the mob.

Louis-Philippe, some years later, when he was King of
France, declared that Danton had boasted to him of his responsibility for the massacres.   Danton perhaps tried only
to divert the hatred of the people from the prisoners to
the invaders: "The tocsin that is about to ring," he had
announced from the tribune of the Legislative Assembly
in his immortal address of September 2, "is not a signal of
alarm, it is the charge against the enemies of our country."
There is some reason to believe, too, that Danton, had he
taken the proper precautions, might have saved the prisoners whom Fournier, called the American, was transferring
from Versailles to Paris for trial and on the way slaughtered

without provocation. But even if Danton were not assuming the responsibility of the outrage for the sake of preserving factional peace inside of France, even if he were not, in Aulard's phrase, playing the part of "patriotic hypocrisy," yet there is no convincing proof of his guilt in starting the massacres. Nor can the Jacobins, as a party, be held guilty. If the Jacobins were anxious for a demonstration that would keep the conservatives away from the polls in the election of the delegates to the National Convention, they were doomed to disappointment, for the elections had already begun and turned out to be a Jacobin defeat (except that in Paris no candidate who had been opposed by Marat's journal succeeded in being elected). The Commune, in open conflict with the Assembly, which refused to recognize it as properly elected (having annulled its election on August 30, recognized it again on August 31, and annulled it again on September 2) might also have profited from the massacres as a means of inspiring the Brissotin Assembly with a wholesome fear of its power.

But all these facts do not fix the responsibility anywhere. They merely show the complication of forces at work, the state of the public mind, and the conflict of authorities that made possible these September lynchings. There were others than the Committee of Surveillance who ought to have exerted every effort to preserve order. The Girondin Mayor of Paris, Pétion, and the Girondin Minister of the Interior, Roland, certainly were equally responsible for the tranquillity of the city. Not only did they not put forth all their endeavors to prevent the massacres, but Roland, a leader in the party that afterward tried to throw the entire responsibility for them upon the shoulders of the Jacobins, referred to them on September 3, apologetically:

> Yesterday is a day over the events of which we must perhaps draw a veil. But I know that the People, terrible as its vengeance is, has yet tempered it with a kind of justice.

To the patriotic Frenchman in September, 1792, the massacres were a regrettable but entirely pardonable example of popular justice. It was not to be the last time in

history that the best citizens regretted but forgave, others
encouraged, while the official class found justification for
their indifference in the need for, strenuous popular measures
against undesirables.

The final meeting of the Legislative Assembly took place
on September 20, 1792.   On that same day, at Valmy.
Dumouriez, who had now taken command of the Army of
the North, was able to stop the invading enemies and force
them to retreat.   The cannonade of Valmy, in which only a
few hundred casualties occurred on both sides, thus saved
France from further invasion, perhaps from conquest and
partition.   It was under favorable conditions, therefore,
that the Legislative Assembly came to a close.   It had met
at a time when one series of revolutionary events had come
to a successful conclusion.   It adjourned at a moment when
another, more savage and yet inspiring more devotion and
self-sacrifice, was to be inaugurated.   The events of 1789–
92 were but a preparation for the drama of 1792–95, as
essential to, as like and yet as unlike that drama as a re-
hearsal is to the *première*.   The fate of Louis XVI and his
family was still to be determined; even the form of government to take his place was not yet decided.   But it was
clear that constitutional monarchy — or at least Louis XVI
as constitutional monarch — had failed.   The Constitution
of 1791 had been torn into shreds by opposing forces, all of
whom favored certain parts of it, none of whom favored it
as a whole.   The Legislative Assembly had thus had the
career of a transitory body.   It served merely to bridge the
gap between absolutism and the republic.

BOOK III
THE FIRST FRENCH REPUBLIC

CHAPTER I
THE GIRONDIN SUPREMACY IN THE CONVENTION

On September 20, 1792, when the National Convention met at the Manège in Paris (they were to move to more sumptuous quarters in the Tuileries only on May 10, 1793), it was divided into three distinct parties. The great majority of the seven hundred and eighty-three deputies to the Convention sat in the Center. That meant that they were a party of moderation, unwilling to commit themselves to either extreme and prepared to vote upon each measure according to its merits or in compliance with popular pressure. Barère, who had held a very similar position in the National Constituent Assembly, acted at first as their leader. They soon acquired the name of the "Marsh" or "Plain," because their seats were on a level immediately in front of the President's desk. On the Right and the Left sat the Girondins and the Jacobins respectively. There were about one hundred and sixty-five Girondins and fewer Jacobins or Montagnards, as they came to be called from the fact that they sat in the "Mountain" or raised seats.

At the beginning of the preceding Assembly, the Girondins had been among the staunchest attendants at the meetings of the Jacobin Club. But there had been a rift between the leaders of the Jacobins and those who had followed the deputies from the Gironde on the question of war with Austria; and now, although no one doubted the necessity of prosecuting the war to a victorious conclusion, the rift remained. The Girondins now no longer appeared at the Jacobin Club. Instead, they held their rendezvous at the salon of Madame Roland, where that zealous lady, as well·

beloved by these gentlemen as she was despised by the Jacobins, played a rôle equal to her husband's or any other's in determining their policies.

To the old quarrels between the Girondins and the Jacobins, there was now added the one over the position of Paris in national affairs. The Jacobin leaders represented Paris and the Girondins had begun to be afraid of that city. There was some reason to believe that the Commune of Paris had been more responsible for the September massacres than any other group of individuals, and the Girondins now were more scandalized by these massacres than they had been disposed to be immediately after their occurrence. They began to agitate, cautiously at first, for removal to another city, maintaining that there was constant danger of disorder and duress in the capital that would not have to be contended with elsewhere.

Lamartine, poet rather than historian, is the author of the Girondin legend. His *Histoire des Girondins* is an epic of the struggle of patriots and gentlemen against self-seekers and guttersnipes. Much has been done to destroy this legend by a number of more recent investigators. In spite of their efforts, the historian is now hard put to it to discover what was really the cause of the mortal conflict between the two factions. Aulard claims that fundamentally it was nothing more than this question of whether the interests of Paris or those of the departments should predominate. True, Robespierre, Danton, Marat, and the others who were the leaders of the Mountain, represented Paris, while Vergniaud, Roland, Brissot, and the other leaders of the Girondins represented the departments. But that alone hardly serves to explain the unremitting hatred that existed between the two parties. It leaves out of consideration the personal enmities that, incidental at first, soon seemed to become the motivating force behind all the ensuing attacks and counter-attacks. It takes no account of the fact that even well-informed contemporaries believed that the one party represented a desire to bring the revolution to a halt, while the other held that there was more yet to be accomplished.[1]   It disregards the issues on which, as we shall see, the Girondins frequently took a moderate stand and the Jacobins an extreme one.

Yet there undoubtedly were charges made by one party against the other which were without foundation.   Thus the Girondins accused the Jacobins of what we to-day would loosely call communism, and the Jacobins replied with a charge of federalism, a desire to break France up into a loosely knit group of small republics.   Neither accusation was wholly true, and, indeed, not always made with entire sincerity.   But there was enough of a social philosophy in the Montagnard dogma to make the enemies of social reform fearful of them.   In his private notebook, for example, intended for no eyes but his own, Robespierre once wrote:

> Our internal dangers come from the bourgeoisie.   To conquer the bourgeoisie, it is necessary to rally the people.

And there was enough of a desire among the Girondins for the equality of the provincial cities with Paris to furnish a basis for the accusation of decentralization.   The leaders among the Jacobins, it must be remembered, were the delegates from Paris — men who, with the exception of Robespierre and Égalité alone, had never sat in a national assembly, and who, like Danton, Marat, Panis, Manuel, Sargent, had been directly connected with the Commune of August 10.   The leaders of the Girondins, on the other hand, had almost all sat in either the Constituent or the Legislative Assembly — most of them in the latter.   Now, to sit in the Legislative Assembly, at the time they were elected, one had had to meet the property qualification of a *marc d'argent*, which only about fifty thousand of the entire population of France could fulfill.   The Girondin leaders were, therefore, among the wealthiest men in France. The Jacobin leaders were not ne'er-do-wells; quite the contrary, many of them were influential professional men. But they had come into political prominence by virtue of

[1] Cf. Barère in *Archives Parlementaires*, LX, March 18, 1793, pp. 291–92.

lower-class support, their championing of popular measures, and the success of revolutionary movements. While the Jacobins and the Girondins were, therefore, both of bourgeois lineage, the first represented the industrial city of Paris with its large population of unpropertied artisans and shopkeepers and workers; the second represented the commercial towns of Bordeaux, Marseilles, Toulon, etc., in which the ruling classes were the merchants, many of whom had held landed property before the Revolution and more of whom had secured new lands since the distribution of the property of the Church.

Even before the Convention met, the issue between the two parties was clearly drawn upon social lines. The Jacobins had already advocated and the Girondins had already opposed certain measures by which the cost of the war would be borne by the wealthier classes. As the war and the Revolution progressed, this question as to who were to pay for the war and another as to who were to fight the war were to make the two extremist parties in the Convention more and more unalterably antagonistic to each other. Political and social issues were to be inextricably merged, but it was to be no mere matter of country against city, Paris against the departments, or even of federalism, defeatism, and socialism alone.

The first meetings of the Convention, opened at a time when the cannonade at Valmy had momentarily relieved France from the fear of invasion, evinced a spirit of coöperation that was rarely again achieved in its sessions. On September 21, amidst a burst of enthusiasm, royalty was abolished, and on the next day it was decreed that September 22 should be regarded as the beginning of the First Year of the French Republic. Thus, in indirect phrases, was the First French Republic created. Nature and chance had conspired to have this event take place on the first day after the autumnal equinox, so that, some months after, when disgust with Christianity went even to the point where the old Christian calendar was found obnoxious, the new revolutionary calendar was easily made astronomically more logical than the Gregorian. There had been no enthusiasm for royalty among the electoral assemblies that had chosen the members of the Convention. But only one, and that the one of Paris, had spoken in favor of a republic. It is significant, therefore, that while none of the chiefs of either party, excepting Collot d'Herbois, who introduced the subject, objected to the critical step, neither did any of them take part in the debates that led up to it, and Marat, at least, made no secret of his lack of enthusiasm. Royalism was by no means extinct. France had become a republic because there was nothing else for it to become. On September 25, on the motion of Danton, the Convention declared the Republic "one and indivisible."

The coöperation of the rival forces in the Convention barely survived the earliest days. On September 21, Danton had tried the rôle of mediator. The Executive Council had sent a number of commissioners into the departments. Two of them, Dufour and Momoro, staunch Jacobins, had issued a manifesto in which they made cautious promises of equality of property. The fear of the "agrarian law," as the vague propaganda in favor of social reform was currently called, was so strong and constant, that, perhaps sincerely, perhaps only to take advantage of the errors of their opponents, the Girondins opened the Convention on September 21 with an accusation against the Mountaineers of preaching social revolution. Danton proposed, and the measure was carried amidst resounding applause, that property be placed under the safeguard of the nation. This amiability lasted four days. On September 25, the Girondins attacked Marat and the Mountain for preaching a dictatorship and for having fomented the September massacres. A hot debate came to a close only after Marat spoke of suicide there and then, and eloquently replied to or skillfully avoided the accusations of his enemies. On October 29, Louvet delivered himself of a vitriolic attack upon Robespierre's ambitions, which, with equal skill, the Incorruptible brushed aside. To all of these attacks the Jacobins replied in kind, though, not having the support of the Plain, they preferred the press rather than the tribune for their purposes.

The struggle between the Jacobins and the Girondins for the control of the Convention, thus begun, soon became merged in a problem that, for the moment, demanded immediate attention. Now that France was a republic, what was to be done with the former king? He and his family had been well-treated but carefully guarded prisoners at the Temple ever since his deposition on August 10. Should he be freed now as a private citizen? On the whole, all parties agreed that he was far too important a figure to be set at large; he would be at liberty then to conspire for his restoration and to rally the enemies of the Republic. How then should he be disposed of? Life imprisonment? Exile? Execution? The Girondins favored leniency, the Jacobins the capital penalty. After a prolonged discussion, it was finally decided to try the former monarch on a charge of treason. Enough evidence had been found in a secret iron closet at the Tuileries to convince even the most hesitant of juries. He had been in correspondence with the enemies of France; he had opposed the reforms that had been effected; he had even planned to bring about a civil war in order to rehabilitate himself.

Realizing that this was no ordinary case and could be handled by no ordinary court, the Convention constituted itself a tribunal for that purpose. On December 11, 1792, the trial began. The King's manner at his first appearance was very courageous but not altogether wise. He seemed to forget too many things of which there was substantial proof. He was permitted three very good lawyers — Malesherbes, formerly his Minister of the Household, Tronchet, one of the greatest of former parlementarians, and Desèze, a younger man, who did the actual pleading. The trial dragged on for over a month. The Girondins, in control of the Government and its foreign policies and dependent upon the conservative elements of France for support, favored a decision that would not alienate the still friendly neighbors of France. The Jacobins, feeling that the death of the King would mean the death of counter-revolution, and representing the extremist elements of France, favored capital punishment. Despite the earnest efforts of the ex-monarch's advocates, there could be no doubt of his guilt. The question of punishment was thus political rather than judicial. Was Louis Capet more dangerous dead than alive? Would not his execution rally to the standards of the enemies of France a number of the countries that were now awaiting only some such pretext to join forces with the coalition of Prussia and Austria? Would not the hope, if he remained alive, that he might yet be delivered create plots and conspiracies and add strength and fervor to the counter-revolutionary cause?

The case came to a head on January 18. That the King was guilty of treason only a few deputies denied. The Girondins, for the most part, however, wanted him to be punished by imprisonment for life. They were outvoted in favor of the death penalty by a small majority, but this majority can be made to seem as low as one (as is sometimes asserted) only by counting all those not voting or voting conditionally as opposed to the death penalty. The Girondins then attempted to have the decision re-ferred to the people for its approval, but this measure, too, failed to pass the Convention. And when they proposed to postpone the carrying out of the penalty until some more expedient time, the Convention voted for its immediate execution. On January 21, 1793, Louis XVI paid upon the guillotine the penalty for what were principally the sins of his fathers. Up to the very last, his conduct was such as to call forth admiration even from his bitterest critics. On the eve of his doom, he took a tender farewell of his family, like himself prisoners of state at the Temple, and then dismissed them that he might spend his last hours alone. A non-juring priest accompanied him to the guillotine and blessed him at the moment of his death: "Son of Saint Louis, ascend to Heaven!" Louis XVI endeavored to make some comment upon the scaffold, but the drums were ordered to beat and to drown his voice. There were cries of *Vive la nation!* as the knife dropped.

Were it not for a few accidents or mistakes (who can tell which?), Louis might have ranked as a great reformer along with his contemporaries, Catherine and Frederick. But there is very little room for the sentimentality that has so often been poured forth in his behalf. There was enough guilt upon his conscience to have caused the execution of a score of ordinary men even in less troublous times. He failed to realize that revolutions respect only principles and not persons, and that in revolutionary times a king who every now and then dug in his heels was an obnoxious principle, no matter how likable and well-meaning a person. And the Girondins, whose chief offense had been that they believed it impolitic to kill one of the fraternity of crowned heads, now had the charge of royalism thrown at them by their opponents of the Mountain, while their proposition to appeal to the people on the matter of the King's punishment furnished ammunition to those who fought them as federalists. On the night of the execution of the King, Lepeletier de Saint-Fargeau, one of the members of the Convention who had voted for the immediate execution of Louis, was assassinated by a frenzied royalist in a Paris café. The first member of a French national assembly to die a violent death was thus a "Martyr of Liberty" at the hands of a reactionary. Manuel, who had guarded the royal prisoners as the representative of the Convention, had been won over to their side; he voted for incarceration until the peace and then banishment, but resigned as deputy before the final votes were taken. The Girondins lost one of their number, likewise, by the withdrawal of Kersaint, who refused any longer to sit in a body "in which blood-thirsty men dominated" and "where Marat triumphed over Pétion."

As had been feared in certain quarters, some of the nations that had hitherto preserved a grudging neutrality found in the execution of Louis Capet a pretext for war. Chief of these was England. At the beginning, the English people had sympathized with the revolutionists. It is easy to be enthusiastic about those who are avowedly following a precedent that you have yourself set. But as soon as the French went beyond the English scheme of things, and adopted a republican form of government, English statesmen began to feel that England was uncomfortably close to the French shore. Burke had never shared Fox's faith in the glory of the Gallic cause nor even Pitt's assumed indifference. In his *Reflections on the French Revolution* he had maintained that the Revolution, as a revolt against properly constituted authority, would soon lead to excess and destruction. A number of more or less able replies had been printed — by Mackintosh, Priestley, Thomas Paine, Mary Wollstonecraft, and others. But Burke could now point to the September massacres and the execution of the King as proofs of the excesses that he had predicted.

Furthermore, the proclamation of the Legislative Assembly that the war which it had declared on April 20, 1792, was not a war of conquest, even though the Convention itself had repeated it recently, had not been strictly observed in spirit. Custine had erected a series of German republics as fast as his army conquered the Rhineland bishoprics; and the Republic of Mainz, fearful that the Convention's avowals of disinterested war aims might indicate a desertion by its creator, appealed to the Convention for a dependable pledge of support. On November 19, 1792, the National Convention declared that "it would accord fraternity and aid to all peoples who should wish to recover their liberty," and on November 27, gave an example of the way in which this might be done by the annexation of Savoy, which General Montesquiou's victories over the Sardinian army had put at the disposal of the French. Though the Savoyards, through a carefully manipulated "National Assembly of the Allobroges," had requested this action, an empire of which the Irish were a part could not regard imperturbedly such a policy of "aid to all peoples who wish to recover their liberty." Indeed, it was well known that Wolf Tone, the Irish leader, was already avowedly republican; in fact, he was soon to get in touch with the statesmen of France on behalf of his Society of United Irishmen. On December 15, the November propaganda decree was carried to its logical conclusion by putting at the command of French generals the wealth and the welfare of occupied territories; France was going to force freedom upon all territories under her control and would "treat as enemies the peoples who, refusing liberty and equality, or renouncing them, may wish to preserve, recall, or treat with the prince and the privileged castes."

Actually what these propaganda decrees portended was the intention of France to surround herself with a series of dependent buffer republics, which, from the point of view of British foreign policy, was bad enough; but, in addition, even some of the coolest heads in England thought, with some justice, that they detected an attempt to rouse the radical elements against George III and the aristocracy. The Revolutionary Society, the London Correspondence Society, and a number of less conspicuous organizations that had come into existence upon the wake of the pro-French wave in the earlier days of the Revolution, though hitherto regarded as quite harmless, now began to acquire formidable significance. If Bolshevik Moscow has more recently been considered the source of all dangerous ideas, to the good subjects of the English monarch Jacobin Paris was then no less so. England now experienced a political reaction. The reforms that the younger Pitt had planned or actually inaugurated — the India Bill, providing for a more carefully supervised government in India, the sinking fund for the reduction of the public debt, the agitation for the abolition of the slave trade, the proposed concessions to Ireland, the incipient plans for the decrease in the number of rotten boroughs — all were forgotten. There were bread riots in the fall of 1792 that were ruthlessly suppressed. Steps were taken to increase the army and navy. An Alien Act placing all foreigners under surveillance and permitting the Government to deport unwelcome ones, was passed by Parliament in January. Repressive measures bearing down upon native Britons followed. Ill-feeling and fear of France pervaded all circles in England. Wordsworth, who in 1789 had found that

> Bliss was it in that dawn to be alive,
> But to be young was very heaven,

now discovered, more in indignation perhaps than in inspiration, that

> Frenchmen had changed a war of self-defense
> For one of conquest, losing sight of all
> Which they had struggled for.

In the mean time, the Convention had considered the fate of Belgium. A series of victories by Dumouriez, culminating in the battle of Jemmapes (November 6, 1792), had placed the former Austrian Netherlands under the control of the French at the same time as the conquests of Custine in the Rhine Valley had relieved all pressure from that quarter. Danton, sent on mission to Belgium and the army of Dumouriez, had fallen in with the General's plans for treating the Prussians gently and pushing them little, in the hope that they might be persuaded to desert Austria, and for punishing Austria by depriving her of the Netherlands. Dumouriez might have preferred a Belgium that would be under his own control and which he might use as a base in his dealings with the Convention. A great number of Belgians (probably a majority) looked forward to independence. But the Convention naturally paid more attention to the group that sued for annexation to the French Republic. Actually, it was not until March, 1793, that Belgium was formally annexed to France, almost at the very moment (April 13, 1793) that the Convention defiantly declared "that it will not interfere in any manner in the government of other powers, but . . . it will sooner be buried under its own ruins than suffer any power to interfere in the internal régime of the Republic." But as 1792 came to a close, indications were not lacking as to which way the wind was blowing. In annexing Savoy, the Convention had spoken of "the limits set by the hand of Nature to the

French Republic." Before the New Year was a month old, Danton announced that the limits of the Republic were "marked by nature"; they were the Rhine, the Ocean, and the Alps. Small wonder that conservative old gentlemen in London could see very little difference between the foreign policy of the despotic Richelieu and that of the democratic Jacobins — save the difference that the Jacobins were on the verge of success.

For England it was essential that Belgium should not pass into the hands of any energetic state, since Belgium was in a position to rival English commercial supremacy (Antwerp, if traffic on the Scheldt River is open, can be made one of the best ports on the North Sea), and was a good avenue of trade with Central Europe. In the hands of France, it was afterwards remarked and now no less felt, Antwerp would be a pistol pointed at the heart of England. France, already near enough to England strategically and commercially, must not be allowed to come nearer. The Convention had already opened the Scheldt to international commerce, though it was closed by the Treaty of Westphalia (1648) and subsequent understandings; and now Dumouriez was planning to invade Holland, England's ally, in pursuit of the Austrians. Pitt, who was not entirely indifferent to the growing need of foreign markets, now that the Industrial Revolution was well advanced in England, began to believe that decisive action was necessary.

Then came the news of the execution of Louis XVI. Talleyrand, unofficial Ambassador, had been dismissed from England upon the dethronement of Louis XVI in August; Chauvelin, official Ambassador, was thereafter no longer recognized; and the English Ambassador to Paris was recalled. Danton and the Girondin ministers on the Executive Council tried, nevertheless, to keep England passive, and Talleyrand had again been sent to London on an unofficial mission. But on the day of the execution of Louis XVI, Chauvelin was given eight days in which to leave England. On February 1, 1793, the Convention declared war on George III and the stadholder of Holland, assigning as reasons England's failure to observe the Treaty of 1786, their preparations for hostilities, and their unfriendly attitude in recent affairs. The Government of Spain, having made valiant efforts to save Louis' life, soon (March 7, 1793) joined forces with Austria, Prussia, Sardinia, England, and Holland. Thus republican France stood alone against a coalition of five of Europe's oldest monarchies and one of her proudest republics. Russia remained neutral, jealously watching the revolution in Poland that, if let alone, might have enabled the Poles to withstand further partition; but Catherine made no secret of her hatred of French revolutionary principles. The smaller states within the Empire likewise remained neutral, but it was a neutrality that at any moment might change into bitter hostility against the oppressor of German princes, which was establishing republics in the Rhineland as fast as Custine's victories made it possible. Thus, practically all of Europe joined forces physically or spiritually to bait the Revolution and to resist its conquests. The advantages of numbers, wealth, organization, prestige, and training were on the side of the Coalition. Could revolutionary fervor and the propaganda spirit alone counterbalance these?

Despite the gathering of forces on the outside, despite the efforts of peacemakers within, the struggle between the Jacobins and the Girondins continued unabated. The lack of precise party organization in the Convention makes it difficult to say conclusively that the execution of the King was a Jacobin victory. The voting had been along what we should now call "party lines," but there were, nevertheless, such curious anomalies as the behavior of Vergniaud, one of the recognized Girondin leaders, who, after voting for the death penalty, insisted that a separate roll-call be taken on the question of delay in its execution and then, on that roll-call, voted for immediate execution; and the vote of Manuel, hitherto a popular Paris deputy, who, having expressed himself in favor of banishment after the war, resigned from the Convention before the question of execution was finally settled. The defeat of the referendum on the question of how to punish the King and of the proposal to delay final sentence is quite a clear indication that the Plain did not follow wheresoever the Girondins chose to lead. And yet, the Girondins remained superior in the Convention. Their attacks upon Robespierre and Marat continued to rouse cries of animosity on all sides against the attacked. Futility alone resulted from the efforts of men like Anacharsis Clootz, who in a pamphlet entitled *Ni Marat ni Roland* pleaded for unity, and like Danton, who, despite the persistence of the Girondins in considering him a leader of the Mountain, was trying anxiously to effect a compromise between the two parties.[1] The Girondins still controlled the Legislature; they were able to elect their partisans exclusively to the chair; they were able to name only members of their party and of the Plain to committees; their general, Dumouriez, was in command at the front and was the idol of Paris. They were going to destroy the Mountain, if they could — by calumniating its leaders, whom they declared to be guilty of preaching dictatorship, pillage, massacre, and communism (charges not altogether without foundation), or, if possible, by expelling them from the Convention.

Much of the prestige of the Girondins depended upon the success of Dumouriez. Faced by an army of English, Dutch, Prussians, and Austrians, Dumouriez' plan of action was first to conquer Holland. The odds against him, however, were too great. Moreover, he had long been in touch with the Prussians, hoping that they would withdraw from the war. Success seemed to be about to reward these negotiations. Prussia, supporting Austria against France more out of a jealous fear of allowing Austria to stand alone as the champion of the German cause than out of any antipathy to France, was unwilling to let Russia handle the Kosciusko revolution in Poland single-handed. By warily guarding his every interest when Catherine intervened on

---

[1] Dr. Catharine E. Young, in her forthcoming biography of Madame Roland, maintains that Danton made serious efforts to conciliate Madame Roland but succeeded only in rousing her antipathy.

behalf of her puppet, King Stanislaus Poniatowski, against
the Polish insurgents, Frederick William II of Prussia succeeded in securing another slice of Poland in the second
partition of 1793, as compensation for the even larger share
that Catherine acquired.   Austria was left to learn of this
maneuver after it was completed. Before this second partition of Poland was settled, Dumouriez, taking advantage
of this double-dealing of Prussia with her ally, almost succeeded in weaning Frederick William away from his alliance
with Austria.

But the execution of Louis XVI brought all his efforts
to naught.   The anti-Jacobin fervor of the Hohenzollern
monarch once more became his predominant passion, and
with renewed vigor he coöperated with his allies.   Dumouriez had good cause to damn the Jacobin leaders. What his
plans were at this time cannot be stated with certainty.
They seemed to have included, however, the erection of an
Orléanist dynasty upon the throne of France, with the son
of Philippe Égalité, Louis-Philippe, formerly Duke of
Chartres, who was serving as a general under his command,
as king and himself as major-domo; Belgium would serve
as a base from which to achieve this revolution.   Whether
it was because the forces facing him were too powerful or
because he put forth only half-hearted efforts against his
opponents, Dumouriez failed in his intrigues because of his
inability to remain a victorious hero.   He was defeated at
Maestricht and at Neerwinden in March, 1793, while
Custine was obliged to fall back upon his fortifications at
Landau, leaving his puppet republics in Germany to shift
for themselves.   The Convention, becoming suspicious,
sent a commission to investigate Dumouriez' conduct.
Dumouriez arrested the commission and turned them over
to the Austrians as prisoners of war (Carnot, merely by the
chance of having delayed in joining the other commissioners
being saved to reorganize the armies of the Republic that
were soon to win victories once more).   Dumouriez threatened to march upon the Convention, to oust the "satellites
of Marat and Robespierre" and leave "the sane majority"

in control, but his army refused to follow him. On April 5, he deserted to the enemy, taking Louis-Philippe along with him. One of France's most capable generals now became merely an apologist, spending the remainder of his days in England living on an English pension and constantly intriguing against France.

The defeats and desertion of Dumouriez and the retreat of Custine had annihilated all the advantages that the overwhelming successes of the previous fall and winter had won for the French cause. In Paris fear and panic took possession of hearts but yesterday filled with pride and confidence. Since the death of Louis XVI, there had followed a series of misfortunes one upon the other. And always there was the precarious food situation and the depreciation of the assignats to complicate affairs! The *Enragés*, a group of men especially strong in the Commune, talked, heatedly enough to justify their name, of punishing speculators and profiteers. On February 25, there had been a bread riot. On March 1 had come the defeat at Maestricht. News began to arrive of revolts in the departments. At Lyons there were moderate men in control, and Chalier, the Montagnard mayor, was soon to become another Jacobin martyr. In the Vendée, the simple peasants wanted their old priests back, and resisted conscription to fight a war that did not concern them.

The first step that the Convention took to avert the impending disaster was to decree the levy of an army of three hundred thousand soldiers and to appoint deputies to go "on mission" into the departments to superintend the enrollment. It was the beginning of a huge scheme of national conscription that was to be perfected during the course of the Revolution and under Napoleon and eventually to be adopted by all of the large Continental countries. Between March 9 and 11, the Convention vehemently debated Danton's proposal to erect an extraordinary tribunal to try the murderous conspirators that every one was sure lurked everywhere, while the mob outside sent petitions and expressed its wishes in no dubious manner.

and individual agitators clamored for insurrection. The attempt at insurrection failed, but Girondin opposition was finally overcome and the court created on March 13. This court, as constructed on March 29, was controlled by Girondin appointees, however, and was not very effective until reorganized. A Commission of Six, all of them Girondins or Centrists, was to initiate and prepare the indictments to be placed before the court, and effectively neutralized its activity. For a moment (March 18 and 31), the mutual dread of communism united both parties long enough to enable a unanimous decree of death for all supporters of the "agrarian law." On March 21, revolutionary committees of twelve each for the stricter surveillance of foreigners were created in each canton. On March 28, émigrés were declared civilly dead and their property confiscated. The next day, a strict censorship of the press was inaugurated, punishing with death the advocates of the dissolution of the Convention or the reëstablishment of the monarchy.

All of this occurred before Dumouriez' defection. His desertion was the signal for even more rigorous action against the enemies of the State. Between April 3 and 7 the former Committee of General Defense (erected in January) was made into a Committee of Public Safety, that the Government might be more definitely centralized to meet invasion. This Committee was vested with authority to supervise the ministers, to deliberate in secret, and to spend a sum of one hundred thousand francs without rendering any accounts. It was originally intended to last only one month, though actually its career was prolonged. On April 23, the opposition of the old Church was once more debated, and it was decided to deport non-juring priests. On April 30, the deputies who had been representing the Convention in the departments in raising the new army were given extraordinary and almost arbitrary powers as *Representatives on Mission*. Despite the fact that the Girondins had always opposed any measures interfering with business freedom, on May 4 a maximum price was established for the sale of corn. Thus, step by step, between February and May, 1793, there was designed a form of government that might be able ruthlessly to organize the nation against invasion and counter-revolution, if leaders could be found capable and willing to exercise the necessary ruthlessness.

As long as the Girondins remained in control of the Convention, however, the personnel of this governmental machinery remained moderate. Though Girondin leaders had sat in the chair when these measures were passed, some of them became law despite Girondin opposition. The demands of the Paris press and populace, expressed in petitions from the sections and demonstrations from the galleries and the gardens of the Tuileries, induced enough of the Plain to vote with the Mountaineers to pass these measures. Once they were passed, however, the bodies that they created were filled with Girondin sympathizers. The Revolutionary Tribunal, the Committee of Public Safety, the Commission of Six, were packed with Girondins and Centrists, save for Danton, the only reputed Jacobin sympathizer on the Committee — and Danton was still trying to effect a compromise, or perhaps to be on both sides at once. Among the deputies on mission, the Jacobins predominated, but, whether their opponents had premeditated it or not, that meant only that their numbers in the Convention were proportionately diminished.

The debates and the disorders attending all of these decrees, particularly those of March 9–11, had shown how bitter was the feeling of the Jacobins against the Girondins. Petitions had already been read in the Convention demanding the expulsion of certain members of the Girondins. Were they not Royalists, Moderates, Federalists? They replied to these charges by attacking their adversaries' weakest point. Marat had demanded a dictator, preached insurrection, vilified the Convention. All of these, in the new revolutionary statutes, were dread offenses. They had tried to quiet him, since his *Journal de la République française* was one of their opponents' most formidable weapons, by passing a measure requiring members of the Convention who edited papers to choose between the professions of legislator and journalist. Marat, changing the name of his journal temporarily to *Observations to My Constituents*, cheerfully got around the intention of the law. The Girondins now repealed the provision of the Constitution that the person of a representative of the people was inviolable, inducing the Convention to declare that a representative might be impeached before the Revolutionary Tribunal by a majority vote of his colleagues. Marat had long advocated such a measure himself. Several attempts followed to have Marat brought for trial before the new Extraordinary Revolutionary Tribunal. Finally on April 12, after he had accused them of being in league with Dumouriez, the Girondins put forth their best efforts and succeeded in carrying an act of impeachment against him on the grounds that he had signed an insurrectionary appeal to the popular societies. For ten days he went into hiding, at which, out of frequent necessity, he had become quite expert; but, having assured himself of a friendly audience, he at length submitted to trial. The court, though filled with Girondin nominees, proved friendly likewise. He was not only acquitted of all the charges, but even commended for his patriotism. An admiring mob carried him back to the Convention upon their shoulders. The "triumph of Marat" that day (April 23) in the Convention and three days later at the Jacobins' was celebrated by crowds that went wild with shouts of *Vive Marat! Vive la Montagne! A bas les Girondins!*

The number of petitions against the Girondins now increased. In order to protect themselves, the leaders of the Girondins demanded that the Convention be transferred to another city where it would be free from the influence of the Paris populace. This the Committee of Public Safety, led by Barère, its spokesman, and by Danton, both unwilling to commit the Government to anything but a compromise measure, refused to permit. Upon the Committee's suggestion, it was finally agreed, instead, that it was more advisable to remain at the capital, but to appoint a Commission of Twelve to investigate and quell the disorders. This Commission, controlled by the Girondins, immediately made a bad situation worse by arresting Hébert, Dobsen, and other popular idols. The arrests were quite in keeping with the purpose of the Commission. Hébert was the editor of the most scurrilous popular sheet in Paris, *Le Père Duchesne*, and, as substitute procureur of the Paris Commune, one of the most outspoken of the enemies of the Girondins; Dobsen was a bitterly anti-Girondin President of the congested, lower-class Section de la Cité.

To preserve a Girondin sense of order in a Jacobin city, the arrest of these two men might have seemed logical. But it now appeared as if the Commission of Twelve, intended only as a protection of the Girondin party against the tyranny of Paris, had itself become an instrument of tyranny by the Girondins over Paris. Protests of their action from a number of sections of the city poured in upon the Convention. One petition demanded the expulsion from the Convention of all the members of the Commission and of the leaders of the Girondins. Incensed at this audacity, Isnard, President of the Convention at the moment (May 25), himself included in the petition, made his famous retort: if any harm were to come to the national representatives, "Paris would be destroyed, and it would be necessary to inquire upon the banks of the Seine whether Paris had ever existed." It would have been an unwise speech to make, even if it were true. It grated on the ears of Paris like the Brunswick Manifesto. On May 27, in a Convention that expected to be surrounded by an armed mob at any moment, the Commission of Twelve was suppressed. Danton now aligned himself unmistakably with the Jacobins, since the Girondins had consistently refused all his advances. On the next day, the Girondins demanded a reconsideration of the motion and the Commission was reëstablished. The sections of Paris began to prepare for insurrection. On May 30, the Central Insurrectionary Committee which had installed itself at the Évêché, under the leadership of the

group called the Enragés, declared itself *en permanence.*
When the Convention met on May 31, it was surrounded
by a mob of thirty thousand Parisians. The Convention
consented once more to the abolition of the Commission
of Twelve, and the mob dispersed.

On June 1, petitions against thirty-two Girondins were
again introduced, and on June 2, the mob again surrounded
the Tuileries, intent upon nothing less than definite action
on their petitions. A feeble attempt of the Convention to
avoid the issue by leaving in a body was resisted by the
National Guard. At eleven o'clock, after a twelve-hour
session, the Convention decreed the arrest of thirty deputies, including all the members of the Twelve, and two
ministers. The Girondins had fallen.

There was no intention, as yet, to do any more with the
Girondins than to nullify their influence in politics. They
were put under arrest in their own homes to await trial by
the Revolutionary Tribunal. The Paris Commune, to reassure their constituencies, offered to send hostages from
among their own number. It was clearly the popular impression in Paris that, while these men were guilty of ob-
structing patriotic measures and tyrannizing over patriotic organizations, they might be left to the courts for trial
and punishment. Their ultimate fate was determined not
now, but by the errors of their partisans later. With the
removal of the most influential Girondins from the Convention, however, power passed into the hands of the
Mountain, who could depend upon the Paris mob for
support, whenever, indeed, the mob did not direct them.

CHAPTER II

JACOBIN SUPREMACY IN THE CONVENTION

THE Constitution of 1791 provided that, in order to amend it, a Constitutional Convention must be convened. It was in accordance with this provision that the Convention had met, but so completely had the pressure of other problems drawn its attention in other directions that it was not until after the execution of the King that it seriously took up the matter of a new constitution. On February 15, 1793, a Girondin committee, of which the venerable Condorcet was the chairman, proposed a new instrument of government. It was immediately attacked by the Mountain, particularly by Marat, as Federalist, since it put too many powers in the hands of the primary assemblies. It actually did propose to vest them with a kind of referendum and recall. It was sent back to the committee, from which it never emerged again, the fall of the Girondins intervening to prevent its completion.

After June 2, 1793, the Mountain busied itself with drawing up a new constitution. In several important details the plan now proposed was found to resemble that which the Girondins had previously advocated. But Marat, who had bitterly attacked the latter, was enthusiastic in his praise of this. The belief that there was very slight difference between the social program of the Girondins and the Mountain is based largely upon a comparison of Condorcet's project with the Montagnard Constitution of the Year I (1793). If the Constitution of 1793 really represented the doctrine of the Mountain, there would be a very justifiable basis for this belief. Both documents provided for universal manhood suffrage, a unicameral legislature, a responsible ministry, electoral assemblies (though deputies were to be chosen directly by the Constitution of 1793), and a bill of the usual rights of man.

But the Constitution of 1793 was really a compromise measure. A number of the Girondin victims of May 31–June 2 had refused to place themselves under arrest. Joined by others of their party, they had fled to the remoter sections of France — Bordeaux, Lyons, Toulon, Marseilles, Caen — and were now engaged in raising armies to lead against the Convention. Federalism seemed about to become a reality. It was necessary to disarm the Federalists, whose chief weapon was the fear of Paris tyranny in the departments, by showing that the Mountain did not intend to place the capital in a position of predominance over the rest of France. Hastily, the new constitution was drawn up. It was completed within a few days (June 24, 1793) of the overthrow of the Girondin leaders. It carefully avoided any mention of social equality that might frighten the commercial classes of the provincial cities. Though Robespierre's well-known proposal of a Declaration of Rights, delivered to the Convention on April 24, 1793, was used as a model for the declaration in the new constitution, care was exercised to omit Robespierre's article to the effect that " citizens whose incomes do not exceed what is necessary for their subsistence are exempted from contributing to the public expenses; the others shall support them progressively, according to the extent of their fortunes," and other bold provisions of his were softeningly paraphrased, though the right of insurrection was recognized. In fact the Declaration of Rights had been accepted, on Barère's motion, on May 29, in the hope of drawing Girondin and Jacobin forces closer together. Furthermore, all primary assemblies were placed on a basis of equality in the election of officers; and — the cleverest move in the theft of Girondin thunder — it was provided that the Constitution was not to become effective until it was accepted by a majority of the primary assemblies in a referendum to the people. The Constitution of 1793 was thus more of a weapon of propaganda in the campaign against the Federalists than a true reflection of Montagnard social philosophy. Even the loud burst of approval it called forth from Jacobin organs must be somewhat dis-counted as anti-Girondin rhetoric.

But it was destined never to be put in force. Situations on the battle fronts began to develop with which the leaders of the Convention believed a new government would be unable to grapple. For one thing, the insurrection in the departments had assumed startling proportions. The in-surrections at Bordeaux and Caen involved very little fighting. Being almost exclusively Federalist in origin, they fell of their own accord when the Constitution of 1793 was seen to be all that the departments could desire. At Marseilles, Lyons, and Toulon, however, the Federalist movement soon developed into a Royalist movement, and threatened to overrun the entire Midi. In the Vendée, where the insurgents, roused originally by their devotion to the old Church, were now being led by aristocrats like Charette and La Rochejacquelein, the movement was thoroughly royalist and completely counter-revolutionary, and therefore the more persistent and formidable. In Corsica, the Francophile Bonaparte family, led by Lucien and Napoleon, who was on leave most of the time from the French army, was unable to keep the Corsican patriots, under the leadership of their old chief Paoli, from striking for Corsican independence; the Bonapartes were obliged to flee to France, as their home went up in flames, and shortly afterward Paoli invited the English to protect the island.

The immediate result of the Girondin activity in Nor-mandy was the determination of the romantic Charlotte Corday to seek martyrdom by the assassination of Marat. Abetted by Barbaroux, Pétion, and Duperret, she stabbed the Friend of the People to death (July 13, 1793) at a time when he was obliged to take medicated baths for his health and was rapidly losing his influence anyway. Rumor had it that Robespierre and others were likewise intended as victims of this Girondin "angel of assassination." The dramatic setting of the murder, the state of mind produced by suspicions of a gigantic counter-revolutionary plot suc-ceeded in making of the already decrepit Marat a powerful symbol of republican hagiolatry. A veritable cult, borrow-ing its ceremonies and fetishes from that Christianity which advanced revolutionaries feigned to despise, sprang up around the new saint. For a brief interval after the fall of the Girondins, there had been a danger of a pro-Girondin reaction. Seventy-three deputies had signed a protest against the events of June 2, and protests poured in from the departments. Now the probability of success for such a reaction became negligible.

The month following the assassination of Marat wit-nessed the inauguration of a series of laudable measures. On July 17, all the remaining vestiges of feudalism were abolished without compensation. On August 1, the metric system of weights and measures was adopted. On August 8, the conservative old academies were abolished. On August 9, granaries were voted for each district. On Au-gust 14, the State assumed responsibility for property de-stroyed by the invaders. But these salutary acts were lost sight of in the flood of terroristic measures that accom-panied them. Eight deputies who were suspected of having aided Corday and the Girondins were, within two weeks, decreed " of accusation." On July 28, eighteen of those who had escaped were outlawed. Eleven were ordered to be brought before the Revolutionary Tribunal. By August 6, the number proscribed had mounted to fifty-five. Death was decreed as the penalty for food monopolists and prof-iteers. The property of all outlaws was confiscated. The arrest of all foreigners who had come to France since July 14, 1789, was ordered. Investment of property abroad was prohibited. Refusal to accept an assignat at its face value was made punishable by twenty years' imprisonment. And on August 1, the gates of Paris were closed, and hundreds of young men arrested as aristocrats.

On August 10, the first anniversary of the fall of the mon-archy, representatives of the primary assemblies came to announce the result of the referendum on the Constitution. It had been overwhelmingly accepted, but (and probably Robespierre instigated this suggestion) a new government could not successfully be established in circumstances of war, insurrection, and treason such as then surrounded France; therefore, until the close of the war, the representatives asked, let the Constitution of the Year I be suspended, a goal to be realized only with the dawn of peace, and let the Convention in the mean time rule the country by extraordinary measures. The Convention hesitated, however, and it was not until October 10 that the government of France was declared "revolutionary until the peace."

In the mean time, on the battle front, disaster followed disaster. Metz, Valenciennes, and Condé fell successively into the hands of the Austrians and Prussians, while the Vendéans, skilled in guerrilla warfare and dispersing immediately after battle, cut to pieces several armies led against them. On August 28, the citizens of Toulon welcomed the English Admiral Hood into their harbor. But, grave as the emergency was, the Convention was prepared for it. In the previous March and April, as Dumouriez had retreated and then deserted, the Jacobins had provided for a vigorous revolutionary government. To be sure, it had not functioned very vigorously, having been filled by Girondin nominees. But it was now deemed sufficient merely to find a new personnel for the existing governmental organs and to supplement them rather than to supplant them by other tribunals and committees.

The rejuvenation of the revolutionary government began in July. On July 10, 1793, the Committee of Public Safety was reorganized. On that day, Jeanbon Saint André, Barère, Gasparin, Couthon, Hérault-Séchelles, Thuriot, Prieur de la Marne, Saint Just, and Robert Lindet were named members. A Jacobin majority in the Convention failed to rename Danton, whose creation, in a sense, the Committee originally had been, for well-founded rumor had it that Danton had opened peace negotiations with the Coalition. On July 27, Gasparin resigned and was replaced by Robespierre. On August 14, Carnot and Prieur de la Côte d'Or were added. All during August, the question of conscription was discussed, and on August 23, the *levée en masse* put all Frenchmen "in permanent requisition for the service of the armies":

> The young men shall go to battle; the married men shall forge arms and transport provisions; the women shall make tents and clothing, and shall serve in the hospitals; the children shall turn old linen into lint; the aged shall betake themselves to the public places in order to rouse the courage of the warriors and preach hatred of kings and the unity of the Republic.

Buildings, arms, and horses were requisitioned. Every unit of France's man-power and resources was concentrated against invader and rebel. For the first time, a whole nation was mobilizing every human being and every sou in a national cause.

The fall of Toulon, the chief naval base of France on the Mediterranean, to the English at the end of August created intense emotion in Paris. Hitherto the rebels had been content to fight alone, but Toulon had sought the aid of an inveterate foreign foe! How long it would be before all of southern France might be in the enemy's hands, no one dared say. The Convention was obliged by the state of the public mind to yield to the popular extremists, called *Enragés*, who, led by a former constitutional priest, Jacques Roux, demanded social measures that even a Jacobin Convention was reluctant to grant. The maximum price to be paid for corn was reduced by a law of September 3. On the same day, following a precedent already created by the Commune of Paris, the incomes of all citizens were made subject to loan by the country on an ascending scale, all incomes being liable to a hundred per cent loan beyond nine thousand livres. The sum thus to be raised was to total a billion livres. On September 5, Hébert and the Enragés instigated a noisy bread demonstration at the Tuileries that the Convention could not resist. A Revolutionary Army of six thousand was established to enforce the laws against reactionaries. Houses were thrown open to search, and men were paid forty sous a day for attending the meetings of their sections. In order to expedite action against traitors, the Revolutionary Tribunal was divided into four parts of equal authority. And on September 6, Billaud-Varenne and Collot d'Herbois, two deputies of Hébertist affiliations, known to favor the most drastic methods of suppressing counter-revolution, were added to the Committee of Public Safety.

With the adherence of Billaud-Varenne and Collot d'Herbois and the resignation of Thuriot (September 20), the Committee of Public Safety now consisted of twelve of the most capable men in the Convention. Barère, Collot, and Couthon were entrusted with the correspondence with the officials and representatives of the government. Saint Just was in charge of constitutional legislation, though he was frequently sent on special missions to the army. Jean-bon Saint André was in charge of the marine, Carnot of the army. Prieur de la Côte d'Or controlled munitions, Lindet subsistence, clothing, and transportation, Prieur de la Marne, finance, Barère and Hérault-Séchelles, foreign affairs, and Robespierre, public instruction. Not until the World War was a similarly centralized and dictatorial war cabinet given such complete authority over a nation. On September 9, the Committee of General Security, created by a decree of October 2, 1792, was reorganized. Its nine members, among whom were Lebas, Amar, Vadier, and David, were named by the Committee of Public Safety with the consent of the Convention. The duties of the Committee of General Security were never precisely defined, but they included responsibility for the internal police and the preservation of order.

There is some difference of opinion among historians as to when the Terror began. Taine would date its outbreak on July 14, 1789, with the fall of the Bastille. Ternaux begins his admirable, if biased, *Histoire de la Terreur* with the massacres of September, 1792. There is no doubt that these were terrible and terrorizing acts, but by the Terror (as distinguished from the Reign of Terror, a phrase used chiefly by unfriendly English observers) historians generally mean that period in the French Revolution when the

Government of France, embodied in the Convention, deliberately adopted a terroristic policy in order to put fear of the Republic in the hearts of royalists, traitors, counter-revolutionaries, and war profiteers. Logically, then, it cannot be regarded as having begun earlier than these sweeping laws of September, 1793. It was this legislation that created the octopus-like revolutionary government, focused in the Committee of Public Safety, working in Paris through the Committee of General Security and the Revolutionary Tribunal and thrusting its tentacles out into the departments through the representatives on mission, the Revolutionary Army, and revolutionary committees. Two laws, passed likewise in September, soon brought plenty of victims within the reach of the octopus. On September 17, the Law of Suspects decreed the arrest of all "suspect-persons" and required the Committees of Surveillance (Revolutionary Committees) throughout France to execute the law. These were suspects:

> 1st, those who by their conduct, their connections, their remarks, or their writing show themselves the partisans of tyranny or federalism and the enemies of liberty; 2nd, those who cannot justify their means of existence and the performance of their civic duties; 3rd, those who have been refused certificates of civism [which each citizen was required to get from his local committee and carry about with him]; 4th, public functionaries suspended or removed in virtue of the decree of August 14th last; 5th, those of the former nobles, all of the husbands, wives, fathers, mothers, sons or daughters, brothers or sisters, and agents of the émigrés who have not constantly manifested their attachment to the Revolution; 6th, those who have emigrated from France in the interval from July 1, 1789 to the publication of the decree of March 30–April 8, 1792, although they may have returned to France within the period fixed by that decree or earlier.

To fall under this law as a "suspect" incurred imprisonment until a trial would either convict or acquit the imprisoned of "suspicions." It was a drastic means that the rulers of the Republic were adopting to make sure of catching all the agents of the émigrés and the spies of the enemies, of whom there were an appreciable number actively engaged inside of France. Yet it was a Draconic law, and justifies the acrimony of a later critic: "No one feels safe; no one is safe. If not a suspect, one may be suspected of being suspect."

A decree passed a short time afterwards (September 29, 1793), in reply to the English blockade of the French coast, enlarged the scope of the Law of the Maximum to include a long list of necessities other than corn, and subjected to huge fines and to treatment as suspects all those who sold the specified products above the maximum price. An effort was made even to regulate wages in accordance with these prices and the depreciation of fiat money. As if the meaning of all this were not clear enough, on October 10, 1793, the Convention finally decreed that "the provisional Government of France is revolutionary until the peace." In other words, until the war was over, the Constitution of 1793 was to be laid aside. To use a phrase quite common at the time, Terror was "the order of the day."

The number of executions by the guillotine began to mount rapidly. Charlotte Corday was guilty of murder and put up no defense; she was guillotined on July 17. The fear of counter-revolutionary plots and the danger that she might be freed by her sympathizers (of whom Danton was probably one) led to a demand for the trial of Marie Antoinette. Unnecessary and gratuitous accusations were made against her by the leaders of the Commune; and her fortitude was all the more winning because of the baseness of her slanderers. But like her husband's, her treason was clear; her trial was prolonged because of the importance of the defendant rather than because of any doubt as to her deserts. On October 16, Marie Antoinette traveled "through the little door to heaven." She was followed soon by the leaders of the Girondins. What might have been their fate if their colleagues had not fomented insurrection and the assassination of Marat, it is difficult to say. Now, however, there could be no doubt of what it would be. A number of Girondin leaders who had not been included in the petitions of May, 1793, were placed under arrest by the

Committee of Public Safety as conspirators, until the list of the proscribed ran to fifty-five. After a trial of several days' duration. twenty-two of them were sentenced to death. Valazé committed suicide in prison. The others were guillotined the next day (October 31, 1793). The seventy-three members of the Convention who had protested the events of May 31–June 2 were imprisoned. The Girondin strength was now not only broken; it was almost entirely eliminated. Madame Roland, dramatic to the last, was guillotined with an apostrophe to Liberty upon her lips. Her refugee husband committed suicide with a sword cane upon learning of her death, perhaps only, however, to save his property from confiscation. Condorcet, almost starved to death, took poison, after having found time and inspiration, while hiding from his pursuers, to erect a significant, if pathetic. monument to the theory of progress in the form of his *Esquisse d'un tableau des progrès de l'esprit humain*. Pétion, Barbaroux, and other outlaw Girondins came to equally sad ends.

On December 4, 1793, the numerous statutes that had created the Government of the Terror were codified in a single document commonly called the Constitution of the Terror. The ministers and the Executive Council were made directly responsible to the Committee of Public Safety. Deputies on mission were to report to the Committee every ten days. The only Revolutionary Army that was permitted existence, that appointed by the Convention, was made subject to its orders. The revolutionary armies that the Commune had created of its own accord thus were abolished. To complete the subjugation of the entire nation even in local affairs to the Committee, the powers of the department assemblies were limited to taxation; all other departmental offices were abolished; the old district officialdom was to be purged; thenceforth all district officers were to be known as "National Agents" and to be appointed by the Executive Council, with the approval of the Committee; and all municipal police were to be under the domination of the Committee of General Security,

Thus the independence of the departments that had been created by the Constitution of 1791 was destroyed, and the entire nation was brought directly under the domination of the Committee of Public Safety. The only official body in the country that could claim any independence of the Committee of Public Safety was the Convention itself, to whom the Committee was still nominally responsible.

Historians who have been primarily interested in the destructive side of the French Revolution have depicted all of the harrowing details of the Terror. Many of its horrors cannot be exaggerated, even if some particularly barbarous practices — for example, the "republican marriages" by which a man and a woman were supposed to be stripped naked, bound together, and thrown into the Loire to drown — never occurred, and streets did not run red with blood, and rivers were not stopped up with corpses. Émigré literature carried many hysterical details that were mere figments of the imagination. Boats loaded with suspects, however, actually were sunk in the river at Nantes, though recent investigations tend to prove that the number executed by these *noyades* was considerably smaller than is generally supposed, perhaps no more than twenty-eight hundred, certainly no more than forty-six hundred.[1] In the Vendée, columns of soldiers did march through already devastated lands in order to ravage systematically what was left. Large parts of Lyons were destroyed, when that city was finally subdued by the Republican Army, about sixteen hundred of its citizens executed, and the name of the city changed, euphemistically enough, to Commune-Affranchie. Huge numbers were shot or guillotined whenever a rebellious city was forced to surrender — whether at Marseilles, Bordeaux, Toulon, or elsewhere. In Paris, the situation was no less appalling. Although in October, 1793, the guillotine was fed only fifty victims, in July and June of the next year the total sacrifice was 1376.

---

[1] Velasqué: *Études sur la Terreur à Nantes*, in the *Revue Historique de la Révolution Française* XV, 1923, p. 224: Lavisse: *Histoire de France contemporaine*, II, 203.

But such episodes and numbers, presented *en masse*, give an erroneous impression. Abbé Sieyès was once asked, after the Revolution, what he had done to distinguish himself during its most crucial period; he answered sardonically, " I lived." For one of Sieyès' prominence, if not caution, that was a considerable achievement; but, after all, a great many people succeeded in living through the Terror. Despite the extravagant pictures that have been painted of wholesale butchery by historians and pseudo-historians, there probably were not more than twenty thousand victims all told in France between September, 1793, and July, 1794. Twenty thousand is a large number, but it is well to remember that the Terror did forestall counter-revolution and rebellion for years to come; a civil war would have reaped a harvest of many more than twenty thousand lives; and, furthermore, the Terror did prevent the conquest of France by her enemies. When Billaud-Varenne and Collot d'Herbois were admitted into the ranks of the Committee of Public Safety, Austrian and Prussian troops were invading France from Belgium and the Rhine, and the Spanish army had crossed the Pyrenees; England controlled Toulon and was blockading the Atlantic coast. In July, 1794, France had driven out the invaders and again controlled Belgium and the left bank of the Rhine. It was the Terror that made possible this achievement.[1]

The Terror was always, in the minds of its chief proponents, a purely defensive measure. The committees, agents, and tribunals through which it worked, were conceived in March and April, 1793, as the Vendéans cut the national armies to pieces, Dumouriez and Custine retreated, and Dumouriez deserted. The Committee was provided with a more vigorous personnel only when Federalist revolts had become a reality and the Vendéan revolts a serious menace. Robespierre was added when the " foreign plots " had apparently gained one prominent victim, Marat, and threatened others. Carnot and Prieur were made members with the express purpose of reorganizing the armies and muni-

[1] For the military details of 1793-94 see below, pp. 265-266.

tions service. Up to this time generals acted as they pleased; munitions were provided in a haphazard way; armies were made up mostly of volunteers. Now came the advantages of centralized command, food and munitions, dictatorships, selective draft (*levée en masse*), and many other of the war measures that more recent governments in even less appalling crises have felt obliged to use. Billaud-Varenne and Collot d'Herbois were added as Toulon voluntarily surrendered to England and the Duke of York set out to capture Dunkirk. In October, terror was declared "the order of the day," though the demand for such a declaration had come from radical quarters early in September. On October 23, the Committee was able, in a proclamation to the armies, to say:

> The cowardly satellites of tyranny have fled before us. . . . They have abandoned Dunkirk and their artillery. They have hastened to escape, to their complete ruin, putting the Sambre between them and your victorious columns. Federalism has been struck down in Lyons. The republican army has entered Bordeaux to give it a final blow. The Piedmontese and the Spanish have been driven from our territory. The defenders of the Republic have just destroyed the rebels of the Vendée.

To be sure, the Vendéans were not destroyed; they were merely closely pressed. Yet, by the end of October, the Terror, as a defensive measure, had justified itself in the eyes of those who felt the Revolution was worthy of sacrifice.

Up to October, the Terror was largely for military and patriotic motives, and only incidentally for social and economic purposes. After October it became largely economic. The program of the Enragés, though opposed step by step by the Convention, was gradually adopted. As early as September the Maximum Law was made to cover all necessities of life and even wages. All royal assignats and bonds were replaced by republican assignats and bonds, and the national debt was funded. Speculation and hoarding were direly punished. Assignats were, by severe penalties, forced into circulation at face value. Forced loans, or what we should call "capital levies," supplied the revenue for support of the armies. A distinct line was drawn between "rich" and "poor" by popular orators. The "rich" were conceived of as unpatriotic, counter-revolutionary, pro-English war profiteers. The "poor" were the supporters of the Republic, the war, and the Revolution. The "rich" were always suspect; the "poor" ran the section meetings and applauded the Commune. Finally, Saint Just, by the famous Ventôse decrees (February 26, March 3 and 13, 1794), induced the Convention to declare the lands of suspects sequestered and subject to distribution among the poor. The Ventôse decrees were the zenith of the social program of the Robespierrists. For most of their colleagues on the Committee of Public Safety and the Committee of General Security, they went too far. The Committees were willing to support such measures up to a certain point in order to win popular support, but they were unwilling to follow the Robespierre faction completely. Through a policy of obstruction they succeeded in preventing the effective execution of Robespierre's program until he died, and his social program with him. The assignats actually mounted in value between July, 1793, and July, 1794, and proportionately the cost of living came down to an appreciable degree, though the reason for this was probably the increased confidence in the Government that issued them because of its military fortune rather than the economic legislation of the Convention.

Step by step, as each of these new measures was passed, the Committee of Public Safety increased in power. Originally it was a temporary committee, with limited funds, answerable to the Convention. As each new restrictive measure or executive decree was passed, its execution was entrusted to the Committee, the natural instrument for carrying it out. Thus the Committee concentrated in its hands the execution of all the extraordinary revolutionary legislation, and the control of the deputies on mission and of local committees and authorities. This was not done without a struggle. Two of its members (Gasparin and Thuriot) resigned, at separate times, because they did not agree with the policies of their colleagues. In the Convention, there were groups that opposed its increasing authority over the Convention itself and attacked it in principle and in personnel. It always managed to come out of these debates with votes of increased confidence, not alone because its members were the most capable men of the Convention, but because it was a vital necessity. It was a War Cabinet, an emergency dictatorship, standing not only between France and her foes, but between the Convention and the super-patriots, the radicals, the Enragés. The laws of October 10 and December 4 that gave the dictatorship of the Committee a legal basis were but confirmations of already existing conditions; they rendered *de nomine* what already, by a series of steps (inevitable if France was to be saved), had actually become *de facto*.

A series of political successes for Robespierre were soon to follow that were to render him the outstanding figure of France. Whether, as some believe, he had cleverly and unscrupulously made himself dictator of France, or, as others would have it, he was merely a tool in the hands of less popular but more able men in the Committee of Public Safety, or, as still others put it, his ability and patriotism had made it necessary for him to put himself to the fore, he now occupied the center of the stage. Robespierre had from the very first been dear to the Paris electorate. They called him " the Incorruptible," and always allowed him to wear *culottes* and powdered wig and once even to trample upon the red, white, and blue cockade — each an offense that would have made things go very hard with a less idolized offender. The fact that he was the most popular man in France made him an important figure on the Committee of Public Safety. Fixing prices and wages, rationing supplies, conscripting manpower, devoting an entire nation and mobilizing all its resources to the business of winning a war, are thankless jobs. Carnot, Lindet, Prieur, and the rest gladly permitted Robespierre to assume the responsibility in the Convention and in the public eye for the measures that originated with them, but which the popularity of Robespierre was necessary to carry. Thus Robespierre, whose official business on the Committee was the supervision of Public Instruction, became the personification of the Committee to every one else. The individual members of the Committee found it desirable at first to win his consent to any plans they had for their separate provinces of government in order to assure their success. Though the indefatigable Barère still acted as official spokesman, it was made to appear as if the Committee were under Robespierre's domination. Actually, however, this was not true. Sometimes, indeed, they persuaded him to advocate certain measures with which he was not entirely in sympathy. But knowing his popularity, they allowed it to appear to others that he was the guiding genius of the Committee.

The Committee of Public Safety was bound to maintain the Terror. Carnot, whose special province was military affairs, wanted to keep control of officers through deputies on mission who could bring to immediate trial any generals who were suspected of faltering or of treason. The number of high officers who were guillotined, including men like Custine and Beauharnais, indicates severity, however, rather than lack of discrimination. Lindet, whose task it was to supply the army, wanted to be in a position to punish summarily all violations of the Law of the Maximum, though he refused to be dragged into political conflicts. Billaud-Varenne, rare example of a college professor turned revolutionist, was sure that, as soon as the Terror ceased, counter-revolution would stalk the country. Any plea, therefore, for the moderation of the Terror seemed to them treasonable; who dared urge moderation with the enemies at the gates and rebellion within? And Danton, Fabre d'Églantine, and all the old Club of the Cordeliers, who, following Danton's lead, were beginning to plead for a more lenient policy, were looked at askance by them. For the moment, however, Danton's attitude was valuable to the Committee. There were those in France who were accusing the Committee itself of moderation, of not ferreting out the enemies of the Fatherland vigorously enough. These people must be silenced; they were as dangerous to the revolutionary cause as the moderates; and Danton's moderation might be welded into an effective weapon to use against them.

The turn of the Enragés came first. Led by an ex-priest, Jacques Roux, they had opposed profiteering so vehemently that they had attacked even the Constitution of 1793, which everybody respected but few wished to see put in force, because it was silent on that question. They kept constantly agitating for effective measures against speculators. The overthrow of the Girondins and the Laws of the Maximum (as we have seen) were due to their demands. Other measures of September and October had been passed because of Enragé agitation, though the leaders of the Mountain were themselves not heartily in accord with their ruthlessness. Such were the execution of Marie Antoinette, the arrest of all enemy aliens (October 16) and the terrible penalties against ecclesiastical suspects (October 20). When they began to attack the Convention itself for its moderation, however, that was too much. First they were expelled, through Robespierre's efforts, from the Jacobin and Cordelier Clubs. Eventually their leaders were arrested. Roux himself committed suicide upon hearing his sentence (January 15, 1794), but some of his followers were guillotined, and the organization now passed under the leadership of Hébert.

Hébert had been one of those who had aided in destroying the Enragés. He was one of the leaders of the Commune that since August 10, 1792, had held sway at the Hôtel de Ville. His rabid sheet, *Le Père Duchesne*, was the most scurrilous of all the journals in Paris. He had joined in the attack upon Roux because he was not particularly concerned with profiteers and speculators, but he too had long felt that the Convention was not sufficiently active in suppressing defeatism and rousing the patriotism of the lower classes by measures aimed at the rich. The Revolutionary Commune had on previous occasions, as on June 2 and September 5, 1793, been obliged to force the hand of the Mountain; it must do so now or the Terror might not be as fruitful as it ought. Everybody labored under an uneasy fear that there was a " Foreign Conspiracy " (*Complot de l' Étranger*). Barère himself added to this dread suspicion by announcing the arrest of a spy whose papers revealed that Pitt was spending large sums for hired assassins to kill the leaders of the Revolution. The Hébertists demanded counter-measures and accused the Convention of laxity. On March 4, 1794, both Danton and Robespierre were vehemently attacked at the Commune. If Hébert could have got the people of Paris to follow as they did on the previous June 2, there might have been another purging of the Convention. But the people of Paris were for the most part loyal to the Committee. Moreover, they considered their food difficulties attributable in part to the Revolutionary Army that had been ravaging the neighborhood of Paris; and the Revolutionary Army had been created upon the insistence of the Hébertists; its chief, General Ronsin, but recently released from prison, where he had been placed on a charge of excessive severity, was loudest in his attacks on the *Endormeurs* (Pacifiers), as they called the Committee. The Committee of Public Safety realized the danger of Hébert's and Ronsin's attitude; if they succeeded, the Committee's influence would be undermined. Furthermore, the extreme religious policy of the Hébertists alienated many and shocked Robespierre. Hébert had succeeded in getting the old Cathedral of Notre Dame converted into a Temple of Reason. At the inaugural ceremonies, while Reason — impersonated, some say, by a street-walker, but, more probably, by the wife of Hébert's right-hand man, Momoro — was enthroned in the Temple in the presence of the entire Convention, her devotees went to extremes that some considered unreasonable. Within less than a month twenty-four hundred and thirty-six churches had been converted into Temples of Reason. The popularity of the movement demonstrates the eagerness of a naturally religious people, cut off from their old church allegiance, for a new national church. But it also meant a menace to the authority of the Convention, the creation of a spirited national movement under the leadership of the Commune.

The Committee of Public Safety determined upon the destruction of the Commune's opposition. The Dantonists, who were naturally opposed to the Hébertists because they were unwilling to permit any further extension of the Terror, were pressed into action. Camille Desmoulins, whose pen had done valiant service before, was encouraged to begin a new journal. He called it *Le Vieux Cordelier* (*The Old Cordelier*) as if to recall the revolutionary but unsanguinary policy of the original society. In it he attacked the Hébertists and spoke of the necessity for leniency. Robespierre read and approved the first numbers at least. The campaign against the new Cordeliers bore rapid fruit. The policy of the Indulgents quickly became as dangerous to the Committee as that of the Hébertists, and it was soon called upon to wage a battle on two fronts against both Hébertists and Dantonists. The Ventôse decrees made a splendid weapon for such a fight. The French populace was inclined to believe that only the unpatriotic rich were made to suffer by the Terror and that the Committee would actually take measures to make the poor happy while the Hébertists mouthed only empty phrases. Shortly after the attack by Hébert upon Danton and Robespierre, the Committee of Public Safety felt itself strong enough to proceed against the Commune. Hébert, Momoro, and their supporters were arrested on March 17, and executed a week later, on the grounds that they had plotted to starve Paris, establish tyranny, and annihilate the Convention.

The time had now come for the Dantonists. Robespierre told Camille Desmoulins bluntly that the later numbers of *Le Vieux Cordelier* had displeased him by their too obviously sincere demands for clemency. Number 3 of *Le Vieux Cordelier* had spoken of the "crimes" of the Terror. It was read everywhere, and on December 20, 1793, a deputation of weeping women came to the Convention to demand the release of their friends and relatives awaiting judgment in the prisons. The Convention decreed that the Committee appoint commissioners to investigate the means of setting at liberty any patriots who might unjustly have been incarcerated. The Indulgents, as Danton's party came to be called, were thus becoming a serious check in the effectual working of the Terror machinery. Several notes of warning were given them. Danton's friend Fabre d'Églantine was imprisoned on a charge of embezzlement in the management of the French East India Company. Chabot, ex-priest, now brother-in-law of the bankers, the Frey Brothers, was arrested soon after for an effort to defraud the Government. Had Danton retained some of his one-time energy, he might yet have rescued himself and his friends. But the death of his first wife while he was on mission in Belgium (he had had her body dug up that he might kiss her good-bye) and his recent marriage to a mere chit of a girl seem to have distracted his mind from politics.

Besides, his actions of late had not been altogether above suspicion. He now preferred to spend his time at his estate at Arcis-sur-Aube (which in the course of the Revolution he had mysteriously built up to magnificent proportions) rather than at Paris. To his natural bourgeois scruples, Danton now added the wealthy property-holder's objections to a *sans-culotte* republic whose victories on the front were made possible by taxes on the rich, regulation of industry and commerce, suppression of personal liberties, and the rapid punishment of suspects. His appeals were now addressed more and more to the moderates inside and outside the Convention whose property was of large enough proportions to convince them of its sacrosanctity. Inside the Convention, the moderates, the wealthy, were led by Bourdon de l'Oise, who, from the very beginning of the Terror, had captained an able but ineffective opposition to Bouchotte, the *sans-culotte* Minister of War, to the Revolutionary Army and to the Committee. These moderates now lent a willing ear to the Dantonist cry for indulgence; and at the same time, former deputies on mission, such as Ysabeau, Fouché, Fréron, and others, who had good reason to believe that Robespierre did not approve of their revolutionary fervor or motives at Marseilles, Lyons, or elsewhere, joined forces with the moderates. Whether from a soft-hearted feeling for sufferers, or from an honest conviction that the Terror was no longer necessary after the fall and winter victories of the revolutionary armies, or from patriotic concern over the increasing power of the unpropertied in social and political affairs, or only from a natural if not entirely praiseworthy desire to keep their own heads, the opposition parties to the Committee in the Convention had reached proportions that rendered its position precarious.

There is an anecdote to the effect that a mutual friend of Danton and Robespierre tried to bring about a reconciliation by inviting both of them to dine at his house; Danton inadvisedly broached the subject of the Terror: he did not object to the punishment of the guilty, but why involve the innocent in their destruction? "And who told you," Robespierre is said to have asked, "that a single innocent man has lost his life?" The anecdote, like so many anecdotes, is probably too good to be true, for it is too typical of the attitude of the two men. But *si non e vero, e ben trovato*. Danton, longing for peace and the leisure to enjoy his new home, probably still negotiating with Pitt at the time, and always of an easy-going nature that permitted a few laxities without necessarily surrendering all principle, could not see the hard necessity of a terror so severe that even some innocent might be involved in the destruction of the guilty, particularly since his own skin and those of his friends were in danger. Robespierre, unwilling to surrender one jot or one tittle until the accomplishment of the ideal which he was now perhaps in a position to attain, blindly wedded to principle to the exclusion of mercy even for himself, until mercy became a weapon on behalf of principle, could conceive of no innocents who had incurred the penalty of the guillotine; suspicion alone was quite enough proof of guilt. That this was the Robespierre who only a few years before had pleaded for the abolition of capital punishment shows the power of an ideal to make zealots.

Already steps had been taken for the ruin of the Dantonists. Robespierre at first refused to sacrifice his former friends. No more proof of this is necessary than that at a

later date Billaud-Varenne accused him of moderation on
that account. He had gone to school with Camille Desmoulins, it must be remembered, and was said to have once
looked upon the sister of Lucille, now Camille's wife, quite
sentimentally. But he was eventually convinced, probably
by the argument that Danton and Danton's party, by their
moderation and laxity of behavior, stood in the way of the
establishment of that ideal Republic of Virtue for which he
and Saint Just were striving, and he yielded. Saint Just
led the attack against the Dantonists in the Convention; a
number of charges were made, some of them true, others
untrue. Only Legendre rose in the Convention to defend
Danton, and he was speedily discountenanced. The Convention voted for the impeachment of the entire group,
some of whom could hardly be considered followers of Danton.[1] They were allowed no counsel. Danton made no
strenuous effort to defend himself or his partners. He depended upon his still great popularity and his eloquence as
an orator to win his acquittal. But he was not to return
from the Tribunal to the Convention in triumph as had
Marat. The Committee pushed through the Convention a
decree providing that if at any time in the course of a trial
the judges felt convinced of the guilt of the accused, they
need hear no further evidence. Even so, some agents of the
Committee had illegally to speak to the jury in private, introducing some evidence that even to-day is shrouded in
mystery, before the defendants were found guilty. On
April 5, when the prisoners were returned to their cells,
Danton crying for pardon of man and God for having
created the Revolutionary Tribunal, they were already ad-
judged guilty, though they did not know it. L'Huillier
committed suicide. The rest made their last sacrifice for
the Revolution on April 6. "Show my head to the people,"
said Danton. "They do not see the like every day."
Robespierre, apparently at least, was now supreme.

[1] Danton, Desmoulins, Hérault-Séchelles, Westermann, Delacroix, and
Phillipeaux were accused of royalism. Fabre d'Églantine, Delaunay, Chabot,
Basire, Abbé Espagnac, the Frey Brothers, Gusman, L'Huillier, and Diderich-
sen were accused of graft and corruption.

During the months of April and May, 1794, a series of minor measures — the abolition of the Executive Council, the decree to try all conspirators at Paris, the creation of popular commissions for the hastening of preliminaries to the trials of suspects — had strengthened the power of the Central Government. Nothing now seemed to stand in the way of the Republic of Virtue save Atheism and the insincerity of some patriots. The opportunity to create the democratic state, the underlying principles of which he had portrayed in his proposal for the Rights of Man in April, 1793, Robespierre now hoped to seize by the forelock. His was to be a Republic of Virtue — that virtue which Montesquieu and Rousseau had maintained was the foundation of republics and which popular orators more recently had dilated upon, love of equality and love of country, democracy and patriotism. France, still tainted with the character that under a monarchy had been a virtue but now was a vice, must wash away the stain, in blood if necessary. After France had been made into a nation of free, equal, and devoted citizens by the sacrifice of those who could not be made such, because their roots were bedded too deep in a soil that had once been monarchical, then a return to internal peace, normal legislation, regular courts, and the Constitution of 1793 might be possible. Until that time, mercy was a kind of cruelty, tolerance a mere continuation of bloodshed. The sooner all of the enemies, conscious or unwitting, of the Republic of Virtue were destroyed, the sooner good will and happiness might once more reign. In the mean time, the Committee continued the policy of Terror, simply in order to clear away the guilty — counter-revolutionaries or supposed counter-revolutionaries already in the prisons. After the death of Danton, not many new arrests were made; most of the provincial tribunals were shut down; but the number of executions in Paris mounted appallingly; and for this the Committee rather than Robespierre was responsible.

Robespierre, though in no sense a sectarian, was essentially a religious man. Like him, the patriots of France.

great and obscure, had lost faith in both the old Catholic
Church and the new Constitutional Church. These had
created only discord and danger to the Republic. What the
French needed was a religion that would nourish their tremendous spiritual cravings, their fervor on republican holidays, their ardor in pursuit of this religious fad and that —
the cult of Marat, the Worship of Reason, the Messianic
obsession of Catherine Théot — and convert it into a great
national, revolutionary, and republican sect. Thus, Robespierre was merely crystallizing a popular demand when he
instituted the worship of the Supreme Being, a religion
borrowed largely from Rousseau's Savoyard Vicar. The
quondam Cathedral of Notre Dame, already the witness of
three types of religion and destined to behold others, now
became the Temple of the Supreme Being. On June 8,
Robespierre, happening to be President of the Convention
at the moment, led a solemn procession to the Garden of
the Tuileries, and with his own hand set fire to large images
representing Atheism, Discord, and Selfishness; a mechanical contrivance had been arranged so that from their ashes
rose the figure of Wisdom. The Festival of the Supreme
Being wound up with an oath of allegiance to the Republic
on the Champ de Mars. It was all very impressive, but a
few influential members of the Convention were heard to
grumble.

Atheism having thus been handled, now came the turn of
insincere patriots. On June 10, 1794, a measure with this
end in view was introduced by Robespierre, though advocated by all of the Committee. The Revolutionary Calendar, itself a splendid instrument for the protection of a
national, republican religion against international Christianity, with its months named after natural phenomena
and its holidays after good republican characteristics, was
now in force. In accordance with this calendar the law was
known as the Law of the 22d Prairial. If it passed, it would
place the Convention completely under the dictation of the
Committee of Public Safety. It was a step, therefore, which
the Committee wished to see prevail, and which the oppo-

nents of the Committee and men whose patriotism would
not stand close scrutiny in the Convention were equally
anxious to prevent. The struggle in favor of the proposal
was led by Robespierre. The principal antagonist was
Bourdon de l'Oise. Robespierre's advocacy secured its
passage on June 10. But the next day its opponents rallied
and repealed the part of the law which placed members of
the Convention under the authority of the Committee,
only, however, to have it passed again on the next.

The Law of the 22d Prairial provided for the death
penalty for all enemies of the people, even for offenses
that had hitherto been punishable by deportation or imprisonment, and so defined " enemy " as to leave no margin
of safety for any of whom the Committee of Public Safety
wished to be rid. No witnesses need be examined or
counsel given the accused if the Revolutionary Tribunal
was assured of his guilt. Moreover, the members of the
Convention, hitherto impeachable only by their colleagues,
might now be brought before the courts by the ordinary
authorities. Finally, the Revolutionary Tribunal was
itself reorganized by the dismissal of its most inactive (and
therefore most merciful) members. The result was that in
the next seven weeks more than the entire number in the
preceding fifteen months were guillotined. The total of
the executions in Paris since the fall of the Girondins was
2627, of whom more than half died between June 10 and
July 27, 1794. From April to August, 1793, the number of
guillotined averaged three a week; from September, 1793, to
May, 1794, thirty-two a week; but in June and July, 1794,
there were one hundred and sixty-six a week.[1]

But things were coming to pass that were soon to destroy
Robespierre. The Committee of Public Safety had divided
into two groups, one centering about Robespierre, Saint
Just, and Couthon, and the other about Billaud-Varenne

[1] In palliation of the Committee's sanguinary activity, it has been pointed
out that during the World War more people in France were shot unjustly and
later cleared by the Court of Cassation than the total number executed by the
Revolutionary Tribunal during the Terror. See Mathiez: *Robespierre ter-
reuriste*, in *Annales Révolutionnaires*, 1920, XII, 178–79.

and Collot d'Herbois. At their meetings, it had become plainly a question of whether or not Robespierre was actually to become the guide and master that he was popularly supposed to be; he refused to send to the Revolutionary Tribunal the seventy-three Girondin sympathizers or the followers of the fanatic prophetess Catherine Théot, and signed very few of the warrants that sent hundreds to their death in Prairial and Messidor of the Year II. And in the Convention Robespierre's quest of Virtue created contempt, while his all-inclusive laws created fear. No one knew who next would fall under his displeasure, though all were troubled in their consciences. Finding his faction in the minority in the Committee of Public Safety, Robespierre had recently absented himself more than was wise from their conferences. And in the Convention there were two parties opposed to him; there were those who were sure that Robespierre was the soul of the Terror, while Billaud-Varenne saw to it that others believed him a moderate. Tallien's young and beautiful wife had but recently been imprisoned and she wrote him impassioned letters accusing him of cowardice, which encouraged him to stir his colleagues on to action. The members of the Committee of General Security, resenting the power that had been acquired by the Committee of Public Safety, fixed their displeasure upon Robespierre. Fouché, who had recently had a stormy interview with Robespierre regarding his mission at Lyons, filled the ears of gullible Conventionals with stories of huge proscription lists that Robespierre was alleged to be preparing.

The adversaries of Robespierre adopted the attitude that the Terror was no longer necessary now that the armies of the Republic were everywhere victorious. On July 25 (7th Thermidor), Barère attacked those whose confidence in the victories of France was so small that they demanded new proscriptions. The Convention ordered his speech to be printed and circulated among the municipalities. Robespierre, on July 26, attempted to defend himself and suggested the reorganization of the two committees, naming a number of his enemies very definitely, but also making vague threats against others without accusing them by name. Everybody in the Convention was left to wonder whether he was marked for proscription or not. For if Robespierre's proposal to reorganize the two committees were to pass, there could be no doubt of his suzerainty over France. That evening at the Jacobin Club, Robespierre made the same appeal. Collot and Billaud, both of whom were present, were not permitted to reply and barely escaped with their lives. Overnight the two men became feverishly active, an activity instigated not alone by a desire to save the State from a wrong-minded master, but also to save themselves from the fate of Hébert and Danton. Carnot, Tallien, Barère, Barras, Legendre, Vadier — all joined in the conspiracy. The Moderates of the Plain were convinced that Robespierre was the soul of the Terror, which now that the armies of the Revolution were triumphant was no longer needed. The Montagnards were convinced that Robespierre was the soul of the opposition to the Terror. Had he not tried to save Danton? Had he not saved the seventy-three Girondin sympathizers awaiting trial in the prisons? They pointed out that he was lenient toward Catholics and was addressing himself more and more to the Plain.

But the Robespierre faction had not been idle either. When the meeting of the Convention opened on July 27 (9th Thermidor), Saint Just went to the tribune. Accusing Billaud and Collot of having taken advantage of the absence of the other members of the Committee to make themselves dictators, he meant to propose a definite statement by the Convention that, while the revolutionary power of the Government would be kept intact, it must in no way be made to favor tyranny, ambition, or oppression. But he never finished his speech. Tallien interrupted with a short speech demanding that "the curtain be completely torn away." Immediately, there were shouts against Robespierre all over the house. The opposition against him had been thoroughly organized. Collot d'Herbois, sitting in the chair as presiding officer, persistently refused to give him the floor to answer the taunts that were being hurled at him on all sides. Soon Collot surrendered the chair to Thuriot that he might himself join the attack. Finally, when Robespierre did start to speak, he was so angry that he could not talk. "The blood of Danton chokes him" some one cried. "It is Danton, then," he replied, "whom you wish to avenge." Was there regret or accusation in that retort? Finally a decree of impeachment was passed against Robespierre, Saint Just, and Couthon. His friend Lebas and his brother Augustin asked to share his fate, and were included in the decree.

Ever since the reorganization of the Commune upon the fall of Hébert, the Hôtel de Ville, led by Hanriot as Commander of the National Guard, Fleuriot-Lescot as Mayor, and Coffinhal, had been completely under the domination of Robespierre. Hanriot, with a small force, tried to wrest the five victims from the Convention, but was himself placed under arrest by the Convention's guards. The Commune immediately issued orders to the governors of the prisons not to receive the several prisoners. Only some of the governors obeyed, and the result was that the arrested deputies found themselves in separate jails. Before long, Hanriot was freed by his followers and went himself to free the others. Robespierre and Couthon, however, refused to leave their cells. Not knowing the strength of his popularity in the city, and hoping, like Marat, to be acquitted of the charges against him by the Revolutionary Tribunal and returned in triumph to the Convention, Robespierre feared to incur outlawry, which would mean death without trial, if he broke jail. The others of the accused, however, had already met at the City Hall. The Convention, learning of this disregard of its decrees, took advantage of their opponents' error, outlawed them, and appointed Barras, a former army officer, to take the necessary steps to capture the outlaws and to defend the Convention against any insurrection on their behalf. The Convention had at last learned how to defend itself. When Robespierre heard of the decree of out-

lawry, he consented to join his fellows at the Hôtel de Ville.
They determined to appeal to the sections and the army in
the name of the people against the Convention. It was
about 1 A.M. before Couthon consented to leave his prison
cell and to join the others. Plans for an insurrection were
progressing rapidly by that time.[1] But the guards and adherents of the Commune from several of the sections had
been drawn up and ready since six o'clock. Tired out by
their long wait and expecting no action till the morning,
they had dwindled away. In the mean time, Barras had
raised an army and had gone out to capture the insurgents.
Having learned the password from one of Hanriot's men,
Barras' force easily made its way into the Hôtel de Ville,
and broke into the room where the conspirators were gathered. Robespierre probably shot himself, but succeeded
only in shattering his jaw. Lebas made a better target of
himself. Paralytic Couthon hurt himself trying to escape
down the stairs. The younger Robespierre jumped out of a
window, but was captured. Saint Just did not resist arrest.
Only two made their escape, one of them but to be captured
the next day. No trial was necessary, since they were outlaws. Merely upon recognition, they were executed on July
28 (10th Thermidor). The Thermidorians, as the leaders in
the overthrow of Robespierre were soon to be called, had
brought to an end the Republic of Virtue knowingly. They
did not know that they had also destroyed the ascendancy
of the Mountain.

[1] The old story is that Robespierre, out of certain legalistic scruples, delayed
so long in signing an appeal to arms that when he finally was persuaded, he had
time only to sign *Ro* when the troops of the Convention broke in upon him. It
has recently been shown, however, that this particular appeal, addressed to the
Section des Piques, though signed only *Ro*, was written long before the force of
Barras arrived and actually was delivered to the section. In other words,
Robespierre was actively leading the insurrection rather than delaying it by
petty inhibitions. See Mathiez: *The Fall of Robespierre*, chapter x.

CHAPTER III

THE THERMIDORIAN REACTION

AMONG the troop that had followed Barras to the Hôtel de Ville on the 9th of Thermidor, many came from the wealthier sections of Paris. These were the people who had endured the brunt of the Terror, from whose families the "suspects" had been taken, who, because they had had to lose by the mobilization of capital during the war, were considered the most likely to join in intrigues with émigrés and foreigners. As long as there was an invader upon the soil of France, they had followed the Convention, not alone out of fear, but likewise out of patriotism, none the less lamenting the severity that bore more heavily upon their class than upon the *sans-culottes*.

But now the need for severity had passed. The purpose of the Terror had been achieved. La Rochejacquelein had been killed in battle in the Vendée. Charette and Stofflet, who had been his ablest allies, were inclined to accept peace. The people of the Vendée, beaten by *noyades*, epidemics, companies Marat, and the scourge of Carrier, were willing to return peaceably to their agricultural pursuits when invited by a proclamation of the Convention to do so. The Federalist movement inside of France had come toppling down with the capture of Toulon, made possible by the daring and expert skill of a young artillery captain named Bonaparte (1793), and the English fleet under Admiral Hood was obliged to sail out of the harbor. Hurried through the intermediary ranks by friendly deputies on mission, Bonaparte, as one of the generals of the Army of the Alps, was now coöperating with older officers in driving the Sardinian army back toward Turin. The Spaniards were being chased by General Dugommier, his former superior, back from the eastern Pyrenees into Catalonia, and on August 1, 1794, General Müller captured San Martial and Irun, which caused San Sebastian to fall to the French force operating on the southwestern front. In the north, the mutual dislike of Austria and Prussia and the impending third partition of Poland fought on the side of the tricolor. At the close of 1793, Victory, until that time partial to the Allies, began to smile upon the young generals of the Republican Army. The British advance upon Dunkirk was stopped at Hondschoote (September 8, 1793) by Houchard. The Prussians and Austrians under Coburg were checked at Wattignies (October 14, 1793) by Jourdan; and Hoche and Pichegru in Alsace-Lorraine had recaptured the Wissembourg lines and the fortress of Landau. Thus the winter of 1793–94 found the French successfully defending their country against the advance of their enemies.

In the spring of 1794, the plans of Carnot called for an offensive. Moreau captured Turcoing (May 17–18), and on June 25–26, while the Deputies Saint Just and Lebas looked on and took a valiant part, Jourdan's army, gratefully to be renamed the Army of the Sambre and Meuse for this exploit, crossed and recrossed the Sambre five times in order finally to take Charleroi and to defeat Coburg at Fleurus. On July 9, the combined armies of Pichegru and Jourdan entered Brussels, and on July 24, three days before the 9th Thermidor, Antwerp was once more in French hands. As the British and the Dutch were thus being driven back into Holland, Prussia, whose loyalty to the Coalition, up to this point, was attributable to a monthly subsidy of £150,000 that Pitt had arranged to pay Frederick William, withdrew from Trèves, with some persuasion on the part of Schérer's army. Only upon the high seas was the eloquent Barère, who officially announced these victories to the Convention, unable to sing of triumphs. Carnot acquired the sobriquet of "Organizer of Victory," but to Lindet, who acted as "Food Dictator," to Prieur de la Côte d'Or, who provided the armies with munitions, and to other members of the Committee of Public Safety, who labored indefatigably upon some phase of the Government that made victory possible, must go some of the glory, too.

Where were the enemies now and what the danger to justify one hundred and sixty-six weekly executions any longer? Those who had husbands or brothers or fathers or sisters or friends in prison as "suspects" now felt that they dared to protest. Their protest was the support that they gave the Convention when insurrection threatened on the 9th Thermidor. Even the sections that had been loyal to the Commune up to this point did not anxiously rise to defend their idols; and when Robespierre and his fellow outlaws were guillotined on July 28, there were no uprisings — not even a commanding demonstration in his behalf. The truth is that, if Robespierre had prevailed on the 9th Thermidor, the Terror would have continued. For to him the Terror was no longer merely an instrument of victory; it was a means toward a better state. Even among the lower-class sections, though more of their sons had fallen on the field of battle than on the Place de la Guillotine, the Terror had brought enough grief, and they welcomed the chance to bring it to an end.

But the leaders in the overthrow of Robespierre — men like Billaud-Varenne, Collot d'Herbois, Tallien, Barras — were not in favor of reaction. Quite the contrary, they were men who as much as or more than he had promoted Terror and still wished to see it progress. They were genuinely afraid of a royalist restoration, of plots by foreign agents, of efforts to assassinate the leaders of the Revolution, of what we to-day should call *defeatism*, of a number of other things that were not altogether hallucination. Louchet, on August 19, when Robespierre had been dead only three weeks, delivered a long speech to the Convention, in which he pleaded for a continuation "of that inflexible severity to which the judicious and profound Marat never ceased to recall us." It was now considered desirable to lift Marat's memory to a higher pinnacle than Robespierre's had ever been so that Robespierre's might proportionately be dimmed. Accordingly, on September 21, 1794, the last day of the revolutionary year, with the most elaborate ceremonies, arranged in minutest detail by the Convention itself, Marat's body was transferred to the Panthéon, the former Church of Sainte Geneviève, now used as a Revolutionary Hall of Fame. Mirabeau, the only other revolutionary leader so to have been honored, was removed in disgrace at the same time.

But these were the last bolts in the Montagnard defense. Even before they were shot, definite steps had been taken in the direction of reaction against the Terror. Public opinion expressed itself now largely through young fops, the so-called *Jeunesse dorée* or *Muscadins*, among them many moderates, even royalists, who began to appear upon the streets of Paris, where before they had not dared to show their faces, and to attend the meetings of the Convention. Leading this *Gilded Youth*, who, dressed in the height of fashion, fought with the *sans-culottes* in street brawls and gave vent to their feelings by smashing the busts of Marat wherever they saw them, was Fréron, once the disciple of Marat, once editor of a popular sheet called *L'Orateur du Peuple*, and once deputy on mission, who at Marseilles had caused the execution of hundreds. Despite all that Billaud-Varenne and his confrères could do, the Terrorist edifice erected since March, 1793, was torn down brick by brick. The Law of the 22d Prairial was softened and eventually repealed. The Revolutionary Tribunal was reorganized in the interests of clemency; large numbers of prisoners were released amid great rejoicing on the part of anxious relatives; and Public Prosecutor Fouquier-Tinville, who was generally regarded as the evil genius of the Tribunal, was himself tried and finally executed. In December, 1794, the seventy-three deputies who had been proscribed for their sympathy with the Girondins were allowed to return to their places in the Convention and were joined later by the Girondin refugees who still survived — Isnard, Louvet, Lanjuinais, Kervelégan, Larivière, La Révellière-Lépaux, and Lesage. Carrier, who had been responsible for the *noyades* of Nantes, was brought before the Revolutionary Tribunal and sentenced to death for excessive severity. The Law of the Maximum was repealed. Liberty of worship was again permitted. The Committees of Public Safety and General Security were revised and brought under the control of the Convention. In January, 1795, a mob of *Jeunesse dorée* burned Marat in effigy in the garden of the Jacobin Club. In February the campaign of the *Jeunesse dorée* was rewarded with a decree providing that no one who had been dead less than ten years might be Panthéonized. Marat's remains were removed from the Panthéon to an obscure grave near by. In March, 1795, Billaud, Collot, Barère, and Vadier were themselves brought to trial. Within less than a year after the downfall of Robespierre, the leading figures in the Terror had received some kind of punishment or other; its most effective branches had been abolished or revised; its supporters were now as suspect as once its opponents had been. The reaction was thorough.

All of this did not occur without a struggle. It was attended by street fights, participated in chiefly by Jacobins on one side and Muscadins on the other. These brawls resulted in the closing of the Jacobin Club by a decree of the Convention. The trial of Carrier caused great public emotion. On the stand Carrier put up a brilliant defense. "When I acted," he said, "the air still seemed to resound with the patriotic songs of twenty thousand martyrs, who had cried *Vive la République* in the midst of their torture. How could the voice of humanity, which had died in this terrible crisis, be heard? I saved the Republic at Nantes; my life has been devoted to my country; and I am ready to die for it." It was obviously a patriot and not a homicidal maniac who spoke. The sections of the poorer quarters of Paris were deeply moved. On the 1st Germinal (March 21, 1795) and the 12th Germinal (April 1, 1795) there were demonstrations. These were too late to save Carrier, but the trial of Billaud, Collot, Barère, and Vadier was already on. It was hoped that the reorganized Revolutionary Tribunal might take cognizance of public agitation on their behalf.

But it was more than a protest against the execution of patriots that called these *sans-culottes* sections forth. The people of Paris were once more hungry. The repeal of the Maximum Law had made it again difficult for them to get bread. Furthermore, the moderate majority of the Convention had appointed a Commission of Eleven to examine the Constitution of 1793 and the feasibility of putting it into immediate practice. Word had gone abroad that they were planning to draw up a new and more conservative document. At both the March and the April demonstrations, therefore, the slogan of the crowds, as they marched through the Tuileries, was "Bread and the Constitution of the Year I." The disorders were limited to noisy remonstrance, however. The Muscadins fought the demonstrators out before any serious harm was done. The only effect of these uprisings was to seal the fate of Billaud, Collot, Barère, and Vadier, who were ordered deported by a decree of the Convention. Only Billaud and Collot actually were sent to Cayenne; Vadier managed to escape; and Barère's case was reconsidered. A number of other Montagnards were arrested on a charge of having instigated the disorders. The sections of Paris were disarmed.

On May 20 (1st Prairial, Year III), another insurrection broke out. This time one of the members of the Convention, a deputy named Féraud who was mistaken for Fréron, was decapitated by some of the mob, and his head paraded on a pike before his colleagues. Boissy d'Anglas, one of the leaders of the Plain and sometimes suspected of royalism, who up to this time had taken only a minor part in the political affairs of France, sat in the chair. Very courageously he refused to permit the meeting to go on, despite the demand on the Left, as long as armed men remained in the house. The head of Féraud was threateningly placed before him; he is said to have bowed respectfully to it, and remained adamant. Only the timely arrival of armed Muscadins prevented more serious trouble. In reprisal, the Convention had more Jacobins arrested, put the Faubourg Antoine under martial law, and inside of two days made ten thousand arrests. Six Montagnards, who were accused of being accomplices in the insurrection of the 1st Prairial,

were arrested and tried, not by the Revolutionary Tribunal,
but by a military commission. They were condemned to
death. They all stabbed themselves, crying *Vive la République!* as they passed the knife from one to the other. Only
three of them died; the other three were guillotined. They
were referred to as "the last of the Montagnards." These
were but six of the seventy-six Montagnards who, since
the 9th Thermidor, had been either executed or imprisoned.
The Girondins, eighty of whom had recovered their seats in
the Convention, were once more supreme.

The Convention had at last learned how to protect itself.
Even now, however, it would probably not have succeeded
in doing so had it not been in accord with the spirit of a large
part, perhaps the majority, of the Paris populace, led by the
wealthy middle class. Finally, on June 12, 1795, the official
use of the word "revolutionary" was suppressed. Since
the 9th Thermidor there had been a veritable "white Terror," particularly in the departments where "Companies
of Jesus" and "Companies of the Sun" armed themselves
against the Jacobins and perpetrated atrocities that might
have shamed a Carrier. The Revolutionary Tribunal,
which had had to share with special military commissions
the honor of delivering sentence upon Jacobins and Montagnards, had alone ordered three hundred and twenty-six
deaths between July, 1794, and May, 1795. But on the last
day of that month, by the decree of the Convention, it
passed into limbo.

In the mean time, the Convention had been engaged in
negotiations that were to break up the coalition against
France. Victory still continued to smile upon French
standards. In December, 1794, Pichegru began to invade
Holland. Before long, he was master of Amsterdam. In
February, Charette, leader of the Vendéans, agreed to peace
at La Jaunaie, although it later developed that he could
not enforce the peace himself. In April, Prussia, fearful lest
Austria and Russia might conspire to divide what remained
of Poland between them and leave her out just as Austria
had been left out in 1793, negotiated peace with the French

Ambassador at Basel.   By this treaty, Prussia surrendered
to France all of her possessions on the left bank of the Rhine,
while France withdrew all her troops in Prussian territory
on the right bank.   In secret articles, Prussia was promised
eventual compensation for her territorial losses and France
agreed not to carry warfare into the countries of the Empire
north of a stipulated line of which the Main River was the
most conspicuous part.   The treaty was quite acceptable
to both sides; to France it offered peace with a formidable
foe and a strong claim to some of her conquests, while Prussia, who was to receive a promise of compensation for her
losses by a supplementary treaty in August, 1796, was free
to claim her share of the Third Partition of Poland and was
recognized as the paramount influence in the northern half
of the Holy Roman Empire by a powerful neighbor.   The
Third Partition of Poland soon occurred, after Kosciusko,
badly wounded upon the field of battle in defense of the
last shreds of his country, was made a prisoner, and his
followers were scattered.   When Russia, Prussia, and
Austria had each taken her share, there was nothing left of
Poland but a memory and a name.

Nor was the Treaty of Basel the only diplomatic success
for France.   In Holland, Pichegru's invasion was soon
followed by a revolution.   The Stadholder fled to England
and the Republic of the United Provinces was set up.   By
a treaty completed at The Hague on May 16, 1795, this
republic not only surrendered the Dutch Flanders to France
and promised to pay an indemnity of one hundred million flor-
ins, but also formed an offensive and defensive alliance with
France, pledging herself to support a contingent of twenty-
five thousand French soldiers and to put her own army and
navy under French commanders.   Thus was the amity of
the two republics assured.   Further fortunate events followed.   A huge expedition of émigrés financed by the
English and coöperating with the Vendéans, which landed
at Quiberon Bay in June, was captured in July, 1795.   The
death of the Dauphin in the Temple (of which, despite the
persistence of a number of pretenders to the title of Louis

FRANCE

in 1795

☐ The Old Provinces and the
    Modern Departments

▦ French Conquests by 1795
    Peace of Basel

SCALE OF MILES

0   25   50   75   100   125   150   175   200

Longitude 2°   West   0°   Longitude   2°   East   4°   from   6°   Greenwich

XVII, there can be little doubt) had removed a formidable obstacle to the way of peace with Bourbon Spain. Encouraged by the presence of French armies on Spanish soil, Spain withdrew from the war, surrendering only the Spanish part of San Domingo by the Treaty of Basel (June 22, 1795).   England still retained control of the seas.   The only naval victory for the French, if it was a victory, was "the glorious 1st of June" (1794), when an English fleet was prevented, at great loss to the French fleet, from capturing a huge convoy from America.   The victory was spiritual rather than real, for Barère, in reporting it, manufactured out of whole cloth the story of how the Vengeur, rather than surrender, had sunk with all colors flying and all hands defiant to the end.   The only truth in the story was that the Vengeur had been sunk, the sailors whom the British had not rescued crying *Vive la République!* as they went down, but it was a great moral victory.   Otherwise Britannia still ruled the waves, and the colonies of France (and now her Dutch ally) washed by those waves had passed under her empire.   The only means of offense France had against England was intrigue with Irish patriots that, as yet, had yielded no result save the removal of Wolf Tone to America.   English gold also kept Austria, Sardinia, tho Empire, and Portugal faithful to the Coalition.   But the effective alliance against France had now been reduced to only England, Austria, and Sardinia; and all of these were on the defensive.

While the Convention was thus engrossed in reaction and peace, it was also engaged in drawing up a new constitution for France.   In March, a Commission of Eleven, headed by Boissy d'Anglas, had been appointed to reconsider the Constitution of 1793.   The original intention of the Convention had been to draw up a series of organic laws that would fill in the outline of the government it provided.   The insurrections in April and May, precipitated by the demand for the Constitution of 1793, convinced the Commission that the Constitution was but "the organization of anarchy." Accordingly, they determined to present an altogether new project, and, with the approval of the Convention, drew up an instrument that once again concentrated all power in the hands of the middle class.

It began with the usual declaration of rights; and, in addition, freedom of worship and freedom of opinion were made the subject of several special articles in the text of the Constitution. But not a word was said therein about the rights of resistance to oppression and the right to subsistence that had been contained in the Constitution of 1793. Moreover, there was a declaration of the duties of the citizen, for which there had been some demand in 1789, but which had been omitted in both of the earlier constitutions. Conspicuous among these duties was the reminder that "it is upon the maintenance of property that . . . the whole social order rests," although, by article 373, it was expressly declared that the estates of émigrés were "irrevocably acquired for the profit of the Republic."

Citizenship was granted to Frenchmen of twenty-one only if they paid a direct land or personal property tax and were enrolled upon their cantonal civic register. Those who could not read, write, and follow a mechanical calling (including agriculture) might not register. No one, besides, might exercise the rights of citizenship unless he was enrolled in the Reserve National Guard; the Active National Guard, consisting of the regular army and navy, was to be made up of volunteers, except in cases of emergency. All citizens might vote in the primary or cantonal assemblies for electors. To be an elector, one had to be proprietor, usufructuary, or occupant of a habitation producing an income ranging from one hundred to two hundred days of labor (depending upon the size of the commune in which it was situated). The electors were to choose, among others, the national representatives, the departmental officials, the members of the Court of Cassation, and certain other magistrates. Even by these low property and literacy qualifications for voters, over a million adult males in France were deprived of the right to vote; and since only persons with certain landed properties might be electors, the number of Frenchmen excluded from that honor was considerably greater, even among the bourgeoisie, though, by this time, practically every man of means owned some land. The Legislative Body (*Corps Législatif*) was divided into two houses, the Council of Five Hundred and the Council of Ancients. The latter council was to consist of two hundred and fifty members. Only citizens who were thirty years old and before their election had lived ten consecutive years on French soil might sit in the Council of Five Hundred (though until 1799 twenty-five was to be considered a sufficient age). This council was to originate all legislation. The Council of Ancients was to be made up of only married or widowed men, at least forty years of age, who for fifteen years before their election had lived upon French soil. The chief privilege of this upper house was to veto the resolutions of the Five Hundred. If they accepted the proposals of the lower house, such proposals formally became laws. Only by decree of both houses might a legislator be brought to trial. The two houses together made up the *Corps Législatif;* on certain important occasions, such as this, they might meet as a single body. The legislature was a permanent institution and might be adjourned only for periods of its own determination.

The administrative power was vested in an Executive Directory of five members, chosen by the Ancients from a list of ten nominees per Director to be drawn up by the Five Hundred. Directors were to be forty years of age and were to be chosen only from among former ministers or deputies. The Directors appointed the ministers, ambassadors, generals, tax administrators, and certain other officers. They were empowered to declare war and to make treaties, but only with the consent and ratification of the Legislative Body. One Director was to withdraw every year and a new one to be elected, the order of retirement of the first four to be determined by lot. Each member was to preside over the Directory in rotation for a period of three months. Local government was once more divided into departments. cantons, and communes, with the corresponding administrators and assemblies, but by means of a commissioner appointed by the Directory, each department was made more thoroughly subject to the Central Government than by the Constitution of 1791.

Each department was to have its civil tribunal, with the right to hear appeals from the tribunals of adjacent departments, from three to six correctional courts, and a number of justices of the peace. The chief courts of the land were to be a Court of Cassation (which might, only if it found there had been some violation of the proper court procedure in the trial of a case on appeal, send it back to the proper court for retrial), and a High Court of Justice, chosen from among the members of the Court of Cassation to hear impeachments of Directors and Legislators. The Constitution further provided for a system of public instruction and a national system of finances. To guarantee freedom of trade, corporations and associations contrary to public law were forbidden.

The Constitution of the Year III was a longer document even than the Constitution of 1791. But actually it provided for little more than the fundamental laws adopted by the National Constituent Assembly. Except for the executive power, the bicameral legislature, the greater authority of that legislature in the making of the laws and of that executive power in departmental affairs, and the complete divorce of Church and State, the Constitution of 1795 was a repetition of the Constitution of 1791. The differences between the two documents that existed only further emphasized the power of the middle class. Even the Jacobins might not have gone back to the Constitution of 1793 if they had triumphed, but the Thermidorians deliberately turned from that document. If there were any serious debates on the Constitution of the Year III, they were on the question of whether even bourgeois natives who owned no landed property might safely be given the right of suffrage, since stocks and bonds were not always considered sufficient as hostages to fortune.

But the Constitution of 1795 did not prevail without a

critical struggle. Hardly had the discussion on the proposed constitution come to a close when a royalist outbreak took place in Normandy, and Charette again resorted to arms in the Vendée. The danger of a royalist reaction was by no means negligible. Large numbers of the population, some of them influential in the government itself, were known to favor a return of the monarchy, and more would probably reveal their true feelings as soon as pressure was removed. A royalist restoration would have spelled ruin for the members of the Convention. It was they who had voted for the death of Louis XVI and had created the Republic. In the eyes of the old aristocracy they were regicides and traitors. They must see to it, therefore, that the old aristocracy did not regain power. They must retain control of the new government just as they had had control of the old. In Fructidor of the Year III (August 22, 1795), therefore, they passed the famous "two-thirds decree": two thirds of the seven hundred and fifty members of the two houses in the coming *Corps Législatif* must have been members of the Convention! Immediately there was a general outcry against this high-handed procedure of the Convention. The two-thirds decree was submitted to a plebiscite, but, as it was not carefully distinguished from the Constitution itself, it received a majority vote, much smaller, however, than the Constitution itself received. In Paris it was defeated.

Led by the Section Lepelletier, the National Guard of the capital and several thousand civilians attacked the Convention on October 5 (13th Vendémiaire). But the Convention had taken the proper precautions for its protection. Barras was again put in command of the troops in Paris and called to his aid a young brigadier-general, then in disgrace and crossed off the army list for having been friendly with the Robespierre faction and having, more recently, refused as an artilleryman to take command of an infantry brigade ordered to the Vendée. This was the Corsican Napoleon Bonaparte (originally Buonaparte), still unknown except for his part in the recapture of Toulon from the English in

December, 1793. Having got possession of some artillery,
Bonaparte poured grapeshot into the advancing insurgents
until they broke and fled. Desultory fighting completed the
activities of the day. There had been four or five hundred
casualties, about equally divided on both sides. Despite
the great number involved in the uprising, Paris on the
whole had taken no part in it. The royalist cause had suffered tremendously by an unwise declaration made by Louis
XVIII from the Italian city of Verona, upon his assuming
the title of King after the death of Louis XVII. The Declaration of Verona boldly rejected all of the new liberties
and economic modifications, and threatened dire punishment for all revolutionaries. Many of the most stalwart
royalists reluctantly underwent a change of heart upon
learning of this reactionary stand. The Convention could
therefore afford to be lenient. Only two executions resulted
from the events of the 13th Vendémiaire, and the "patriots" as well as the National Guard were disarmed. Bonaparte soon became commander-in-chief of the Army of the
Interior.

The days of the Convention were fast drawing to a close.
On October 25, it passed a law that renewed the three hundred, more or less, bills that had been passed against the
émigrés and non-juring priests. On October 26, it met for
the last time. Its final measures were decrees to the effect
that there should be a general amnesty for all except deported priests, émigrés, and Vendémiairists; that the death
penalty be abolished on the day of the coming of the general
peace; that the name of the Place de la Révolution, where
the guillotine had stood, be changed to the Place de la
Concorde. Its last chapter makes much more pleasant
reading than the earlier ones. But whatever harsh judg-
ments must be pronounced against it, however bitterly some
of its work must be condemned, its acts were not alone
destructive. Several of the measures that were to form the
most glorious features of the Napoleonic era — the reorganization of the school system, religious toleration, the codification of the laws, the creation of a national financial system,

the formation of a well-trained and equipped army, the prefect system of local government — were inaugurated by the Convention. In addition, it had created the metric system of weights and measures, which has lasted, and a logical calendar, which has not. It completed the task of destroying feudalism and of freeing the slaves in the colonies. Amid the stress of war and terror, the Convention had not neglected the arts. Literature, music, painting, each had its great exponent. Some one has described the Revolution itself as "a lyrical drama, verse by Chénier, music by Gossec, setting by David." With Martini, Méhul, Grétry, and Chérubini to understudy for Gossec, music flourished upon the emotional atmosphere of the day. In 1793, the national school of music that to-day makes France a musical center was created; in 1795, it was given the name of Conservatoire de Musique. The theaters were constantly crowded, though actors and playwrights were frequently imprisoned for royalist sentiments. All art, sometimes because of artificial pressure, took on a revolutionary manner. That the Convention did not do more is attributable to the monopoly of its efforts by the civil war within and the foreign war without. Indeed, the greatest accomplishment of the Convention was neither its constructive nor its destructive enterprises. What made it great was its preventive measures — its armies, its committees, its deputies on mission, its Terror saved the Revolution. That the restoration of the Bourbons came only in 1814 and not in 1793 or 1795 was the glory of the Convention. Had the restoration come in 1793 or 1795, who can say that the Bourbons would have been as clement, as liberal, as yielding, as willing, in defiance of Bourbon tradition, to learn and forget, or the allies as sparing of French soil, as they were in 1814–15? And who can say that the message of the Revolution would ever have reached beyond the boundaries of France?

CHAPTER IV

THE DIRECTORY

IT was a badly organized and muddled body that met on October 26, 1795, as the "Electoral Assembly of France," made up of the members of the Convention who had been elected to the *Corps Législatif* of the new government. They did not number the stipulated "two thirds" or five hundred.[1] In fact, there were only 379 of them. Consequently they proceeded, as the "two-thirds law" required, to make good the deficit themselves. It is typical of the chaos in which the Directory began its régime that they elected 127 others instead of the requisite 121, and therefore there were 506 Conventionals in place of the legal 500. The new third, which should have numbered 250, contained only 235, making a total of 741 members in the *Corps Législatif* in lieu of the constitutional figure of 750. One Félix Hamon was put upon the roll and even appointed to committees. Almost two years afterwards, it was discovered that there never had been such a person. On October 27–28, from those who were forty years old and married, 243 instead of 250 members were chosen by lot to form the Council of Ancients. On October 28, the two bodies met separately, the Council of Ancients at the Tuileries, the Council of Five Hundred at the Manège.

Their first task was to choose the Directors. In a list of fifty nominees drawn up by the Five Hundred, there were forty-four totally unknown candidates for the position. In this way, the Council of Five Hundred actually determined who the Executive Directory were to be. Restricted to a choice of five out of six, the Ancients chose La Révellière-

[1] As the maritime possessions of France were in English hands, no elections could take place in Corsica and the Colonies. Hence the seventeen representatives of these districts in the Convention were decreed elected to the Corps Législatif. Thus, only 483 members of the Convention were to be elected to the latter body inside of France.

Lépaux, Le Tourneur, Reubell, Sieyès, and Barras — all of them regicides. Sieyès was too cautious to act as an executive in a government not of his own contrivance, and Carnot was chosen in his stead. The Directors, who were assigned the Luxembourg Palace as their official residence, on their first day (November 2, 1795) found it cold and unfurnished, and were obliged to hold their inaugural conference on rickety chairs over a three-legged table. The Convention had fixed by law the costumes that the various bodies were to wear, more with an eye toward the bizarre, it would seem, than the practical. The Director's official dress made him appear like a prosperous merchant dressed up for a party, and the Council of Five Hundred looked strikingly like twentieth-century moving-picture portraits of pioneer Kentuckians save for the bright colors of their costumes. Their first public appearance was thereafter dubbed the "Masquerade of the Luxembourg."

The problems that the Directory had inherited from the Convention were numerous and knotty. The Government was in a worse financial position than ever before. In January, 1796, the assignats were worth, in actual value, less than one per cent of their face value. There was a theoretical value of almost 40,000,000,000 livres of this worthless paper in circulation. Certain kinds of goods cost five hundred times as much as they had in 1789, or as they might yet be purchased for in gold. Moreover, the war was still being waged on several fronts, and civil war likewise threatened. The Vendée had again to be pacified. There were many inside of France, some in the very legislature, who were royalists, while there were others who wished a return to the days of the Convention, a new constitution like that of 1793. and even a new Terror. Of the people who clung to these Jacobin principles, perhaps the staunchest were some of the generals of the army.

Even if the Directory had been made up of capable men, it would have found it difficult to steer clear of the danger points. None of them, however, was particularly able, save Carnot, and he was a soldier rather than a politician.

Barras soon arrogated to himself the leadership of the Directory. Barras was not a very capable man. He was not even a particularly honest or patriotic man. He owed his reputation to the fact that on two occasions (9th Thermidor and 13th Vendémiaire) he had been in a position to save the Convention against attack. This was due to chance more than to any merit of his own. But his repute was none the less real. The other members of the Directory were second-rate men. La Révellière was deeply interested in the new religion, Theophilanthropy. Reubell had some small reputation as a diplomat, having taken part in the negotiations of the Treaty of The Hague. Le Tourneur had distinguished himself in naval affairs when a deputy on mission. Such men, acting under a constitution that greatly restricted their authority and that permitted no coöperation between the executive and the legislative authorities, were not likely to achieve startling successes.

Hardly had the Directory been inaugurated when it was faced by both royalist and Jacobin plots. General Pichegru had got in touch with the émigrés and on the last day of the year 1795 signed an armistice with the Austrians. He was immediately removed from his command and ordered to Sweden as ambassador, though he declined to go. While the suspicion against him was by no means confirmed, it is very probable that he would not have been dealt with as leniently two years previously. At about the same time, an active young Jacobin named Babeuf, editor of the popular newspaper *Le Tribun du Peuple*, organized meetings of persons with radical ideas in a building near the Panthéon. There had been considerable agitation for socialistic measures since 1789. Had not Rousseau, Mably, Morelly, and other eighteenth-century philosophers preached equality of property as well as of civil rights? Had not Robespierre proposed a Declaration of Rights that envisaged social equality? Had not Babeuf, designedly calling himself "Gracchus Babeuf," written tracts upon the *loi agraire* that had gained some notice under the earlier assemblies? He now organized the *Society of Equals.*

Many of its recruits were one-time Jacobins, who had resented the closing of their club. It met at an establishment near the Panthéon and became popularly known as the "Club of the Panthéonists." At their meetings and in their writings, Babeuf, Buonarotti, Darthé, and the other leaders of the Society advocated frankly communistic policies — a reduction of wealth to a basis of equality by the redistribution of surplus property. Despite the law that prevented the organization of corporations and societies, the Society of Equals gained adherents rapidly. It had about two thousand active members and probably seventeen thousand followers in all. Though Babeuf and the other leaders of the Equals were themselves middle-class intellectuals, many of the members were poor *sans-culottes* and working men.

Its strength grew until it became a menace to the kind of peace and order established by the Constitution of the Year III. In February, 1796, the Directory considered it advisable to order General Bonaparte of the Army of the Interior to close the Panthéon Club. The movement continued, nevertheless, and gained valuable converts. A group of former Conventionals, led by Lindet and Amar, joined forces with them. Drouet, the hero of Varennes, gave them an ally in the Council of Five Hundred. But in April, Babeuf's paper was suppressed, and on May 10, Babeuf and his principal followers were arrested. The "anarchists" then attacked the military post at Grenelle (September 10, 1796), in the hope that the garrison would fraternize with them. Perhaps governmental *agents-provocateurs* led them on in this foolhardy attempt. Several deaths resulted, and one hundred and thirty-two, who were severely dealt with later, were arrested. In the mean time, the trial of the Babeuvist leaders proceeded. Finally, after a year's delay, on May 27, 1797, Babeuf and Darthé were condemned to death, the rest of the group being acquitted or sentenced to deportation. Thus ended the last candid attempt to make of the French Revolution an essentially socialistic movement

But by the time that the trial of Babeuf came to a close, attention had already been called to other quarters. Hoche had defeated and killed Charette and, by a skillful combination of tact and severity, had succeeded in again restoring peace in the Vendée, Normandy, and Britanny. This glorious victory was soon thrown into the shadow by the brilliance of a new commander. In March, 1796, Bonaparte had been named general-in-chief of the Army of Italy. He found a large corps of soldiers, ragged and badly equipped. It did not take him long to decide to make war support war; otherwise his army would receive no pay or supplies and would lose its morale. Almost immediately, in accordance with a plan for the conquest of Austria, which he himself had outlined and the Directory had endorsed, he took the offensive at the same time that two other armies invaded Germany farther north. A few preliminary victories succeeded in separating Sardinia's army from the Austrian troops. On April 28, the Sardinians agreed to an armistice at Cherasco, giving to the French the right of passage through Sardinian territory. On May 15, 1796, the Sardinians signed a treaty of peace at Paris, by which they surrendered Nice and Savoy, which had long been incorporated in France, and agreed to pay an indemnity of three million livres. Bonaparte had, meanwhile, continued to press the Austrians, and by victories at Lodi and Borghetto, had forced them to shut themselves up in the fortified Quadrilateral centering upon Mantua. Bonaparte's triumphal entry into Milan was unopposed. The success of the French in Italy had induced the smaller Italian states to join forces with Austria against the invader. While besieging Mantua, Bonaparte sent smaller contingents to impose armistices with heavy indemnities upon Parma, Modena, and the Papal States. Naples was obliged to withdraw her contingent from the Austrian army, and Tuscany to drive out the English fleet that had been making its base at Leghorn. At the same time, at San Ildefonso (August 19, 1796), the Spanish Government formed an anti-British alliance with the Directory. This made it necessary

for the English to give up Corsica, which surrendered to an
expedition sent by Bonaparte in October, 1796; and for a
time the French were masters of the western Mediterranean. In Bologna, Ferrara, Modena (which drove out its
Duke), and Lombardy, Bonaparte set to work to reorganize the government upon a republican basis. Wherever
possible, the French commander made the recipients of
these political benefits pay for them not only in cash, but
in the finest of their works of art.

The Austrian Government soon sent expeditions to relieve
Mantua. In July, an overwhelming force under Wurmser
forced Bonaparte to raise the siege, but a battle at Castiglione was so disastrous to Wurmser that he had to retreat.
When he returned, he was again defeated at Bassano. A
third attempt, this time under the command of Alvinzi,
failed at Arcola. Here Bonaparte was almost killed. His
aide, a young officer named Muiron, stepped in front of him
to receive the death blow; and afterwards, at St. Helena,
Bonaparte wished to take the *incognito* of Muiron. The
fourth and last effort to raise the siege ended in another
French victory at Rivoli. Mantua capitulated on February
2, 1797.

While thus engaged in reducing one of the most strongly
fortified positions in the world, Bonaparte had undertaken
the first step in his empire-building. In October, 1796, he
created the Cispadane Republic out of a few of the small
states in Italy in the southern valley of the Po, including
Modena and some of the recently reorganized papal dominions. After the fall of Mantua, he obliged the Pope to accept the Treaty of Tolentino (February 19, 1797), by which
the Pope renounced Avignon, the Comté Venaissin (which
were already included in France), Bologna, Ferrara, Ro-
magna, and the fortified city of Ancona (which were already
included in the Cispadane Republic), and promised an
indemnity of 330,000,000 francs. Negotiations entered into
with Austria for the exchange of Madame Royale, as the
daughter of Louis XVI was called, who alone survived of
the victims of the Temple, had culminated in the return of

eight important French prisoners and the renewal of the war spirit in France. Sardinia, not entirely voluntarily, had also formed an alliance with the French Republic in April, 1797. Only Austria and England remained of the first coalition against France, which now had the support of Holland, Spain, Sardinia, and the Cispadane Republic.

These diplomatic successes were slightly offset, however, by the growing hostility of the United States of America, verging almost upon war, over the commercial rights of neutrals. The French had insisted that the alliance of 1778, formed at the moment that France had declared war against England during the War of the American Revolution, bound the United States to support France in her war against England. When Washington issued the Declaration of Neutrality in 1793, Frenchmen were bitterly disappointed, affecting to see in it the arbitrary act of an aristocratic government unsupported by the people. The high-handed policy of Genêt as French Minister to the United States, when he acted, in disregard of the wishes of the American Department of State, as a propagandist for the Revolution, had occasioned his recall upon the fall of the Girondins and the recall of Gouverneur Morris as Minister at Paris.

Genêt's successor, J. A. J. Fauchet, was more tactful. But ill-feeling remained. The naval war between England and France now began to make trouble for Yankee shippers. Each side, without sufficient marine power, endeavored to prevent neutral trade with the other. A series of British Orders in Council blockading the French coast were answered by the decree of October 31, 1796, prohibiting the sale, advertising, or importation of any product of English manufacture or commerce within the entire extent of the French Republic; a long list of common articles of trade, "whatever their origin," were designated as English and automatically excluded. The principle that "free ships" made "free goods" was thus completely ignored. Both countries captured and searched American merchant vessels for breaking blockades that existed only on paper. War by the United States with both countries seemed possible at one moment, but John Jay, sent to England by President Washington, had succeeded, in 1794, in drawing up with Grenville, British Secretary for Foreign Affairs, a treaty that settled, more or less satisfactorily, the outstanding difference between the two countries. The treaty was formally ratified by the Senate in July, 1795, but the pro-French Republicans in the House of Representatives blocked the appropriation of sufficient funds for its execution until April, 1796.

The decree of the Directory of October, 1796, coming after this point, made relations with France much more strained than ever before. A commission, sent by President Adams to negotiate with Talleyrand, French Minister of Foreign Affairs, was given to understand that, if they paid a huge sum to the French diplomats, their errand would be more likely to succeed. The practice of "diplomatic gifts" was not uncommon in eighteenth-century Europe, but when the request became known in America, through the famous X Y Z letters, it occasioned a huge scandal. The American Government began to fit out privateers and to order the capture of armed French merchant vessels. An actual declaration of war was not forthcoming from either side, but there were several encounters between ships of the two countries; and it was not until the Directory had passed out of existence as a government that its successor settled this problem.

In March, Bonaparte again renewed his offensive against Austria. Not even the defeat in Germany of Jourdan by the Archduke Charles, the subsequent retreat of Moreau, and the dispatch of the Archduke with a new army against Bonaparte could stay his seemingly invincible advance. By April, the Tyrol was in his hands; and while the Archduke Charles unsuccessfully tried to stop his progress, the Army of the Sambre-et-Meuse under Hoche marched through the Black Forest and the Army of the Rhine-et-Moselle laid siege to Frankfort. On April 18, the Emperor agreed to discuss the terms of an armistice at Leoben.

While the peace negotiations were proceeding, Bonaparte established himself at the palace at Mombello (or Montebello) near Milan. Here his wife and some of the Bonaparte family joined him. Mombello became a veritable court, and Bonaparte, partly for reasons of diplomacy and expediency, partly out of ambitious satisfaction, played the rôle of monarch. Unconstitutionally taking the treaty-making power into his own hands, as he had already done on several occasions, Bonaparte planned to oblige the Austrian Government to renounce Belgium (which had again been made an integral part of France on October 1, 1795), the left bank of the Rhine, and Lombardy.

But he was still a good distance from Vienna, and Austria was not so badly beaten that she would consent to losses without proper compensation. It was agreed at Leoben that the compensation would be at the expense of Venice. Finding a pretext in some disorders in the Republic of Venice, which he had himself aided in fomenting and in which some French were killed, Bonaparte sent an army into that city. While he was announcing that his men had come to protect the liberties of the ancient republic, its independence disappeared, never again to be regained. A short-lived democratic republic, under French protection, was put up in the place of the old oligarchy until the negotiations at Leoben might mature his plans. This was in May, 1797. Bonaparte performed a similar reorganization of the equally venerable Republic of Genoa, although there he saw fit to leave some vestiges of independence. On June 15, 1797, he created, out of the old city and its environs, the Ligurian Republic, bound by an alliance to France, and based upon institutions such as the Republic of France then boasted.

After prolonged negotiations, during which the young general showed diplomatic abilities as splendid as his military prowess, using threats, ruse, and even displays of anger as weapons, a peace was finally concluded. Austria, in return for her cessions of territory, received large parts of the former possessions of Venice. The Ionian Islands were re-

tained by the French, for Bonaparte already had his eyes
fixed upon the Orient, and a goodly share of the terra firma
was added to Lombardy and the short-lived Cispadane
Republic to form the Cisalpine Republic. It began to appear that Bonaparte, himself an Italian by birth, who had
spent much of his youth in dreaming of Corsican independence of France, and whose mother never learned to speak
French without an Italian accent, was planning to bring
about the unification of Italy. On October 17, 1797, these
terms of peace were ratified at Campo Formio. In secret
articles it was provided that German princes dispossessed
by the French occupation of the left bank of the Rhine
would receive compensation on the right. At whose expense
the compensation was to take place was more than vaguely
intimated by the acquisition of the ecclesiastical state of
Salzburg by Austria to indemnify her for the loss of Breisgau, which, in turn, was handed over to the Duke of Modena
to counterbalance his loss of his hereditary state. A congress of the German States was to be called at Rastatt to
consider such a redistribution. As a result of the Treaty of
Campo Formio, France now faced England alone.

While Bonaparte was engaged in planting the glory of the
Republic upon foreign soil, the Republic was only with difficulty maintaining itself at home. For a time, its chief
source of trouble was financial. For several months, the
worthlessness of republican paper currency had made it
necessary to conduct business upon a basis of gold and silver.
The Directory determined to recognize by decree a situation
that already was generally recognized by practice. On
February 4, 1797, the assignats, estimated at a face value of
39,999,945,428 livres, were repudiated. The financial dis-
turbance that such an act might have created was lessened
by the fact that it had long been foreseen. Only some poor
unfortunates who had no wealth except in paper and some
others who had been speculating upon its rise in value were
very greatly affected by its repudiation. The behavior of
the Directory with regard to the national debt was the
cause of greater dissatisfaction. The national debt, due to

the liquidation of feudalism and the expenditures of the war, had steadily increased. Despite the valiant efforts to reduce it by means of assignats, in 1797 it was about 2,500,-000,000 francs. The Government was unable to pay even the interest upon this debt. Finally, on September 25, 1797, the Legislature decreed that two thirds of the public debt would be paid in bonds (*bons*) which would be received (as the assignats originally had been) in payment for the public lands. Like the assignats, these bonds depreciated rapidly; within a year they were worth only three per cent of their face value. In 1801, when the Government of the Consulate under Bonaparte was to call them in, they were credited at about one twentieth of their nominal value. Thus almost two thirds of the national debt was repudiated. The one third that was not, the so-called "Consolidated Third," was no less worthless, since the Government could neither pay it nor the interest upon it.

One result of the unstable financial condition of the Directory period was its reflection in social behavior. A generation that lived in war, whose young men, alive to-day, might be dead to-morrow, whose money was always worth less to-day than it was yesterday, could not be expected to improve upon the somewhat easy standards that they had inherited from pre-revolutionary society. Ladies of the highest rank, like their predecessors of the *Ancien Régime*, conducted their amours just as freely but more openly than before. The wife of General Bonaparte nad been the widow of a guillotined marquis and the mistress of a Director; Bonaparte knew it, and did not care, though he was quite an unsophisticated lad at the time of his marriage. It was only after he was married and had himself followed the *mores* of his age in this respect that he began to be jealous of his wife's more recent lovers. Josephine was merely typical; she was no better and no worse than many of her neighbors. The "flapper" of the Directory ("*sans-chemises*" they were called) might have shocked even the twentieth century by her lack of costume; solemn English gentry were scandalized. Such, at least, was the manner of society in the city. In the country districts, though the young men were at the front, the ordinary course of daily life had not much changed. With the grant of religious tolerance by the new constitution, despite the unfriendly attitude of the Directors, there was a revival of the Catholic Church. Though sometimes the old houses of worship might not be used, new congregations arose, and regardless of the Republican Calendar, Sunday was once more a day of rest. Even where Catholicism was considered an anti-republican superstition, the new Theophilanthropism, fostered by La Révellière, made a number of converts, though its following was never very large. Freedom of behavior and devotion to God flourished side by side.

The high-handed policy of Bonaparte in negotiating the peace on his own authority had been very much resented by the Directory. But already they were too much in his debt to dare to protest too vehemently. His victories afforded the only relief from their otherwise unpopular régime. His levies in money and art treasures alone kept the penurious Government in a position to carry on its functions. The disgusted people gave up all hope that they had ever had in the Directory and had confidence now only in the dashing young general who had humbled the proud Hapsburgs.

During the time that he had been laying a foundation for his future greatness by his campaign in Italy and Austria, royalism had again begun to show its head at home. The law prohibited the formation of clubs or even the sitting of members of the Legislature of like political views in any one section of their respective chambers. But what was to prevent a member of the Five Hundred from entertaining guests at his home on the Rue de Clichy? And if these friends of his eventually came to be known as the Clichian Club, certainly the law was not violated. Some of the Clichians were royalists, and, as more and more émigrés and deported priests succeeded in making good their return to France, the royalists took heart. But the actual royalists in the Clichian Club and in the Councils were very few. The conservative party there, made up mostly of those who had never sat in the Convention, were Constitutionalists. They wished to return to a normal government as provided by the Constitution of 1795. Hence, they favored peace and the repeal of the law of October 25, 1795, by which the Convention had codified its several hundred decrees against the émigrés and the old Catholic priests. Public opinion was probably on their side throughout France, but the Two-Thirds Decree had given control of the Councils and the Government to the regicides and their supporters, who formed the Revolutionist Party, pledged to a continuation of the war and hatred of priests and émigrés. At Madame de Staël's salon, the Cercle Conventionnel, of whom Sieyès, Benjamin Constant, and Talleyrand were the leaders, the more moderate of the Revolutionists held forth.

In 1797, the first elections to the Legislative Body took place. Two hundred and sixteen of the old Conventionals retired and only eleven were reëlected. The Department of the Seine, which was practically Paris, returned Constitutionalists alone. Le Tourneur was chosen by lot to leave the Directory and his place was filled by the selection of Barthélemy. Barthélemy had been ambassador to Switzerland and had been instrumental in drawing up the two treaties of Basel; at heart, he was a royalist, and he had never sat in the regicide Convention.

The Directory, still controlled by Conventionals, and the Councils, now largely run by the conservative faction, soon were in bitter strife. One of the first acts of the new legislature was to permit each commune to determine its religion. The Directors were worried. Then there arose a dispute over the control of the ministers. Barras saw fit to order General Hoche to concentrate his troops in the neighborhood of Paris, but, as it was contrary to the Constitution, he did not dare to employ them. In the Councils, Pichegru, now a member of the Five Hundred, was in negotiation with Wickham, the English agent in Switzerland. The Directory learned of this through information that Bonaparte had acquired by the capture of one of their intermediaries. Since the army was whole-heartedly republican, the Directors appealed to its generals. One of the Council of Five Hundred had been unwise enough to attack Bonaparte on his Venetian policy. Bonaparte was at this time engaged in making peace with Austria at Leoben, but he sent one of his most reliable and dullest generals, the blustering Augereau, to handle the emergency. Acting on the orders of three of the Directors, Augereau took command of all the troops in Paris, surrounded the Tuileries on September 4, 1797 (18th Fructidor, Year V) and purged it of a number of its conservative members. Some of those that resisted were arrested; Pichegru was sent to Cayenne. Barthélemy, who refused to resign from the Directory, was made a prisoner, and Carnot, who had from the very first worked in sympathy with the Constitutionalists, had to take refuge in flight. The dominant Directors spread the story, which Pichegru's activities gave some semblance of truth, that they were acting thus arbitrarily in order to prevent a royalist *coup*. One hundred and forty deputies were deprived of their seats by this Fructidor *coup d'état*. Merlin de Douai, originator of the Law of Suspects, and François de Neufchâteau, who had been a member of the two preceding assemblies and until now had been Minister of the Interior — both of them safely regicide — were chosen to fill the vacancies in the Directory. The Government had been delivered from the danger of an anti-regicide reaction, and again the victory was largely due to Bonaparte.

The Treaty of Campo Formio had provided for a Congress of the German States at Rastatt, in order to take up the questions raised by that treaty with regard to the reapportionment of German lands. The Congress opened in December, 1797. It was hoped that it would end in a peace between France and the Empire, since Campo Formio had made peace only between France and Austria. Bonaparte had had himself appointed one of the French representatives at the Congress. Cobenzl represented Austria, and Hardenberg, Prussia. But Bonaparte stayed only long enough to ensure the ratification of the Treaty of Campo Formio, and then returned to France. While the Congress was in session, the Directory sent General Hatry to besiege Mainz, the only place now left to an imperial prince on the western bank of the Rhine, and on December 29, 1797, it fell.   The German princes were now willing to adhere to the terms of France and to yield their claims to the left bank.   But the negotiations dragged on.   Austria demanded all of the Papal States but Rome, as compensation for her losses on the left bank of the Rhine, and this France was unwilling to grant. Prussia, whose new king, Frederick William III, gave to Hardenberg the same confidence as had his predecessor, Frederick William II, who died while the conference was in session, was unwilling to accept French offers of an alliance, despite a secret mission of Sieyès to Berlin.   Even the promise of Hanover did not win her over.   At one time the Congress came near to breaking up over a brawl in Vienna, where General Bernadotte, the new French Ambassador, was attacked by an infuriated mob upon displaying the tricolor at his embassy.   But the Congress continued through numerous vicissitudes, until April, 1799, and ended in an attack upon the French representatives, in which two of them were killed and the third badly wounded.

Having convinced himself that the time for the reorganization of Germany was not yet, Bonaparte had returned to Paris on December 5, 1797.   Hoche had died, probably of tuberculosis, on September 19, 1797.   Bonaparte now took over the Army of England that Hoche had organized.   It did not require a long time for him to decide that an invasion of England was impossible.   Various methods of attack upon the seagirt kingdom had been tried and had failed.   It was hoped that an insurrection in Ireland might bring "perfidious Albion" to her knees.   Wolf Tone had returned from America to France and was in close touch with the Directory on this matter.   An uprising in Ireland broke out in May, 1796, and was speedily suppressed. Hoche had embarked with an army of sixteen thousand to bring the insurgents aid, but even the elements fought on England's side and he was obliged to return to France on

New Year's Day, 1797, without ever reaching English soil. In 1798, two smaller expeditions were sent by France to Ireland to support the rebellion, but they arrived too late and were captured after their arrival. Wolf Tone, who was with one of them, cheated the executioner by suicide. At the same time, the Directory planned a more extensive invasion of England. A widespread mutiny in the English navy at Nore was quelled just in time to prevent the junction of the Spanish, Dutch, and French fleets at Brest. The naval forces of the Spaniards were badly crippled by their defeat at St. Vincent at the hands of a smaller British squadron under Jervis, with Nelson second in command, in February, 1797. In the following October, the Dutch suffered a like fate at Camperdown, where Admiral Duncan earned his peerage. As long as inferior forces of England, despite the disaffection among her sailors, could thus control the straits, Bonaparte felt that some other means of attack must be employed.

The Directory did not want peace, though the English Government was willing to offer highly advantageous terms in 1797. Peace would mean a Constitutionalist victory at the polls. And what would they do with the army? Likewise, the Directory had good reason for wishing Bonaparte away from France. He was too popular to remain for any length of time in France without soon overshadowing them. Bonaparte himself was anxious to go away, because he was afraid that his popularity would wear off with inactivity. He confessed in his *Mémoires* that he had already been urged to place himself at the head of the Republic; so "he determined to set out for Egypt, but resolved to reappear if circumstances should arise to render his presence useful or necessary." It was not a mere fantasy that urged him to lead an expedition to the Orient. Romantic glamour, no doubt, it had. But there were more important practical considerations to be taken into account also. The overland route to India, upon which England was largely dependent for her commerce and wealth, was still very much in use. If Egypt could be captured from its Mameluke rulers and

their Turkish suzerains, he expected that Syria would soon
fall likewise, and the English would be obliged to use the
longer and more arduous route around Africa exclusively.
The engineers that he took with him would cut through the
Suez Isthmus, as it once had been cut through in the days
of the Pharaohs, and thereby enable France to compete on
more favorable conditions with the English for supremacy
in India. That the plan also involved the possibility of an
actual attack upon India is evidenced by the fact that the
Directory formed an alliance with Tippoo, Sultan of My-
sore, who was to wage war on the British in India while
Bonaparte kept them occupied in Egypt. Lord Wellesley,
the brother of Arthur Wellesley and Governor-General of
India, spoke with some anxiety at this time of "the French
state erected by M. Perron on the banks of the Jumna."
In any event, control of Egypt and Syria would mean control of the Mediterranean world. This would interfere with
English trade to such an extent that the commercial classes
of England would soon urge their Government to sue for
peace. If all other schemes miscarried, at least a large part
of the English fleet would have been diverted to the Mediterranean, making possible a quick return to France and a sudden swoop down upon the British Isles.

Bonaparte set sail from Toulon on May 28, 1798. Twice,
Nelson's fleet, which had recently arrived in the Mediterranean, barely missed overtaking him. As the French hove
into sight of Alexandria, having on the way captured the
Island of Malta from the Knights of Saint John, Nelson's
fleet, which had anticipated them at Alexandria and set out
again to search for them, disappeared over the horizon.
The French easily effected a landing on July 1, 1798, and on
the 21st the spectacular defeat of the Mamelukes in the
battle of the Pyramids, while, as Bonaparte announced to
his soldiers, forty centuries gazed down upon them, put
them in control of the country. The victory was short-
lived, however. For Nelson had returned. On August 1,
he engaged the French fleet, exposed in an unfortunate position in Aboukir Bay, and practically annihilated it. Only

three French ships made good their escape. Gloriously
successful though Bonaparte's army was, it was now virtually a prisoner, cut off from all hope of communication or
reënforcements from the home country. "Well," said
Bonaparte, "we must remain in these lands, and come forth
great, as did the ancients."

If he ever seriously entertained the ambition to conquer
Constantinople, and from it, as a base, to create a huge
empire, it was suggested to him by his curious position now
as both master and prisoner at the same time in Egypt.
Having skillfully won the confidence of the Mohammedans
in Egypt by pretending to be greatly impressed with their
cult and culture, and having suppressed a revolt in Cairo
that very nearly brought his adventure to a premature end,
he started upon his conquest of Syria. After the battle of
Aboukir Bay, the Porte had been induced to declare war
against France, and now, with the support of a British fleet
under Sir Sidney Smith (aided by a French officer, Picard
de Phélippeaux, who had sat on the same bench as Bonaparte at the École Militaire, where Bonaparte for a brief interval had studied upon leaving the military school at
Brienne), the Sultan undertook to defend his Syrian cities.
Gaza was easily captured by the French, but Jaffa fell only
after a stern resistance. At Acre the invaders were checked.
On March 19, Bonaparte settled down to besiege the city.
During all of April and May, he ineffectually wasted his
men, whom the plague had already attacked, against its
fortifications, which were reënforced by the guns of the
British fleet. On May 20, fearing that a Turkish army
would land behind him in Egypt, he reluctantly admitted
his failure and raised the siege. In the middle of June,
after a most inglorious retreat, in which some of the
wounded and sick had to be abandoned to take their own
lives or to fall into the hands of a merciless enemy, he ironically made a triumphal entry into Cairo. On July 25, he
fought his last battle in Egypt by destroying a Turkish
army that had landed at Aboukir, just as he had expected.

Meanwhile great things had been happening in Europe.

When Bonaparte set sail in May, 1798, from the harbor of Toulon, he had left a prosperous France, at peace with all its neighbors save England, surrounded by allies in Holland, which had been converted into the Batavian Republic, in Switzerland, which was now the Helvetic Republic, in the Papal States, which, the Pope having been driven out by a French army, had recently become the Roman Republic, as well as in Spain and the Cisalpine Republic. The King of Sardinia had been forced out of his possessions on the mainland, and Piedmont, as his continental lands were called, was now garrisoned by the French. Bonaparte had not been long in Egypt when the King of Naples was driven from his realm and it was reorganized as the Parthenopæan Republic (January, 1799).

But in August, 1799, when Sir Sidney Smith, whether out of kindness or malice, sent him a packet of the latest newspapers, after they had discussed the exchange of prisoners, Bonaparte, who had been deprived of news from Europe since the battle of Aboukir Bay, learned that the face of things had now been very much altered. England had busied herself with renewing the coalition against France. Russia, first approached by Francis II of Austria, had readily joined. Paul, the son of Catherine the Great, accepted an English promise of subsidy the more eagerly because the attack upon the Knights of Saint John at Malta had offended him as Protector of their order; and furthermore, he feared the French aggressions in the eastern Mediterranean. Austria, irked by the rankling humiliation of Campo Formio, fearful of continued French aggression in Italy, and unable to get the terms at the protracted Congress of Rastatt that she wished, lent a willing ear. And the attacks upon Egypt and Syria had so overbalanced the inveterate hatred of the Turks for the Russians that the Sultan likewise decided to join the common cause. Shortly after hostilities began again, Moreau was repulsed in Italy and forced to shut himself up in Genoa by the Russians and Austrians under a capable Russian general named Suvaroff. Joubert was killed in the battle of Novi. The

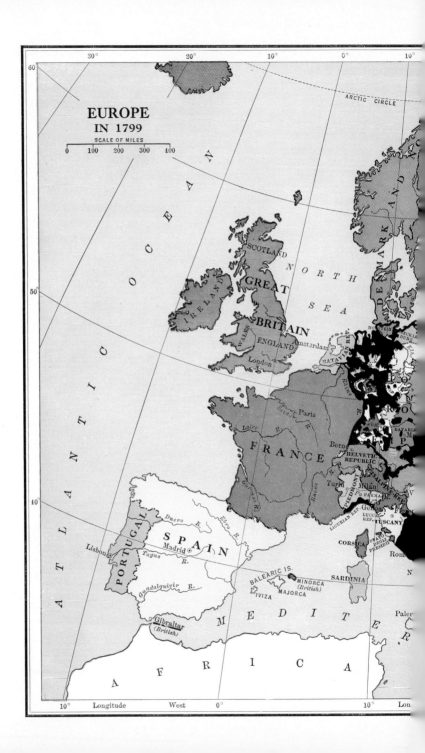

EUROPE
IN 1799

SCALE OF MILES

0   100   200   300   400

ATLANTIC OCEAN

NORTH SEA

SCOTLAND

GREAT BRITAIN

IRELAND

WALES

ENGLAND

London

Amsterdam

BATAVIAN

Paris

Loire

Berne

HELVETIC REPUBLIC

FRANCE

Turin

Milan

PIEDMONT

PARMA

LIGURIAN REP.

Genoa

LUCCA REP.

TUSCANY

CORSICA

SARDINIA

PORTUGAL

Lisbon

Duero R.

Ebro R.

SPAIN

Madrid

Tagus R.

Guadalquivir R.

BALEARIC IS.

MINORCA (British)

MAJORCA

IVIZA

Gibraltar (British)

MEDITERRANEAN

AFRICA

DENMARK

HOLSTEIN

MECKLENBURG

BAVARIA

Rome

Palermo

ARCTIC CIRCLE

Longitude   West

20°   30°   40°   50°   60°

White Sea

Gulf of Bothnia

Lake Onega

Lake Ladoga

St. Petersburg

Stockholm

L. Peipus

BALTIC SEA

Dwina R.

Moscow

R U S S I A

Niemen R.

Volga R.

P. RUSSIA

Vistula R.

Warsaw

Pripet R.

Don R.

Dnieper

AUSTRIA

Dniester

Vienna

Buda-Pest

Sea of Azof

R.

O T T O M A N

Pruth R.

Danube R.

BLACK SEA

Ragusa

Constantinople

SEA

E M P I R E

ÆGEAN SEA

RHODES

CRETE

CYPRUS

N   E A N   S E A

50°

40°

several Italian republics disappeared, as they had been created, overnight, and the old aristocracies returned in the train of the victorious allies. The Archduke Charles, who under another government and with better troops might have rivaled Bonaparte's reputation, had invaded Switzerland, while a combined English and Russian force landed in Holland.

The disasters thus wreaked on the front were mirrored by domestic confusion. The elections of 1798, since the Constitutionalists had learned by the events of the preceding Fructidor to stay away from the polls, had resulted in a Jacobin victory. Even before Bonaparte's departure for Egypt, the Directory, without even a pretense at constitutionality, had had the outgoing legislature, which it controlled, declare enough of the elections annulled to assure it a favorable majority in the Councils. This was the infamous *coup d'état* of the 22d Floréal, Year VI (May 11, 1798). The elections of 1799 again went against the Government, but this time the Directors did not dare to take any action. Reubell retired and Sieyès was chosen to fill the annual vacancy in the Directory and remained in alliance with the opposition in the Councils. Taking advantage of his support, the Councils declared Treilhard, elected in 1798 as a result of the Floréal *coup*, to have been illegally chosen, and obliged La Révellière-Lépaux and Merlin de Douai to resign from the Directory. Three friends of Sieyès — Gohier, Roger Ducos, and General Moulin — were named in their places. Only Barras remained of the original five Directors. This Conciliar *coup d'état* of the 30th Prairial, Year VII (June 18, 1799), was followed by a reorganization of the Ministry in the interests of the friends of the Councils. Hitherto, the Directory, with the support of the army, had manipulated the Councils to their hearts' desire. It remained to be seen whether the Councils could now do as they pleased with the Directors. Sieyès appeared to be master in both bodies.

Such was the internal chaos and military catastrophe of which Bonaparte learned in August, 1799. It did not re-

quire much cogitation on his part to make him decide that
he was needed more in France than in Egypt.   Confiding
his intentions to several trusted men, he left his army behind him under the command of the gallant Kléber and, accompanied by only a few devoted officers and men, landed
at Fréjus on October 9, having on the way passed in the
dark an English frigate off the coast of Syracuse.   Had
Bonaparte deserted his army, as has so often been maintained?   The army undoubtedly had been left in good
hands, but its position, as Bonaparte later admitted he then
knew, was hopeless, and in 1801 it was obliged to surrender
to the British.   But did Bonaparte have any other choice?
Even if he had no ulterior motive, as a good patriot he must
have discerned that his continued presence in Egypt was
futile, whereas he was vitally needed in France.   Though he
could not have known it, since English control of the seas
prevented any communication with him, the Directory had
already ordered him to return.   The only lasting result of
the whole campaign, dramatic and heroic though it was,
was the added renown it brought to Bonaparte, whose
victories alone were chronicled and remembered in France,
and the discovery of the Rosetta Stone by the archæologists
accompanying his expedition, the inscriptions on which
made possible the deciphering of Egyptian hieroglyphics.
The endeavors of Tippoo Sultan to drive the English from
India led only to the conquest of his lands by Lord Wellesley.   In France, however, before Bonaparte made harbor
at Fréjus, the military crisis that had been his pretext for
coming had already passed.   On September 16, Masséna
had inflicted a decisive defeat upon the Archduke Charles
at Zurich and had saved the Helvetic Republic.   The
Anglo-Russian forces in Holland had been checked by
Brune; and the Allies had already begun to quarrel among
themselves over the spoils in Italy, Austria claiming territory that Russia was no more willing than France to
grant.

    The journey from Fréjus to Paris was a triumphal proces-
sion for the returning hero.   Master of propaganda as he

was, Bonaparte had taken care that the glorious details of the Egyptian campaign should be well known in France, and had managed to arrive at about the same time as the first tidings of his overwhelming victory at Aboukir over the Turks. He reached Paris on October 16. Sieyès was already conspiring to overthrow the Directory and was casting about for a general to aid him, for no conspiracy could be complete now without the tramp of boots and the clank of swords. Jourdan, Augereau, and Bernadotte were radicals and were themselves engaged in planning a Jacobin reaction. Moreau refused to meddle in politics and suggested Bonaparte. Sieyès would have preferred some one whom he could more easily have directed, but he had no choice. Bonaparte listened willingly to his project, but for the time being affected neutrality. He had had enough experience with the Directory's meddling and ineptitude to realize that no effectual government could be possible as long as the Constitution of the Year III remained in force, but he preferred not to commit himself until he felt himself on firmer ground. His neutrality was well rewarded when the Council of Five Hundred elected his brother Lucien as its president.[1] Perhaps Bonaparte would have preferred using the constitutional means of gaining control of the Directory, but as he was far younger than the age required of Directors (forty), he had to surrender that notion, if, indeed, he ever seriously entertained it. In November, Bonaparte had assured himself of the support of most of the generals and Sieyès had won over a large part of the Council of Ancients. With Lucien presiding over the Council of Five Hundred, everything seemed ripe for a *coup d'état.*

Taking advantage of the constant fear of a Jacobin uprising, on November 9 the Council of Ancients, in accordance with the powers vested in it by the Constitution, convoked the Legislature to meet the next day at Saint-Cloud, across the Seine River, and ordered General Bona-

[1] Lucien was born at Ajaccio in 1775. He was therefore under the constitutional age even to be a member of the Council of Five Hundred. Through his brother's influence, he had nevertheless been admitted on a technicality.

parte to take command of the troops in Paris in order to
carry out its decree and protect it against attack.   The
next step was the resignation of Sieyès and Ducos as Directors.   Barras was wheedled by threats and bribes to
hand in his, likewise, and the Directory ceased to function,
since the signatures of at least three Directors were necessary for the legality of any act.   Moulin and Gohier were
detained by Moreau at the Palace of the Luxembourg.   In
compliance with the decree of the preceding day, the two
Councils met at Saint-Cloud on November 10 (19th Brumaire).   The Council of Five Hundred did not prove as
docile as had been hoped and set up a cry of "Down with
Dictators!" and carried a motion to renew the oath to the
Constitution of the Year III.   Bonaparte thought it high
time to act.   He visited the Ancients first.   How about the
Constitution, he was asked, and answered:

> The Constitution?   You yourselves have rendered it of no
> account.   You violated it on the 18th Fructidor, you violated
> it on the 22d Floréal and on the 30th Prairial.   It is appealed to
> by all parties, and all parties have sinned against it.   It cannot
> afford safety to us, for no one respects it any more.   Let us find
> the means of assuring to every one the liberty to which he is
> entitled and which could not be guaranteed to him by the
> Constitution of the Directory.

Bonaparte's cards now were on the table, and they had
made an unfavorable impression.   His mere presence in
arms was a flagrant violation of the law.   He had worse
luck with the Five Hundred, where it had just been agreed
to take a new oath of allegiance to the constitution that he
had just attacked.   The deputies gathered around him and
jostled him.   According to some accounts, there were even
threats to kill him.   For a moment he lost either his nerve
or his consciousness, and fell into the arms of his grenadiers,
who led him away, followed by cries of "Outlaw him!"
His brother Lucien tried to save the situation by refusing
to put a motion of outlawry and addressing his colleagues
on his brother's behalf.   But he was unable to make himself heard above the din and was glad when some soldiers,

sent by his brother, arrived to escort him from the chamber. So far, the attempted conspiracy had been a failure. It looked as if the Councils would succeed in preserving the Constitution of the Year III and punishing the conspirators.

Everything now depended upon the use of force. Lucien seemed to grasp the situation better than Napoleon, who was in somewhat of a daze, or Sieyès, whose coach was near by ready for flight. He appealed to the troops. The Council of Five Hundred, he declared, was held in terror by representatives armed with daggers and inspired by the English Government. This had its effect. The soldiers hurrahed for Bonaparte, but still they did not move. Seizing a dagger and pointing it at his brother's breast, Lucien swore to kill him if ever he violated the liberties of the French. That proved more than the troops could resist. They followed General Murat into the hall, and the members of the Council of Five Hundred fled through the windows as the soldiers entered. Apparently a bit of *opéra-bouffe* had changed the course of history, though it would be rash to assert that, even if Bonaparte had failed on this occasion, the Directory would have maintained itself, and the dictatorship would not have come.

The Council of Ancients now proved more docile. It adjourned both chambers and appointed a provisional government of three consuls until a new constitution might be completed. In every way the forms of legality were observed as far as possible. A remnant of the Council of Five Hundred was assembled that evening in order to confirm these measures. Sieyès, Ducos, and Napoleon Bonaparte were named provisional consuls. A commission of twenty-five from each of the chambers was designated to coöperate with them in drawing up a new constitution. At first, the three provisional consuls had equal authority. But it was not long before Bonaparte arrogated to himself the supreme position. Ducos withdrew from active politics almost altogether, while Sieyès devoted himself to his favorite pastime of constitution-mongering. At the first meeting of the three Consuls, Sieyès is said to have asked, "Who shall preside?" and Ducos answered, "Don't you see that the General is in the chair?"

An ostensibly republican form of government was retained for several years more. By the Constitution of the Year VIII, which (we shall see) was completed before the year 1799 came to a close, Bonaparte was named First Consul with two innocuous assistants in the form of Second and Third Consuls. In 1802 he was to be made Consul for life, and in 1804 he was to become the Emperor Napoleon. Until that time the fiction of the Republic was officially maintained. Indeed, even after the Empire was created, it was for some time designated upon the coins as the *République française, Napoléon empereur*. But actually France had ceased to be republican, and, since the 19th Brumaire, was under the guidance of one man. "Gentlemen," Sieyès had said on the evening of the 20th Brumaire, "we have a master; he knows how to do everything, he is able to do everything, he is willing to do everything." [1] Sieyès' weakness for epigrams this time permitted him to be not only clever but profound. Bonaparte, who, in his own words, was the son and testamentary executor of the Revolution, had received his bequest. How much of it he was to squander, how much he was to save, how much he was to add, the next fifteen years were to tell.

[1] *Il sait tout, il peut tout, il veut tout.*

PART II
STABILIZATION AND REACTION

BOOK I

THE RISE OF NAPOLEON BONAPARTE

INTRODUCTION

THERE is an old story of a parvenu American millionaire who, to prove his interest in culture, ordered for his library everything that had ever been written upon Napoleon Bonaparte; soon his agent telegraphed him to ask what disposition was to be made of the thousands of volumes that had already been collected, as there was not room enough for the several thousand more that had been bought and were ready for delivery. The story may not be true, but it is not at all improbable, for there are many more than parvenu millionaires who are not aware that Napoleon Bonaparte is perhaps the most written-about individual in history. A French scholar named Davois has published a bibliography of Napoleon which alone comprises three volumes of ordinary size and a more complete one, by the German scholar Kircheisen, is in the process of publication. A larger one by the Italian scholar Lumbroso is likewise unfinished. Probably for no other human being has it been necessary to allot so much space to books about books about him.

Yet this is not strange. For the history of Napoleon from 1797 to 1815 is the most important part of the history of France, of Europe, at times even of a goodly portion of the non-European world. Never before had Europe been under the influence, direct or indirect, of one man so thoroughly as in the last decade of that period. It was inevitable, therefore, that Napoleon should receive a large share of the historian's supply of paper and ink.

It was equally inevitable that historians should quarrel over his grave. As long as Napoleon himself was his own historian — or, more accurately, his own press agent —

there could be no quarrels. Everything then was carefully portrayed by official bulletins in the manner best calculated to inspire the French people with unstinted admiration and enthusiasm for the Consul or Emperor. But when Napoleon fell and the Bourbons again controlled the press and the purse of France, the writers of the Restoration found him to have been always a deep-dyed scoundrel. About 1840 the submissive policy of Louis-Philippe in foreign affairs and his conservative policy in domestic affairs roused the martial and liberal spirits of the French and they turned once more to the Little Corporal. He had himself written his apologia at St. Helena; Béranger and Hugo had sung his glory in lyrical verses; his body had been pompously returned to the banks of the Seine to win a vicarious honor for the Bourgeois King; Thiers had begun his panegyric *History of the Consulate and the Empire*. Through the heavy veil that the intervening generation had drawn, the Napoleon of 1815 appeared to have been a paladin of liberty defending France and the Revolution against a conspiracy of enemy tyrants. It was a legend — the Napoleonic Legend — but it served to elect as President (1848) and then to elevate to imperial rank (1852) the nephew of the great Napoleon, himself barely known as the author of two harebrained Bonapartist escapades. But as Shaw points out in the fifth act of his *St. Joan*, the canonized must not be reincarnated if their legends are to remain respected. Despite all the hothouse cultivation of the Legend under the careful gardening of the Third Napoleon, it withered until it turned to dust at Sedan. The Legend has since had its Masson, Vandal, and Houssaye and the counter-Legend its Taine and Lanfrey — and more recently its Wells, Guedalla, and Guérard.

As is so often the case in questions where there are two extremes of opinion, neither the Legend nor the counter-Legend is true. Napoleon was neither angel nor devil, neither paladin nor villain. He was as much the product of heredity and environment (in which must be included the political circumstances of his time) as any one of us, and on the whole as little responsible for the things that happened to him or happened to others through him as any one of us. To condemn or to exalt would be equally superfluous. He was the tool of Destiny as much as he was the Man of Destiny. Whatever he did was dictated by no diabolical cunning or divine revelation, but by the needs of an occasion as interpreted by a mind that was more energetic, more capable, more comprehending than most, although frail and human. In other words, Napoleon did not create events; he was created by them. If he is great in comparison with other men, it is only because a rather unusual mind in rather unusual circumstances is bound to produce rather unusual results, be they the committing of murder, the founding of a religion, the hitting of home-runs, or the conquering and ruling of an empire. The unusualness, the importance, the conspicuousness of what Napoleon did, measured by whatever norms of greatness there may be, are the best guarantees of his title to greatness.

CHAPTER 1

NAPOLEON BONAPARTE BECOMES MASTER
OF FRANCE

THE rocky island of Corsica lies in the Mediterranean in the northwest corner of what the Romans used to call the Tyr-rhenian Sea. It had at one time formed part of the Carthaginian Empire, later had been conquered by Rome, had then become one of the many island possessions of the Republic of Genoa, and finally in 1768 had passed into the hands of the King of France. Yet in spite of its checkered career, nothing had happened until that time to bring the little island into prominence. Its larger neighbors, Sardinia and Sicily, had each given its name to a kingdom, but Corsica, the home of a romantic race from whom later Mérimée was to derive his *Colomba*, had had to remain in obscurity.

But fate had reserved the period of its French dependence for its crowning achievement. On August 15, 1769, the second son of Carlo Buonaparte and Maria-Laetitia Ramolino was born at Ajaccio, the metropolis of Corsica, and was christened Napoleon. Joseph was the name of Napoleon's older brother. There had been a son born before Joseph. He died in infancy, however. Upon his death, Joseph, whose name up to that time had been Napoleon, took his name, Joseph. When another son was born in 1769, he took the name that once had been Joseph's. It is very likely that, in confusing Joseph with Napoleon, because of this change of names, the difficulty about the date of the latter's birth has arisen. It is now quite certain that he was born in 1769 and not at some previous date, as some maintain who would begrudge the future Emperor of France even his claim to have been born at a time when Corsica was a French possession.

When but a boy of nine, Napoleon was sent to a military

school at Brienne in France, where he was destitute and unhappy a large part of the time among a strange people, but where he first learned to exercise a military genius that has never been equaled or surpassed. After graduating at Brienne in 1784, he spent a brief interval at the École Militaire at Paris, and in 1785 was commissioned a sub-lieutenant of artillery in the French army. He was then only a lad of sixteen. There is still extant a comment that he made in his notebook at about this time: *St. Helena, a little island.* Little islands were to play a great part in the life of this big man, who was born on Corsica and died on St. Helena, after spending a brief interval of exile on Elba.

Barrack life in a time of peace was not strenuous and the young lieutenant found plenty of leisure in which to absorb the writings of the eighteenth-century philosophers — particularly Rousseau and Raynal. He tried his own hand at the fashionable pastime of philosophizing, writing essays and novelettes, and lovingly planning an elaborate history of his native island. But the French Revolution broke out while he was in the midst of his literary endeavors and plunged him into the stream of revolutionary intrigue. His father, who had died while Napoleon was at school in France, had been a conspicuous Corsican patriot in the struggle for independence, first of Genoa, and then of France. The father's mantle now fell upon the shoulders of Napoleon's elder brother Joseph and himself. Securing a furlough in September, 1789, Bonaparte returned to Ajaccio. There he organized the National Guard with the intention of striking a decisive blow in the cause of Corsican independence. The presence of a French garrison, however, discouraged any open activity, and when the French National Assembly raised the island from the status of a conquered territory to that of a department of France and Pasquale Paoli, the Corsican national hero, became president of its Council of Administration, enthusiasm for independence died down and Lieutenant Bonaparte returned to France in February, 1791, to rejoin his regiment. The emigration of the nobility after the fall of the Bastille on July 14, 1789, had so depleted the higher ranks of the French army that not only was Bonaparte not asked to explain his behavior during his absence, but was, on July 1, 1791, promoted to a first lieutenancy. He has himself left us a colorful picture of his life in those hungry days:

> I found means of sending money to pay the board and lodging of my younger brother. Do you know how I managed it? It was by never setting foot inside a café or appearing in the social world; it was by eating dry bread and brushing my clothes myself so that they should remain the longer presentable. In order not to be conspicuous among my comrades I lived like a bear, always alone in my little room with my books — then my only friends. And those books! By what strict economies, practiced on actual necessities, did I purchase the enjoyments of possessing them! When, by dint of abstinence, I had at length amassed the sum of twelve livres, I turned my steps with the joy of a child toward the shop of a book seller who lived near the bishop's palace. I often went to visit his shelves with the sin of envy within me; I coveted long before my purse allowed of buying. Such were the joys and dissipations of my youth.

At this time he even tried to make money in an unsuccessful attempt to win one of the prizes offered by the numerous learned societies of France. In the mean while, also, he was acting as secretary of the Jacobin Club at Valence, where his regiment was stationed.

But again in September, 1791, he secured a leave of absence and with it an opportunity to reëngage in Corsican politics. He managed by means of his first *coup d'état* to detain by force an unfriendly commissioner of elections and thus succeeded in having himself chosen lieutenant-colonel of the volunteer battalion of Ajaccio. But his radical stand, particularly upon the relations of the Church with the State, won him a large number of enemies. Responsibility for an uprising during Easter Week of 1792 in the streets of Ajaccio was placed upon him and for a while there was danger of his being court-martialed. He decided to return to Paris, having lost not only his influence in Corsica, but also having had his name struck off the French army list for failure to report when his leave had expired.

There followed lean days worse than any he had ever had to endure before. This was the period when the sentiments of the people of France were fast turning anti-monarchical and when the threats of Austria and Prussia, who had just effected an anti-revolutionary coalition against France, led to the downfall of Louis XVI on August 10, 1792. Bonaparte witnessed the attack upon the Tuileries on that day and he later confessed that he was shocked at seeing civilians attacking men in uniform; he would gladly have defended the King had he been called upon to do so.

But the fall of the monarchy proved to be Bonaparte's good fortune. The new ministry pardoned his military offenses and made him a captain in his old regiment, and a third September — this time in 1792 — found him again in Ajaccio, where he had gone on the pretext of having to escort his sister Marianne home from her school in France. Bonaparte, despite Paoli's protests, again assumed control of the Corsican volunteers. But Paoli had by this time become opposed to the radical measures of the Convention and had refused to bear arms against the English, who had been his hosts in the time of his exile. A warrant was issued for his arrest, and though most of the people of Corsica rallied about their aged leader and though the older Bonaparte had been one of the staunchest friends of the Corsican Washington, Napoleon threw in his lot with the French Convention. He was declared an outlaw by a Corsican popular council, his home sacked and burned, and his mother and family forced to flee from the town. Bonaparte had tried to capture Ajaccio, but his plan failed, and in June, 1793, he was obliged to leave Corsica for France with his family. Thereafter he ceased to be a Corsican and devoted himself entirely to the cause of France and the fortunes of war.

His astonishing career as a French soldier began at Toulon. The disaffected population of that city had called in the English and Spanish squadron sailing outside the harbor to aid them against the army of the Convention. Bonaparte's capable work with the artillery won him the rank of colonel early in December, 1793. On December 17, he was able to capture the peninsula commanding the harbor of Toulon and force the Spanish and English to retire. The city fell to the dire vengeance of the besiegers on December 19. Only the moderation of the commanding general Dugommier and perhaps also of Colonel Bonaparte prevented Fréron, the representative of the Convention, from making the punishment meted out to the rebels worse than it actually was. Bonaparte, for his part in the siege of Toulon, received his second promotion and became a brigadier-general of artillery on December 22, 1793. In May, 1794, he was detailed to the Army of Italy.

While the siege of Toulon was on, Bonaparte had found time to write an account of an imaginary conversation of four travelers at an inn at Beaucaire, which he called *Le Souper de Beaucaire*, in which he presented the case of the Jacobins against the Brissotins. Through the influence of the younger Robespierre, whom Bonaparte had come to know during the operations before Toulon, the *Souper de Beaucaire* was published by the Convention. Bonaparte had thus become associated with the Jacobin and Robespierrist cause. When Robespierre fell in July, 1794, Bonaparte was deprived of his rank and imprisoned. But as nothing implicating him in Robespierre's "conspiracy" could be found, he was soon released and reassigned to the Army of Italy.

In the mean time, the rebellion in Corsica had advanced to the point where the islanders decided to place themselves under the protection of England. The Committee of Public Safety of the Convention determined to reconquer it and Bonaparte was appointed to take charge of the artillery in the army that was to subdue his once dearly beloved native land. Saliceti, representative of Corsica in the Convention and Bonaparte's patron on several former occasions, was to have charge of the expedition. The destruction of the fleet which was to have carried the troops to Corsica, however, forced the abandonment of the scheme and Bonaparte found himself again without a command. He received orders to join the Army of the West as an officer of infantry under General Hoche, who was only one year his senior. The infantry as a branch of service and Hoche as commanding officer did not appeal to the young artillery officer, and he proved reluctant to proceed as directed. He tarried at Paris as long as he dared, in the mean time trying to interest the war authorities in his scheme for the conquest of Italy. In September, 1795, he was again taken from the active list of officers for failure to join his regiment. Again he appeared to be a hopeless failure.

But the course of political events in Paris soon lifted him higher than he had dared to hope. The Convention, having drawn up a new constitution for France, and wishing to make sure of predominance in the new government therein provided, had passed its notorious "two-thirds decree." The result was the insurrection of the 13th Vendémiaire (October 5, 1795). And it was Bonaparte who, on the 13th Vendémiaire (October 5, 1795), broke up the attacking forces and saved the Convention.

What followed afterwards is all a part of the history of the first French Republic and has been narrated elsewhere.[1] If from October 5, 1795, until November 10, 1799, the French Government is somewhat lost sight of because of the concentration of public interest upon the activities of Napoleon Bonaparte, from November 10, 1799, onward, Napoleon Bonaparte is the French Government and the history of Napoleon Bonaparte becomes the history of France.

When Bonaparte became one of the three Consuls named by the decree of November 10, 1799 (19th Brumaire, Year VIII), France was in no immediate danger of invasion. Masséna had checked the Russians and Austrians at Zurich; Suvaroff had already begun to lead the disaffected Russians out of Switzerland; and Brune had stopped the Anglo-Russian advance upon Belgium. The losses to France since

[1] See above, pp. 283-304.

Bonaparte had left for Egypt had nevertheless been tremendous. He had had every right to ask the Directory on
the 18th Brumaire:

> What have you done with this France which I left so bril-
> liant? I left you peace, I find war. I left you victories, I find
> defeat. I left you the millions of Italy, I find laws of spoliation
> and misery.

Thanks to Masséna and Brune, France was for the moment safe. But for many a Frenchman of 1799 that was
not enough. Fired by two ambitions — the inveterate
desire for "natural boundaries" and the novel one of propagating liberty, equality, and fraternity — he wished to see
France in control of the neighboring states. Italy must be
reconquered; the Austrians must again be forced back not
only from there but also from Switzerland; a firmer hold
must be established upon Holland. Even for less aggressive imperialists the fear of the rejuvenation of the coalition under jealous England's guidance and the danger of a
Bourbon restoration through the increasing activity and
intrigues of the émigrés, the staunch adherence of Chouans
and Vendéans, and the sympathy (not always passive) of
troubled Catholics and clandestine royalists were reason
enough for a vigorous military policy.

For the moment, however, France stood on the defensive
until the provisional government of France might be converted into a permanent one. The decree of 19th Brumaire
had provided that each of the legislative councils (the
Council of Ancients and the Council of Five Hundred)
should appoint twenty-five of its members, who with the
coöperation of the Consuls were "to prepare the changes to
be brought about in the organic arrangements of the constitution." Sieyès saw in this provision another opportunity
for exercising his well-trained powers of constitution-mak-
ing, and proceeded to propose a fantastic scheme providing
for a Grand Elector with two Consuls, a Council of State, a
bicameral legislature, and a College of Conservators. For
the source of this fantasy he had transgressed the fashionable limits of the eighteenth-century philosophy to seek

inspiration in the seventeenth century and Spinoza. This elaborate machinery appealed to Bonaparte for reasons of his own, save that he feared that the Grand Elector might become the "fleshless shadow of a do-nothing king." Knowing that the office would undoubtedly be conferred upon him, he manipulated the constitutional committee in such a way that the Grand Elector became the First Consul, the other two Consuls having but a consultative capacity. Sieyès and Ducos, the other two Consuls, refusing to act in so inferior a position, were named the first members of the Conservative Senate (Bonaparte's version of Sieyès' proposed College of Conservators). Cambacérès and Lebrun were appointed Second and Third Consuls in their stead. On December 13, the Constitution of the Year VIII was ready for a referendum to the people. The executive power was vested in the three Consuls named in the document, chosen for ten years [1] and indefinitely reëligible. The First Consul was practically a dictator; articles 41 and 42 stated:

The First Consul promulgates the laws; he appoints and dismisses at will the members of the Council of State, the ministers, the ambassadors and other foreign agents of high rank, the officers of the army and the navy, the members of the local administrations, and the commissioners of the Government before the tribunals. He appoints all criminal and civil judges, other than the justices of the peace and the judges of cassation, without power to remove them.

In the other acts of the Government, the Second and Third Consuls have a consultative voice; they sign the register of these acts in order to attest their presence; and if they wish, they there record their opinions; after that the decision of the First Consul suffices.

The legislative power was placed in the hands of four assemblies: the Tribunate and the Corps Législatif, which together made up the Legislature, the Council of State and the Conservative Senate. The Council of State, under the direction of the Consuls, initiated bills and sent a committee to argue for them before the Legislature. The Tribunate,

[1] Lebrun was named for only five years.

consisting of one hundred members, debated the project and decided to stand for or against it. It then chose three of its members to present its point of view before the Corps Législatif. The Corps Législatif, a body of three hundred members, having heard the orators of the Government and the Tribunate, without debate and by secret ballot either enacted or rejected the bill. If either the Tribunate or the Government believed a law unconstitutional, they might refer it to the Conservative Senate for annulment or sustention. The Conservative Senate also performed an important function in the election of officers. The citizens of each commune chose one tenth of their number to form a "communal list." These in turn chose one tenth of their number to make up the "departmental list." One tenth of these finally were chosen to constitute the "national list" or "Notables of France." From these the Senate chose legislators, tribunes, Consuls, judges of cassation, and commissioners of accounts. The Senate also filled its own vacancies by coöptation from nominees proposed by the Corps Législatif, the Tribunate, and the First Consul respectively, and taken from the "Notables of France."

The system of judicial administration was practically that created by the Constitution of 1791 and retained in the later documents, save that now many of the chief judicial officers were appointed by the First Consul. Perhaps as a concession to Bonaparte's objections to *idéologues*, there was no Declaration of Rights, but in the division designated "General Provisions" there were granted inviolability of the home, freedom from arbitrary arrest, *habeas corpus*, and the right of petition. There was nothing said about freedom of opinion and several other rights that even the Constitution of the Year III had conceded. And yet this brief document of the Year VIII (it ran to only about eleven octavo pages in print) contained much of what there was in the earlier instruments and a few new devices besides. Like them, too, it declared the goods of the émigrés "irrevocably acquired for the profit of the Republic," though it did speak of the possibility of "indemnification by the Public Treasury." Finally, it provided for a referendum of "the present Constitution" to the French people.

It was not a very liberal constitution. Although every male twenty-one years of age, born in France or having lived there for ten consecutive years, was eligible to vote, once the lists of notables were drawn up, he could vote only every three years to fill vacancies in the lists or to remove therefrom the unfit. Power was concentrated in the hands of the First Consul. Since the Council of State was appointed and dismissed at will by him, it was hardly likely that any measure to which he objected would be proposed for enactment and, while there was no certain way of assuring the passage of all his proposals, the manner of choosing the Legislature and of permitting it to function was one eminently adapted to deprive it of the courage necessary to veto a bill that he was known to advocate. The only body that might claim authority independent of the First Consul was the Conservative Senate, the majority of whom had been chosen by Sieyès, Ducos, Cambacérès, and Lebrun and had themselves named the remainder of their number. They filled their own vacancies, selected important officials, and interpreted the Constitution. While not completely independent of the First Consul, for he was empowered to designate one of the three nominees for each of their vacancies, they were yet the body that formed the chief obstacle to complete control by the First Consul.

Disguised, however, by resounding titles and complicated machinery, the Constitution of the Year VIII seemed liberal enough. Even those who opposed Bonaparte — and they were not at this time very numerous — voted for it. Although the plebiscite was not completed until February 18, 1800, the early voting was so heavily in favor of the Constitution that on December 25, 1799, the new government was installed and the Legislature convoked for January 1, 1800. The dates were officially announced in the manner of the Revolutionary Calendar, but it was obvious that Bonaparte was seeking to associate the red-letter days of his régime with the holidays of the Christian Calendar.

When the vote on the Constitution was finally counted, it was found to have passed by 3,011,007 ayes against 1562 noes. "What is there in the Constitution?" one lady was overheard to ask another. "There is Bonaparte!" was the answer.

CHAPTER II

NAPOLEON BONAPARTE BECOMES MONARCH IN FRANCE

THE first step of the new government, taken upon the very day of its inauguration, was a bid for peace. Whether this action was forced upon an unwilling First Consul by a weary public, riven by eight years of incessant warfare, or the First Consul, anxious for the leisure necessary to stabilize his incipient régime, earnestly sought for peace in spite of the militant attitude of a large part of his people, is a moot point that it would be of no value to discuss, since, in any case, the bid for peace was made in full assurance that it would be bootless. It was addressed only to George III of England and Francis II of Austria. The Czar of Russia, disgusted by Austria's own aggression upon the Italian principalities, and magnanimously promised the evacuation of the Island of Malta by Bonaparte, who was unable to hold it any longer against the English, had already withdrawn from any active part in the Coalition to become a staunch admirer of the Consul for the remainder of his unhappy life.

The surrender of Malta did not actually take place until July, 1800, and peace between Russia and France was not formally concluded until October, 1801, when Alexander had already succeeded Paul as Czar. But as Bonaparte now began his peace offensive against the Coalition, he had no longer need to take Russia into consideration. The debate on Bonaparte's letter in the English Parliament was bitter, but in the end a negative reply was sent. England could not afford to make peace with any country in control of Belgium and the Rhine and with pretensions to the best ports of Italy. As the wags of London remarked, England had contracted one half of her national debt to get the Bourbons out of France and was contracting the other half to restore them. Austria's pride and her fears for her supremacy in Italy could be depended upon to ensure her support of England.

Peace on French terms, then, would have to be won by war. Moreau, the most capable general under Bonaparte, was put in command of an army for the invasion of Germany. Bonaparte himself took charge of the Army of Italy. He achieved the spectacular and difficult feat of crossing the Alps while the Saint Bernard Pass was still covered with snow, entered Milan unopposed on June 2, 1800, and reëstablished the Cisalpine Republic on June 3. Then followed a struggle with the Austrian General Melas for control of the road to Mantua. At Marengo (June 14) Melas decided to attack. Bonaparte, believing Melas' early maneuvers only a feint, dispatched eleven thousand men under Desaix, Monnier, and Lapoype in different directions to look for the main body of the Austrians. By eleven o'clock Bonaparte was hard-pressed; by three his entire army was in retreat. But in the mean time messengers had reached Desaix and he returned, arriving at Marengo at five. Immediately Bonaparte took the offensive again. At eight the French were in possession of Marengo. Both sides had lost heavily and among the French dead was the gallant Desaix, who had retrieved Bonaparte's error and turned defeat into victory.

Had Marengo resulted in a French defeat, Lebrun and others were prepared to overthrow Bonaparte. These men were not altogether sure that the Constitution of the Year VIII was best for France. Moreover, some of them — Sieyès, Barras, Fouché, Talleyrand, even his own brother Joseph — could not forgive Bonaparte, a new man, for having gained a supreme position, while they, some of them famous since 1789, had to be content as subordinates. Their plans were altogether vague; it was a wish rather than a conspiracy. Some of them were in touch with the "King of France," Louis XVIII. From Mitau, in Russia, he directed correspondence and intrigues with England, Prussia, Russia, the émigrés, and royalists inside of France. Dumouriez even conceived of bringing back Bonaparte's

old Army of Egypt to fight against the First Consul, who
had deserted them.   One reversal for Bonaparte was all
they asked; that would be enough to assure his overthrow
and the return of the Bourbons.

Marengo upset all these careful calculations.   Louis
XVIII was asked by his Russian hosts to leave Mitau, and
had to seek the hospitality of Prussia.   The English disbanded the Army of Condé, the émigré forces that up to
this time they had maintained.   Bernadotte proceeded
with increased vigor against the Vendéans, among whom
systematic war had given place to brigandage since February, 1800; and by May, 1802, it became possible to
abolish the Army of the West, that ever since 1793 had been
necessary to fight Vendéans and Chouans.   The Companies
of Jesus, bandits who paraded under the cross as monarchists and Catholics, were all that remained of the vast
royalist uprising that had been expected inside of France.
And by a decree of October 20, 1800, Bonaparte, unconstitutionally and illegally, but very cleverly, permitted certain classes of émigrés to return to France if they would
take an oath of allegiance to the Constitution.   Louis
XVIII rapidly lost about half his loyal subjects, who now
willingly came back to France as subjects of the usurper.
Marengo was not only the defeat of Austria by France; it
was also the conquest of Bourbonism by Bonapartism, now
for the first time firmly established in France.

The nine thousand casualties suffered by Melas at
Marengo convinced him of the advisability of a truce.   At
Alessandria on June 15 he agreed to withdraw to the Mincio
River, leaving Piedmont and Lombardy in the hands of the
French.   Negotiations were immediately begun for peace
but came to naught and hostilities were resumed in November.   On December 3, Moreau won the most important
battle of the war at Hohenlinden, inflicting about fifteen
thousand losses upon the enemy at the expense of only
about twelve hundred French.   The Austrians were so
hard-pressed that on December 25, 1800, they agreed to an
armistice in Germany.   In the mean time Bonaparte's

forces had driven them beyond the Mincio and continued to drive them back even after peace negotiations were again informally opened. Diplomatic transactions, begun on January 2, 1801, resulted in the Treaty of Lunéville on February 9. On the whole it confirmed the violated provisions of the Treaty of Campo Formio, giving France the Rhine as a boundary and Austria the control of Venetia. The Duke of Modena again received Austrian Breisgau as an indemnity for his surrender of his realm to the Cisalpine Republic; the Grand Duke of Tuscany got the Archbishopric of Salzburg; and it was again declared that the lay princes dispossessed by the French from the left bank of the Rhine were to receive compensation on the right. The precedent of the Archbishopric of Salzburg indicated only too well that this indemnification would be at the expense of the ecclesiastical states.

A treaty with Naples on March 29. 1801, practically put that country under French military occupation and restored peace to the Continent. Again, as in 1797, the landrat France faced only the water-rat England. France exulted. The pacification of the Continent had given her control not only of Belgium, but tacitly recognized her suzerainty over the Batavian, the Helvetic, the Cisalpine, and the Ligurian Republics — over what had formerly been Holland, Switzerland, Northern Italian Duchies, and Genoa. Though the dead Desaix and the living Moreau had won the two most significant battles of the war, Bonaparte was the focus of all the glory. France was satisfied; it wanted peace.

But would England listen to French proposals? Certainly not without pressure. So Bonaparte, not especially anxious to challenge English naval supremacy directly, busied himself with the neutral nations. At Mortefontaine on September 30, 1800, he had come to a friendly understanding with the United States, which was so incensed by the ineffectual endeavor of the French to prevent her trade with England as to be actually, though not officially, at war with France. France recognized the prin-

ciple that "free ships make free goods" and thereby was
able to pose as the champion of the freedom of the seas
against England's arrogant domination.   Taking advantage of his friendly understanding with Czar Paul, Bonaparte put forth his energies to try to make more effective a
league of armed neutrality of Russia, Sweden, Denmark
and Prussia that had been erected under the Czar's leadership for the protection of neutral commerce against England's high-handed policy upon the seas.   It was a means
of attack upon the Mistress of the Seas that had succeeded
well in the War of the American Revolution.   But now the
English adopted a more vigorous policy.   Admiral Nelson,
despite the scruples of his superior, Admiral Parker, attacked Copenhagen (April 2, 1801) and forced Denmark to
withdraw from the league.   Russia now lay open to the
English fleet, but to take the offensive against her was no
longer necessary, for Napoleon's friend, Czar Paul, had
been assassinated on March 24 with the secret complicity of
his successor Alexander; and the latter leaned toward an
alliance with England.   "The English failed to strike me
on the Third of Nivôse," [1] Napoleon said, ". . . but they
have not failed to strike me at St. Petersburg."   England
probably was not involved in the assassination of Paul, but
there was no doubt that it was glad at the new turn that
affairs had taken.   The Armed Neutrality of the North now
fell of its own accord.

But already the English had themselves taken steps to
bring about peace.   Pitt had fallen from power over a
matter of internal politics — the grant of political rights to
Irish Catholics — and Addington had succeeded him
(March 14, 1801).   Pitt had decided upon treating with
Bonaparte for peace even before his ministry was obliged to
resign; and Addington, who was more peacefully inclined,
continued his policy in that respect.   The disruption of the
League of the North came at about the same time as the

---

[1] The "Third of Nivôse" is a reference to a royalist attempt to assassinate
Bonaparte on December 24, 1800, which Bonaparte believed or pretended to
believe was due to English instigation.

army that Bonaparte had left behind him in Egypt in 1799 was obliged to take the defensive against a force of English and Turks sent over to drive it out. On August 30, 1801, the French Army of Egypt was obliged to surrender. The failure of the League of Neutrals and the disastrous fate of the Egyptian army convinced Bonaparte of the necessity for peace.

Negotiations that had been begun on March 21, 1801, dragged on for more than a year. Finally on March 25, 1802, the Treaty of Amiens was signed. It is much more important for what it left unsettled than for what it settled. England was allowed to keep Spanish Trinidad and Dutch Ceylon, but was obliged to restore to their original possessors the Cape of Good Hope, Malta, and the French colonies. The Republic of the Seven (Ionian) Islands was recognized; Portugal and Turkey were guaranteed their integrity; the House of Nassau was to be compensated for its losses in Holland. Nothing was said of Italy, the Rhine, and above all of Belgium, which was the chief bone of contention between the two countries. Even as the treaty was signed, threats of renewal of war were in the air. It was to prove nothing more than a short reprieve.

But there was great rejoicing on both sides of the Channel. For the first time since England had taken up arms in 1793, she was at peace; and France had been at war a year longer. In France the First Consul became more than ever the idol of his people. The Legislature cast about for some means of expressing the gratitude of the nation. On May 8, the suggestion was made that he be created Consul for life. The Senate, unwilling to go so far, chose him First Consul of the Republic for the ten years after the expiration of his first term. That was not enough for Bonaparte and his followers. Nothing short of a consulate for life would satisfy them. They conceived the idea of appealing from the Senate to the people.

On May 9, Bonaparte wrote to the Senate thanking it for the honor it had bestowed upon him and added: "You judge that I owe the people a new sacrifice. I will make it

if the will of the people commands what your vote authorizes." The Council of State, meeting on May 10, proposed
to hold a plebiscite on the question, "Shall Napoleon Bonaparte be Consul for life and shall he be empowered to name
his successor?" Bonaparte and his chief adviser Cambacérès believed this asked too much. The question as finally
submitted to the French electorate was simply, "Shall Napoleon Bonaparte be Consul for life?" The vote was
3,568,885 in favor of the question against 8374. Though
the total number of votes cast represented but a small part
of the adult male population, it was probably typical of the
attitude of France as a whole. The ayes were not alone due
to Bonaparte's blessedness as a peacemaker. He had won
the support of several classes of the hitherto persecuted by
his moderate policy toward the Church and the émigrés.
Nor does the figure 8374 measure the extent of the opposition against him. The die-hard Republicans had learned
not to make themselves heard. The first elections (March
27, 1802) of new members of the Legislature had resulted in
the Senate's removing many of the Jacobins in both houses
and choosing supporters of Bonaparte in their places.
Shortly afterwards a plot led by the liberal generals Bernadotte and Moreau was frustrated by effective espionage.
The homes of some of the most conspicuous women of the
country, such as Madame Helvétius and Madame de Staël
became centers of dissatisfied liberals who aired their grievances and did nothing. For the police, under the very
capable and very unscrupulous Fouché, were efficient and
the press carefully censored. On the whole, therefore, the
liberals had preferred to remain away from the polls. Even
so the number of negative votes was higher than in 1799.
But the neo-monarchists held the whip hand; only insignificant minorities opposed the new trend; a mere fiction now
distinguished the Consul for life from a king. While ap-
pearing reluctantly to yield to popular demands upon the
initiative of the Senate, Bonaparte had exceeded the Senate's wish for only a second decennial term. He now
schemed to make himself not only ruler for life, but also
hereditary ruler.

The plebiscite of 1802 should have entailed but one change in the Constitution of the Republic. But the occasion to operate upon it having once been offered, it was not to leave the surgeon's table without several major and more minor operations. By a Senatus Consultum of August 4, 1802, a long series of decrees was issued that practically formed a new constitution of the Year X. It changed the method of elections, abolishing the communal, departmental, and national lists of notables and substituting electoral colleges for them over which the First Consul had significant powers, including the right to appoint their presiding officers. It reorganized the Senate, making it necessary for that body, on the First Consul's "presentation," to choose forty new Senators and allowing the First Consul to appoint forty others at his pleasure. Thus the First Consul practically controlled eighty out of a possible one hundred and twenty seats in the Senate, or enough to give him a favorable majority in that body at any time. Bonaparte had now secured control of the only branch of the Government that had hitherto enjoyed an independent existence. Furthermore, there was erected a Privy Council, composed of appointees of the First Consul, vested with the privilege of initiating decrees of the Senate (Senatus Consulta). The Tribunate was reduced to fifty members chosen by the Senate and divided into five sections debating secretly. The entire legislative machinery was thus revised in the interests of more effective dictatorship. The boldest change of all, however, was the provision that the First Consul might in any manner he saw fit name his own successor. It was a prerogative that Bonaparte had not dared to ask of the people in his plebiscite, but which now he took through his control of the body that was supposed to conserve the Constitution. From 1802 onward the name Bonaparte was less frequently heard and the prænomen Napoleon came into regular usage. The question of the inheritance was to be a source of much intrigue and family squabbling. Bonaparte's brothers, particularly Joseph, the oldest, felt that they ought to be considered as

Napoleon's heirs. Josephine, Napoleon's wife, entertained hopes for her son Eugène, and later for her grandchildren by Hortense and Louis Bonaparte. Bonaparte himself could never be content until there should be an heir who would be his own son.

Great as had been the rejoicing of the people of France and England when peace was reëstablished, the entire period of the Life Consulate was but a preparation for the renewal of war. For Bonaparte war was a necessity. His chief claim to the affections of his people was his glory as a warrior. By making peace and by granting reforms, he might strengthen his hold, but, he felt, let him once lose a square foot of his conquests or rest overlong upon his military laurels and his position would become insecure. England, on the other hand, could not be blind to the fact that, while the ravages of the Revolution were being healed and France grew stronger under the administrative genius of Bonaparte, France's influence in foreign affairs likewise continued to grow. In Italy, Elba, Piedmont, and Parma were added to his possessions and the constitution of Genoa was reformed so as to allow Napoleon Bonaparte to name its Doge. In Switzerland the Valais, a district at the source of the Rhone hitherto subject to the Swiss cantons, was made autonomous with a constitution like that of France, and by the Act of Mediation (1803) Switzerland itself was given a more centralized government than it had ever had, allied with France and neutralized under French protection. The policy of the First Consul was ruthless and egocentric, but nevertheless — and not unwittingly — he had taken great strides in the direction of Swiss and Italian nationalism.

The most difficult and most important work of reorganization that Bonaparte had to undertake was in the Holy Roman Empire. There it was necessary to make order out of a chaos of over three hundred ecclesiastical and lay states — archbishoprics, bishoprics, kingdoms, duchies, counties, republics — some of them so small that knowing wits would say that a dog sitting on the hearthstone of the castle of one

principality would wag his tail in the capital of another.
Bonaparte had first come into contact with the German
problem during the negotiations of the Treaty of Campo
Formio.   Since it was too difficult to arrange a peace with
the Holy Roman Empire at the same time as peace with
Austria was concluded, it was decided to call a congress at
Rastatt for that purpose.   There for a short period Bonaparte had served as the First Plenipotentiary of the French
Republic.   But as the Gordian knot refused to be untied
and the time was not yet ripe for cutting it, Bonaparte
caused himself to be recalled.   He had already determined
that French interests lay in the secularization of ecclesiastical territories and in the attachment of the German princes
of the west to French rule.   His opportunity came in 1803,
when a German diet, meeting at Ratisbon in order to solve
the problems created by the transfer to non-German powers
of 150,000 square miles of Imperial territory containing
3,500,000 inhabitants, decided it was unequal to the task
and appealed for mediation to him and Alexander of Russia
as the rulers of the two powers most interested in Germany
and, by various treaties since Westphalia, most bound to
aid.   Paris became the center of the secular princes of the
Empire and of their envoys, who came to fawn upon Bonaparte, upon Talleyrand, his Minister of Foreign Affairs,
and upon Madame Talleyrand's poodle in order to win
indemnity for their own possessions and to purchase the
land of the Church.   A series of conventions and treaties
was drawn up by the French with German princes and
towns, and having received the assent of Russia, was reluctantly enacted by the Diet of the Holy Roman Empire
(March 24, 1803) and approved by the Emperor (April
27).   Almost the only evidence of dignity about the entire
procedure was the title given to the Diet's decision in "the
awful German language" — *Reichsdeputationshauptschluss.*
By it the number of German states was reduced to half.   Of
the numerous ecclesiastical states only three remained.   Of
the nine in the College of Electors, the highest body of the
Imperial Diet, two of the ecclesiastical electors had van-

ished and to the remaining seven had been added the rulers of Württemberg, Baden, and Hesse-Cassel. These three states, together with Prussia and Bavaria, had been strengthened far out of proportion to the losses they had suffered by French annexations on the left bank of the Rhine, for Bonaparte desired to lessen the dominance of Austria in Germany by erecting large rival states, and to render powerful the principalities that would therefore feel friendly toward him. It was a veritable German Revolution, but German unification advanced at the tremendous price of German independence. German princes began seriously to consider forming a league under the protection of France.

But whatever the motives that actuated Bonaparte, in Italy, Switzerland, and Germany his achievements spelled progress. It makes no difference that his interest in his neighbors' welfare was prompted by nothing more noble than the desire to have well-disciplined and therefore well-organized vassals; the results for the national development of Italy, Switzerland, and Germany were none the less tremendous. Wherever Napoleon Bonaparte went, the ideals of the French Revolution went with him, and if in France he was beginning to betray those ideals, outside of France even their betrayer was the incarnation of the modern spirit and the destroyer of medieval feudalism. Bonaparte was not a sport. The times demanded one like him. As early as 1794, Catherine of Russia had foreseen his coming: "If France emerges from all this . . . she will be as obedient as any lamb, but what she needs is a man of superior intellect, skillful, courageous, above all his contemporaries, and perhaps even his century." Bonaparte was, perhaps, not the only man who might have fulfilled these qualifications. It is conceivable that Moreau, Talleyrand, or even Fouché might have played the requisite rôle for France. What distinguishes Napoleon Bonaparte and sets him "above all his contemporaries, and perhaps even his century," is that he worked for the salvation not only of France but of a number of other countries as well. His tasks lay ready for him; there is nothing astonishing in his discovering them. What is astounding is that one man did, in a dozen or a score of matters, what in each case might have been the life work of a lesser light.

England, of course, did not sit by idly watching Bonaparte strengthen his hold upon Italy, Switzerland, and Germany, improving his alliances with Spain and Holland, and endeavoring (as we shall see) to build up a retinue of colonial settlements. English writers and artists poked fun at Bonaparte in pamphlets and cartoons that, being too much of a parvenu to allow to go unheeded, he answered in kind in the *Moniteur*. French royalists and émigrés found a haven in English homes. The English Government refused to grant exequaturs to French consular agents. Because French troops delayed in evacuating Naples, England refused to evacuate Egypt and Malta, and still held them even after Naples had been cleared of the French. On March 7, 1803, George III declared that, in view of the military preparations then going on, ostensibly for colonial enterprises, in France and Holland, the English military forces ought to be mobilized and organized. Parliament gave its immediate consent. On March 13, at a public reception Napoleon rudely cried aloud to Whitworth, the English Ambassador, "Malta must be evacuated or there will be war!" Negotiations were begun between the two countries for the evacuation of Malta that lasted without result for two months. England's final word was a demand for the occupation of the island for ten years. Whitworth left Paris on May 12, and the ship that took him to England brought the French Ambassador with it on its return voyage. On May 16, England forbade commerce with France and the Batavian Republic and on the 18th declared war. Two days later, Bonaparte announced the declaration of war to the assemblies and after another two-day interval France in her turn declared war. Bonaparte ordered the arrest of all British male subjects between the ages of eighteen and sixty — about ten thousand in all — that were to be found in France. These included a number of friendly observers who, as soon as peace had been signed, had flocked across the Channel to see how the new political experiments in France were progressing.

The immediate cause of the new war had been the dispute over the evacuation of Malta. But the cause of enmity lay deeper than a quarrel about one of those small islands that loom so large in Napoleon Bonaparte's career. England, it must be remembered, was far ahead of the rest of the world in industrial organization. The improvement during the eighteenth century in the manufacture of textiles, bringing in its train improvement in transportation, communication, mining, agriculture, and eventually spreading to every branch of industry, had gradually created an industrial revolution that now, at the beginning of the nineteenth century, had made England more than ever the workshop of the world. To the English nation of shopkeepers it was essential that the ports of Europe and the world at large should be kept open to English trade. If France were to be allowed to retain her control of Belgium, Italy Holland, Switzerland, Germany, and Spain, burdensome restrictions would be placed upon English commerce that these nations would never have laid if they were entirely independent. And furthermore, if Bonaparte were allowed to carry out his plans in peace, the time would not be far distant when America, India, and the thousands of islands in the South Seas would traffic with French rather than English merchants. Naturally, then, the Englishman began to hate this "Boney," as English cartoonists called him, who ruled his own people with an iron hand, ruthlessly suppressed the freedom of nations, and sought to dominate the whole world. If they withdrew from Malta at his bidding, would he not then take control of the island himself and abuse it as he had Switzerland and Germany? If only for the island's sake (to say nothing of its strategic position in the Mediterranean) the English must remain there.

And so, after fifteen months of peace, the two old enemies again faced each other for a twelve-year struggle that was to end in Elba and Waterloo. The English immediately proceeded to capture the few remnants of the French colonial empire that they had not already absorbed. St. Lucia fell on June 2; Tobago followed three days later. Bonaparte's first steps were to take Hanover, of which the King of England was the Elector, and to encourage the rash Robert Emmet in his brave but forlorn rebellion against England in the summer of 1803. The aid that Bonaparte had promised the United Irishmen was neither forthcoming nor even expected. Emmet's handful of followers were dispersed or captured and its leader hanged.

Bonaparte had promised Emmet that he would invade England in August, 1803. In the preceding June, elaborate preparations were begun that seemed to indicate that Bonaparte seriously intended to do so. He later maintained that he merely wished to bluff the English into a panic; and the memoirs of several people in a position to know give the same impression. But if it was a bluff, it was an extraordinarily good one. An army of one hundred and fifty thousand men was concentrated at Boulogne and trained to disembark from flatboats under fire. Medals were struck in commemoration of "the Descent upon England" and bearing the further legend, "Struck at London 1804." Elaborate plans were made for the coöperation of the French fleets with the army of invasion. But if the plan was ever seriously contemplated, it had to be abandoned when the formation of a third coalition against France demanded the devotion of all Bonaparte's attention to England's Continental allies and when Nelson annihilated the French and Spanish fleets at Trafalgar in 1805.

But before these events took place, the Consulate had come to an end and the erstwhile Italian Napoleone Buonaparte had become Napoleon I, Emperor of the French. It had long been obvious that such a change was in the wind. Ever since he had become Consul for life, Bonaparte had usurped the prerogatives of royalty. His head was to be found stamped upon coins. He held court at the Tuileries in the grand manner of the Bourbons. He used only his Christian name in official documents. It required, nevertheless, a stirring crisis before the fiction of the Republic could definitely be discarded. In August, 1803, Georges Cadoudal, leader of the Vendéans and accomplice in several previous plots against Bonaparte, came from England in a cutter attached to the English navy and provided with English money in order once more to conspire against the safety of the First Consul. He communicated with several influential royalists, among them Pichegru, and tried to effect a union with Moreau, who was known to be the leader of the liberal opposition. Moreau, although he committed the fatal error of meeting the conspirators, would not be involved in a royalist plot. The police, under the astute guidance of Fouché, soon discovered what was afoot by methods that would have put to shame the Third Section of a Russian Czar. Moreau, Pichegru, and Cadoudal were arrested within a month of each other· (February–March, 1804) together with more than forty less conspicuous offenders.

The most tragic case of all the conspirators was that of the Duc d'Enghien. The testimony of the witnesses at the trials implicated as the guiding genius of the entire plot an unnamed émigré prince. This was probably the Count of Artois, brother of the dead Louis XVI, but suspicion fell upon the Duc d'Enghien, who was then living at Ettenheim in Baden, not far from the French border. Caulaincourt, one of Bonaparte's most trusted diplomatic agents, was sent to the Margrave of Baden, not to apologize, but to announce what was about to happen. Then, without so much as a "by your leave," Bonaparte sent an expedition into Baden, made the Duke a prisoner and had him conveyed to Paris. After a hard journey of sixty-five consecutive hours, the young prince was hastily court-martialed. He had arrived at the fortress of Vincennes at 5.30 P.M. on March 20, at 2.30 the next morning he was shot before an open grave, leaving to his wife a ring and a lock of his hair that were never delivered. In explanation of his merciiessness, Napoleon afterwards wrote: "I caused the Duc d'Enghien to be arrested and judged because it was necessary for the safety, the interest, and the honor of the French people, when the Comte d'Artois, by his own confession, was supporting sixty assassins in Paris." The act was at the same time a reprisal, a warning, and an indication of the undying enmity between the sons of the Bourbons and the son of the Revolution.

The trial of the other conspirators in the mean time went on. Several of the accused were undoubtedly subjected to torture. Pichegru was found strangled in his cell on April 15, whether by his own hands or by the order of Bonaparte is unknown. Moreau's trial was a *cause célèbre*. Public opinion was with the hero of Hohenlinden. He had, after all, merely seen the conspirators only long enough to tell them he would not join with them. Crowds cheered, and even the soldiers on guard presented arms as their prisoner passed. Some suspected that Bonaparte was using Moreau's association with the plot merely to rid himself of a powerful rival for popular adulation. Indeed, it was only after Bonaparte had himself brought adverse pressure to bear against the defendant that he was finally found guilty. He was sentenced to two years' imprisonment, but was allowed by Bonaparte (who could be generous to a brave adversary when it was to his advantage so to be) to go into exile to New Jersey rather than undergo the humiliation of jail. Moreau, one of the last of the Jacobins, was soon to join the counter-revolutionary forces and to die in battle against his former comrades. Cadoudal and nineteen other conspirators were condemned to death, but upon the prayer of Josephine Bonaparte, eight of the latter were sent to prison instead.

For the first time since the beginning of his ascendancy was there any general feeling of revulsion against Bonaparte. Fouché, who certainly was not likely to err on the side of clemency, said that the execution of D'Enghien was "worse than a crime; it was an error." And Moreau was perhaps the only man who (though for that very reason it was desirable to get him out of the way) could win popular support despite Bonaparte's opposition. After the execution of the Duc d'Enghien, the stock market wavered and Bonaparte had to spend millions in order to stabilize it again. But if Bonaparte had sacrificed some of the affection of his people, he had not diminished their confidence in the advantages to be derived from his rule. Lucchesini, the Prussian Ambassador at Paris, saw this: "It is possible that he knows the French better than they know themselves; perhaps he has been taught by the example of Cardinal Richelieu, who ordered the execution of a Montmorency, that in France just those most daring political acts tend rather to secure than to shake the supreme power."

Lucchesini was right. Even while the trial of Moreau and the others was in process, intrigues, which even now are hidden in a veil of obscurity, were hatched with a view to making the rule of Bonaparte a hereditary empire. If assassins were to succeed in killing him then, the entire Bonaparte family would have to be wiped out in order to make room for a Bourbonist restoration, and the assassins, realizing this, would probably not be so eager to take his life. The argument of Bonaparte's henchmen was, therefore, that in order to save Bonaparte and France, in order to stabilize the advantages thus far secured, it was necessary to convert the Life Consulate into an empire. In that event, too, there would be no further room for the hope entertained by many, both within and without France, that Bonaparte was willing to play the part of a General Monk and escort the Bourbons back to their royal dais. It is even possible that Bonaparte tried to buy up the Bourbon claims by an offer of a huge yearly payment to the pretender, Louis XVIII. In any case, he warned Louis, shortly after Marengo, not to come back: "You will have to cross over one hundred thousand dead bodies. Sacrifice your interest to the safety and happiness of France."

On March 27, 1804, a week after the assassination of the Duc d'Enghien, the Senate delivered to Bonaparte a plea to perpetuate the new era which he had founded, "to calm and tranquillize all France by giving to it institutions which will cement the edifice which you have erected and which will

338 BONAPARTE BECOMES MONARCH IN FRANCE

continue to the children that which you have given to the
fathers." On April 25, the tribune Curée, chosen in advance by Bonaparte for the purpose, moved that Napoleon
Bonaparte be declared Emperor of the French. The motion
came up for discussion and vote on April 30, and only Lazare
Carnot, whose organization of the revolutionary armies between 1793 and 1797 and whose work as Minister of War
under Bonaparte until 1801 had been a tremendous factor
in Bonaparte's successes, dared to vote against abolishing
the fiction that separated the Consul for life who might
name his successor from the position of Emperor. Bonaparte himself set to work to draw up the new constitution
(of the Year XII) and it was adopted as a Senatus Consultum on May 18, 1804 (28 Floréal) with only three negative
votes and two abstentions.

By the Constitution of the Year XII, Napoleon Bonaparte, formerly First Consul of the Republic, became
Emperor of the French. The imperial dignity was made
hereditary in the direct male line in order of primogeniture.
Titles of nobility were given to members of the imperial
family and a list of "grand dignitaries of the Empire" provided for with specific duties to perform. The Senate was
reformed so as to consist solely of appointees and relatives
of the Emperor and with few powers except that of having
"strong presumptions that —— is arbitrarily detained" or
"strong presumptions that the liberty of the press has been
violated" or "the opinion that there is no need to promul-
gate" any law just brought before it by the Corps Législatif. In the last case, the Emperor had the privilege of
doing as he pleased, and there is a "strong presumption,"
since no other provisions were made, that he might do the
same in the other two cases. The Council of State, the
Corps Législatif, and the Tribunate were kept with all their
original innocuousness, but a new High Imperial Court,
empowered to take cognizance of treason, impeachments,
crimes of high officials, etc., was erected. The last article of
the proposed constitution called for a referendum upon the
question.

The people desire the inheritance of the imperial dignity in the direct, natural, legitimate and adoptive lineage of Napoleon Bonaparte, and in the direct, natural, and legitimate lineage of Joseph Bonaparte and of Louis Bonaparte, as is regulated by the organic Senatus Consultum of this day.

This was not a fair statement of the question. For the "imperial dignity" was taken for granted as an established fact, and all that the people were asked to vote upon was the manner of its inheritance. The results of the plebiscite were announced by the Senate on November 6, 1804. There were 3,572,329 affirmative and 2579 negative votes. But since everybody on the departmental lists of voters was counted whether he had gone to the polls or not and since silence was taken to be acquiescence, the vote was not a true index of the state of popular feeling. There had, for example, been no voting in the army and navy, but 450,-000 ayes were counted as having been cast by the armed forces of the nation.

Napoleon was now an Emperor. Georges Cadoudal, about to die, saluted him: "We have done more than we wished; we came to give France a king and we have given her an emperor." And so the Corsican adventurer, who was at one time thought to be a Monk and had himself for a time pretended to be a Washington, was found to be a Cæsar with a generous admixture of unadulterated Napoleon. And he had already begun to have visions of being a Charlemagne!

The time had passed when the republican institution of the plebiscite was sufficient to please Napoleon. He felt now that he must have a further hold upon his throne than the consent of those he governed. Charlemagne had been the anointed of God; Napoleon I must be no less divinely sanctioned. Otherwise there might be lacking in his new dignity something of the glory and splendor of emperors. Negotiations were immediately begun with the Pope. Pius VII, hoping that by making this new concession to the upstart Emperor, he might acquire increased privileges and even new possessions for the Church, consented to a religious coronation. He arrived in Paris in November, 1804.

But whatever expectations he had had that Napoleon would prove a compliant son of the Church were doomed to disappointment. With regard to his own personal affairs Napoleon would make only one concession. On the prayers of Josephine, he yielded to a religious celebration of the civil marriage they had contracted in 1796. Josephine, an attractive rather than beautiful woman of Creole stock, had then had a number of admirers, of whom Barras was said to have been the most favored. She was the widow of the General Beauharnais, by whom she had had two children, Eugène and Hortense. Napoleon had fallen in love with her shortly after he had saved the Convention in Vendémiaire, 1795; and when he became commander-in-chief of the Army of Italy, he asked her to marry him. She did not appear to care for him very much at this time, but nevertheless consented. She was not faithful to him during his campaigns in Italy nor even, despite her tearful promises upon his return to Paris in 1797, while he was in Egypt. For that matter, neither was Napoleon to her. But of recent years she had become greatly devoted to him, largely out of ambition for her two children, and her great fear now was that he would set her aside. She had rejoiced when her daughter Hortense, recently become the wife of Napoleon's younger brother Louis, had given birth to a son who was looked upon as the heir of Napoleon. Now she hoped by the performance of a marriage ceremony according to Catholic rites to make it impossible for Napoleon ever to divorce her. Though Cardinal Fesch, the Emperor's uncle, secretly performed such a ceremony for the imperial couple on December 1, 1804, the poor woman was eventually to find it of no avail.

The coronation of Napoleon took place on the next day in the Cathedral of Notre Dame. All of the new nobility were there with their most resplendent regalia. The Pope himself was to officiate. Napoleon kept His Holiness waiting until he was ready to appear. During the coronation, lest he seem to be beholden for his crown to any other, Napoleon himself seized the golden laurel and placed it upon his own head. The Pope had little to show for his pains other than the abandonment of the Revolutionary Calendar and the return to the Gregorian Calendar with its Saints' Days and Church holidays, and the promise that the clergy who still clung to the Civil Constitution would return to the papal fold. The greater prize undoubtedly was Napoleon's. He had gained formal recognition by the Church of his new title; no earthly power could easily challenge the validity of his claim now. The ruler of the Holy Roman Empire had recently taken also the title of Emperor of Austria, and in return for the recognition of his newer title granted Napoleon the recognition of his.

Francis II was more fearful when Bonaparte, believing that it was incongruous for the Emperor of the French also to be the President of the Cisalpine Republic, on May 26, 1805, had himself crowned in the Cathedral of Milan as King of Italy with the iron crown of Lombardy. It began to look as if Napoleon planned to control all of the Italian peninsula. Austria not only saw her influence in Italy waning, but now had reason to fear even for her hold upon Venetia; and when Pitt, recently returned to power in England, promised her subsidies if she would join forces against France, she declared war on July 7, 1805. Russia, outraged by the execution of the Duc d'Enghien, had already broken with France on account of Napoleon's intrigues in the Balkan peninsula, his occupation of Naples, and the consequent danger to Russian supremacy in Corfu, Malta, and the whole of the eastern Mediterranean. It was therefore a powerful coalition of England, Russia, and Austria that Napoleon now had to face. The foreign relations of the new Empire did not seem to augur a happy future. But Napoleon faced the coalition with a calm assurance that for a time was justified by the outcome.

CHAPTER III

THE CRYSTALLIZATION OF THE REVOLUTION

POLITICAL revolutions are hardly ever the work of the most advanced nations of the earth; they, on the whole, are too well satisfied to exert the energy that is necessary to overcome the native inertia with which mankind ordinarily views its circumstances. Nor are revolutions the work of the least advanced; they are generally too completely subdued and too much concerned with the more pressing and immediate problems of food and shelter to create the opportunity for revolt. Revolutions generally originate among the peoples who have fared neither too well nor too ill. And because they are not too badly off, revolutions generally begin with comparatively mild demands and measures. What causes excess is not so much the innate viciousness of revolutionists as a class, but the degree of opposition with which they have to contend. The greater the opposition to the early demands of the disaffected, the more radical these demands will become and the more violent their measures.

In the French Revolution, where foreign intervention formed an enormous share of the opposition, radicalism reached the point of fanaticism. French political appetite had never before been whetted upon a diet of democracy. Now it suddenly began to feed upon rich dishes of imported Rights of Man and French constitutional pastry. After ten years of such fare, Dr. Bonaparte, skillful political diagnostician, decided that the country was suffering from acute political indigestion. What was needed was a proper admixture of the old diet with the new. As the son of the Revolution, Bonaparte began to apply the treatment that as diagnostician he considered advisable. He proceeded to restore enough of the Ancient Régime and to cast off enough of the fantasies of the Revolution to stabilize and solidify what he regarded as the most desirable institutions in his bequest. Jacobins and royalists were to be equally disappointed.

Among his most important reforms were the efforts he made toward the unification of Italy, Germany, and Switzerland. These, like his other reforms, were not original with him. Dante and Machiavelli, Maximilian the Dreamer, and Ulrich Zwingli had fondly conceived of them centuries before he was born. But the Cisalpine Republic, the *Reichsdeputationshauptschluss*, the Act of Mediation were almost the first practical measures toward the realization of a hope for which they had merely sighed. And these were but the first steps toward making united states out of the congeries of Italian and German principalities and Swiss cantons that Napoleon himself undertook There were equally definite measures to follow, until, at the time he was to go in exile to Elba for a brief respite, there were to be one strong confederation in Switzerland, one strong confederation on the Rhine, and but two states, both under his sway, in Italy. Possibly, in Italy, there was some sentiment attached to Bonaparte's activity. But even there, and more so in Germany and Switzerland, it was a genius for organization that urged him onward. These states, as well-organized political units, were in themselves an end for the great organizer, but they were also, for the great soldier, better as military allies, because more effective politically.

The Congress of Vienna was to undo his work in Italy almost entirely, and in Germany in large part, though, since there were not as many international rivalries and claims of local aristocracies to take into consideration, they made arrangements for Switzerland even better than Napoleon's. But the nineteenth century was to witness the undoing of the Treaty of Vienna and the realization, to an even more radical degree, of the centralized effectiveness in Italy, Germany, and Switzerland that Napoleon Bonaparte had endeavored to create. *Risorgimento* and unification might have come without him; they were, perhaps, destined by those laws (if there are any such) that determine historical developments. If so, Bonaparte was, at least, one of the tools in the structure; if not, he was, at least, one of the architects.

If Bonaparte had fixed his gaze solely on Europe and its infinite problems, it would be possible to credit him with a record of almost unbroken, even if sometimes unfortunate successes as a reformer, as long as he remained a power. But he always looked for other worlds to conquer — in Asia, Africa, America; and there, invariably, he met with failure. Except for the purchase of the freedom of over two hundred prisoners by his youngest brother Jerome from the Algerian corsairs, which was celebrated as a great feat of arms throughout the Empire (1805), and for the acquisition of fifteen million dollars, to which he was hardly entitled, by the sale of Louisiana to the United States, his whole extra-European program was a failure. Nevertheless, it was inevitable that, while Bonaparte improved his hold on the Continent, he should also engage in an attempt to rebuild the glorious French colonial empire that had been dissipated by Louis XV and that Louis XVI had already tried to recreate. Colonel Sebastiani had been sent to the Orient to investigate the advisability of colonization in Tripoli, Egypt, and Syria. His report spoke of the ease with which the English forces in Egypt could be driven out and a French colony established. Published in the *Moniteur*, which on December 27, 1799, had become the sole official journal of the French Government, this report had the single result of rousing English apprehensions.

In other quarters Bonaparte's imperialistic schemes were no less unproductive. In order to promote agriculture and to win the support of the planters in the French West Indies, slavery, which had been formally, though not actually suppressed by the Convention, was reëstablished and the marriage of blacks and whites forbidden. Martinique still remained under English occupation despite the terms of the Treaty of Amiens. In Guadeloupe an uprising of negroes in 1801 was put down at the end of 1802 only after the complete devastation of the island. In San Domingo the negroes had found a remarkable leader in Pierre Domin-

ique Toussaint l'Ouverture, who not only established his
supremacy over the French portion of the island (what is
now Haiti), but also succeeded on October 27, 1801, in taking over the Spanish portion (what is now Santo Domingo)
and giving an effective government to the whole island.
Bonaparte determined to reëstablish French control over
the colony and dispatched there an expedition under his
brother-in-law, General Leclerc, husband of the very pretty
and very wayward Pauline. Leclerc, by a ruse, succeeded
in capturing Toussaint l'Ouverture (June 7, 1802), and sent
him to a French prison to die of consumption, less than a
year later. The negroes of the island continued to fight for
their freedom, however, and climate and disease fought on
their side. Of thirty-three thousand men put at Leclerc's
disposal, twenty-four thousand died and seven thousand
were in the hospitals. Leclerc himself succumbed on
November 2, 1802. His successor, Rochambeau, was
obliged to capitulate to Toussaint's successor, Dessalines
(November 19, 1803). In 1804, the colony declared its
independence. The entire expedition had been a humiliating and unsuccessful massacre. More than half of the
population of the island had perished. The remainder
swore a solemn oath of undying hatred of France.

The most successful colonial undertaking of Bonaparte
was in Louisiana. By the Treaty of San Ildefonso (October 1, 1800), Spain had surrendered this former French
possession to France in return for the establishment of a
Spanish princess and her husband upon the throne of the
Kingdom of Etruria. France took possession of the huge
extent of territory on March 21, 1801. It was not organized until September, 1802. General Victor became cap-
tain-General of Louisiana, but did not reach New Orleans
until March, 1803, and by August the entire territory had
been sold to the United States of America for fifteen million dollars. Bonaparte, constantly expectant of a new
war with England, was not sanguine of his ability to keep
the colony against the English navy. Rather than have it
fall into the hands of the enemy, he preferred to sell it for a

song to President Jefferson's Government, which was anxious to have control of the Mississippi River and to prevent the establishment of a vigorous European colony as its neighbor. Bonaparte's plans for colonization in the East Indies and in Algeria likewise miscarried. Of all of the schemes hatched by the brain of Napoleon Bonaparte, none proved to be a greater fiasco than his dream of a vast colonial empire.

But the greatest glory of Napoleon Bonaparte is that he consolidated the changes, begun in the Ancient Régime by the ablest ministers of Louis XV and Louis XVI, and too rapidly hastened onward by the Revolutionary Assemblies. The first important internal reform of the Consulate was a pat example of this process of grafting the old upon the new. One of the finest features of the Ancient Régime had been the centralization of the government. It had unfortunately been carried to a tyrannical extreme and therefore had been one of the first institutions to be amended by the Constituent Assembly of 1789–91. Instead of the old "Thirty Tyrants," as the royal intendants had been called, it created eighty-three (in 1804 there were one hundred and four) departmental governments with a goodly share of local administrative authority. Subsequent assemblies had permitted the departments to have a reasonable amount of autonomy, save during the rigorous régime of the Terror Government, when they had been put under the dictatorial sway of the representatives on mission.

Uniformity of administration throughout the various parts of a large nation may not be a virtue, but for a country at war centralization is certainly a desideratum. On February 17, 1800 (28 Pluviôse, Year VIII), a decree revising the form of government in France was issued. The departmental divisions were kept, but instead of leaving power to elective departmental councils with vague powers, each department was put in charge of a prefect with definite powers. who, while he had the aid of a council of prefecture and a general council, was alone responsible for its administration. In each cantonal district there was to be a sub-prefect and a district council, and in each municipality a mayor and a municipal council, and, in the larger cities, a commissioner of police. Prefects, sub-prefects, mayors, and members of the councils were to be appointed by the First Consul and the departmental budget fixed by the Government. France is still ruled by the same system of local government, the President (or rather the Premier), however, having taken the place of the First Consul. Thus a scheme of government devised by Richelieu, plus a geographical division fixed by the first Revolutionary Assembly, plus a few titles arbitrarily borrowed from ancient Rome, totaled a lasting Napoleonic reform.

Having revised the system of local government, Bonaparte had now to adapt the judicial hierarchy to it. This was done by a series of laws of which that of 27 Ventôse, Year VIII (March 18, 1800), was the most significant. A system of "courts of the first instance," courts of appeals, criminal courts, and a national Tribunal of Cassation was erected and most of the magistrates made appointees of the First Consul. Much more important was the codification of the laws of France. This was an enterprise that had been contemplated by the Constituent Assembly, which had indeed taken the first steps toward drawing up a code through a committee of which Adrien Duport, former parlementarian, had been the chairman. Under the Convention and the Directory, the inadequacy of this code had been realized, and Cambacérès had been engaged in an effort to revise it for some years before the Napoleonic régime. On August 12, 1800, a committee, headed by the eminent lawyer Tronchet, was appointed to draw up a Civil Code. Its report, printed on June 21, 1801, was examined and amended by other bodies. Napoleon and Cambacérès took important parts in the discussions. Enthusiastic eye-witnesses have left their impressions of the inexhaustible labor and astute understanding that the former applied to the task. The work was not completed until March 21, 1804, when the Civil Code was made law by the Corps Législatif. Here again was a union of the old and the new

France; much of the legal tradition and common law of the Ancient Régime had been welded together with revolutionary legislation to make the new Civil Code. The part of the Code that drew the strongest attack, and one for which Bonaparte was himself largely responsible, was its reactionary attitude toward the position of women. A wife was debarred from all control of her own property and in the family the father was lord and master. Perhaps with a view to ensuring his own succession, as well as to reduce the power of the Church, Bonaparte did not vigorously reënforce family ties in his Code. Divorce was permitted upon the mutual consent of both parties; heirs might be adopted by the head of the family; and in cases where dubiety existed regarding parentage, the matter was to be solved always so as best to protect the interests of the child.

Besides the Civil Code, there was a Code of Civil Procedure, which was begun in 1802 and put into operation in 1807; a Criminal Code, which was begun in 1801 and passed as law in 1808; a Penal Code, begun in 1808 as a complement of the Criminal Code and adopted in 1810; a Commercial Code begun in 1801 and completed in 1807. The Penal Code permitted confiscation of property, branding, cutting off the hands of parricides before execution, chaining with ball and chain, capital punishment for theft and brigandage, and in certain cases, for perjury and corruption. But it must be remembered that this was before the great humanitarian movement of the nineteenth century, when it was still regarded as the purpose of penal law to punish rather than to correct or to protect. No matter how primitive the Code may appear to twentieth-century minds, it was decidedly less barbarous than contemporary practices in England or any of the Continental countries. On the whole, it was probably, as Napoleon himself thought, the greatest achievement of his career. A modern historian, by no means a subscriber to the Napoleonic cult, has called it "a reasoned and harmonious body of statutes such as had not appeared since the days of Justinian." [1]

[1] J. Holland Rose: *Personality of Napoleon*, 139.

The Code Napoléon not only codified the Revolution; it is still in force in France, Belgium, Luxembourg, and Geneva; it has had obvious influence upon the codes and legislation of Italy, Switzerland, Roumania, Egypt, Canada, Louisiana, Bolivia, Haiti, and Japan. Until the advent of the German Empire, the Rhenish principalities of Germany that had come under the domination of Napoleon were guided by it. In Holland until recently it formed the established system of law. With the changes that a more advanced age has deemed it wise to make, it is still more general in its application than any other system of laws. Ironically enough, the same day that saw the enactment into law of the Civil Code, the most significant part of this great work of justice, had already seen the execution of the Duc d'Enghien.

The immediate cause of the Revolution had been the financial instability of the Government of the Bourbons. The Revolutionary Assemblies had done little to remedy this defect save to confiscate the territory of the Church and of the émigrés. They had then squandered most of the wealth thus acquired and the Directory had had to resort to forced loans. One of Bonaparte's first acts was to abolish the practice of forcing loans and to substitute instead a system of direct taxation. In this respect he had the direct taxes created by the National Constituent Assembly as a precedent to follow. His system of taxes met with more success, however, as there was a vigorous government behind it that not only put tax collectors to work, but punished malfeasance of finance officials and kept careful accounts. Bonaparte also tried to reduce the amount of paper money in circulation. He organized a special Council of Finance, which was the only body in which the ministers deliberated in common. To stabilize the national debt he established a sinking fund and a national bank — the Bank of France, which, unlike the earlier experiments of John Law under the Regent, and the Caisse d'Escompte of Turgot and Necker, is still functioning. At times he threw large sums of his own private fortune into the market to keep the

Bourse from breaking. For the first time in a century France was financially sound. This was almost entirely a Consular reform; in finances Bonaparte had inherited only confusion and chaos from the Ancient Régime and the Assemblies, except for four hundred million francs in unsold national domain which enabled him to do much more than he might have done if he had started empty-handed. But even here, some sort of beginnings had already been made before he appeared upon the scene.

Of this four hundred million francs, over a fourth was set aside to be devoted to the cause of public education. Except for military schools, education had been exclusively in the hands of the Church in the Old Régime. The Constitution of 1791, having destroyed the educational organization of the old Catholic Church, provided that there should be a system of public instruction. The machinery for such public instruction was not created by the Legislative Assembly. The Convention had drawn up a scheme of public instruction which it was unable to carry out beyond the creation of three or four professional schools of doubtful vigor. In 1802, provision was made for a national system of primary and secondary schools, *lycées*, and "special schools," or professional colleges, to be maintained at national expense. Sixty-four hundred students, most of them the children of soldiers, were to be supported by the Government.

The schools soon became seminaries of patriotism and shrines of Emperor-worship. Napoleon Bonaparte realized the value of propaganda as well as any man, and he made good use of the school system for that end. French school children pledged allegiance to their Emperor as regularly as, in more recent times and in other countries, they have pledged allegiances to their flags; and a disloyal teacher was not allowed to remain in the school system very long. Yet this school system merely took over the propagandist spirit of the Revolution. Its catechisms, exalting the Emperor, were merely translations of similar ones that had exalted the Republic. With all their weaknesses. they constitute the first public school system of Europe, and they formed in 1808 the nucleus of the University of France, then created, which to this day controls the French educational system.

The necessity of thus putting education completely in the hands of the State was more than ever urgent because Bonaparte had already permitted the Church to return to France. His attitude toward the émigrés and the Catholics had in it none of the bigotry of blind revolutionaries. Even while Provisional Consul, he had acquired the right to authorize the return to France under suitable surveillance of certain of the deported and had availed himself of that privilege. After becoming Decennial Consul, he offered religious peace and political amnesty to the rebels of the West if they would submit. Troops had to be used, but the leaders of the Vendéans and Chouans soon learned to fear the Consul's forces and accepted peace. Hundreds of them were made prisoners and executed. By February, 1800, the Vendéan rebellion, which had gone on intermittently since 1793, was definitely over. The Vendéans having been pacified, it was now necessary to seek the support of the royalists in France. On March 3, 1800, the list of émigrés was closed; only those who were already regarded as émigrés were to be subject to the disabilities imposed by the laws of emigration. This decree was tremendously reassuring to several thousand former nobles and relatives of émigrés still inside of France. The plot of the Rue Saint-Nicaise (December 24, 1800), in which a bomb aimed at Bonaparte struck a number of bystanders, caused a slight flutter of reaction, but the innocent Jacobins were made to bear the greater share of the persecution.

No sooner had the smoke of the infernal machine cleared away than France found itself again in the bosom of the Catholic Church. Napoleon, though a deist or perhaps even an agnostic himself, believed in religion for others. He once (June 10, 1801) had said to the Councilor of State Thibaudeau in words that, as nearly as Thibaudeau could remember them, at once explain both his motives and his intentions:

Last Sunday I was walking here alone when I heard the church bells of Ruel. I felt quite moved by the sound: so strong is the power of early association. I said to myself, "If such a man as I can be affected in this way, how deep must be the impression on simple believing souls?" What have your philosophers and *idéologues* to say to that? A nation must have a religion, and that religion must be under the control of the Government. At present fifty émigré bishops, pensioned by England, control the French clergy. Their influence must be destroyed, and nothing but the authority of the Pope can do that. He will deprive them of their sees and induce them to send in their resignations. We shall issue a declaration that the Catholic religion, being that of the majority of the French nation, must be recognized and organized. The First Consul will nominate fifty bishops, whom the Pope will institute. They will appoint the curés, and the State will give them all salaries. All alike shall take an oath of fidelity to the Government. Those who refuse to submit shall be banished, and those who preach against the Government shall be handed over to their ecclesiastical superiors for punishment. The Pope shall confirm the sale of Church property, and give his blessing to the Republic. We shall have "Salvam fac rem Gallicam" chanted at mass. A papal Bull is here: there are only a few expressions to be changed. People may call me a Papist if they like. I am nothing. I was a Mohammedan in Egypt: I shall be a Catholic in France for the sake of the people.

This is so complete a description of the Concordat of 1801 that it is likely that Thibaudeau, when he wrote these words, did more than simply recollect the statement of Napoleon; he probably had a copy of the document near at hand. Negotiations with the Pope had been begun shortly after the battle of Marengo. They dragged on until Easter Day, 1802, when the Concordat of 1801 was solemnly proclaimed at Notre Dame. The Concordat was very unpopular in France, for the Catholic Church, to many of the leading figures of the nation, was a reincarnation of the Old Régime. To allay the opposition, Bonaparte had presented to the Assemblies, together with the proposed Concordat, a series of Organic Articles, never approved by the Pope, which reaffirmed the old Gallican liberties and subordinated the Church completely to the State. Likewise, there were

attached thereto provisions for a similar public recognition
and support of the Protestant churches.   The three documents became law on 18 Germinal, Year X (April 8, 1802).
Bonaparte had won over a powerful enemy of the Revolution without endangering the religious freedom that the
Revolution had gained, and at the same time, had made
more difficult a return to the social order of the Ancient
Régime by securing the Pope's consent to the land confisca-
tions of the Revolutionary Assemblies.   The Concordat of
1801 formed the basis of the relationship of the French
Government and the Catholic Church until the Act of
Separation of 1905.   In 1807, seeking to win the support of
the Jews of Europe, Bonaparte called a meeting of the San-
hedrin of Rabbis, modeled closely upon the ancient Sanhe-
drin of Jerusalem.   It held its meetings in February and
March, endorsed a series of resolutions by which Napoleon
hoped to make more malleable subjects of the Jews, and
devised a scheme of local government for Jewish communities by Consistories that was sanctioned by a decree of
March 17, 1808.   The Jews of France and of the countries
on the borders of France were won over to the Napoleonic
cause then, and have since remained loyal to the Consistory
form of religious governance.

Bonaparte realized the important part that vanity plays
in a republic.   Since the time had not yet come for the
restoration of the nobility of the blood, he adopted the
course of creating a nobility of honor.   On May 19, 1802,
the Legion of Honor was created.   It was nothing more
than a handful of silver and a riband to stick in one's coat,
but it formed the basis of the new nobility.   Already the
celebrities of the Consular Court were attending classes in
etiquette taught by Madame Campan and other ladies of
the Bourbon household.   Bonaparte likewise revived the
old Academy under the name of the Institute of France on
the basis of a new foundation previously laid by the Convention.   Thus there was also established an aristocracy of
learning and letters.   Both organizations have long outlived their founder.

As the life Consulate merged into the Empire, Napoleon had made good his claim to be the heir of the Revolution. A return of feudalism no longer seemed possible. The old privileged orders had weakly assumed the positions assigned to them in society and politics. The cry for equality was almost completely satisfied. If there was a Legion of Honor, if some held exalted positions, both the Legion and the positions were open to all of talent. Bonaparte had translated political equality into *la carrière ouverte aux talents* (careers open to talent). For all, there was, at least, an equality of opportunity. To be sure, liberty was in great danger. Since 1800, on the grounds that the newspapers were instruments in the hands of the enemy, only thirteen newspapers had been allowed to exist in Paris and provision was made for strict censorship elsewhere. In certain cases, trial by jury had been abolished.

But if the liberty of the press and of the courts had been encroached upon, the Concordat granted liberty of worship, the new attitude toward émigrés granted liberty of movement, the new code and judicial reform granted liberty from arbitrary arrest. Too often those who personally offended the Emperor were to find these liberties altogether too theoretical. Madame de Staël, daughter of Necker and a writer of considerable reputation, was made the victim of a studied persecution on account of her leadership among the liberals and Bonaparte's personal dislike. Eventually she was exiled from France because of her quarrel with the Emperor. But most Frenchmen were indifferent to the hardships of Madame de Staël. Furthermore, mankind as a whole — and it is said to be especially true of Frenchmen — cares less about being free to do a certain thing than it does about being free to do that which some one else may do; in other words, it values equality more highly than it does liberty. Napoleon Bonaparte, in so far as he believed equality more important than liberty, was a disciple of Rousseau, even if he once did say, "It would have been better for the repose of France if that man had never existed."

Gladstone once maintained that Napoleon was the greatest administrator in history. Persons less qualified to judge than Gladstone have repeated this dictum. However questionable Napoleon's motive may have been, they detract, after all, not one iota from the importance of his reforms. It is more significant that some of his works — as, for example, the Concordat, the bureaucracy that he created, and some of the provisions of his Code — became the root of great difficulties afterward. But whether for good or evil, his influence upon France and upon the parts of Europe that came under French domination, even after only five years of his administration, was greater than any other man's had ever been. Until 1804 that influence had exerted itself largely for good — for France at least. Would the Empire continue that happy precedent?

CHAPTER IV

NAPOLEON BECOMES MASTER IN EUROPE

No man is as vicious as he can be painted. Certainly few famous men can conceivably have been as black as historians sometimes would have us believe — megalomaniacs devoid of all but selfish motives, impelled by the lust for power and blood, as all the great conquerors, at times, have been represented. True patriotism is rare, sincerity of conduct is rarer yet, and many since Diogenes have flashed their lanterns in vain; but no great man has submitted to self-scrutiny without some illusions of righteousness. Alexander, Cæsar, Napoleon probably thought themselves altogether justified, altogether admirable in following the courses that they took. The last two have told us so in their memoirs; the first might have if he had lived long enough. And who are we, asks Romain Rolland, who do not know our own friends, who do not know ourselves, who are we to judge the acts of those long dead? And yet, he adds, we have to judge, we have to act.

In judging Napoleon, the world's greatest conqueror, let us remember that he rode with a current which he did not create, but in which he knew well how to pilot. One group of historians has tried to reveal him to us as a scoundrel who attempted the impossible out of sheer malice and egotism. Napoleon, they say, was the conqueror personified; he occasionally granted reforms, but only to increase the efficiency of the nations behind him, to make for himself a greater and more effective man-power; conquest came first, reform was only incidental. It is possible, however, to argue differently — to maintain that conquest was forced upon Napoleon; that England, with the aid of her willing allies, would never have permitted him to build up a strong France that would have succeeded in rehabilitating French prestige in Europe and restoring the once glorious French colonial empire; that if he hoped ever to make France a great state, to realize the platonic ideal of philosopher-king, he had first to become the world-conqueror in order to overcome England. Certainly there is as much truth in this argument as in the other. Neither, however, is entirely true. Napoleon was no more the ruthless world-conqueror than the philosopher-king. He fell just short of being either, and the cause of his shortcoming in each case is England as much as himself.

Indeed, until the outbreak of the second war with England in 1803, Napoleon may be said to have come very close to the Greek ideal of the philosopher on the throne. He had established peace; he had brought about reforms; he had solidified many of the most desirable achievements of his revolutionary antecedents. If the period of peace was short-lived, the reforms continued even after the war broke out; and if the peace was soon broken, the fault was as much England's as Napoleon's. War was declared in May, 1803; actual hostilities on the Continent did not begin until the end of 1805. In the mean time, Napoleon, as he was later to admit, on at least one occasion, at St. Helena, was arduously preparing to invade England. And in the interval between the declaration of war and the outbreak of actual hostilities, there was as much aggressiveness on the part of the one government as the other. Napoleon formed alliances with the Dutch and the Spanish and had himself crowned Emperor (December 2, 1804); the English recalled the imperialistic Pitt to power and created the Third Coalition. France, with the ineffectual aid of Holland and Spain, found herself faced by England, supreme upon the seas, and a combination of Austria and Russia that might easily prove to be supreme upon the land.

The negotiations by which Pitt had been able to complete the Third Coalition, promoted as they were by Napoleon's aggressive policy in Italy, where he annexed the Ligurian Republic outright and had himself crowned King of Italy at Milan (May 26, 1805), had reached a successful conclusion by August, 1805. If Napoleon had ever previously considered it advisable to invade England and to force the proud nation of shopkeepers to her knees by the application of crude force to her most sensitive spots instead of by the more subtle methods that had hitherto been used — even if, as is likely, he still regarded the invasion of England as the master stroke of his policy as soon as it might become feasible, certainly he could no longer regard it as possible for the moment. With Austria and Russia ready to spring upon a defenseless France as soon as the Army of England should have left her shores, it required much less than the military insight of Napoleon to decide upon a temporary abandonment of the expedition to England and a quick thrust against her Continental allies. The Army of England suddenly became the Army of the Continent; between August and September, 1805, it marched from Boulogne to Bavaria. It was joined at Strassburg by Napoleon on September 27.

In Bavaria the Austrian General Mack had concentrated an army of about thirty thousand men. This army Napoleon determined to capture. By a series of brilliant feints, he succeeded in surrounding Ulm and cutting off the bulk of Mack's army from its base of supplies and reënforcements. The Archduke Ferdinand was able to extricate a few thousand men, but Mack persisted in the groundless illusion that the French were in retreat, and did nothing. On October 22, he confessed his error by surrendering twenty-three thousand men to a vivacious and good-natured French Emperor dressed in the uniform of a common soldier. Napoleon wrote home to Josephine with characteristic exaggeration: "I have made sixty thousand prisoners. . . . I have lost only fifteen thousand men, of whom two thirds are slightly wounded."

Indeed, it was a great victory and at a very low cost. The other armies of Austria fell back while Russian troops hurried to the defense of their ally's capital. On November 13, Napoleon led his soldiers into Vienna and the next day established his headquarters at the palace of Schönbrunn. But if Napoleon had hoped to negotiate a peace with

Austria while in possession of Vienna, he was disappointed. At Olmütz, one hundred miles north of where he was then encamped, lay a force of ninety thousand Austrians and Russians, and in Italy the Archduke Charles still controlled an undefeated army. Napoleon tried diplomacy, urged on in his course not only by a natural desire to separate Russia from the Coalition, but also by the fear of the threatening attitude that Prussia was now taking and by the news that had just reached him of a great naval defeat that his Admiral Villeneuve had suffered at the hands of the English under Napoleon's old Nemesis, Admiral Nelson.

This battle had taken place shortly after Napoleon's own glorious victory at Ulm, but the Emperor learned of it only when he sat in possession of his enemy's capital. Napoleon had spoken of Villeneuve in harsh and unconfident tones a month before the battle. Napoleon's plan, it seems, was to have Villeneuve sail toward America as if to land troops there, allowing the English fleet to follow him, and then return suddenly to the Channel, arriving there long enough in advance of his English pursuers to permit the French army to cross unmolested. But Villeneuve did nothing, while Napoleon raged. His vehemence was largely without good reason, for Villeneuve's inaction at Cadiz, where he had under his command thirty-three Spanish and French vessels to as many of the English, was justified in view of the rawness of most of his men and officers and the tried expertness of his adversary.

On October 20, smarting under Napoleon's accusations of "treason" and "cowardice" and having already been superseded by Vice-Admiral Rosily-Mesros, who had just arrived at Madrid, Villeneuve determined to risk battle. Nelson, guessing from the allies' signals what they were about, determined to block their passage through the Straits of Gibraltar. He sailed toward Cape Trafalgar and there on the following noon the forces of the English admiral, reduced by six ships that he had sent for water, engaged a larger but more reluctant enemy. England, expecting "every man to do his duty," was not disappointed. Admiral Collingwood, second in command, rushed his Royal Sovereign into battle before the others, and for twenty minutes endured alone the concentrated fire of the nearest enemies. The others came up in two lines of battle, prow to stern, headed against the center of the perpendicular line that Villeneuve had formed of his fleet. After two hours' fighting, the skill of the English sailor triumphed over the lumbering courage of the French and Spanish. Eighteen of the allied fleet were destroyed or captured. Villeneuve himself was made a prisoner, and after a brief period of captivity in England, died mysteriously on his return to Paris. Of the fifteen ships of the allied line that succeeded in making their escape, eleven found safety in a retreat to Cadiz, and four that had managed to sail out into the open sea later fell victims to English cruisers. Not a single ship of the English squadron had been lost, but among her many dead lay the greatest sailor that the world's greatest naval power has ever been able to boast.

The victory, no doubt, was colossal. And yet its importance has too often been overstated. Great as was the rejoicing in England, which not even the death of Nelson could dampen, bolstering as it was to the falling stocks upon the Exchange, there had never been any real danger to England from a French invasion. Even if Napoleon had ever seriously intended to undertake the difficulty of such an enterprise, and even if Villeneuve had succeeded in joining his fleet with that in the Channel, there was still little likelihood that the French forces would have been able to get control of the straits long enough to land a sufficient force for the purpose. The battle of Trafalgar had merely made assurance doubly sure. And, from the French point of view, the defeat was not as irreparable as might at first glance have appeared. Hope was still buoyed up by the but recent victory at Ulm and the continued progress of Napoleon toward Vienna. There were enough French ships left in the various yards to form a nucleus, if the Emperor had been minded to construct another formidable navy. It was Napoleon's indifference to the importance of

naval maneuvers as much as the discouraging effects of the
annihilation at Trafalgar, that prevented him from making
another bid against England's mastery of the seas.
But Napoleon's *revanche* was at hand. The diplomatic
negotiations that he had undertaken with Alexander and
Francis had come to naught because neither side truly
wished to sacrifice anything for the sake of peace. Czar
Alexander had a military reputation to make and sought it
in the defeat of Napoleon. Despite the better judgment of
his general Kutusoff, he took the offensive. Napoleon
could not have arranged his opponent's movements more
to his own advantage if he had been allowed to issue the
orders himself. His superior knowledge of the terrain
enabled him to foretell almost every move that the enemy
was to make. The belligerents met near Austerlitz on
December 2. The battle, begun in the early morning,
lasted until two in the afternoon, for the Austrians and
Russians outnumbered the French force by twenty thousand men. But when the Allied center broke and the
Allies fled before the onslaught of Murat's cavalry, they
left behind them twenty-six thousand men, most of whom
had been drowned in the mad rush for safety. The French
had suffered a loss of only nine thousand casualties. The
"sun of Austerlitz" had witnessed a magnificent celebration
of the first anniversary of the new Empire. "The battle of
Austerlitz," wrote Napoleon, "is the most splendid of all I
have fought."
The outcome of Austerlitz settled temporarily the attitude that Prussia was to take. Frederick William III was
pacifically inclined, and, realizing that the strength of
Prussia was more show than substance, had been quite
willing to follow the lead of the French Emperor as long as
he could do so without humiliation. Napoleon titillated
his ambition by secret offers of Hanover all the time that his
own troops held the Electorate. But in 1804, when Napoleon's men had invaded Hamburg and carried off the British envoy Rumbold, as the Director of the Circle of Lower
Saxony, Frederick William was stirred to protest this

violation of North-German neutrality. Again he was appeased by the release of Rumbold and the bestowal of seven Golden Eagles of the Legion of Honor; and when the Third Coalition was formed, Prussia was not one of its number. But Napoleon, depending upon it that "the Prussians do not declare so quickly," had, in preparing his trap for General Mack's forces at Ulm, marched some of his troops through Ansbach, thus violating Prussian neutrality. On November 3, Frederick William signed with Russia and Austria the Treaty of Potsdam, by which he agreed to offer armed mediation and, if it were refused by Napoleon, to declare war against him, the Czar promising to use his influence to secure Hanover for Prussia. Haugwitz, the Prussian Foreign Minister, was commissioned to carry this ultimatum to the French, but he delayed until the Prussian forces should be prepared for any contingency; and when he finally did set out on his errand, Napoleon had already become master of Vienna. When he arrived in the French camp, he was kept moving futilely between Talleyrand, Napoleon's Foreign Minister, at Vienna and the Emperor himself at the front, without daring to create the breach that the delivery of his message would have entailed.

All this was changed by Austerlitz. On the very night of the battle, the Emperor Francis sued for peace, and on December 6 an armistice was signed by which the Russian army was to be removed and the Prussian army excluded from Austrian territory. Frederick William, in view of the imminent disruption of the Third Coalition, despite Russian importunings became unwilling to accept any act of Napoleon's as a *casus foederis*. Haugwitz in the mean time had become deeply involved in protestations of friendship for France; and after negotiations were resumed between him and Napoleon, he was induced on December 15 to sign the Treaty of Schönbrunn. Prussia surrendered Ansbach to Bavaria, France's ally, and Clèves and Neuchâtel to France, entering into an offensive and defensive alliance with Napoleon, in return for the cession of Hanover, long coveted by Prussia, which his troops held, but which he had no legitimate authority to give to Prussia.

Thus obliged to surrender the support of Russia and Prussia and having already accepted unfavorable terms of truce, Austria was for a third time at the mercy of the Corsican Emperor-General. Despite Napoleon's anxiety for a speedy arrangement, peace was not finally concluded until December 26. By the Treaty of Pressburg, proud Austria was made to yield all her outlying possessions to France or France's allies. In Italy she conceded Venetia, Istria, and Dalmatia to Napoleon as King of Italy. In Germany she surrendered to her unfriendly neighbors, Bavaria, Württemberg, and Baden, all of her Swabian possessions as well as Tyrol and Vorarlberg. The former two of these duchies now became kingdoms and the last a Grand Duchy. Thus, while weakening Austria, Napoleon strengthened her old rivals and his staunch allies.

Fearing that all his efforts in creating a strong alliance against French aggressions were soon to be blasted, Pitt undertook to try to outbid France for Prussian friendship. Negotiations, that had already been begun before the battle of Ulm, were now pushed more vigorously. Unwilling to surrender the ancestral realm of his master, Pitt tried to turn the attention of Prussian statesmen from Hanover to Belgium and the Rhine Basin. The Prussian Government on the whole preferred Hanover to any other part of Europe, but some of its members owned tender consciences that would not permit the robbery of an erstwhile friend in this fashion; and there was a large Allied force in the neighborhood of Hanover to strengthen their consciences. The Prussian State Council therefore decided to favor a revision of the Treaty of Schönbrunn with Napoleon by which Hanover would be occupied only provisionally.

Pitt, however, was deeply worried. The result of the battle of Austerlitz had more than offset in his mind the splendor of Trafalgar. Worn out by fifteen years of constant labor, suffering like his father from the gout, he now began to take on what his friends called "the Austerlitz look." He had been at Bath for his health when the news of the disaster came to him. He returned, broken in spirit, to his home in Putney. A map of Europe hung on the wall. "Roll up that map," he is said to have exclaimed; "it will not be needed these ten years." Despite the impression that many historians give, however, it was not the news from Austerlitz but the situation in Berlin that killed him. Harrowby, his envoy to Prussia, was on his way to bring a report that was more hopeful than the facts warranted, for Frederick William had not allowed the English diplomat to know his full intention. But Pitt died, before Harrowby could reach him, on January 23, with the despondent cry: "My country! Oh, my country!" He thought he had failed.

In normal times Pitt would have been a giant, but he was now matched with a personality with whom he was dwarfed in comparison. Pitt nevertheless had done great things for the internal development of England; greater yet might have been possible if the wave of revolution in France had not created a reaction in England. And in foreign affairs, dark as the future might have appeared in 1806 as he lay on his deathbed, the policy of Pitt — a policy that had been inaugurated by his father — of subsidizing allies on the Continent while maintaining control of the seas, brought Great Britain once more out on the top of the struggle and left her commercial supremacy unquestioned and unrivaled. It was not the first time that the plodding of a tortoise was to beat the genius of a rabbit.

In the mean time, Prussia had continued negotiations with Napoleon. Feeling unaccountably sure that the Emperor would accept his revision of the Treaty of Schönbrunn, Frederick William reduced his army to a peace footing. But when Haugwitz went again to interview Napoleon on that question, he was greeted with a torrent of reproaches. Why was the Anglophile Hardenberg still kept in the King's good graces? Why were English and Russian troops admitted into Prussia? Why were Prussian troops about to enter Hanover before Prussia had formally ratified the Treaty of Schönbrunn? But if Prussia still wanted Hanover, she might have it if she consented to close the entire coast of Germany to English commerce. With these terms the thoroughly subdued Haugwitz returned to Berlin — to a Queen and a people who now hated him heartily as the tool of an oppressor, but to a King who was in no position to repudiate his negotiations. Despite the patriotic impulses of the followers of Queen Louisa, Prussia proceeded to close the German ports on the Baltic. Peace might yet have been kept between France and Prussia save for the fact that now England began to consider the possibility and desirability of peace.

Fox had become the Minister of Foreign Affairs in the so-called Ministry of All the Talents, which succeeded the Pitt Ministry; and Fox, the radical who had been a staunch friend of the revolutionists in America, had likewise been a champion of democracy in France. He had defended the French Revolution and now was anxious to bring about an understanding with its heir. Russia was willing to comply. Napoleon, too, would have liked a breathing space in which to develop his schemes for the creation of a huge Oriental Empire. Negotiations looking toward a cessation of hostilities were begun between Fox and Talleyrand, the Imperial Minister of Foreign Affairs, as early as February, 1806. Meanwhile, however, Napoleon kept himself busy in Europe. The Bourbons of Naples, having welcomed an Anglo-Russian force within their realms, were attacked, on the grounds of having broken their neutrality, and driven from the mainland into their island possession of Sicily. Napoleon now created his brother Joseph King of Naples and instructed him to acquire Sicily also. In order to bind the Batavian Republic more closely to the destinies of France, Napoleon had, in March, 1805, placed it under a Grand Pensionary of his own appointment. But in June, 1806, he converted the Batavian Republic into the Kingdom of Holland and made his brother Louis its King.

His most important achievement at this time, however, was the displacement of the Holy Roman Empire by the

Confederation of the Rhine. In the Treaty of Pressburg the Holy Roman Empire had been designated by the ominous title of "German Confederation"; and on August 1, 1806, Napoleon announced to the Imperial Diet at Ratisbon that he no longer recognized the existence of the old Empire. Francis II consented to surrender his title of Holy Roman Emperor and became exclusively the Emperor of Austria. Sixteen states in southern Germany now organized the Confederation of the Rhine, accepted the Code Napoléon, named Napoleon Protector and agreed to furnish him with sixty-three thousand soldiers. New mediatizations were now carried out, by which the Free Cities of Augsburg, Nuremberg, and Frankfort were incorporated with larger states. Germany gained much in the way of unification and efficient government, but again at the price of independence.

The negotiations between Talleyrand and Fox meanwhile progressed, but as the English captured more and more Dutch and French colonies and as Joseph proved in the battle of Maida (July 4, 1806) unable to capture Sicily, Napoleon refused to grant peace on the basis of *uti possidetis* (present possession), as the English wished. The Russians likewise refused the French terms, and Fox, a few days before he died (September 13, 1806), despaired of peace. Negotiations came to a close on October 6. England, however, had not lost by them. In a draft treaty prepared in July there had been included a provision for the restoration of Hanover to George III. Yarmouth, the semiofficial English envoy, took special pains to see that the Prussian Ambassador learned of this. A new source of grievance between Napoleon and Frederick William had arisen in the ambition of Murat, Napoleon's brother-in-law. Napoleon had recently made Murat Duke of Berg and Clèves. Murat immediately undertook to increase his territories at Prussia's expense. The news of Napoleon's double dealing with regard to Hanover reached Berlin just after a collision between troops of Murat and Blücher's Prussians had been prevented only by the anxiety of Frederick William to preserve peace.

Even now Berlin might have been wheedled into believing that Napoleon had not intended to humiliate Prussia and might have listened to the bargain terms that Napoleon was willing to offer for continued neutrality, had not the French ruler here committed one of the most brutal and glaring errors of his career. Palm, a peaceful, law-abiding bookseller of Nuremberg, was arrested one day, despite his protests that there must have been a mistake, and taken to the Austrian town of Braunau to be tried by a French court-martial. It developed that he was guilty of having sold a pamphlet entitled *Deutschland in seiner tiefen Erniedrigung* (*Germany in Its Profound Humiliation*), an appeal to Saxony and Prussia to save Germany from the deep shame of French suzerainty. Palm was shot on August 25, 1806. Napoleon was living up to the opinion that he had once confided to Madame de Rémusat, that *la clémence proprement dite est une si pauvre petite vertu* (mercy, properly defined, is a very petty virtue). Frederick William, forced into action by the rage of a people for whom the more belligerent Queen Louisa was an idol, now became the hero of German patriots by demanding the withdrawal of all French troops from German territory and Napoleon's consent to the formation of a North German Confederation under Prussian hegemony. When the ultimatum reached Napoleon, the period of respite allowed had already expired.

On October 7, both forces began to move. But the Prussian army of 1806 was not a worthy descendant of the army of Rossbach, and the Duke of Brunswick, its commander-in-chief, was only a shadow of the dashing soldier who had won the hearty praise of Frederick the Great. Within a week Napoleon had cut off the Prussian army from its capital and had forced the King to divide his forces in two parts. On October 14, Napoleon routed Hohenlohe at Jena, while at the same time Davout at Auerstädt defeated the divisions under Brunswick and the King. The honors of the day belonged to Davout, for he had faced a larger army than his own (sixty-three thousand and twenty-

five thousand respectively) and had inflicted a more telling
rebuff upon his enemy than Napoleon, whose command
(ninety-five thousand) outnumbered Hohenlohe's (fifty
thousand).   As a reward Davout's corps was permitted to
march into Berlin first of all the French (October 25).   Panic
seized the remnants of the Prussian army and they surrendered in batches.   At Stettin, a well-built fortress, a garrison of five thousand men capitulated without firing a shot
to a brigade of hussars who had gone out only to recon-
noiter.   Inside of a month the French had captured over
one hundred thousand prisoners.

Napoleon tarried at Berlin only a short while.   On
November 25, he was again in the field, for to his east lay
the rest of the Prussian army and a powerful unbeaten
Russian force.   In the dead of winter, Bennigsen, commander of the Russians, attempted to surround Bernadotte's forces and brought on a battle at Eylau (February
8, 1807).   The losses on both sides made this one of the
most bloody of all of Napoleon's conflicts.   Of the sixty
thousand men on each side engaged in this battle, one third
were among the killed, wounded, captured, or missing when
night fell and the Russians decamped.   Even Napoleon is
said to have been affected by the horror of a spectacle that
has become familiar through Baron Gros' famous picture of
Napoleon at Eylau.   Although Napoleon claimed the
victory, so did Bennigsen.   The advantage lay with the
French, however, as they were able to march on.   Except
for the capture of Danzig (May 26, 1807), operations did
not begin again until June.

Napoleon in the mean time opened negotiations with
nations as far south as Egypt and as far east as Persia, all
with a view toward strengthening his hand against England
and Russia.   Napoleon's skill as a diplomat is revealed in
the clever way in which he took advantage of the new
situation in Egypt to induce the Ottoman Turks to join
forces with him against their traditional enemy, Russia, and
their erstwhile ally, England.   In this work, he was ably
seconded by Sebastiani, his ambassador at Constantinople,

who, in large part, was responsible for his interest in the
Near East.   His intrigues in Egypt and the Levant met
with greater success this time than they had on an earlier,
more famous occasion.   An English fleet that tried to land
on Egyptian territory was repulsed by Mehemet Ali, the
very competent Albanian ruler of Egypt.   The Sultan of
Turkey, having declared war against Russia in order to
protect the Roumanian provinces from aggression, was able
to force an English squadron out of the Dardanelles, with
the help of Sebastiani.   Thus the Coalition was being
beaten by the Turks at the same time as the French were
driving the Russians before them farther north.

In England, a new ministry, under the Duke of Portland,
had succeeded the Ministry of All Talents.   In this ministry, the Tory Canning was Fox's successor as Minister of
Foreign Affairs.   Canning tried to instill new vigor into the
Fourth Coalition.   In April, 1807, the Baltic Powers,
Sweden, Prussia, and Russia, had formed the Convention of
Bartenstein against France.   This was now almost forgotten, as the French swept irresistibly through Prussian
territory.   England now agreed to join this alliance and,
as usual, to furnish the necessary subsidies (June 27, 1807).
But her action came too late.   On June 10, Bennigsen was
defeated at Heilsberg and four days later again at Friedland.   Here Lannes' forces, greatly outnumbered, would
have had to retreat but for the timely arrival of Napoleon
himself with enough troops to equal Bennigsen's army.
Bennigsen again withdrew.   At Tilsit on June 21, Napoleon
granted the Russians a month's armistice.

Alexander, his territory still untouched by an invader, was
prepared to desert Prussia and England and ally himself
with France.   Neither of the former had given him the aid
he wished, and England, whose traditional policy was to
resist any encroachments in the eastern Mediterranean,
could be expected to be nothing but hostile to his aggressive
plans regarding Turkey.   The two Emperors agreed to
meet in private to discuss their relations.   Napoleon had a
profound, perhaps comic, sense of the dramatic.   Further-

more, he sought to appeal to his younger and more inipres-
sionable contemporary.   In deference to his wishes, the
two Emperors met alone (June 25, 1807) in a pavilion on a
raft moored midstream in the Nieman River, in full view
of their two armies drawn up on either bank.   The first
words that Alexander uttered on that occasion were supposed to have been: "I hate the English as much as you do,
and I will second you in all your actions against them."

There is a contemporary cartoon of the meeting at Tilsit
which shows Alexander and Napoleon embracing so heartily
that the raft rocks and precipitates Frederick William into
the water.   As a mere fact, the cartoon is at fault; Frederick
William was not present except on the right bank, anxiously
pacing to and fro before the Prussian and Russian forces,
although at the meeting on the following day he was allowed
to come to hear the unpleasant things that Napoleon had
to unbraid him with.   But as a caricature of what actually
did happen, it is delightfully apposite in spirit.   The two
Emperors were greatly pleased with each other and proceeded to arrange peace at Frederick William's expense.

Napoleon dreamed of India.   The French Charlemagne
felt the call of the Macedonian Alexander.   The mirage of
the East had never ceased to beckon to him since first in
1797 he had gazed across the Adriatic.   He yielded much
to the Russian Czar in order to win Russian support against
England.   Only when England would be obliged to consent
to French hegemony in Europe could he be free to conquer
new worlds.   At this and subsequent meetings Napoleon
agreed, therefore, that Russia might have a free hand in
dealing with the Sultan, even now his ally, if the Porte did
not accept French mediation in her conflict with Russia;
that Poland would not be revived, lest Russian Poland be
claimed by the reëstablished nation; that Russia might take
from her own ally Sweden the desirable province of Finland.
In return, Alexander acquiesced in advance to whatever
changes in Italy, Spain, and Portugal Napoleon might make
and consented, if England would not accept an offer of
peace, to close Russian ports to English commerce, to make

common cause with France, and, in concert with France, to call upon Sweden, Denmark, Portugal, and Austria to do likewise. As both Emperors thus divided Europe between them, Prussia was picked to pieces. Her Polish provinces were erected into a Duchy of Warsaw, over which, out of respect for Alexander's apprehensions of Polish independence because of his own Polish possessions, the erstwhile Duke, now King of Saxony *Napoleonis gratia*, became Duke, with Napoleon, who had confiscated the crown lands, as his wealthiest subject. The western provinces of Prussia, together with part of the Electorate of Hesse and of the Electorate of Hanover and such states as Brunswick, Hesse-Cassell, Mühlhausen, and Westphalia, were made into the Kingdom of Westphalia. Over this, partially as a reward for having surrendered his Baltimore wife and consenting to marry the daughter of the King of Württemberg, Napoleon placed his youngest brother Jerome. The treaty stated that only "out of regard for His Majesty the Emperor of all the Russias and wishing to give proof of his sincere desire to unite the two nations by the link of an unalterable trust and friendship," did Napoleon leave to Frederick William his intervening lands; even from them choice morsels were thrown to the Czar and the King of Saxony.

On the basis of these agreements, peace was signed between the two powers on July 7, 1807. In a secret treaty of alliance Russia consented to make war with France against Great Britain if by November the latter had not accepted peace and promised to return to France all her conquests since 1805 and to grant complete freedom of the seas; and France agreed to make war with Russia against Turkey somewhat later if the Porte did not accept French intervention between the two countries. The treaty went into minute details as to how this concert of action was to be achieved and what territorial results a victorious issue would have. Two days later, Prussia was obliged to consent to her degradation. Not even the personal entreaties of the beautiful and courageous Queen Louisa could shield her husband from any of the burden of shame that Napoleon had prepared for him. Not only did Frederick William have to consent to the trichotomy of his lands, but he had also to agree to close his ports to his only ally, England, and to make war on her if in November Russia and France decided to do so.

Some historians have maintained that Napoleon was not a first-rate diplomat. Thiers, in closing the first seven volumes of his remarkable *History of the Consulate and Empire* with a survey of the events at Tilsit, said that "in war Napoleon was guided by his genius, in politics by his passions"; and more recent writers have echoed this opinion. To be sure, Tilsit is the beginning of the end, not so much because of what it itself provided, not so much because the proud nation of Frederick the Great was obliged to accept a disgrace that it would always scheme with every secret and open resource at its command to avenge, but because from Tilsit onward Napoleon began to attempt the impossible. He was to rule over more land than he did in July, 1807; a glance at a map of 1810 will show more territory under his direct or indirect control than after the alliance with Russia and the suppression of Prussia, but it will not show how inside that territory there were more forces at work to destroy the Napoleonic Empire than in 1807. The Treaty of Tilsit marks the zenith of the career of Napoleon Bonaparte.

BOOK II

DEFEAT AND REACTION

CHAPTER I

THE CONTINENTAL SYSTEM

"NAPOLEON began to attempt the impossible." The impossible was the Continental Blockade. All other means of attack upon England, which once again, after Tilsit, faced France singlehanded, had failed; invasion was obviously impracticable, since Napoleon had made no attempt to rebuild his navy after Trafalgar; Napoleon's own attack upon India by way of Egypt and Syria had been unsuccessful; the Armed Neutrality of the North had been frustrated in 1801 by the bombardment of Copenhagen; attempts to arouse insurrection in Ireland had succeeded only in feeble rebellions that were soon squelched. One way still remained for Napoleon to fight England, a way that the Revolutionary Assemblies had considered before him and in part carried out. Since England depended so completely upon trade with Europe for her prosperity, cutting off trade with Europe would ruin English business and force her to beg for peace on any terms. If Napoleon could not blockade England because he had no fleet, he could blockade the Continent; by his military control of Europe he could prevent Continental nations from trading with England.

The Continental Blockade was inaugurated before the Treaty of Tilsit. Indeed, Tilsit was itself but one of the links in the chain that Napoleon now wrought to close the ports of Europe to the English. Initiated by the Directory, the Continental System had, until 1806, practically no great effect upon the commerce of Europe. What caused greater havoc among English shipping was the Directory's practice of issuing letters of marque to a multitude of ships of all sizes and kinds as privateers. England lost in this way about five hundred and twenty-four ships a year, or about two and one half per cent of her shipping. She resorted to the convoy and the patrol as defensive measures; and in 1803, at the outbreak of the War of the Third Coalition, when the French occupied Hanover, England as a retort declared the coast of Europe blockaded from the Elbe to the Weser. When the short-lived alliance at Schönbrunn between France and Prussia was drawn up, Prussia agreed to close Prussian and Hanoverian ports to English vessels. England retaliated by the Orders in Council of May 16, 1806, by which the American Minister Monroe was informed that the blockaded coast was extended from the Elbe to Brest; that is to say, so as to cover the entire North Sea and Channel coasts of the Continent. It was Fox, the friend of the American and French Revolutions, who was responsible for this Order in Council that forms the first of the series of Orders and Decrees by England and France that could end only in the exhaustion of France and not until the United States of America had been dragged into the war.

When the Order in Council of May 16, 1806, came to the notice of Napoleon, he had already subdued Austria and Prussia. He determined that there was no course open to him now but to "conquer the sea by the land." On November 21, 1806, during his brief triumphal sojourn in the Prussian capital, he issued the Berlin Decree. Maintaining that the Orders in Council were contrary to international law, since they blockaded commercial ports as well as fortified ports (international law actually drew no such distinction) and that England could not really enforce a blockade of the coast from Brest to the Elbe, he replied by declaring all of the British Isles in a state of blockade and therefore forbade any trade to or from Great Britain. The latter part of the decree was the more important; the blockade of the British Isles could be nothing more than a paper blockade, since the Emperor's fleet was but a powerless refugee from the English navy, but the Emperor had extensive control of the Continent and could prevent any ships of any nationality from entering or departing at many of the most thriving Continental ports. Until the Treaty of Tilsit, however, Napoleon did nothing actually to enforce the Berlin Decree. By secret provisions of that treaty, Russia and Prussia agreed to make common cause with France and to close their ports to English commerce if by December 1, 1807, England had not accepted the mediation of Russia; Russia also agreed to act in concert with France in summoning Denmark, Sweden, Portugal, and Austria to do likewise.

The retort of the English Government to the Berlin Decree was to issue, on January 7, 1807, a new Order in Council, which prohibited trade even by neutral vessels between any two ports under the control of France or her allies. This destroyed American trade in the Mediterranean and threatened to do the same on the other seas. When Napoleon returned to Paris after signing the Treaty of Tilsit in July, 1807, his reply to the January Order in Council was to summon Portugal and Denmark to declare war against England. But the English, already informed of the arrangements secretly prepared at Tilsit by which Denmark was to play her part in the Continental System, stole a march on Napoleon. In August a British fleet sailed into the Baltic, summoned the Danish fleet to surrender for safe-keeping to Great Britain, although war had not been declared between the two countries, and quite appropriately celebrated the fifteenth anniversary of the September massacres by bombarding Copenhagen for four days (September 2–5, 1807) when the Danes refused to comply. Finally Denmark yielded, and the British, to use a phrase that the late Lord Fisher coined from this episode, "Copenhagened" (appropriated) its fleet. The British thus made for France a loyal ally, who now prepared to close her ports to English commerce.

In Portugal, on the other hand, where there had been a constant fidelity to England ever since the highly profitable Methuen Treaty of 1703, the Government refused to

accede to the French summons.   On October 27, 1807, a
treaty was arranged at Fontainebleau between France and
Spain, by which all Portugal, like Cæsar's Gaul, was to be
divided into three parts.   The northern section was to be
made into a kingdom for the young Bourbon King of
Etruria, in exchange for Tuscany, which, with its seaport at
Leghorn, was to be surrendered to Napoleon; the southern
provinces were to be made into a principality for Godoy, the
inamorato of the Queen of Spain; the central section, including the active seaport of Lisbon, was to remain in
Napoleon's possession until the conclusion of a general
peace.   Napoleon therefore gave orders to Marshal Junot
to lead an expedition through Spain into Portugal.   Junot,
by forced marches that worked fearful hardships on his
men, reached Lisbon on November 30.   Portugal passed
under French control, but not before the English fleet had
had time to take the Portuguese court and its treasure to
Brazil.

In the mean time Russia had failed to win British consent
to her mediation and had declared war (November 8).
Prussia and Austria closed their ports to English ships.
Etruria, the Papal States, Bremen, and Hamburg, having
allowed English goods to leak through to the Continent,
lost their independence.   The seaports of the first two
passed by the Emperor's orders under the control of the
Viceroy of Italy, while Napoleon himself annexed the territory of the other two.   At the same time, while he thus
tried with surprising success to shut off English commerce
from the Continent, he also interpreted the Berlin Decree
in such a way as to make subject to confiscation all neutral
goods of English origin.   Theoretically, but only theoretically (as we shall see), English goods could now no longer
reach the Continent even through neutral agents.

In retaliation, the British issued new Orders in Council
(November 11, 1807) declaring that all ports of France and
all other ports from which the British flag was excluded
"shall from henceforth be subject to the same restrictions
. . . as if the same were actually blockaded in the most strict

and rigorous manner"; but exceptions were permitted so
that the possibility still existed of direct trade between
neutrals and colonial ports of the enemy or of indirect trade
with blockaded Continental ports if the neutral vessels
stopped en route either way at an English port. It was
hoped in this way to make England the center of neutral
commerce.   There was to be "no trade except through
Great Britain." Even from these exceptions were excluded
most articles of foreign manufacture or cultivation; these
could be "re-ported" only by special license from the British
Government.   This gave rise to an extensive traffic in
licensed goods. But since English goods did not have to
be licensed, wherever English manufacturers could supply
the Continental demand, English goods were likely to get
the preference.   Thus the Orders in Council were a scheme
not alone of retaliation against the Continental System, but
likewise an endeavor to force English goods upon the Continental market in so far as any imported goods at all
might be admitted.

The next move, of course, lay with Napoleon. On December 17, 1807, at Milan he issued the Milan Decrees,
which made subject to capture any ship that had submitted to search by British cruisers or that sailed to and
from the British Isles. Neutral commerce, particularly
that of the United States of America, had now to choose
between obeying the English Orders in Council (thereby
running the risk of capture by French privateers or by
French port authorities whenever they sailed into a harbor
under Napoleon's control) and adhering to the Berlin and
Milan Decrees by refusing to trade with England. At first
President Jefferson's Government adopted the course of
refusing to permit the importation of certain specified
articles from England. This was done by the Non-Importation Act of 1806, aimed exclusively at England not alone
because the Berlin Decree had not yet been promulgated,
but because English ships had begun searching American
vessels for English sailors, sometimes failing to discern the
difference between an American and an Englishman, often

deliberately refusing to see the difference between a natur-alized American and an Englishman. Good sailors were few, and in times of great stress, like the present, authorities could not take the time to bother about American charges of "press gangs." Furthermore, resistance to England fell in with the desire of certain political leaders in the young Republic who represented a growing demand for expansion. The Western pioneer had long been casting covetous eyes toward Canada.

But when the Berlin Decree was issued, France, too, be-came guilty of aiding in the destruction of American com-merce. Jefferson now determined to have nothing to do with either country and on his request Congress adopted the Embargo Act (1807), which forbade all trade with all foreign countries. Until 1809 the Embargo Act continued to destroy American commerce, while England and France unconcernedly drew tighter the nets that had been pre-pared by Orders in Council and the Continental System. In fact, by a decree issued from Bayonne in April, 1808, Napoleon proceeded calmly to order the sequestration of all American vessels in European ports under his control on the grounds that, since they could not, by the Embargo Act, have come from their own country, they must have come from England. By the Rambouillet Decree of March 23, 1810, ships thus sequestered were definitely con-fiscated. By this time, however, Jefferson had ceased to be the President of the United States and Madison had taken his place. Three days before the inauguration of his suc-cessor, Jefferson had signed the Non-Intercourse Act. By this, all trade with either France or England was prohibited, allowing trade, however, with all other countries, but the President was empowered to open trade with either country should it revoke its decrees against neutral commerce. Madison inherited an intricate problem that his more capable predecessor had not been able to solve.

A large leak in the Continental System ran through Spain. The fate of Portugal presaged the doom of Spain. If Portugal had had to be divided into three parts in order to keep the blockade intact, Spain must not be allowed to go unpunished. There was also the fear that Spain, which was suspected of having coquetted with the Fourth Coalition, might be induced to join a fifth. Furthermore, there was the growing ambition of the large Bonaparte family to satisfy. A pretext for intervention was not hard to find. The shameless scandal centering about the Queen and Godoy, and the crying ineptitude of a weakling ruler eventually caused Prince Ferdinand to put himself at the head of a party that demanded change, at least, if not reform. The King abdicated in favor of his son on March 18. Napoleon thought the moment opportune for intervention. Having called upon the royal family to meet him at Bayonne, he induced the father to confirm his abdication in favor of the son and obliged the son, ignorant of these proceedings, to abdicate in favor of the father (May 10), and, with both abdications in his hands, proclaimed his brother Joseph King of Spain (Louis having refused to accept the honor), naming his brother-in-law Murat in the latter's place as King of Naples and himself annexing Murat's former possessions in Germany.

Machiavelli might have taken a keen satisfaction in this demonstration of the superiority of craft over force as a means of expanding the state. But the crisis had just begun. The proud and united people of Spain were not to be treated in the same manner as the motley group of small states in the Holy Roman Empire. Even before Ferdinand's abdication, the French troops had been all but driven out of the city by an infuriated populace on May 2 (*Dos de Mayo*), which is still celebrated in Spain as a great national holiday. Before June, every quarter of Spain was in revolt against its proposed king. On June 6, 1808, Joseph was crowned king by Napoleon himself and accepted by a reluctant Junta on June 15 at the command of Murat. But about 120,000 French troops had to be called upon to support him after he entered Madrid on July 20. The French in Spain now occupied the position that the Austrians and Prussians of 1792–93 had held, while the Spanish now, like the French then, were fighting for their homes and ideals. Discipline and efficiency once again were obliged to yield to national fervor. At Saragossa a heroic city compelled a besieging army to retire; at Baylen, on July 22, Dupont and an entire corps of seventeen thousand men were forced to surrender. On August 1, Joseph, wishing he had never left Naples for sunny Spain, withdrew from Madrid and ordered all French forces to retreat beyond the Ebro River. At the same time the English landed an expeditionary army in Portugal under Sir Arthur Wellesley. On August 21, this army defeated Junot at Vimiero and forced him to sign the Convention of Cintra on August 30, by which all his troops were to surrender, but to be repatriated. Lisbon for a time remained in English hands and Wellesley lost no time in coöperating with the Spanish patriots.

Napoleon, who at first had been inclined to scorn the Spanish insurrection as a flare of excited *idéologues* and monks, now was seriously disturbed. But for the time being, his interest was drawn elsewhere. Relations with Alexander of Russia had become strained, even though he had now taken Finland from Sweden and had occupied Moldavia and Wallachia. He had never been pleased with Napoleon's high-handed policy toward Prussia, and resented especially the treaty that had just (September 8) been forced upon Prussia (as a sort of annex to the Treaty of Tilsit) by which she was not permitted to have an army of more than forty-two thousand men at any one time. Furthermore, Napoleon had revived his old dreams of a conquest of the Orient, even to the point of building armaments in his Adriatic possessions.

If Napoleon were to undertake an expedition against Spain, to say nothing of India, he must first reassure himself of the friendliness, or at least the passivity, not alone of Russia, but also of Prussia and Austria. He made plans for a splendid congress to meet at Erfurt. There, amidst a fawning assemblage of kings and princes, the Czar and the Emperor entertained each other in luxurious and impressive display (Napoleon succeeding poorly in his attempts to overawe Alexander) from September 27 to October 14. On October 12, it was, however, agreed by a secret convention that the two Emperors would continue in common their hostilities against the English until England should recognize Finland, Moldavia, and Wallachia as a part of Russia and acquiesce to any changes that France might make in Spain. Napoleon, though, at the same time, striving to have the Porte consider him friendly, nevertheless agreed that if Austria or any other power went to the aid of Turkey in case of the renewal of hostilities between the Sultan and the Czar, France would go to the aid of Russia; and conversely, if Austria made war against France, Russia was to declare against Austria.

December 2, the day so memorable in Napoleon's career, found him in Madrid at the head of an army of two hundred thousand men. His numerical advantage enabled him easily to push the Spanish before him and to force Moore, who was now in command of the British, to retreat. Napoleon himself soon hurried back to Paris, recalled by rumors of Austrian recalcitrance and of conspiracies engineered by Talleyrand, his Minister of Foreign Affairs, and Fouché, his Minister of Police. Fouché was too useful a man to be dispensed with just yet and Napoleon had to rest content with administering a verbal flagellation, but Talleyrand, after repeated stormy sessions, was disgraced by being deprived of his office. "What a pity that such a great man has been so badly brought up!" Talleyrand is reported to have said. Napoleon's most capable, though untrustworthy minister henceforth became his secret but no less his bitterest enemy. In the mean time Marshal Soult, to whom the command of the army in Spain had been entrusted, was unable to prevent Moore's army from embarking at Corunna (January 18), though Moore himself was left behind, a heroic sacrifice for the safety of his army. "Not a drum was heard, not a funeral note," as they "left him alone with his glory."

While thus endeavoring to strengthen his hold upon Spain and the western Mediterranean, Napoleon made several acquisitions in Italy and the Adriatic, always with a view toward the Conquest of India and the East and the hermetical sealing of the Continent. Eugène Beauharnais had acted as his stepfather's viceroy in the Kingdom of Italy since 1805. In the south, Joseph and, later, Murat ruled over Naples, though the Bourbons were still able to hold their own in Sicily. In between lay the Papal States. Relations with the Pope had never been cordial since the time the Pope had gone to Paris to take part in the coronation of Napoleon. Napoleon not only refused to recognize the old claim to papal suzerainty over Naples, but actually converted small pieces of papal territory into duchies and principalities for his servants. After the Treaty of Tilsit, when the Pope was peremptorilv ordered to close his ports to English commerce, he hesitatea. Napoleon now drew up a treaty favorable enough in its general terms to the Pope, but carrying the joker that thenceforth one third of the Sacred College of Cardinals was to be French. The Sacred College refused to accept these terms, and in February, 1808, Napoleon's troops seized Rome. The Pope was allowed to remain, but his temporal power passed into the hands of the new Charlemagne. It was only a matter of time until even the nominal control that was still left to the Pope would be destroyed. When, on July 10, the Pope excommunicated the Emperor (for the second time), Napoleon ordered his arrest and imprisonment at Avignon in France. The second Babylonian Captivity of the Church had commenced. The Pope was afterwards removed to Savona, in Northern Italy, and, in 1812, to Fontainebleau, near Paris. On May 17, 1809, the States of the Church in Italy became part of the French Empire. All of Italy now was under the aegis of Napoleon.

In Austria the new Chancellor, Stadion, watched events in Italy and Spain with increasing anxiety and interest. The success of the French in the one peninsula filled him with despair that was lightened by the hope that came from their difficulties in the other. There had been, since Pressburg, a development of national feeling that was especially remarkable in view of the heterogeneity of the peoples of the Austrian Empire. Hungary had been rendered to a large degree autonomous under the amiable and capable Archduke Charles, while in German Austria, Stadion carefully nourished the spirit of German nationality. In the mean time, the Archduke Charles reorganized and drilled the army. The feelings of the Austrians reached a bursting point. They forgot Campo Formio, Lunéville, and Pressburg, smarted under the humiliation of being but a cog in the Continental System, and remembered only Cintra and Baylen. For the moment it was thought that Prussia would coöperate in a war of liberation, but Frederick William would make no move without Russia. England, however, promised not only large subsidies, but also the employment of a large army in the Netherlands. Accordingly, on April 6, 1809, the Archduke Charles issued a proclamation to his army: "The freedom of Europe has sought refuge beneath your banners!" The First German War of Liberation had begun.

The war was not unwelcome to Napoleon. He needed victories to offset the disasters in Spain, and he needed money to balance his expenditures there. He was confident of success. "I am leaving my best troops with Joseph," he said, "and am starting along for Vienna with my little conscripts, my name, and my long boots." On May 12, having won the campaign of Ratisbon (April 19–23), he again entered Vienna. But the main body of the Austrians, under the Archduke Charles, lay across the Danube. On May 21 and 22, Napoleon stormed the villages of Aspern and Essling, but withdrew at last when the bridges connecting the island of Lobau in the Danube with the bank were swept away. The Archduke Charles had proved himself the greatest of the generals who had yet faced Napoleon. Until July 5, Napoleon was obliged to remain inactive on Lobau, waiting for Eugène and the Army of Italy. On that day the French crossed to the left bank of the Danube, and on the next, with a larger force than the Archduke's. defeated the Austrians at Wagram. Forty thousand Austrians and thirty-four thousand French were killed, wounded, lost, or made prisoners. The English kept their part of the bargain and endeavored to create a diversion in the Netherlands at Walcheren, but disease and mismanagement frustrated their attack, and on September 30 they returned to England again.

Francis had by this time had enough of war, although his army was yet in a position to fight. On the 12th of July, an armistice was signed, and on October 14, the treaty, known either after Vienna or Schönbrunn, was signed. Again Austria was stripped of some of her most desirable provinces. To the Illyrian Provinces under his immediate control, Napoleon added Carinthia, Carniola, the cities of Trieste and Fiume. To Bavaria went Salzburg and the Inn Quarter. Warsaw, officially named a Grand Duchy in 1808, received a part of Galicia, including the city of Cracow. By way of compensation for this Polish aggrandizement, Russia had to be reimbursed with the part including Tarnopol and Brody. Austria agreed to reduce its army to one hundred and fifty thousand men and to adhere to the Continental System. If Austria after the Treaty of Pressburg might still have been considered a second-rate power, now she was certainly of a third or fourth rate, and practically without a seacoast. The Treaty of Vienna of 1809 established "a peace of violence, relatively more harsh for Austria than had been the conditions of Tilsit for Prussia."

The end of the year 1809 had come. Every historical atlas of any value in recent times has been very careful to include a map showing the political geography of Europe in 1810. A glance at such a map will show how completely — at least to outward appearances — the Continental System was effective. Napoleon himself was King of Italy, which comprised the territory northwest of the Adriatic, Lombardy, Venetia, and the Marches; Protector of the Confederation of the Rhine, which included among others the Kingdoms of Westphalia,[1] Saxony, Württemberg, and Bavaria; the wealthiest subject of his puppet Grand Duke

[1] Later (August, 1810) annexed in part by France.

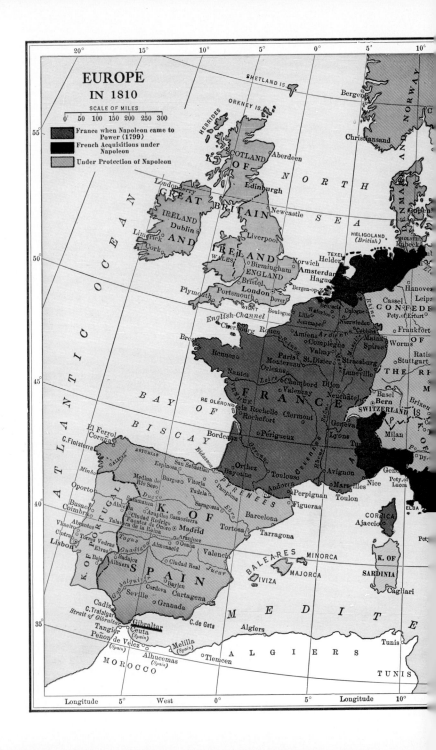

EUROPE
IN 1810

SCALE OF MILES

0'   50   100 150 200 250 300

France when Napoleon came to
Power (1799)
French Acquisitions under
Napoleon
Under Protection of Napoleon

SHETLAND IS.

ORKNEY IS.

Bergen

HEBRIDES

NORWAY

SCOTLAND

Aberdeen

Christiansand

KENMARK AND NORWAY

Edinburgh

NORTH

Londonderry

GREAT

Newcastle

SEA

IRELAND

BRITAIN

Dublin

Limerick

Liverpool

HELIGOLAND
(British)

Cork

WALES

Birmingham

Norwich

TEXEL
Helder

Holstein
Lübeck

ENGLAND

Bristol

Amsterdam

Hanover

Bergen-op-Zoom

Hague

Cassel   Leipz

Plymouth

Portsmouth

London

Dover

CONFEDE

WIGHT

Boulogne

Brussels

Cologne

Pety.of Erfurt

English Channel

Cherbourg

Rouen

Lille

Coblentz

Frankfort

Amiens Ardenn

Oberwinden

OF

Bre

Compiègne

Mainz

Worms

Spires

THE

Rennes

Paris

St. Dizier

Valmy

Strasbourg

Ratis
Stuttgart

Nantes

Orleans

Montereau

Lunéville

RI

Chambord

Loire

Dijon

Neuchâtel

Basel

M

RE OLÉRONS

FRANCE

Valençay

Bern

Brixen

Busento

la Rochelle

Clermont

SWITZERLAND

IS

Rochefort

Geneva

BAY

Périgueux

Lyons

Milan

OF

Garonne

Rhone

Tu

BISCAY

Bordeaux

El Ferrol
Coruña

ASTURIAS

Geno

C. Finisterre

Espinosa

San Sebastian

Orthez

Avignon

Pety.of
Lucca

Minho

GALICIA

Burgos

Vitoria

Bayonne

Toulouse

Marseilles   Nice

Medina de
Rio Seco

Tudela

Pamplona

PYRENEES

Andorra

Perpignan

Toulon

CORSICA
Ajaccio

Oporto

Salamanca

K.   OF

Saragossa

Figueras

Busaco
Coimbra

Albuela

Ciudad Rodrigo

Araples Samosierra

Barcelona

Duero

Fuentes de Onoro

ELBA

Vimeiro
Abrantes

Talavera de la Reina

Madrid

Tortosa

Pety.of

Cintra

Torres Vedras

Aranjuez

Tarragona

Pet

Lisbon

Tagus

Elvas

Ocaña

Almonacid

Beja

Badajoz

Guadiana

Valencia

MINORCA

K. OF

Albuera

Ciudad Real

Jucar

BALEARES

SARDINIA

SPAIN

Baylen

IVIZA

MAJORCA

Guadalquivir

Cordova

Cartagena

Cagliari

Seville

Granada

Cadiz

C. Trafalgar

C. de Gata

M   E   D   I   T

E

Strait of Gibraltar

Gibraltar

Algiers

Tangier
Peñon de Velez
(Spain)

Ceuta
(Spain)

Melilla
(Spain)

Tunis

MOROCCO

Alhucemas
(Spain)

Tlemcen

A   L   G   I   E   R   S

TUNIS

Longitude   5°   West   0°   5°   Longitude   10°

20°   15°   10°   5°   0°   5°   10°

55°

50°

45°

40°

35°

ATLANTIC   OCEAN

PORTUGAL

15° 20° 25° 30° 35° 40° 45°

Bjorn
Tavastehus
ALAND
Abo Helsingfors
Sveaborg of Finland
DAGÖ
Stockholm
G.
Reval
L.Peipus
GOTHLAND
Windau
Riga
ÖLAND
Libau
BORNHOLM
Memel
Königsberg
Tilsit
Danzig
Eylau Friedland
RÜGEN
PRUSSIA
Thorn Pultusk
Vistula
GD. DUCHY
Warsaw
OF WARSAW
Breslau
Lublin
Cracow
Lemberg
EMIA
GALICIA
Austerlitz
Carpathian
Vienna Pressburg
Erlau
EMPIRE OF AUSTRIA
Gratz
Buda Pest
HUNGARY
Drave
Villach
Save
TRANSYLVANIA
Temesvar
Alata
Zara
OTTOMAN
Belgrade
Danube
Ragusa
Nish
Balkans
MONTENEGRO
Cattaro
Uskup
Sofia
Maritza
Adrianople
ADRIATIC
SEA
Brindisi
Avlona
Salonica
OF NAPLES
Taranto
Otranto
Janina
ÆGEAN
CORFU
(Fr. to 1814)
(French to 1864)
SEA
Athens
C.Passero
MOREA
ISLANDS
(British from 1809)
CERIGO
800)
CRETE

Rjorn
Lake
Mörö Ladoga
Kronstadt
St.Petersburg
Novgorod
Pskof
Kholm
Tver
Moscow
Yaroslaf
RUSSIAN EMPIRE
Vitebsk
Smolensk
Kovno
Vilna
Studienka
Grodno
Pinsk
Pripet
Desna
Bielgorod
Kiev
Dnieper
Targovitz
Taganrog
Kaminiets
Dniester
Bug
Sea of Azof
Kherson
Aleshki
Bender
Perekop
Izmail
Bakhchisarai
BLACK SEA
Bukharest
Babadag
Silistria
Sinub
(Sinope)
Bosporus
Kastamuni
Amasia
Brusa
Constantinople
Sea of Marmora
Sakaria
Angora
Krizil irmak
EMPIRE
Kutaia
Kaisarieh
(Caesarea)
Gallipoli
Smyrna
Menders
Konieh
Adalia
RHODES
CYPRUS

55°
50°
45°
40°
35°

N
E
A
N
S
E
A

15° from 20° Greenwich 25° 30°

of Warsaw; and Emperor of France, which contained not
only the France that we know, but also Belgium, all German
territory on the left bank of the Rhine, the Kingdom of
Holland,[1] the Duchy of Oldenburg, the Hanseatic cities of
Hamburg and Bremen,[2] the Republic of Genoa, Piedmont,
Tuscany, Rome, and — detached from the rest — the
Illyrian Provinces.   At Madrid, his brother Joseph still
managed to sit, albeit insecurely, upon the throne of Spain.
In Naples, his brother-in-law Murat ruled.   Prussia and
Austria were cowed and forced into alliances with France.
Russia was also an ally, though by no means cowed.   Den-
mark preserved an independence that Napoleon preferred
not to interfere with, since the Danish resentment against
England was still fresh and potent and helped him to keep
Sweden in subjection; whereas in Sweden, the infirm Charles
XIII, already deprived by Russia of Finland and the Åland
Islands, in September, 1810, was cajoled into adopting
Bernadotte, one of Napoleon's marshals, as son and crown
prince, without Napoleon's enthusiastic approval, however.   In Portugal, the contest for possession with the English as yet seemed to favor the French.   Only Turkey, and
the islands of Sardinia, Sicily, Ireland, and Great Britain
were entirely free of his dominance.   In every other quarter
of Europe the Continental Blockade was enforced by the
allies or the soldiers of Napoleon.

But though in 1810 Napoleon was master of more territory than ever before, his position was fundamentally
weaker than it had been after Tilsit.   To say nothing of the
running sore of Spain, the Continental System had failed to
produce the results he wanted.   The blockade had never

[1] Louis and Napoleon had never exhibited great fraternal affection for each
other. Now Louis, regarding himself as a Dutchman rather than a Frenchman,
frequently balked at the disadvantages of the Continental System.   After
Napoleon's return from the Austrian campaign, he decided he needed Holland
as "one of the principal arteries" of his Empire. He sent troops into Holland
to occupy part of it and Louis, unable to get the Dutch Council to resist, abdicated and fled.   Napoleon then annexed Holland (July 9, 1810).

[2] These were on the North Sea and therefore important points in the Continental System.   To have better control of them, Napoleon annexed all three
regions in December, 1810.

been completely successful; smuggling became as highly developed an art as it has more recently become; clothing, coffins, false labels, and numerous other devices were used to hide importations or to disguise their origin.   The prices of goods thus smuggled became exorbitantly high, but many a Continental could be found willing to run the risks of arrest and to pay the enormous charge for his coffee rather than use the chicory that had recently come into fashion as a substitute, though he might be persuaded to use the beet sugar that the high cost of colonial cane sugar had for the first time made it profitable to manufacture.   The island of Heligoland, taken by the English from Denmark in 1807, had become the chief source of supply for the smugglers, who in every respect had the coöperation of the British Government.

But smuggling was not the only means of getting around the Continental Blockade.   Despite Adam Smith's *Wealth of Nations*, the mercantilist theory of *favorable balance of trade* was still dominant in both English and French governmental circles.   Each felt that the important feature of its economic campaign against the other was to ensure that it would export more than it imported and that the other would import more than it exported.   Consequently, Napoleon did not object to French and Continental goods going to England, nor did England object to British or colonial goods going into France and the Continent.   Both England and France granted licenses to neutral merchants, the one to carry English goods to French ports, the other to carry French goods to English ports, each intending to promote its own trade at the expense of the other.   If a neutral vessel received licenses from both Governments, its chances of capture, even if it did engage in contraband trade, were greatly diminished, since it could show either license in an emergency.   Even if a neutral vessel or, in the case of the French licenses, the vessel of a friendly belligerent, were granted only a French or only an English license, there were enough such licenses issued to destroy the effectiveness of both the Orders in Council and the Continental System.

Since prize goods were sold subject to a huge tax, Napoleon even went so far as to allow certain English goods to be admitted and sold as prize goods. Eventually he adopted the practice of granting licenses to merchants who would carry as much French goods out of the Continent as English goods into it. But English manufactures continued to flourish at the expense of other nations. Even France, though her trade had fallen off considerably since 1806 and more noticeably after 1810, derived some advantage, especially in the textile industries. It is possible to maintain that one of the motives of Napoleon (perhaps the paramount motive) was to bring about this result — to benefit French industry and commerce at the expense of the industry and commerce of other nations to be ruined by the Continental System. It is significant, for instance, that Lyons now began to compete with the Italian cities as a center of the silk trade. But Russians, Germans, Italians, and Dutch had not only to pay high prices for colonial goods or do without, but had, also, to see their business ruined.

England herself did not go unscathed. The wheat imports of England showed an average excess over exports, for the years 1807–12, of 104,000 tons. This in a nation and an age that believed in the mercantilist theory of favorable balance created a greater consternation than the actual figures would justify. In 1809, the exchange began to show a marked fall; in 1810–11 there was a crisis in which a number of merchants and some manufacturers went bankrupt. This period of depression was probably due, however, more to economic disturbances generally attendant upon war conditions than to the Continental System in particular. In general, the Continental System, however magnificent the conception of forcing all Europe into one gigantic scheme for the destruction of England's economic organization, had almost no lasting result upon the developments of the nineteenth century. Professor Rose says ironically of Napoleon's "constant straining after the one final expedient that must assure the ruin of England":

It is difficult to believe that this was the man who, in the domain of thought, sneered at *idéologues*. He himself was the chief *idéologue*, the supreme dupe, of the age. As he looked round on the Europe of his day, he took no count of the mighty forces of the industrial revolution that then were girding England with the strength of youth and were connecting all parts of the world by indissoluble ties; what he beheld was a mirage conjured up by his vivid fancy and boundless egotism.[1]

If there is any apology to be made for such a gigantic, if glorious, failure, Napoleon made it:

It is the English who have forced me to aggrandize myself unceasingly. But for them I would not have united Naples, Spain, Portugal to my empire. I have willed to struggle and to extend my coasts in order to increase my resources. If they keep on, they will oblige me to join Holland to my shore lines, then the Hanse towns, finally Pomerania, and perhaps even Danzig.

The implications of this statement, made in November, 1805 were never fully realized, but already Napoleon's domination in Europe was greater than any conquerer before his time had been able to establish. At the time it was made, therefore, it was only natural that Napoleon should begin to wonder what would happen to it all when he died. Napoleon had at least one and probably three sons, and was expecting to be blessed with a fourth (all by different mothers), but none of these might legitimately succeed to his throne. Josephine had not borne him any children. In her anxiety to preserve her influence over her husband, she had not only had her marriage confirmed by the Catholic Church, but had tried to establish other ties. Her son Eugène had long been a favorite with the Emperor; his relations with her daughter Hortense, wife of Louis Napoleon, were so cordial as to have led to scandalous, though probably baseless, rumors regarding the parentage of the young prince, Louis Napoleon, afterwards Napoleon III. Louis Napoleon's older brother, Napoleon Charles,

---

[1] Quoted from *The Cambridge Modern History*, IX, 380, by permission of the University Press. Cambridge, England.

had long been regarded as the heir presumptive, and when
he died (May 5, 1807), Josephine again found her position
greatly weakened. For the first time, Napoleon suggested
a divorce from Josephine and began to consider Anne, the
little sister of the Czar Alexander, as his future wife. But
Alexander put him off; she was too young, he said — as,
indeed, she was. But after the Austrian campaign he
broached the matter to Josephine again, and though she
fainted or pretended to faint and he was very much moved,
all was eventually arranged. Josephine retired to her villa
Malmaison with the title of Empress, the affections of her
former husband, and a "dowry." The wife whom Bonaparte had taken just before his first Austrian offensive,
Napoleon set aside after his last Austrian offensive. Of
eighteen eligible candidates, Napoleon chose the Archduchess Marie Louise of Austria as her successor — Marie
Louise, who had spoken of him as the "Antichrist" and of
her marriage as a "sacrifice." The Austrian Government
rejoiced at the protection thus acquired and Napoleon at
the honor of an affinity with one of the oldest royal families of Europe. But when on April 1, 1810, the marriage
was solemnized at Saint-Cloud, the populace that loved
Josephine showed no signs of enthusiasm for their new Empress, whom not even the birth of a son, the King of Rome
and the future *Aiglon*, on March 20, 1811, was to make
popular.

Again, between 1809 and 1812, Napoleon had only one
enemy — England. England now, however, had in Portugal a foothold on the Continent that gave her a distinct
advantage she had not hitherto enjoyed. There Wellesley had again been put in command in April, 1809, and
his conduct of the phases of the Peninsular War that ensued
became his greatest claim to glory. By the end of July he
had succeeded in driving Soult's corps out of Portugal, and
on July 28, after two days of fighting, he defeated the French
under Joseph, Victor, and Jourdan at Talavera in Spain.
Wellesley was awarded the title of Viscount Wellington and
Baron Douro. Napoleon sent his ablest marshal, Masséna.

to check the English advance, and Masséna was able to force Wellington out of Spain and, on September 16, to cross into Portugal. Though repulsed at Busaco (September 29), where he lost five thousand men to the enemy's thirteen hundred, Masséna obliged the English to retreat behind the fortifications of Torres Vedras. These were a triple line of trenches with one hundred and fifty-two redoubts, manned by sixty-eight thousand English, Portuguese, and Spanish with seven hundred guns, and reaching for thirty miles from Lisbon to the sea — the first line of trenches of any great length in modern warfare. The French had not even known of their existence. Here Masséna was obliged to stop (October 12) and in March, 1811, after a siege of five months, during which food became increasingly hard for the besiegers to get, he retreated into Spain.

Napoleon again had not thought the Peninsular War important enough for his personal attention. The period of comparative peace between 1809 and 1812 he regarded as another opportunity to weld his far-flung empire together. One step that he took soon after his marriage and perhaps to please his Austrian relatives, justifiable as it was, was indiscreet. He dismissed Fouché, who was contaminated by revolutionary glory and intrigues with England and other enemies of Napoleon, but whose ruthless police system had made Napoleon more a master of his press and his people than perhaps even Napoleon, who acknowledged his debt to Fouché in this respect, was aware. His place was taken by General Savary. In 1810, also came the Tariff of Trianon, another attempt, like its predecessor, the Tariff of 1806, to promote French commerce and manufacture at the expense of England and neutral powers. But unlike that of 1806 — what with the workings of the Continental System and the licenses — it had evil effects upon French business. For in 1810–11 banks began to fail on the Continent, at Lübeck, at Amsterdam, at Paris. "The situation of trade becomes daily more critical," wrote the leading cotton manufacturer of France in January, 1811; "sales have almost ceased, and payments are slow and uncertain. My credit is ruined."

In 1811, also, came the culmination of his quarrel with the Pope, ending in a Senatus Consultum making Rome subordinate to Paris as the second city of the Empire, and the Pope to the Emperor as a stipendiary, at two million francs a year, under oath not to contravene the Gallican Articles of 1682. In August, Napoleon summoned a picked National Council, which decreed that thereafter bishops might be instituted by the Metropolitan if the Pope failed to take action within six months. The Pope, a prisoner at Savona, accepted, but in a brief whose language was unsatisfactory to Napoleon. The matter dragged on, therefore, bringing increasing hostility to the Emperor and proportionate sympathy for the Pope, until, the war with Russia having begun, Napoleon himself sought reacceptance of the decree of the National Council, even at the cost of definite concessions on his part. This was arranged by the Concordat of Fontainebleau on January 25, 1813.[1]

During this period, too, the censorship of the press reached its highest point. Madame de Staël's *Allemagne* was seized and she herself ordered to leave France in 1810. In February of that year the laws upon the press were summarized in a decree the tenor of which may be discerned from article 10:

> Printing or causing to be printed anything which can involve injury to the duties of subjects toward the sovereign or the interests of the state is forbidden.

By October, 1811, only four newspapers remained unsuppressed in Paris. Liberty had long ceased to exist; in 1808, Napoleon had suppressed the Tribunate, the only body that could claim to have authority from the people. Equality was fast going the same way; for Napoleon more and more chose to favor the nobility of the Ancient Régime, whom he had allowed to return to France, at the expense of those who had deserved well of the Republic and the Empire. Careers still were "open to talent," but to a lesser degree than in the days of the Consulate. The marriage

[1] The Pope did not regain his liberty until March, 1814.

with an Austrian Archduchess reminded people of Marie
Antoinette; and when in 1811 Napoleon fixed a maximum
price for the sale of corn inside of Paris, they remembered
the Terror.   Perhaps the only popular measures that he
took during his second reform movement were the completion of his organization of the University of France,
and a series of public works in Paris, Rome, Hamburg,
Genoa, and other cities under his control, where harbors
were dredged, canals built, imposing buildings and monuments erected, parks and boulevards laid out.   If one dared
to assume that genius is an exhaustible human quality
like energy, one might find an explanation for the difference
between the years 1802–03 and 1809–12; certainly the more
successful Napoleon was in his conquests the less fortunate
he was in his internal administration.

Exclusive of his military achievements, however, Napoleon during his imperial career retained one indubitable
title to greatness,   Like Alexander, he hellenized the bar-
barians.   The tyrant in France was still the herald of the
Rights of Man abroad.   Wherever he went, he left the in-
delible mark of the French theory of politics and of his own
unmistakable efficiency in government.   Nowhere was this
more conspicuous than in the very places where he wanted
least to bring about popular reform.   Of Austria's growing
nationalism, something has already been said.   In Prussia,
the humiliation of Tilsit and the noble example of Queen
Louisa *moritura* created an intense feeling of patriotism.
The Treaty of 1808, "wishing to remove the difficulties
which have occurred in the execution of the Treaty of Tilsit," obliged defenseless Prussia to pay an indemnity of
140,000,000 francs, turn over certain districts for French
occupation until it was paid, and reduce her army to forty-
two thousand men.   It simply added to the chagrin.   Dissatisfied Germans, despite the reduction of Prussia, turned
to her rather than to Austria, so largely non-German, for
leadership.   The best hearts and brains of Germany rallied
to the Prussian cause; it is not without significance that
Stein, Arndt, Hardenburg, Niebuhr, Scharnhorst, Gneise-

nau, Fichte, Yorck, and Blücher were not native Prussians.

Of these, Stein was called to the King's cabinet on October 4, 1807. This was his second term as minister, for he had quarreled with Frederick William and had been dismissed in January, 1807. Under his guidance as Minister of Home Affairs, the King's Council and Ministry was reorganized; the edict of emancipation (October 9, 1807) was issued, abolishing serfdom throughout the realm and sweeping away other feudal institutions and encumbrances to political development, so that henceforth nobles might follow professions and peasants rise to higher stations; and (November 19, 1808) a considerable degree of local self-government was granted to the cities and villages. In 1809, when Von Humboldt became Minister of Public Instruction, he reorganized the school system, inducing the King to erect the University of Berlin as its apex. In 1811, Hardenberg carried feudal reform to its logical conclusion by permitting the peasant to get complete control of his land provided he surrendered one third of it to his lord. Unfortunately the international situation prevented a thorough execution of these reforms; Prussia was but slightly better off politically and socially in 1812 than France had been in 1789.

While thus, in civil affairs, Prussia by royal decree achieved in a few years something of what it had taken France a score of years and a revolution to accomplish, a Commission for Military Reorganization, under the presidency of Scharnhorst, undertook to reform the army. Officers who had not conducted themselves ably during the war with France were cashiered; provisions were made for the promotion of able young men. The army, to be sure, was limited by the Treaty of 1808 to forty-two thousand men, but nothing in the Treaty demanded that it must always consist of the same forty-two thousand men. And so, as fast as a man was trained, he passed into the reserve and another came to take his place. In this way, by the year 1812, Prussia could boast of having one hundred and fifty thousand trained soldiers, although ostensibly her army had not exceeded the stipulated limit. The French Revolution had made possible and necessary a Prussian Revolution, and French militarism had produced its antitoxin in Prussian militarism.

Stein was not permitted to carry out his entire scheme for the rehabilitation of Prussia. Napoleon, who at first failed to appreciate the profundity of the feeling he had aroused in Germany, scorned the Prussians as "poor, miserable people." But he soon changed his mind. When he was in Madrid in December, 1808, he declared Stein an enemy of France, sequestered his property, and ordered his arrest. The precedents of the Duc d'Enghien and the publisher Palm left no room for doubt as to what this order meant. Stein sought safety in flight (January 5, 1809), leaving Hardenberg behind to complete his work. For three years Stein remained in retirement in Bohemia, to emerge as a minister of the Czar Alexander when Napoleon was driven out of Russia and Germany.

Those three years saw the rise of a widespread popular movement against the French oppressors not only in Austria and Prussia, but in the states of the Confederation of the Rhine as well. While the princes and aristocracy of the German states fawned upon the conquerer in hope of favors yet to come, the leading intellectual lights formed themselves into a Moral and Scientific Union (June, 1808) which, by its popular name of *Tugendbund*, was to become a significant factor in the moral reawakening of Germany. This was the time when the University of Breslau was incorporated; when Jahn organized his open-air gymnasia for the instillation of physical prowess and patriotic devotion in young Germans; when Arndt, who had already been obliged to flee to Sweden for his attack on Napoleon in *Die Geist der Zeit*, returned and wrote his stirring song, *Was ist das Deutsche Vaterland?* and when Fichte, author of the famous *Reden an die Deutsche Nation*, inspired his faculty and students at the freshwater University of Berlin with an ardor that later made devoted soldiers of them. Minor writers did their share in rousing an enthusiastic emotion; and while daring spirits like Schill and the young Duke of Brunswick-Oels, impatient of restraint, led bold but abortive raids upon the French, the mass of Germany's youth waited eagerly for the moment when the Napoleonic system must fall and Germany be freed. They forgot that in Prussia, Bavaria, Württemberg, Baden, and other German states that had come under Napoleon's domination, French rule had meant the abolition of feudalism, the modernization of the law, the destruction of clerical and aristocratic privilege, and efficiency in government; they remembered only that it meant humiliation.

That the Napoleonic system might fall was now a rising hope among his enemies. For Napoleon and the mighty Alexander had quarreled and were preparing for a struggle that was to be the most eventful and disastrous in the annals of Napoleon. For this rupture there were several causes. Since the Congress of Erfurt relations between the two had not been very cordial. Alexander had never quite forgiven Napoleon for the ill-treatment of his friends, Frederick William and Queen Louisa. He disapproved of Napoleon's marriage with an Austrian princess. He was offended when Napoleon increased his territories at the expense of the Duke of Oldenburg, a relative of his. Napoleon's Oriental ambitions roused his suspicions. Furthermore, the unburied Polish ghost seemed to become more restless when, by the Treaty of Vienna, Napoleon added Galicia to the territory of the Grand Duchy of Warsaw. On the other hand, Napoleon was angered by Alexander's refusal to coöperate with him unquestioningly with regard to the Continental System. Alexander found that many of the chief products of Russia could be sold only to England, while certain necessities could be bought only from England. The Continental System was ruining Russian peasants for the advantage, it seemed, of French merchants. Alexander determined that this must not continue. When, therefore, in 1810, Napoleon, on promulgating the Tariff of Trianon, asked Alexander to adopt it likewise, not only did Alexander refuse, but he issued a ukase (December 31, 1810) levying a tariff on certain French goods and opening his ports to neutrals. He began, too, to prepare plans for the reduction of the Grand Duchy of Warsaw.

At the beginning of 1811 it was clear that a break would come, but the year 1811 passed without any disaster. Both sides, however, began to make ready for war. By divers threats Napoleon succeeded in forcing his reluctant allies, Prussia and Austria, to provide him with contingents of twenty thousand and thirty thousand respectively. He made the mistake, however, of refusing to Bernadotte, the new crown prince of Sweden, a piece of territory in return for his support. Indeed, he even went so far as to occupy Swedish Pomerania. This decided Bernadotte, now actually, if not nominally the ruler of Sweden, and on April 5, 1812, he formed an alliance with the Czar. To this alliance England was admitted on May 3, 1812, and France now faced a sixth coalition. To have a freer hand, Russia made peace with Turkey at Bucharest that same month (May 12, 1812) by evacuating the Roumanian provinces, but annexing Bessarabia. The prospects for the success of this coalition seemed brighter than those that had faced previous alliances.

Help came to France from an undeserved though not wholly unexpected quarter. That was the United States of America. Madison, on entering office, attempted to negotiate the points of dispute between England and the United States, and actually drew up a satisfactory treaty with the English Minister, which, however, the Government at London refused to ratify. Congress then passed the so-called Macon Bill No. 2, by which trade was renewed with the world at large (May 1, 1810), but the President was empowered to close it to England if France revoked her restrictions on neutral commerce, or to France if England revoked hers. Napoleon saw an opportunity to act, and informed the American Minister that on November 1, 1810, his decrees would no longer remain in effect if the United States could force England to respect her commercial rights. In February, 1811, Congress, accordingly, resumed the policy of non-intercourse with Great Britain. As a matter of fact, however, the French decrees were never really repealed in favor of American commerce. Madison, nevertheless, called Congress in special session on November 4, 1811, and asked it to prepare for war against England. On June 1, 1812, the President's message asked for war, and on June 19, Congress complied. Five days later, England revoked her Orders in Council, but it was too late. Hostilities that were to last two years and to have no important results for Europe, save that they diverted a small part of England's attention from Napoleon, had already begun.

Napoleon had got his army ready for a march through Russia before the United States declared war. Six hundred and fifty thousand men, two thirds of whom were not French, lay on the Niemen, ready to advance. On June 24, without even an attempt at opposition, the river was crossed, and on June 28, Napoleon, still unresisted, occupied Vilna. As the smaller Russian force of two hundred and fifty thousand retreated before him, he reached Smolensk, which he captured by assault only after a fire started by the retreating enemy, and the loss of about twelve thousand men. Napoleon had intended to winter at Smolensk and to solidify his conquests, but as his march had been quicker than he had expected and there was still a good stretch of campaign weather to be expected, he decided to go on to Moscow. Although there had been very little fighting, the Grand Army had already lost about one hundred thousand men, through straggling, desertion, fatigue, disease, and hunger.

The Russian army, under the command of Kutusoff, resisted his approach to the holy city of Moscow. Napoleon's speed had been such that he had been obliged to leave the greater part of his army behind. Of these, those who were not casualties of battle were ill, exhausted, unequipped, stragglers, or deserters. Marshal Marmont later maintained that one corps, which had started out with eighty thousand men, reached Moscow with fifteen thousand, and that fifty thousand cavalry were reduced to six thousand at

Moscow. When the Russian army of one hundred and thirty thousand men blocked his progress at Borodino, Napoleon was able to gather but one hundred and fifty thousand troops with which to oppose them. Ninety thousand men fell in that battle, the bloodiest ever fought until more civilized times; of these sixty thousand were Russians. On September 14, 1812, Napoleon and his army entered Moscow. But his exultation was short-lived. By the orders of the governor of the city, Moscow was set on fire that very night and the greater part of the city destroyed. Napoleon's hopes had literally turned to ashes. It was obvious that he could not stay there. The charred walls of the buildings that still remained would offer only poor protection against Russian Cossacks and Russian weather; the feeding of an army would be a difficult task in a deserted city. Napoleon determined, since he did not dare to advance, to order a retreat.

The story of that retreat hardly needs repetition. It is the story of an army constantly attacked in the rear by ubiquitous bands of Cossacks and Russian regulars, obliged to return along the road it had already devastated as it came; now reduced to only fifty-five thousand men and twelve thousand horses fit for service, even before the cold set in; destined to endure death by freezing, by starving, by drowning in icy waters, by bleeding on snowy battle-fields, or by falling into the hands of enraged Cossacks. It is a story made familiar by song, picture, and prose. Only the incredible labors and heroism of Ney, "the bravest of the brave," who sacrificed himself and his men in almost continuous rearguard actions, prevented the retreat that had already turned into a rout from resulting in annihilation. On November 28–29 the army succeeded in crossing the Beresina under fire from two Russian armies, and there twenty-five thousand Frenchmen lost their lives. They reached Vilna on December 8 and were forced out by the Russians on December 10. Kovno, where they then sought refuge, fell to the relentless Russians on December 14; and the pursuit did not end until the French recrossed the Niemen River. Only about one thousand of the Guards had preserved any sort of discipline. The rest, disorganized wings and stragglers, did not number more than one hundred thousand. More than five hundred thousand men, one hundred and fifty thousand horses, and one thousand guns of the Grand Army had been lost.[1] No other single campaign of six months' duration — even in the World War when methods of killing were so much more scientific — was proportionately disastrous. Napoleon, who had carefully studied the campaign of the Swedish Charles XII in order to avoid his mistakes, had committed an error more fatal even than his. And Kutusoff had won a complete victory for Russia and conservatism. England and Russia had proved that Napoleon could not conquer all of Europe. It remained to be seen whether all of Europe might not now conquer Napoleon.

[1] These are the figures of Stschepkin in *The Cambridge Modern History*, IX, 505, but Pariset in Lavisse, *Histoire de France Contemporaire*, III, 427, gives only three hundred thousand casualties. The one is a Russian, the other a French historian.

CHAPTER II

LIBERATION, ABDICATION, AND RESTORATION

ONCE again, as in Egypt, Napoleon felt obliged to leave a routed army to a subordinate and to return to a domestic crisis. Placing his armies (December 5) under the command of Marshal Murat, King of Naples, before it had even arrived at Vilna in Lithuania, he hastened, by rapid posts, to his capital. Murat surrendered the command to Eugène in order to return to Naples to guard his own interests. On December 18, Napoleon arrived in Paris. The cause of his precipitation was the conspiracy of Malet, already the hero of a republican cabal in 1808. Malet had spent eighteen months in prison for this previous plot, but had recently succeeded in getting himself transferred to a prison hospital. Despite all that Napoleon could do, reports of the disasters that the French incurred in Russia had reached Paris. Deciding to take advantage of these rumors, Malet made his escape from the hospital (October 23, 1812), and with nothing but his audacity, a lie about Napoleon's having died before Moscow, and a few forged documents, succeeded in taking over several important posts in Paris before he was recognized and arrested. He was tried and shot together with his fellows. Although the execution was not carried out until some time after Napoleon's return, yet the dénouement took place before his arrival.

The significance of the movement was not so much that it had nearly succeeded as that, on the report of Napoleon's death, no one seemed to have thought of his son as his successor; everybody proved quite ready to accept a provisional government. All Napoleon's clever machinations to found a hereditary dynasty and to secure an imperial princess as mother to his heir, it appeared, would prove to have been quite in vain if he did not now take additional precautions. Hoping to remedy this disloyalty, Napoleon,

by a Senatus Consultum of February 5, 1813, provided for
the naming of the Empress mother as regent for her minor
son during the absence or in case of the death of the Emperor. Having so designated Marie Louise on March 30,
1813, Napoleon left for the frontier again.

The fighting now was in Germany. Napoleon had
managed, by calling classes that were not yet of age and by
making new levies on his allies, to gather another army of
about two hundred and fifty thousand men. But among
these allies, Prussia was no longer to be counted. Even on
the retreat from Moscow, General Yorck von Wartenburg,
who commanded the Prussian contingent, had not co-
operated loyally with the French army; and on December
30, 1812, shortly after Napoleon's army had crossed into
Polish territory again, without authority from his Government, he declared the neutrality of his corps by the Convention of Tauroggen. The sight of bedraggled, emaciated,
disorderly corps returning whence a splendid army of over
half a million men had gone, confirmed rumors that had
reached Berlin of overwhelming defeats. Germany took
heart, and Prussia listened eagerly to the plea of Alexander
for an alliance, though the King was cautious and the
French occupied the country up to the Vistula.   Stein
returned to Prussia, and with Yorck's connivance summoned the people of Prussia to rise against the oppressor.
The King, for a time, did not dare to manifest any open
disloyalty to the French treaties. At first he repudiated
Yorck's treaty with Russia. After a skillful double game,
however, the pressure of public opinion and their own hopeful willingness to risk all in a single blow for liberation
caused Frederick William and Hardenberg to consent to
the Treaties of Kalisch (February 26, 1813) and Breslau
(March 19, 1813) with the Czar: Prussia was to be restored
and enlarged on condition that she furnished an army of
eighty thousand men to fight the French. Troops began to
pour into her army; Germans who were not Prussians
organized themselves into Free Corps; and those who could
not fight pledged their fortunes. After the war had started,

Prussia was able to put two hundred and fifty thousand fighting men in the field. It was to be a War of Liberation à outrance.

Fighting had continued almost constantly during the absence of Napoleon and the French had sullenly retired to the west, yielding Hamburg and Dresden. When Napoleon rejoined his army, the first pitched battle was fought at Lützen and Gross Görschen (May 2) in which Napoleon lost eighteen thousand men to the Allies' ten thousand, but the Allies were obliged to retreat to Bautzen. Here (May 20–21) Napoleon's conscripts again repulsed the Russo-Prussian troops and forced them to seek refuge in Silesia, enabling Davout to retake Hamburg. Napoleon had already reëstablished himself at Dresden.

In the mean time, Austria had taken no part in the hostilities. Between the aggrandizement of Russia and of France there was little choice for her to make. Before she dared risk a fifth humiliation at Napoleon's hands, she wished to be assured of her own advantages. It was largely because both sides were exhausted and each felt that a truce would be of greater benefit to itself than to the other, but also because it was advisable to ascertain exactly what Austria's attitude was, that an armistice was concluded at Pläswitz on June 4, calling for a congress to meet at Prague to draw up terms of peace. It was through Austria's mediation that this armistice was made possible, and Austria now determined to make the most of her favorable position. Napoleon hoped to influence his father-in-law to cast Austria's fortunes with France by promises of concessions. He did not know that shortly after the armistice was signed Austrian, Prussian, Russian, and English representatives had met at Reichenbach, where, on June 14–15, Prussia, Russia, and England formed an alliance by which each agreed not to make a separate peace with Napoleon, England promising a subsidy besides. On June 27, Austria pledged her adherence if Napoleon refused to accept the terms of peace that Metternich, Austria's Minister of Foreign Affairs, had already (on June 7) announced. By

a series of skillful maneuvers Metternich had thus reëstablished Austria's independence of France in diplomatic
affairs, and now meant to delay negotiations until her armies
were ready to take a decisive part in the war.

These terms were not altogether unfavorable to Napoleon.
They required him to surrender Warsaw, the Confederation
of the Rhine, and Northern Germany to their *ante-bellum*
sovereigns, the Illyrian Provinces to Austria, and to restore Prussia. They still left him in control of Belgium,
the Rhine Valley, and part of Italy. But Napoleon could
not bring himself to accept. He stormed at Metternich,
who came to interview him on June 28 and 30; he even
made certain concessions at the futile Congress of Prague
that opened shortly afterwards; but he would not accept
Metternich's proposals *in toto*. This reluctance was partially because of his unwillingness to admit defeat and to
yield his ambitions, but it was motivated by more than
pride. Politically it was unwise for him to admit defeat.
His position in France was no longer as secure as it once had
been; he was still able to control his people by stringent
censorship, but what was suppressed he fully realized. He
had once declared that for usurpers glory in war was an
essential that hereditary rulers might afford to overlook.
To have accepted Metternich's terms would have meant
his first unsuccessful peace and it might have spelled his
downfall in France. He was "in blood stepp'd in so far
that, should he wade no more, returning were as tedious as
go o'er."

While the Congress of Prague was in session and Napoleon's forces enjoyed a respite in Germany, his armies were
enduring not only fatigue, but also repeated reverses in
Spain. In March, 1811, when Masséna had reluctantly
given up the siege of the Torres Vedras lines and retreated
to Spain, Wellington had gone after him in hot pursuit.
Rearguard actions, interspersed with an occasional battle,
were frequent, and Masséna's army, when it regained
Spanish territory, had lost over half of the sixty thousand
men who had started with him on his invasion of Portugal.

On the other hand, Soult had, in the mean time, succeeded in capturing Badajos, and Victor had laid siege to Cadiz. Wellington, however, marched on. On May 11, he took Almeida, while his lieutenant, Beresford, by a hard-won victory at Albuera (May 16), forced Soult to take refuge in Seville. Napoleon recalled Masséna and appointed the inexperienced Marshal Marmont in his place. Beresford and Wellington together now laid siege to Badajos and to Ciudad Rodrigo in turn. After several attacks, retreats, and counter-attacks, on January 8, 1812, they began to besiege Ciudad Rodrigo a second time, and eleven days later (January 19) took it by assault. Here Wellington won his earldom. The Allied army then marched south and by another daring attack succeeded in taking Badajos likewise, on April 7, after fearful carnage. Salamanca's turn came next; here on July 19 one of the most costly battles of the Peninsular War was fought. Beresford was badly wounded.

King Joseph's army now retreated, and on August 12 Wellington entered Madrid. For a time the French forces united and succeeded in driving the Allies back into Ciudad Rodrigo (November 18, 1812), where they went into winter quarters. When he took the field again in 1813, Joseph was obliged again to retreat, and at Vittoria, not far from the northernmost coast of Spain, he made a last stand. Here, on June 21, 1813, the Allies inflicted a decisive defeat on the French and drove them in rout from the field. On June 26, the bulk of the French army abandoned Spain and crossed the Pyrenees. And the Portuguese Government named Wellington Duke of Victory. Wellington did not stop at the mountains. Soult gradually retreated before him, surrendering San Sebastian, which fell on September 9, and Pampeluna, on October 31. These were the last French posts in Spain.

Soult now withdrew to Bayonne. The Spanish, on entering French territory, wreaked such a dire vengeance for what they had suffered at French hands that for a moment Wellington refused to serve as their commander. Soult was again defeated at Villefranque and the Nive before the winter intervened to give him a respite. In 1814, when operations were renewed, Wellington succeeded in driving Soult out of Bayonne (February 14–15) and laid siege to it. The French retreated toward Toulouse and were again defeated in the battle of Orthez (February 27). The partisans of the Bourbons in the neighborhood regained confidence and activity. On their promise to open the gates of Bordeaux to the English, Beresford led an army there, and on March 12 the city surrendered. Napoleon tried desperately to create disaffection in Wellington's ranks by freeing Ferdinand VII, legitimate King of Spain, and having him declare peace, but to no avail. The relentless impetus of the Allies brought them to Toulouse, and on April 12 Soult was once more obliged to evacuate. But the ten thousand men who fell in the terrific struggles around Bayonne and Toulouse after April 6 died in vain, for on that day peace had virtually been declared at Paris. Learning of this, Soult and Wellington agreed to an armistice on April 18. The Spanish had received their hard-won vengeance.

The "running sore," as Napoleon called the Peninsular War, had sapped his strength, but it was a more direct wound that overwhelmed him. The armistice of Pläswitz and the Congress of Prague had produced nothing but aimless bickering, for Napoleon, though, when looking backward from St. Helena, he confessed that he "felt the reins slipping" from his hands, was confident despite the losses in Spain that he could manage the Sixth Coalition just as he had managed the ones before it. The situation in Spain was not encouraging, but Wellington had not yet crossed the Pyrenees. When, therefore, Austria delivered her ultimatum, fixing August 10 as the latest date for acceptance of her terms, he made no reply. On August 12, Austria declared war. On August 14, Napoleon unexpectedly announced that he was willing to accept Metternich's proposals, but Austria replied that it was too late.

The Coalition had about eight hundred and sixty thousand drilled men under arms, against whom the Emperor could muster from France and the Confederation less than seven hundred thousand, of whom many were raw recruits; and the Coalition now had the services of the greatest rivals of Napoleon, the general Moreau, who had been induced to leave America, and the statesman Stein; both of them had joined the retinue of the Czar. The Allies took the offensive with Dresden as their objective. Napoleon, who had left Dresden with the intention of striking at Berlin, was hastily recalled to defend the Saxon capital. For two days (August 26–27), Schwarzenberg, Frederick William, and Alexander attacked and counter-attacked and in the end retreated. General Moreau was one of the twenty-three thousand Allied casualties of the battle of Dresden. The French had lost ten thousand. Against two hundred thousand Austrians, Prussians, and Russians, Napoleon with ninety-six thousand French, Saxons, and Württembergers had won his last great victory on foreign soil.

It was a sorely needed victory, for Oudenot had been defeated at Gross Beeren by Bernadotte, and Macdonald on the Katzbach River by Blücher (August 23 and 25 respectively). On August 30, Vandamme capitulated with more than ten thousand men to the Russians under Barclay de Tolly at Kulm. Even Marshal Ney suffered a defeat at Dennewitz on September 6. By these defeats, Napoleon's offensives against Berlin and Bohemia had been checked, and it was all he could do to hold his own in Saxony. The Allies, despite the disastrous outcome of the attack on Dresden, felt justified in planning a new map of Europe. At Töplitz, on September 9, they agreed to restore Austria and Prussia and to dissolve the Confederation of the Rhine, granting complete independence to the states of southern and western Germany. The Treaty of Töplitz reassured the monarchs of the larger German principalities, who had wavered between a strong desire to be rid of French suzerainty and an equally strong fear that liberation from France would mean only domination by Austria. On October 8, by the Treaty of Reid, Bavaria cast her lot with the Coalition, and the French ranks grew thinner as the German soldiers deserted individually and in contingents.

In October, Schwarzenberg again took the offensive. Napoleon had concentrated his forces at Leipzig. In the rain and mist of October 16 the Prussians opened the attack upon him that was to last for three days and to become known as the "Battle of the Nations." At Mockern, Wachau, Connewitz, Holzhausen, and other villages near Leipzig, the *Völkerschlacht* raged; three hundred thousand Allies pounded away at one hundred and ninety thousand French, Saxons, and Württembergers. In the midst of the battle the German allies of Napoleon went over to the enemy. Fearing to be cut off, Napoleon at length gave the order to retreat, and by a single bridge the French army, defeated in a battle such as, save for Borodino, had never before been witnessed, poured across the Pleisse River. The total loss was one hundred thousand men, of whom about half were French.

It was a Napoleon sick in soul and in body that led his army through the Bavarian forces that endeavored to check his retreat at Hanau (October 30) and across the Rhine. Only about eighty thousand troops, half of whom were stragglers, were left of the French army of a quarter million that had begun the War of Liberation. Most of the casualties were desertions that not only weakened Napoleon's army, but strengthened his enemies. As the imperial forces crossed into France, the Confederation crashed. Württemberg joined the Coalition on November 2 and Baden on November 20. At Frankfort, in November, the Allies had been willing to offer France her natural boundaries, but by December they committed themselves only to the extent of promising "a stretch of territory which France never knew under her kings." Germany was liberated, but the liberators had now become avengers.

Napoleon returned to Paris in the hope of rallying the nation behind him as he had in the past and thereby forcing a favorable peace from the Coalition. But a defeated Em-

408 LIBERATION, ABDICATION, RESTORATION

peror who had suppressed a liberty-loving people for almost
ten years was not to find them as docile as when he came, a
conquering hero, to rule over a nation sick of terror and
anarchy. The imperial session of the Legislature that he
called with more than the usual pomp proved unexpectedly
sullen. The Senate lived up to its best traditions of syco-
phancy, but the Corps Législatif delivered to him, through a
commission intended to examine and approve the Emperor's
diplomacy, an address urging him to continue the war "only
for the independence of the French people and the integrity
of its territory" and "to maintain the complete and constant
execution of the laws that guarantee to the French the rights
of liberty, security, property, and to the nation the free
exercise of its political rights." The Corps Législatif was
immediately adjourned, while a hurt and angry Emperor
raged at them: "The throne is in the nation and you cannot
separate me from it without harming it, for the nation has
more need of me than I have of it!"

As the new year dawned, Napoleon again took Herculean
measures to create an army. Even with the children of the
class of 1815, he could make up a force of only one hundred
and ten thousand men. On January 25, he went to the
front to face three armies moving through Belgium, Lorraine, and the Jura Mountains, each considerably larger
than his entire command. Taking every advantage that a
central position offered, he attacked one enemy and then
another, but, though he fought what some critics have considered the ablest campaign of his career and won most of
his battles, he was obliged to retreat by the sheer weight of
numbers. And as he retreated, the Allies decided upon the
terms of peace that they would offer a vanquished France.
Divided among themselves, jealous of each other's motives,
fearful of the power that was still Napoleon's, they were
willing to talk peace.

Napoleon, who at first gave Caulaincourt *carte blanche* to
accept any reasonable terms that the Allies might offer, had
recently been victorious enough to be willing to consider
only the offer made at Frankfort in the preceding November.

But the Allies now were no longer so magnanimous; at a Congress called at Châtillon they would consent to nothing more than a France with the boundaries of 1791. Metternich, who was still willing to make peace on the Frankfort basis, and the Czar, who wanted to dictate peace at Paris, were both brought around to accept these terms by Castlereagh of the British Foreign Office. England had decided that France's internal affairs were her own concern, but that she must get out of Italy and the Netherlands and return to her "ancient limits." But Napoleon refused to listen to any such terms.

Castlereagh now induced the Allies to sign the Treaty of Chaumont, dated March 1, though actually of March 9, which bound each power to contribute one hundred and fifty thousand men in the war against France, England also undertaking to grant subsidies to the others. The usual clauses about not making peace except in common were there, but here also is to be found the kernel of the future Quadruple Alliance: the four powers bound themselves to protect each other against France for a period of twenty years. If he had dared, Castlereagh might have made of the alliance at Chaumont a league to enforce peace against any power that broke it, and not France alone. But that had to wait. In the mean time the Conference at Châtillon went on ineffectually.

On the day that the Treaty of Chaumont was signed, Napoleon, who had almost succeeded in annihilating Blücher's army at Vauchamps in the Marne Valley (February 10–14), was defeated at Laon. The victories of Wellington in Spain and southern France encouraged the Allies to continue in the path they had begun. Napoleon in a last spasm of energy attempted to cut the enemy's line of communication, but the Allies, perhaps with Talleyrand's connivance,[1] had by this time decided that Paris and not Na-

---

[1] Wilson: *The Greville Diary*, 1, 91. On the authority of Ponsonby and Wellington (neither of whom could have witnessed the events they narrated, however), Greville wrote, January 22, 1820: "Just before the advance of the Allied army on Paris a council of war was held, when it was unanimously resolved to retreat. The Emperor of Russia entered the room, and said he had

poleon was their objective. Schwarzenberg advanced by the Seine, Blücher by the Marne, driving before them a hastily gathered force of National Guards, Home Guards, and students under Mortier and Marmont. The battle of Paris, or Montmartre, in which almost forty thousand men on both sides fell, began on the morning of March 30. Paris surrendered on March 31. As Alexander and Frederick William entered Paris in triumph, Napoleon, who had learned of its surrender when he was only ten miles away in his march to relieve the city, retired to Fontainebleau. Perhaps there he had time to reflect that the *idéologues* and the Terror that he affected so much to despise had been able in 1793 to invoke a *levée en masse* to repel the invaders, while he, practical man of law and order, had been able to rouse only half-hearted alarm.

Talleyrand had, meanwhile, been engaged in negotiations with the diplomats of the Allies. Prompted not alone by his hatred of Napoleon, but also by his patriotic desire to save his country from dismemberment at the hands of the vengeful Prussians, and recognizing that the Bourbons would not be punished by an alliance that had supported them and that favored a return to ancient limits, he had persuaded a willing England and an unwilling Russia to consent to the enthronement of the brother of Louis XVI, who dubbed himself Louis XVIII, King of France. On April 1, therefore, Talleyrand, in his capacity of Vice-Grand-Elector, called a meeting of the Senate and induced it to name a provisional government and to depose Napoleon and his family because of a long series of acts of tyranny and oppression. The army, thus released from its oath of obedience to the "Little Corporal," might yet have risked all before Paris *den Kaiser zu schützen*, as Napoleon himself wished, but the marshals advised, first, a retreat beyond the Loire, and then the abdication of the Emperor. They recognized the futil-

reasons for advancing, and ordered the advance; the generals remonstrated, but the Emperor was determined. Woronzoff told Sydenham that that day a courier arrived at his outposts with a letter for the Emperor in the handwriting of Talleyrand."

ity of further slaughter and the possibility of saving their own ranks and emoluments.

It was a broken but still scheming Napoleon who on April 4 abdicated in favor of his son. He hoped by this step to win over the marshals, who hated the Bourbons as much as he. But Marmont was persuaded by the Provisional Government to march his division within the enemies' lines. Alexander now refused to accept anything but an unconditional abdication; and so by the Treaty of Fontainebleau, on April 13, Napoleon abdicated. In return he was granted the island of Elba, off the coast of Italy, in full sovereignty, with the titles and prerogatives of an emperor; the Empress and other members of his family were amply provided for; he was himself to receive a pension of two million francs a year. Whether Napoleon really attempted suicide at this time will perhaps never be definitely proved.[1] Sad and sobered, the Emperor bade a pathetic farewell to the Guards on April 20. Fréjus, which had witnessed the beginning of his triumphal procession in 1799, was now the terminus of his humiliating journey through a hostile country. The crowning irony came when he boarded a British cruiser (it was named the Undaunted!) to go to his new Empire.

Was the Revolution over? Had Europe seen the last of the Imperial Eagle? Was the world to return to peace and legitimacy once more? Could a man who had ruled over most of Europe be made to remain satisfied with an eighteen-mile island? Would a France that had been stirred and bled by genius, imagination, and glory prefer the dullness and blessings of Bourbon peace and politics to the glamour and heroic misery of Napoleonic conquests and constitutions? Would a Europe that had thrilled to the cries of *Liberty, Equality, and Fraternity* be willing to accept the course in political sanitation that its diplomats were now to prescribe? All this remained to be seen — and to be seen shortly. And perhaps no one yet knew the answers so well as the little

---

[1] It is noteworthy that the most recently published of the memoirs of those who were near Napoleon at this time supports the contention that he did attempt suicide. See Saint-Denis: *Napoleon from the Tuileries to St. Helena*, 66–70

man who on May 4 stepped ashore at Porto Ferrajo on the island empire of Elba.

As the rueful cortège of Napoleon made its way toward Elba in the early spring of 1814, Parisians made ready to welcome back their old rulers. Not even the fickle Romans, who had "climbed up to walls and battlements, to towers and windows, . . . to see great Pompey pass the streets of Rome," strewed flowers in his way who came in triumph over Pompey's blood with a more thorough change of heart. The generation that witnessed the banishment of Napoleon to Elba had been born while Louis XVI struggled futilely to retain some vestige of his absolute sovereignty; it had spent its adolescence listening to the heroic tales of Austerlitz, Jena, Wagram. But the days of its youth were filled with the forebodings that Moscow, Leipzig, and Montmartre portended. There were few signs of rage or sorrow as the humbled world-conqueror journeyed through France on his way to his island empire.

For a moment, indeed, there had been a doubt in the mind of the Czar Alexander whether the Bourbons deserved to be restored to the throne that for over twenty years they had not occupied. The Autocrat of All the Russias had seriously considered one of Napoleon's former marshals, Bernadotte, now crown prince of Sweden and a fervent adherent of the coalition against Napoleon, as the successor of the Emperor. But Talleyrand, made master of France, as President of the Provisional Government created on April 1 by the Senate which had deposed Napoleon, persuaded him that there was no choice save between Bonaparte and the Bourbons. Schemer though Talleyrand was, he yet was a more loyal Frenchman than his critics have been willing to concede; and he already saw that a restoration of the Bourbons would mean the preservation of the independence and territorial integrity of France. Surely the royal allies could not consistently punish a hereditary ruler for the crimes of his most hated enemy.

So the Bourbons were restored. Louis XVIII, who had been Count of Provence during the lifetime of Louis XVI and had proclaimed himself Regent upon the death of his elder brother and King upon the death of Louis XVII, and had lived in exile in Germany, Italy, Russia, and England since 1792, now lay ignominiously suffering from the gout at Hartwell. But his brother, the headstrong Count of Artois, was at Nancy, and at once proceeded to Paris as Louis XVIII's representative. On April 12, he entered the capital from which he had fled soon after the fall of the Bastille on July 14, 1789. The Paris crowds that had sullenly watched the rulers of Russia and Prussia ride triumphantly to the Tuileries but two weeks before burst into an enthusiastic demonstration for the Prince clad in the uniform of the National Guard. "Who could have believed it?" asked Marshal Ney, as thousands sang the *Domine, salvum fac regem*, and wept as they sang.

Had the Revolution, then, failed? Was not the very man who might have been sitting upon the throne of France, even if there had been no National Assembly, no French Republic, no Reign of Terror, no Napoleon, now accepted? Well might Ney and others have been puzzled! And yet the Revolution had not failed. The Senate had surrendered but not unconditionally. On April 6, when it had "freely" summoned the Bourbons to the throne of their ancestors, it had required that "Louis-Stanilas-Xavier of France, bro-ther of the late King," should be proclaimed "King of the French" only after he had sworn to a constitution providing for the maintenance of the new nobility alongside of the old; the preservation of the Legion of Honor; a Senate and a Corps Législatif with exclusive power to initiate taxes; the continuance of the electoral colleges; the irrevocability of the sale of national lands; the retention of the existing system of courts and the Napoleonic Code of laws, henceforth to be known as the Civil Code of the French; a series of natural rights, such as trial by jury, liberty of worship, free-dom of the press, the right of petition, and equality of civil opportunity; and the responsibility of the ministers. The document was to be valid only if accepted by a plebiscite.

When, therefore, Monsieur the Count of Artois accepted

the position of Lieutenant-Governor of the Kingdom that the Senate conferred upon him and announced his belief that his brother would accept the fundamental conditions of the proposed constitution, he put a seal upon the principal achievements of the Revolution that he had suffered twenty-five years of exile to avert.   Even though Monsieur had his tongue in his cheek as he spoke glibly about constitutional rule, he, nevertheless, committed the Bourbons to a constitution much more democratic than the Constitution of 1791 had been, much more democratic than any that Napoleon Bonaparte had granted.   The Revolution had reached, with this Senatorial Constitution, the point where Mounier and the Anglophiles would have left it if they had been able, with the additional advantages to the lower classes that a new nobility had arisen and the old nobility and Church had lost their lands and consequently their power, which were divided among the peasantry and bourgeoisie.   Indeed, the Revolution had not yet failed, even if Bourbon corpulence replaced Bonapartist rotundity upon the throne of France. If the new rulers would keep the faith, France might still be the most democratic country in Europe.

But Monsieur, who in the past had shown himself more reactionary than his brother, and who was to take advantage of frequent occasions to do so in the future, had this once stepped beyond the point where Louis was willing to follow. Louis XVIII was not a good representative of the Bourbon family.   Having begun with somewhat liberal principles, he had learned several lessons from his twenty-two years of banishment.   But he was also willing to take every advantage that his opponents offered him; and having beheld his brother accepted whole-heartedly, even without a complete accession to the Senate's proposal for a constitution, he determined to profit thereby.   As soon as his gout permitted, he had hastened to Paris.   At Saint-Ouen on May 2, "Louis, by the grace of God, King of France and of Navarre" (the ancient title), declared that while the basis of the Senatorial plan was a good one, a number of articles showed signs of haste and it could therefore not become the

fundamental law of the State.   He called the Senate and the
Legislature for June 10 to consider the terms that he would
submit; and the Senate, mustered at Saint-Ouen to greet
His Majesty, sanctioned his decision.

By a simple maneuver, the Constitution had changed
from a series of restrictions imposed by the people upon
their king to a voluntary gift of a divine-right monarch to
his subjects.   The social contract theory was not acceptable to the Bourbons; the French Government was not to
derive its just powers from the consent of the governed, but
from the grants of a sovereign king.   Since Louis had
promised that his proposals would be liberal, France was not
outraged.   But on May 3, as the obese but dignified
monarch rode into Paris between lines of soldiers, among
whom was a troubled regiment of the Old Guard, Paris was
cooler and calmer than it had been a fortnight ago when
hailing the Count of Artois.

The first important political act of the new king was to
create a new ministry in which General Dupont, Minister
of War, the Constituent Malouet, Minister of Marine, and
Baron Louis, Minister of Finance, were old ministers;
Talleyrand held the portfolio of Foreign Affairs; and the
rest were comparatively new men, chosen because of their
royalist tendencies.   The meeting of the Chambers to consider the content of the new Charter was held on May 31,
sooner than originally announced.   The document that
they were asked to consider had already been drawn up
after six days of deliberation (May 22–27) by a commission
of which the royalist ministers were the most important
members.   Several questions roused heated discussion, but
in the end a Charter similar to that proposed by the Senatorial act was accepted.   The principal differences in the
new constitution were that the King alone was given the
right to initiate legislation; that the qualifications of voters
and candidates were now raised; that Catholicism was
declared the State religion, though other forms of worship
were granted tolerance; and that there were no definite provisions regarding the responsibility of the ministry or the
revision of the Charter.

The significant feature of the new Constitutional Charter was that it was a "*concession et octroi*" of the King; it was by his good will and not by natural right that the State of France was to remain at all as the Provisional Government had wished. There could be, of course, no plebiscite of a grant coming freely from a king "in the nineteenth year" of his reign. The former Corps Législatif automatically became the new Chamber of Deputies, and the King chose eighty-four former Senators and seventy marshals and old nobles to form the new Chamber of Peers. Bonapartists and Republicans might rage at the mythical assumption of an uninterrupted Bourbon reign since 1792, and royalists at the liberality of the King's concessions, but the mass of the French people were apparently pleased. For no attempt had been made to disturb the peasant in the possession of his land and the *roturier* in his control of the Legislature.

The new Legislature held its first meeting on June 4, 1814. One of the first tasks of the new Government was to consider the terms of peace that the Allies in possession of the capital were willing to grant. Even before the arrival of Louis XVIII in France, the Count of Artois had signed an armistice (April 23). Frenchmen whose hopes had been raised by the proclamation of the Allies on December 1, 1813, promising France "an extent of territory that France had never known under its kings," were to be bitterly disappointed. To be sure, France was granted the boundaries of January 1, 1792, which included Avignon, Montbéliard, and Mülhausen; but all these had been acquired while Louis XVI still was king, and the desire for Luxembourg and Belgian fortresses had to go unsatisfied. That France was permitted to keep the art treasures pilfered by Napoleon from conquered cities and was not required to pay a war indemnity, as Prussia resentfully insisted, was small compensation for the obligation to surrender the most desirable of her colonies to England and to submit to a deflated national boundary. The peace, which was signed on May 30 and published on the day the new Legislature met, was an initial defeat for the Bourbons that French patriots found it hard to forgive.

Peace having been established and a new government created, France prepared to settle down to a normal, regular existence. Talleyrand went off to Vienna, where the representatives of the Powers had met to discuss the problems created by the break-up of the Napoleonic Empire and the return of the old governors to the various capitals of Europe. Baron Louis, Minister of Finance, ably endeavored to build up a systematic budget. Louis XVIII himself, anxious to avoid labor and difficulties, proved easily amenable to suggestion — too easily, perhaps, for sometimes the suggestions he received were unwise. But though the Government was not devoid of talent, its problems were too numerous and intricate for smooth sailing.

Almost thirty years had passed since the Count of Artois had left Paris and a fallen Bastille; and as men's lives go, thirty years is a long time. A generation had grown up that knew the Count of Artois only as a name unpleasantly associated somehow or other with events that had occurred at the time of their birth; and Artois knew this generation only as the willing disciples of a bloody revolution or guilty subjects of a treacherous usurper. He had conceded enough to the fashions of the younger generation to wear the *sans-culottes* that had become the style in his absence, but his ideas still walked in knee-breeches. A respected, dominating, absolute king; a wealthy, proud, landed aristocracy; an awesome, privileged, powerful church; a well-behaved if ambitious middle class; a submissive peasantry — these he had known and hoped to know again. He and his followers resented that the old order had changed and yielded place to new.

And the younger generation resented their attitude equally.

> The appearance in public life of large numbers of elderly gentlemen, speaking with the accent of the last century and gloomily disapproving of the generation with which they found themselves surrounded, was an inadequate compensation for

the disappearance of those bronzed and booted young men of the Empire who had ridden into every capital in Europe. It cannot have been enlivening to be governed by persons who regarded every achievement of the past thirty years as a manifestation of original sin; and for all the memories which it contained of the conscription and the invasion, the roll of the Emperor's drums must have seemed a friendly sound, when it was compared with the dry rustle of the parchments as the King's ministers searched them for royal precedents.[1]

Chief among the malcontents were the soldiers of the Empire. The tricolor, which for a quarter of a century had floated at the head of the French armies on numerous battle-fields and symbolized a concentrated history of revolution, conquest, empire, and defeat, which for all but the older men in the army was the only flag they knew and for which they had fought as only the soldiers of a Napoleon knew how to fight, was now replaced by the white flag, which was as devoid of meaning as of color to all but those who knew it as a flag which had sometimes flown with enemies' standards on bitterly contested battle-fields. The old Household Corps, along with numerous other ashes of the past, was exhumed and installed in the place of the Imperial Guard. The Order of Saint Louis now took precedence over the Legion of Honor as a military decoration; and marshals who had been cited in battle and campaign from Marengo to Paris found themselves superseded — if not replaced — by émigrés who had figured not nearly as brilliantly on the opposing side. As the new Government had to practice an economy approaching niggardliness, about four hundred thousand men found themselves discharged from the army. In addition to these, there were ten or twelve thousand officers who were put on half-pay. Romance had died and the money-counters had come to preside at the funeral. But the Old Guard secretly cherished their colors, worshiped the Emperor, and guarded their eagles. They had not died; neither had they surrendered.

[1] *The Second Empire*, by Philip Guedalla, New York, G. P. Putnam's Sons, Quoted by courtesy of the publishers.

But a few hundred thousand soldiers alone are not a serious menace. If the restored government had been careful not to make allies for them in the upper bourgeoisie, they might have been left to lick their wounds by unromantic firesides while the money-counters battened. But the money-counters, too, soon joined the ranks of the discontented. Though there had been frequent promises of a reduction of the taxes, Baron Louis had found it necessary in a time of peace to keep all that the Imperial Government had levied in a time of war. The Baron's policy was justifiable; he was endeavoring to amortize a large part of the debt and, despite the angry opposition of the returned nobility, not to repudiate any that Napoleon had contracted. But Baron Louis suffered from the weakness that had caused the downfall of Turgot, an abler Minister of Finance, before him; he attempted too much in too short a time. The plutocrats, who were glad that all of their dues were to be paid them, but resented the high direct taxes that alone made full payment possible, and the émigrés, who were chagrined that he should tax them to pay imperial debts without permitting any restoration of their estates, agreed with the soldiers, by whose discharge only could economy be practiced, that Baron Louis was a representative of a government that punished the wrong persons and rewarded the wrong persons. The Government did not even give French manufacturers the commercial protection that they had been accustomed to receive. Napoleon's Continental System had protected them from English competition to a certain extent, but the Bourbon Ministers not only were in no position to maintain the Continental System; it was only after the sternest pressure that they were brought to consider even a high tariff.

The peasantry, too, were soon aroused. The ministry succeeded in passing a measure restoring to the émigrés all of their lands that had not yet been sold by the Government. No individual lost thereby, and opposition was not strong, but it was feared that this measure was but the first of a series. Indeed, it was openly declared by those about the King that he would greatly have liked to do better for those who had remained loyal to him. Furthermore, liberals of all classes were disquieted by the law which subjected writings of less than twenty pages to censorship. The high-handed action of the clergy, who insisted upon a tithe here and refused the sacraments to purchasers of church lands there; of the nobility, who planned a monument to the "victims of Quiberon" and transferred the remains of Marie Antoinette, Madame Elizabeth, and Louis XVI to Saint-Denis in solemn ceremony; of the Government, which reorganized the University of France in such a way as to put it under the control of a Royal Council of Public Instruction presided over by a bishop — all tended to make even the Constitutionalists who had welcomed the Charter wonder when the constitutional régime would be replaced by the Ancient Régime. With Madame de Staël, the Marquis of Lafayette, and Benjamin Constant at their head, the Liberals seared the new Government in their organ *Le Censeur*, while the émigrés, who were "more royalist than the King," raged in *Le Quotidienne*.

A careful listener in the last months of 1814 and the first months of 1815 would have heard portentous rumblings. Numerous officers on half-pay were arrested for plots against the King. General Excelmans became a popular hero because he had resisted arrest after having written indiscreet letters to Marshal Murat, who was still King of Naples. When the priests refused to allow the body of Mademoiselle Raucourt, a popular actress, to be buried in consecrated ground, the crowd, threatening to hang the priests, broke open the door to the church. Wild rumors gained rapid circulation that a wholesale slaughter of patriots was secretly being planned by the royalists; and Carnot, who had anonymously published a *Mémoire au Roi*, the first direct attack upon the Restoration, barricaded himself in his home all of the night of January 21, when it was expected the transfer of the royal remains to Saint-Denis would be the signal for a general massacre. Madame de Staël was sure that it could not last; and Fouché, inveterate schemer and king-maker, put himself at the head of a cabal which, though undecided what form of government to establish in the event of success, could agree at least upon the overthrow of Louis XVIII. Talleyrand looked to the young Duke of Orléans, once a general in Dumouriez's army; Fouché thought of a regency under the Empress Marie Louise; and devoted Bonapartists cast longing glances Elbaward. Napoleon himself, driven on by an innate restlessness and ingenuity and a cultivated or assumed interest in France's welfare, which not even the meager proportions of Elba could cramp, was soon to fill the hearts of the last with exultation and to bring the indecision of the others to an abrupt close.

CHAPTER III

RESTORATION AND REACTION IN EUROPE

THE problems of the restored monarchy in France were but an enlarged reflection of the tribulations that had to be endured in other countries of Europe after the Napoleonic eagles fled and the monarchical cocks came to crow over the ruins of the Empire. Spain welcomed back Ferdinand VII; Rome received its Pope; Sardinia and the other once independent principalities of Italy prepared to resume their old forms of government, save Naples, where Murat was suffered still to remain; the House of Orange returned to Holland with monarchical authority granted by the Treaty of Paris; Portugal, under a temporary British regency, looked for its rulers to return from Brazil; even the petty knights and princes of the once Holy Roman Empire hoped that the antipathy to all things Napoleonic might involve a restoration of their miniature sovereignties or at least some compensation for their loss. France, then, was but a tittle of the entanglements in which the enforced withdrawal of the knot-cutter to Elba had left Europe bound. Furthermore, there were old treaties whose definitive settlement had been left until the time of victory over Napoleon. These now demanded attention — Kalisch, Töplitz, Chaumont, Paris.

What was to be done with the Grand Duchy of Warsaw, which Napoleon had created against the wishes of the beneficiaries of the Polish partitions? How were the King of Saxony and the King of Denmark to be punished for their loyalty to Napoleon even after loyalty had become unwise? What disposition was to be made of the venerable Republics of Venice and Genoa that had passed under French domination and now must be reassigned elsewhere? What political arrangement must take the place of the Confederation of the Rhine, now that its Protector had abdicated?

How were England, Russia, Prussia, Austria, and other states that had suffered through a generation of French aggressions to be compensated? What was to happen to Belgium, Westphalia, the Illyrian Provinces, the Ionian Islands, and other territories that France had ceded by the Treaty of Paris? What provisions were to be made to prevent another *débâcle* like that of the last twenty-five years? These, and many more like them, were questions that concerned the welfare of Europe as a whole, and could be solved only by a European Congress.

The Treaty of Paris stipulated that a Congress of the Powers was to be held at Vienna to consider the questions left unfinished by that treaty. In September the plenipotentiaries of the great nations began to arrive at the Austrian capital. Rarely, if ever, had such a concourse of celebrities been witnessed before. The Emperors of Russia and Austria, the King of Prussia, the rulers of several minor states graced the Congress with their majestic presence. Castlereagh and later Wellington came to represent the British Empire. Nesselrode and Stein attended to advise the Czar. Hardenberg and Humboldt acted on behalf of Prussia; and Talleyrand was sent to guard the interests of France. And presiding over all of them was Prince Metternich, Austria's Minister of State and Foreign Affairs. No international congress since has been able to boast an abler aggregation of men — not even the Congress of Berlin, where the brilliance of Bismarck and Disraeli was offset by the dullness of a number of others; and the Congress of Versailles might have appeared to some observers but a prosaic meeting of bourgeois mediocrities in comparison.

The Congress of Versailles was not unlike the Congress of Vienna. A long war had exhausted all the nations involved. The defeated power had, in the course of the hostilities, built up a vast empire. Not only had the empire to be returned to its rightful owners, but who the rightful owners were had also to be determined. Moreover, there were all sorts of demands put forth by rulers and peoples that had to be answered. Above all, there was a reaction against war, and a sincere desire for some scheme ensuring universal peace. The spokesman of the peace party at both congresses was the ruler of the belligerent that had suffered the least from the fighting and yet had been the decisive factor in the victory. Alexander I of Russia was the Woodrow Wilson of the Congress of Vienna. There had been international congresses before 1814 to settle the terms of peace after a war. This was the first time that a congress had been convened to consider a settlement of problems other than those raised by the war and to bring about a system of international coöperation. It was the beginning of the Concert of Europe.

The formal opening of the Congress was fixed for October 1, but even before the Congress was officially to begin, the four victorious Powers that had signed the Treaty of Chaumont had come to an agreement upon their joint conduct. Since they believed or pretended to believe that France had been the sole disturber of the peace, it was necessary that they dictate the terms of the settlement without consulting the representatives of France. On September 22, therefore, they drew up a *protocole séparé:*

1. The four Powers alone were to decide on the distribution of the provinces to be disposed of as the result of the late war and the Treaty of Paris, but the two other Powers [France and Spain] were to be allowed to hand in opinions and objections afterwards.

2. The plenipotentiaries of the four Powers would not enter into conference with those of the two Powers for this object until they had arrived at a complete understanding among themselves on the question of Poland, Germany, and Italy.

3. To save time, the plenipotentiaries of the four Powers would, as soon as the Congress opened, consult the two Powers on other matters.

Thus it was the intention of the four great victorious nations to settle all important problems as they saw fit and to submit them to France and the lesser powers for their approval afterwards, allowing France and Spain a voice only in the decision of minor matters. Truly, Gentz, the secretary of the Congress of Vienna and Metternich's right-hand man, spoke more profoundly than he knew when he said: "If ever the Powers should meet again to establish a political system by which wars of conquest would be rendered impossible and the rights of all guaranteed, the Congress of Vienna, as a preparatory assembly, will not have been in vain."

When Talleyrand arrived at Vienna (September 24), he at once protested against the arbitrary decision of the four Powers, but his protests were unavailing. Alexander even talked of war again. Talleyrand set about, therefore, to organize the lesser Powers. The German states were exercised particularly by the pending fate of Saxony. Alexander, even as a boy, had set his heart upon the liberal notion of re-creating the Kingdom of Poland, which, however, was to be under Russian control with the Czar as its King. In order to do so, he desired to incorporate with Russian Poland the former Grand Duchy of Warsaw, which had been made up almost entirely of the Polish territory that before the Treaty of Tilsit had belonged to Prussia. Prussia had already been promised compensation by the Treaty of Kalisch, and there was a certain ironic justice in the arrangement that this compensation should be made at the expense of the King of Saxony whom Napoleon had made the Duke of Warsaw. Prussia insisted that the territory of Saxony, whose King had remained loyal to Napoleon until the very end, should be granted entirely to her.

The representatives of the German states, fearing the results that such a precedent might spell for them, met, at Talleyrand's instigation, under the leadership of the Bavarians, to protest against such a usurpation. The attitude of the several German states encouraged Austria in her opposition to Prussia and Russia. A huge increase in the size of Prussia and Russia would obviously not be to the advantage of their southern ally; and England, which was not eager to improve Russia's strategic position in Europe, was inclined to support Austria. The discord thus produced among the four Powers made it necessary to postpone the opening of the Congress to November 1, and

Talleyrand was asked to consent to the postponement. Before long the "effective cabinet" of the Congress was increased by the admission of all the other Powers that had signed the Treaty of Paris — Spain, Portugal, Sweden, and France. Even on November 1, however, the formal opening of the Congress did not take place; and, as Gentz said, the Congress as such came into existence only by its Final Act. In the mean time, the Committee of Eight, in which the Committee of Five (excluding Spain, Portugal, and Sweden) concerned itself with the most pressing problems, carried on most of the work of the Congress. Talleyrand's manipulation of the smaller states of Europe had enabled him to convert the Big Four, so to speak, into a Big Five. France was not, thereafter, to be treated as a prisoner at the bar, obliged to accept, without consultation, whatever decision unfriendly judges might see fit to render. Less important matters were left to minor committees.

Castlereagh now tried to settle the problem of Saxony by compromise. But though he could bring the representatives of Austria and Prussia to agree to the absorption of Saxony by Prussia and compensation elsewhere for Austria and Frederick Augustus of Saxony, he was unable to get any satisfactory reply to his several letters to Alexander. The Czar, in endeavoring to establish the Kingdom of Poland despite the opinion of his advisers, regarded himself as the champion of "European ideals" and "the faith of treaties." Besides, the independence of Poland was inextricably bound up with his larger conception of the scheme of things — a vision of a European confederation of free, nationalistic, and liberal states.

The idea of an international organization of states for the preservation of peace was not a new one. To say nothing of the *Pax Romana*, the Catholic Church, and the Holy Roman Empire, there had been many before Alexander to dream of a league of nations to promote international amicability. Dante, Pierre Dubois, Henry IV of France, Grotius, William Penn, Rousseau, Franklin, Mably, Jeremy Bentham — men of various ages and nationalities had likewise had this vision, but none so clearly as the Abbé de Saint-Pierre, whose experience at the Congress of Utrecht (1713) had led him to write a *Projet de paix perpétuelle* that pleaded for an international congress. La Harpe, a Swiss like Rousseau, had, in his younger days, sat at the feet oi his compatriot; and in those days he was the tutor of the young Russian prince who now, as the Czar of All the Russias, graced the table of his imperial host at Vienna. The impressionable mind of the young prince had gained much from these two Swiss, master and disciple. A curious composite of autocrat and statesman, of the Oriental mystic and the Occidental liberal, Alexander had never rid himself of the influence of La Harpe, though it was an older and somewhat chastened La Harpe who now acted as one of his corps of advisers. In 1804, in a dispatch to Novosiltsov, his envoy to London, Alexander had sent an extraordinary letter of instructions, in which he had portrayed a Europe comprising a single confederation of constitutional states, demarcated by their national boundaries and by homogeneity of population. The Abbé de Saint-Pierre had at last found a disciple, a fervent reader of his *Projet de paix perpétuelle*, in the Czar of All the Russias.

But Alexander's very insistence upon this scheme of peace was to become a most serious obstacle to the establishment of peace. It was the *idée fixe* of Alexander that there must be an autonomous Kingdom of Poland with himself as King; this was a necessary part of his plan of world confederation. His more skeptical colleagues in diplomacy were perhaps not altogether mistaken in their feeling that he would like to have Poland, world confederation or no world confederation. His plans appeared to them to be nothing more than a new twist to an old trick. But Alexander would listen to no arguments to the contrary, and Castlereagh was forced to the conclusion "that, unless the Emperor of Russia can be brought to a more moderate and sound course of public conduct, the peace, which we have dearly purchased, will be but of short duration."

On November 8, therefore, when Alexander's provisional

Governor of Saxony, Prince Refnin, turned over the administration of Saxony to the Prussians and the Prussians accepted, and the Grand Duke Constantine called upon the Poles to defend their country, Austrian troops marched toward the frontiers. The European situation became tense. Castlereagh continued to work for a peaceful solution, however. The liberals in England did not oppose Alexander's plan for an independent Poland, and public opinion in general felt that Prussia was entitled to compensation provided she did not insist upon all of Saxony. Negotiations with Talleyrand had assured Castlereagh of French support on condition that in return he advocated the expulsion of Murat from Naples. Consequently Castlereagh secured the creation of a committee to consider the Polish-Saxon question, in which France's representative was present.

But Hardenberg's unwillingness to yield and his threats of war in a special conference, called on December 29, determined Castlereagh on his next step. On January 3, 1815, a Secret Defensive Triple Alliance was drawn up between France, Austria, and England, each promising to contribute an army of one hundred and fifty thousand men if attacked by Prussia. Talleyrand, when he had urged the German states to protest against Prussian annexation of Saxony, had thus engineered a *coup* by which he had converted France from an unwelcome outsider at the Congress into an ally of the Power that presided and of the strongest Power present at the Congress. England had just signed a peace with the United States of America at Ghent (December 24, 1814) on the basis of the *status quo ante bellum*, thus leaving undecided all of the disputes about which the United States had gone to war. She was still, because of the tardiness with which the news of the peace reached the front, to suffer defeat at the hands of General Andrew Jackson in the battle of New Orleans. Yet now she began seriously to contemplate a war with Prussia.

But news of the Secret Alliance somehow reached the ears of Alexander and had a desirable effect. Prussia realized that she had to yield, but negotiations dragged on for five weeks more. It was finally agreed, before Castlereagh left Vienna and Wellington came to take his place, that Prussia should receive but two fifths of Saxony, including the fortresses of Torgau and Erfurt, and that Russia must remain content with the Duchy of Warsaw, excluding Thorn and the Prussian share of the first two partitions of Poland, which were returned to Prussia, and Austria's former Polish possessions, and Cracow, which was erected as a free city under Austrian tutelage. Thus Russia received only that part of Poland which had been taken by Prussia in the third partition. Castlereagh urged the three Pole-ruling Powers to grant the Poles special privileges and the Czar especially to recognize Polish independence. It was not until May 18 that Saxony acquiesced in this settlement. And it was only after the Congress had adjourned that the Czar proclaimed a constitution for the Kingdom of Poland (November 27, 1815), made up of the Polish lands awarded to him by the Congress of Vienna together with Russia's share of the three partitions. Then the world was faced with a paradox; the Czar of Russia in his own hereditary realms remained an unrestricted autocrat, but in the territory that he had acquired by the right of conquest, he was now merely a constitutional monarch.

In the mean time, other questions, not so thorny, had been settled. In general, these settlements, as in all treaties, were arrived at by a process of bargaining, the stronger Powers being able to drive hard bargains that the weaker had to accept. But the diplomats at the Congress of Vienna usually found ready rationalizations of their actions. They explained that they had been guided by three principles. The first of these was the discovery of Talleyrand. On the plea of *legitimacy*, he had saved France from partition when the Bourbons were returned; on the same plea he had acted as the champion of Saxony. Wherever it was convenient and advantageous to do so, the old, "legitimate" Governments of Europe were confirmed in the reacquisition of their territories. Whatever had existed in 1789, before the outbreak of the French Revolution, was now regarded as legitimate. Hence Spain, Portugal, Austria, Prussia, and the Italian states, when other factors did not have to be taken into consideration, were restored to the boundaries and the rulers they had had in 1789. But, sometimes, the doctrine of legitimacy encountered obstacles, as, for example, when it was regarded as desirable to despoil the King of Saxony of two fifths of his legitimate territory. Then two other "principles" were brought into play — *compensation* and *guarantees*. States that, like Prussia, had in the course of the settlement lost territory must be compensated for their losses, the compensation being generally at the expense of some other state that, like Saxony, had remained loyal to Napoleon too long. In certain cases, even where no loss of territory had been suffered, an increase in the frontiers was regarded as desirable in order to "guarantee" it against the possibility of further French aggressions.

Thus, before Castlereagh left Vienna, a number of significant changes in the map of Europe had been effected. Some of these were mere confirmations of arrangements concluded before the Congress. The Kingdom of the Netherlands was guaranteed against future Napoleons by the annexation not only of Belgium but also of Luxembourg, which, however, was still to remain part of the German Confederation. These additions to the Dutch nation were also to be regarded in the light of compensations for the loss of her colonies (Ceylon and the Cape) to England. Prussia was given the Rhenish Provinces on the left bank as a further guarantee both of the Netherlands and Prussia herself. Hanover was secured by the acquisition of East Frisia. Austria had to be compensated for the loss of Belgium, which in 1789 had been a white elephant on Joseph II's hands; and compensation was found in Italy, where the Congress, forgetting "legitimacy," became accessory to the crime of Napoleon in destroying the independence of the ancient Republic of Venice; Venetia and the Illyrian Provinces now became Austrian possessions. To these were added the whole of Lombardy in addition to Milan and Mantua, which alone had been hers in 1789. For returning the Tyrol and Salzburg to Austria, Bavaria was granted a district on the Rhine around the cities of Landau and Kaiserslautern, corresponding very roughly to the "legitimate" Bavarian Palatinate, and thenceforth to be designated as the Rhenish Bavaria. Norway was severed from Denmark, which had been altogether too faithful to Napoleon, and granted to Sweden as compensation for the loss of Swedish Pomerania, which was awarded to Prussia, and of Finland, in the possession of which Alexander was confirmed. The Norwegians refused to accept the Treaty of Kiel (January 14, 1814), by which the King of Denmark yielded his claims to Norway. Bernadotte undertook an invasion of Norway and several months of negotiations resulted eventually in the Act of Union (1815). Denmark had to be satisfied with the small Duchy of Lauenburg, which was also to remain a part of the German Confederation, as her compensation.

There were some phases of Napoleon's work, however, that it was regarded as inadvisable to tamper with, principle or no principle. Nobody but a few dispossessed princes cared to see restored the havoc of the several hundred states that had once paraded as the Holy Roman Empire. The secularizations that had taken place within the Germanies would therefore have to be affirmed, even if to do so violated the principle of legitimacy. Consequently, the states that had formed the Confederation of the Rhine, of which Napoleon had been the Protector, became the foundation of a new league that was to be known as the Germanic Confederation. The Kingdom of Westphalia, as a purely Napoleonic creation, was broken up into its component parts. Otherwise the changes established by the various treaties and mediatizations since 1803 were retained. Together with restored Prussia and Austria, the thirty-eight states of Germany made up the total of forty members of the new Germanic Confederation. A Diet was provided that might meet either as a General Assembly of sixty-nine votes, which represented all the states of the Confederation in proportion to their size, or as an Ordinary Assembly of seventeen votes, in which the larger states had one representative each, the smaller states being obliged to combine in groups represented by a single deputy. War between members or between a member and an external state was forbidden. A promise of constitutional laws for each of the separate states was also made.

This Federal Constitution resembled the constitution of the former Confederation of the Rhine, but the centralized efficiency of that Confederation had now given way before the imperial interests of Austria, which was made permanent president of the Germanic Confederation. It was clear, however, that the long step that Napoleon had taken in the direction of German unification was not to be altogether retraced; there would, at least, be no return to the hopeless chaos of the Holy Roman Empire. A definite settlement had by no means been reached when Castlereagh left for England. Various delays had been occasioned by the resentfulness of certain smaller German principalities and by the conflicting plans of patriots inside the German committee of the Congress. But a solution was well on the way by February, 1815, particularly after Austria and Prussia had settled their differences on the Saxon question. Before the Congress adjourned, the Federal Act creating the Germanic Confederation was signed (June 8, 1815) by thirty-eight member states. Württemberg and Baden, displeased by certain provisions of the new constitution, held out until July 26 and September 1, respectively.

In Switzerland, too, the mediatization of Napoleon was allowed to remain in some respects undisturbed. To the nineteen independent cantons that had been created by Napoleon, however, there were now added three new ones, fashioned out of the Swiss territory that had been annexed by the French. These were Geneva, the Valais, and Neuchâtel, the last of which, formerly a Prussian possession, was officially surrendered by Prussia only in 1851. Furthermore, the close confederation that Napoleon's insistence upon centralized efficiency had demanded was now practically destroyed by allowing each canton to accept a constitution without the approval of the Federal Diet and by permitting internal customs. There was to be a diet, made up of delegates from the separate cantons, under the presidency alternately of Zurich, Berne, and Lucerne. The Swiss Confederation was, by an agreement arrived at after the Congress of Vienna, placed under the protection of the Powers and neutralized. The distinction between free cantons, allied cantons, and subject countries was never revived. The work that Napoleon had done for Swiss unification was thus not completely undone.

But in Italy the claims of the King of Sardinia and of the Pope were too well supported by political and diplomatic interests to permit of disregard. Furthermore, there was the fact that Austria had enjoyed control of Italy before 1789 and was unwilling to relinquish it in 1815. The frequent invasions of French armies through the Italian Alps into Austria had taught her the strategic importance of an Italy under her own domination; and Italy could best be dominated if it were disunited. Napoleon had gone far toward the unification of Italy. Except for the Kingdom of Naples, which was ruled by his brother-in-law Murat, all of Italy had been under his own control. At the time of his abdication, a united Italy under an Italian Emperor seemed more than an illusion. The return of the King of Sardinia from the island portion of his realm to his capital at Turin, where he proceeded to tear up the botanical gardens that Napoleon had planted; the restoration of the Pope to Rome, where for a time the street lights installed by Napoleon were required to remain unlighted, were the first disruptions of this union. The award of Genoa to Sardinia as a free port and of Lombardo-Venetia to Austria as a kingdom continued the process of decentralization. The necessity of finding a principality for Marie Louise, still the daughter of the Austrian Emperor if also the wife of the Elban, resulted in the creation of Parma, Piacenza, and Guastalla into a realm to be ruled by her without her son, the erstwhile King of Rome, securing hereditary rights over them. At her death they were to pass into the hands of the former King of Etruria, who until that time was to rule Lucca. Tuscany, and eventually Lucca, were turned over to the Grand Duke Ferdinand, the uncle of the Austrian Emperor Francis, and another relative of the Hapsburg House was made Duke of Modena.

King Murat was reluctantly allowed to remain in Naples for the present; and Murat dreamed, like his master, of a united Italy. But Murat's foothold was insecure. The Bourbons in France wished for his overthrow and the restoration of the Bourbons to Naples. By inadvisedly supporting Napoleon and taking up arms in his behalf, when (as we shall see) Bonaparte returned to France from Elba, King Murat was to incur defeat at Tolentino (May 3, 1815) at the hands of the Austrian army, and to be obliged to flee from his short-lived kingdom. The Bourbons established themselves on the mainland immediately, and when Murat returned later in the year to attempt a reconquest, he was captured and shot. The mark of the French heel upon Italy was now filled in by an Austrian boot, for the Austrian Emperor seemed to want to find employment in Italy for a goodly flock of relatives.

Most of these arrangements were accomplished through the insistence and diplomacy of Castlereagh. Since England had no vital interests on the Continent as long as the markets and trade routes were kept open, she was anxious to bring about a definitive peace as quickly as possible. Castlereagh had frequently, by permission or by threat, expedited a decision that might otherwise have been dragged out indefinitely. On the whole, what little justice in the Treaty of Vienna there was, was due largely to the fact that the English representatives, unconcerned with the merits of Continental disputes, sometimes threw the weight of their influence on the side of justice. But when it was a matter of colonies that was to be discussed, the Mistress of the Seas did not act indifferently. Practically all of the colonial possessions of France and her allies in the wars since the Treaty of Amiens had fallen into English hands.

EUROPE

IN 1815

0   250   500

ENGLISH MILES

P = Parma   M = Modena

ICELAND
Den.

FARÖE IS.

SHETLAND IS.

ORKNEY IS.

ROCKALL

HEBRIDES

NORWAY

Trondhjem

Christiania

Bergen

Skagerrack

Gothenbu

Cattegat

DENMARK

Copenhagen

BA

SCOTLAND

Edinburgh

NORTH

SEA

HELIGOLAND

BRITISH ISLES

Belfast

IRELAND

Dublin

Liverpool

Manchester

Cork

St. George C'H.

ENGLAND

Birmingham

London

Southampton

Hamburg

Bremen

Elbe

Berlin

Hanover

Leipzig

Dresden

KINGDOM OF

GERMANY

Prague

Nuremberg

CONFEDERAT

Munich

EMPIRE

Danube R.

English Channel

CHANNEL IS.

Str. of Dover

Amsterdam

THE HAGUE

NETHERLAND

Antwerp

Brussels

Lille

Brest

Le Havre

Seine

Paris

Strasbourg

FRANCE

Loire R.

Lyons

Bordeaux

Geneva

Bern

SWITZERL'D

Milan

LOMBARDY

Graz

Triest

ATLANTIC

OCEAN

C. Finisterre

BAY OF

BISCAY

Opto

Ebro R.

Burgos

Toulouse

Bayonne

ANDORRA

Marseilles

Saragossa

Lisbon

PORTUGAL

SPAIN

Salamanca

Madrid

Toledo

Barcelona

C. St. Vincent

Valencia

BALEARIC IS.

Seville

Granada

Malaga

Gibraltar

Br.

Str. of Gibraltar

Tangier

Meilla

Fez

MOROCCO

BARBARY

Oran

ALGERIA

Algiers

Tunis

MEDITE

KINGDOM OF SARDINIA

GR. DUCY. OF TUSCANY

CORSICA

Rome

SARDINIA

Naples

Palermo

MALTA

Br.

C. Po

R

RR

Tripoli

TRIPOLI

TIA

ADRIAT. SEA

KINGDOM OF

50°

40°

30°

20°

10°

0°

10°

10°   West Longitude   Greenwich   East Longitude   10°

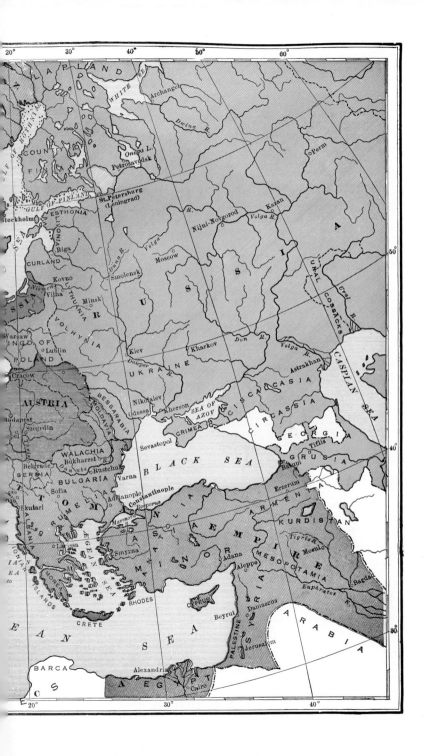

Some of these were too valuable to surrender now. England, where the Industrial Revolution had gone so far that there already was an organized Chamber of Manufacturers, had learned that the colonies make good markets for the disposition of surplus products, good sources of raw materials, and good points of strategic value. By the Treaty of Paris, England had already been confirmed in her possession of the former French islands of Mauritius, Tobago, and Saint Lucia. From Holland she now acquired Ceylon and the Cape of Good Hope. From Spain she took the island of Trinidad and was reconfirmed in her possession of Honduras, Spain being compensated by Olivenza, a slice of Portugal, England's loyal ally, on the Spanish side of the Guadiana River. From Denmark she received the island of Heligoland. The Knights of Saint John surrendered the island of Malta, which gave England a commanding position in the center of the Mediterranean. And a protectorate over the Ionian Islands enabled her to command the Adriatic.

To be sure, England had "borne the chief pecuniary stress of the war and had been more instrumental than any other Power in overthrowing Napoleon," but her compensation was in proportion to her losses rather than, as has been claimed, less than any other country's.[1]   Not only did she render the *coup de grâce* to the Dutch and French colonial empires, whose destruction had been a most important aim of British foreign policy since the time of the Commonwealth, but she also beheld the dissolution of the greater Spanish Empire in the revolts against Joseph Bonaparte in the Latin-American states that never again returned to their former allegiance. Not only did she destroy whatever naval prestige France had regained by the War of the American Revolution, but she also secured a commercial supremacy that was never again to be questioned until two younger states — Germany and the United States — were to do so. France, which, since Philip Augustus' and the Lion-Hearted's day, and even before, had

<hr>

[1] Stephens: *Revolutionary Europe*, 348.

been the inveterate foe and the constant opponent of England — whose support, indeed, in any controversy (save for a brief interval in the minority of Louis XV) would have completely upset the calculations of British military and diplomatic officials, was thereafter to take a part second to Russia and Germany as an adversary of English supremacy. The Lion had once more secured his proverbial share.

The Congress of Vienna also discussed two points of international law. The first was the status of the slave trade. England, still under the influence of Wilberforce, having already abolished the iniquitous traffic in English territories in 1807, adopted a holier-than-thou attitude that puzzled Castlereagh's colleagues. The most Castlereagh and the more eager Sir Sidney Smith could obtain was a declaration condemning the trade in slaves and the promise of France to prohibit it after five years, and Spain after eight. The second of these international problems was the question of the control of rivers flowing between two or more states. It was finally decided to regulate commerce upon such waterways by an international code that was thereupon drawn up and accepted. The Rhine was the principal river thus affected, and by the agreement, the Scheldt River, which had been closed by the Treaties of Westphalia (1648), Utrecht (1713), and Eden (1786), was again open to commerce.

Many of these decisions had not been definitely reached when Castlereagh was recalled to England to attend a meeting of Parliament. The problems of a German constitution and of the deposition of Murat particularly were among those that still defied solution. Nevertheless, on February 15, 1815, Castlereagh left Vienna, having entrusted England's part in the negotiations to the Duke of Wellington. Hardly had he arrived in England when it was learned that Napoleon had left Elba and returned to France. At Vienna the same news speeded up negotiations. Although Wellington and the royal personages soon departed for the battle front, the work of the Congress went on. The final terms of the Treaty of Vienna were submitted for the gen-

eral approval of the nations represented at the Congress on
June 9, 1815. Thus, on that day, the Final Act of the Con
gress of Vienna, in which the Committee of Eight had incorporated all the decisions previously arrived at, was also
the first and only act of the general Congress.

A cynical irony has frequently been the tone of the discussion of the Congress of Vienna by contemporaries, as
well as historians. Irony will probably and deservedly be
the weapon that liberal observers will aim at peace conferences where delegates come to establish a wilderness of
political, commercial, and diplomatic advantages for their
respective countries, and call it peace. Yet the Congress of
Vienna was not altogether a reaction or a failure. It might
have done more. It might have taken up the question of
Greek independence, which the Greek patriot, Prince Ypsi-
lanti, one of the many advisers — none of them Russian —
that Alexander had about him, urged upon the Czar, and,
with it, the Near Eastern Question in general, which in the
early nineteenth century might have been capable of acceptable solution. It might have taken up the question of international coöperation for peace, which was the goal of
millions of hearts that had beat for a generation of almost
incessant war and which found its spokesmen, as yet ineffectually silent, in Alexander and Castlereagh. In what it
did do, it might have considered the current political spirit,
the rising slogans of *Democracy* and *Nationality* — the
nineteenth century's translation of the eighteenth century's
cry for *Liberty, Equality, and Fraternity* — instead of the
outworn principles of legitimacy and compensation. Belgium and Norway might then have been saved years of dissatisfaction ending in ultimate revolution. Italy and Germany might have been unified without the necessity for impatient waiting, international complications, and wars.
Had the Congress of Vienna done some of the things that it
did not do and not done others that it did do, Europe might
have been in 1815 at least as far advanced politically as it
was in 1870.

Yet the Congress of Vienna had a difficult group of problems to examine, when suddenly the responsibility of a vast empire, hitherto under the guidance of an unsurpassed administrative genius, was thrown upon its shoulders. If it had done nothing more than preserve the secularizations and mediatizations in the Germanies, it would have accomplished a difficult task, in view of the epidemic of Napoleonphobia that it had to encounter. That it also helped create a constitutional régime in Poland; that it Germanized Prussia; that it organized and neutralized Switzerland; that it refused to tear up France; that it put an end to factional strife in Holland; that it achieved an international arrangement of European problems that for forty years permitted no war between any of the world Powers, who ever since the rise of modern nationalism had hardly known a decade of peace with each other — all entitle it to pity that it did not do more as well as irony that it did so little. "The treaty, such as it is," said Gentz, "has the undeniable merit of having prepared the world for a more complete political structure. . . . A number of vexatious details have been settled, and the ground has been prepared for building up a better social structure." Gentz might have added that it was the Revolution, spread through Europe by Napoleon Bonaparte, that had made the preparation of this ground a possibility.

CHAPTER IV

THE HUNDRED DAYS

ON the island of Elba, discerning and experienced eyes carefully watched the events transpiring in France and at Vienna. While indulging his passion for efficiency by organizing his little empire of about twenty thousand acres, Napoleon had found time to speculate upon the treatment his vanquishers had afforded him. The annuity of two million francs had not yet been paid him; his son was practically a prisoner in Austria; his wife was put under the tutelage of Field Marshal von Neipperg, who followed out Metternich's instructions "to make her forget France and the Emperor" so well that she eventually contracted a morganatic marriage with him. From newspapers and frequent visitors he learned that there was rampant dissatisfaction in France, that there were conspiracies afoot to oust the Bourbons; that soldiers and officers were already engaged in sporadic but open mutiny; that at Vienna the alliance of Chaumont was on the verge of disruption; that there might be another general war; that his enemies at Vienna regarded his nearness to Europe as a peril and suggested removing him to a safer distance. If he had ever sincerely intended to remain, peaceable and unprotesting, in the Empire that had once been a sub-prefecture, if his occupation with the reorganization of Elba had ever been more than a mask of his real intentions, indignation, the sense of self-protection, and the increased probabilities of success now conspired to present to him the advisability of a new bid for the control of France. On the morning of February 26, with an escort made up of seven hundred of the small army that had been permitted him, he set sail with a fleet of one brig and three smaller vessels from Porto Ferrajo. On the first day of March, 1815, although having encountered a

French brig on the way that had asked after the Emperor's
health, they arrived without mishap in the Gulf of San Juan.
The last flight of the Eagle had begun.

What followed has been spoken of as "the most wonder-
ful adventure in history" and "one of the miracles of history." Without firing a shot or shedding a drop of blood,
Napoleon's little army marched from Cannes to Paris,
growing larger and meeting with more exultant welcome
each of the twenty days of its remarkable campaign. It
took the Alpine paths into Dauphiny, avoiding Provence
as a hotbed of royalty. Marshal Masséna, commanding
at Marseilles, sent a small force to oppose Napoleon; they
joined his little army. Six regiments that were drawn up to
resist his advance upon Grenoble saw him unarmed approach
them and dare them to fire upon their old general; they too
joined his forces. Part of the garrison at Grenoble under
Colonel Labédoyère marched to meet the Emperor with
colors flying; and the people of the city acclaimed their
Emperor as he entered.

When, on March 8, Napoleon set out for Lyons, he had
an army of seven thousand devoted men under his command. On March 10, without a battle, Napoleon took
possession of Lyons, while the crowds in the streets cried
death to priests. At Lyons he decreed the institutions established by Louis XVIII abolished and summoned a *Champ
de Mai*, a revival of the Carolingian popular assembly, to
meet at Paris to aid him in determining "the changes rendered necessary by the need for an intelligent liberty."
Marshal Ney, hastily summoned from Normandy to lead
an army against the marauder, kissed the King's hand as he
prepared to depart and promised to bring Napoleon, whom
he spoke of as "a savage beast or a mad dog," back again to
Paris in an iron cage. But before he had encountered his
former master, his troops were in open mutiny. Ney had
either to do their bidding or desert them. He led them to
Napoleon, who was already at Auxerre (March 17). With
a few choice words appealing to Ney's pride and patriotism, the Little Corporal won Ney over completely. Na-

poleon had met the enemy and, in a very literal sense, they
were his.

In Paris, where no one really believed that Napoleon
could succeed in passing through all of France to the capital,
where the journals of all the parties fulminated against the
military autocrat, where even Lafayette evinced his loyalty
to the royal cause by wearing the white cockade in conspicuous places, the King had begun to be worried. On March
16, he summoned a meeting of the peers and deputies, to
whom he recalled his work for the salvation of France and
swore to continue to maintain the Charter. Even Monsieur the Count of Artois, avowed enemy of the Charter,
swore fealty to the Charter too. But royal theatrics were
no defense against the relentless advance of the constantly
growing forces of Napoleon. On the 19th of March he was
but a day's march from the capital. Louis XVIII, who
but a few days before had boldly asked whether at the age
of sixty he could better end his career than by fighting for
the defense of his people, thought better of it and quietly
withdrew to Lille on the border and, later, to Ghent in Belgium. On the evening of March 20, Napoleon entered the
Tuileries amid delirious cries of *Vive l'Empereur*.[1] It was
iot Napoleon about whom they became thus frantic; they
had grown cold toward him once, and they would do so
again. Napoleon himself was not deceived; "They let me
come," he said to Mollien, "as they let the others go." The
frenzy of the people was but a manifestation of the bitterness with which they had become accustomed to regard the
Bourbons, the priests, and the aristocrats. The Vendée
and scattered districts in the Midi set up an ineffective
resistance on behalf of their royal principles, but France as
a whole eagerly submitted to an all-conquering hero.

Napoleon set to work to reëstablish his government.
Carnot became a count and Minister of the Interior.
Fouché squirmed his way back into the Police Department.

[1] Fournier: *Napoleon the First* (translated by Bourne), 693, does not share the
general opinion that the people of Paris welcomed Napoleon enthusiastically.
He quotes the royalist Broglie: "Every one was gloomy, quiet, indifferent,
without complaining, without hoping, yet not without anxiety."

Cambacérès accepted the portfolio of the Department of Justice; and Caulaincourt, since Talleyrand still represented Louis XVIII at Vienna, was the logical choice for the Foreign Office. Reluctantly, but with full knowledge that such a step was necessary to his pose as an opponent of Bourbonism, Napoleon prepared to carry out his promise at Lyons to grant a liberal constitution. Fictionizing no less than the Bourbons, he prepared to "add" certain provisions to the old Constitution of the Empire, which he was pleased to assume had never ceased to be effective. After a commission, headed by Carnot and Cambacérès, disagreed upon a project, Napoleon entrusted Benjamin Constant, leader of the liberals and a recognized authority on political science, with the task of making the old Constitution conform to the newer exigencies. Constant accepted the Constitutional Charter as his model and drew up a document that won the approval of the Commission and was promulgated as the "Additional Act to the Constitutions of the Empire" on April 22. "Napoleon, by the grace of God and the Constitutions, Emperor of the French" (a title that mixed curiously the theory of divine right with the theory of social compact), benevolently granted to his subjects a bicameral legislature of Peers and Deputies elected by liberal though indirect suffrage; a ministry responsible in theory, at least, to the legislature; a free press; and civil rights. "I would never have left the island of Elba," he said to Molé, "if I had foreseen to what an extent it was necessary to comply with the democratic party in order to maintain myself."

The *Acte Additionnel* was submitted to the people of France for their approval. Only one and a half million votes were cast, less than half the number that had taken part in the plebiscites of 1799 and 1802. At the *Champ de Mai* called for the purpose on June 1, the Constitution was formally accepted. The first elections went overwhelmingly in favor of the liberals; only eighty out of about six hundred members of the lower house were unquestioningly Bonapartist. Lucien Bonaparte, but recently forgiven by his brother for an unsuitable marriage, was the Emperor's choice for presiding officer of the Chamber of Deputies. He got not a single vote. Napoleon secretly resolved, after his first glorious victory, to dismiss the Chamber.

Napoleon had tried, as his less illustrious successor was to do, to make the French believe that the Empire meant peace. He actually made overtures at Vienna and London, but the Allies were in no mood to suffer the reëstablishment of Napoleon, no matter how sincerely he proffered the olive branch. At London, an effort of the Whig leaders to discountenance the renewal of war was snowed under. At Vienna, on the very first news of the return of the "Man of Elba," the plenipotentiaries of Great Britain, Russia, Austria, Prussia, France, Sweden, Spain, and Portugal issued a proclamation pronouncing him an outlaw; and the Four Powers agreed to a renewal of the Treaty of Chaumont (March 25) each pledging itself to put in the field an army of one hundred and fifty thousand men and "not to lay down their arms until Napoleon is rendered wholly incapable of disturbing peace again." The attempt of Napoleon to sow discord among the Coalition by informing Alexander of the exact text of the Secret Triple Alliance of Austria, England, and royalist France against Russia and Prussia, which Louis had left behind him in Paris, was unavailing. Clearly the Empire was not to mean peace. In fact, Murat had already given the signal for a general war. Aware that the Powers were intending to depose him if they could and feeling that Italy would rally to the cause of unification, he had begun an attack upon the Austrians on the Po in March. After a brilliant campaign, he was defeated at Tolentino (May 2–3) and obliged to flee in disguise to France. He offered to serve Napoleon as a general, but his offer was declined because he had frustrated the Emperor's efforts to keep the peace. War was inevitable now, and it was to be a war to the hilt.

On June 12, Napoleon set out for the Belgian frontier. He was to return within nine days. It was good strategy that he take the offensive, for the Allies were not yet prepared. In Belgium there was only a heterogeneous army of English, Dutch, Belgians, and Germans under the Duke of Wellington, and a Prussian army under Blücher. Delay would permit the Austrians and Russians to arrive. Unfortunately for Napoleon, the people of France, even the old soldiers, were tired of war. On paper his army numbered 506,000 men potentially. But actually, only 60,000 responded to his appeal to arms, and even after conscription, he had no more than 200,000 men under his command, part of whom had to be left behind to fight the royalist rebels. Wellington and Blücher could count on at least 215,000, with reënforcements rapidly moving to their support. Napoleon's only chance, in view of the numerical superiority of his opponents, was to engage them singly.

But the old precision of the commander and the old unfaltering discipline of the subordinates were lacking. A whole day was lost in crossing the Sambre River in the hope of cutting the enemy's line, thus allowing Blücher to make counter-preparations. The battle of Ligny (June 16) was, therefore, a more hotly contested encounter than Napoleon had at first expected. He issued urgent orders to Ney, whose wing had been detached from the main line in the expectation of a far different movement, to march to his aid. But Ney was engaged at Quatre Bras by Wellington. Napoleon with only 68,000 men was left alone to fight 86,000 Prussians. But Blücher had engaged in battle only on the promise of the English aid which Ney prevented from reaching him. After a stubborn contest, Gneisenau, believing Blücher, who had fallen with his horse, killed in action, gave the order to retreat. Twenty thousand in dead, wounded, and missing were left behind. The victory was a well-deserved one for Napoleon's veterans, but the Prussians had withdrawn in such a way as to coöperate better with the English.

The army that won the victory was not as efficient a machine as Napoleon had formerly constructed. Twenty thousand men attached to Ney's forces, on their way to Quatre Bras, had turned toward Ligny when an aide-de-camp from Napoleon ordered them to do so, and then turned again toward Quatre Bras, before they had reached Ligny, on insistent orders from Ney. The presence of that corps in either contest would have enabled Ney or Napoleon to crush the opposing force. But the error of Drouet d'Erlon in marching and counter-marching his men without engaging in battle on the 16th was no greater than Napoleon's own in sending Grouchy, only at noon on the 17th, in pursuit of the Prussians whom he believed to have retired upon their own line of communication and away from the English. Ligny was to be the last of Napoleon's victories.

Wellington's army, after its victory at Quatre Bras, had withdrawn to the plateau of Mont-Saint-Jean, south of the village of Waterloo. He had 67,700 men and 174 cannon.[1] Napoleon arrived opposite him on the night of June 17 with 74,000 fatigued men and 266 cannon. On June 18, at half-past eleven Napoleon attacked the superior position of the English, Belgians, and Germans under Wellington. The battle had hardly begun in earnest when the Prussians under the command of General Bülow appeared on the right. Depending upon Grouchy's being not far behind them, Napoleon sent a small force under Lobau to delay their advance, and continued a fearful cannonade against the English lines. At one o'clock an infantry attack was driven back by the English cavalry. At three o'clock it was learned that Grouchy was too far away to be of assistance. Knowing that the Prussians could not be held off much longer, Napoleon determined upon risking all to crush the English before it was too late. Ney attacked the fortified farmhouse known as La Haye Sainte. His first charge was successful, but had been made too soon, without infan-

[1] Cf., however, Wilson: *Greville's Diary*, 1, 83, December 10, 1820: "He [Wellington] said that he had 50,000 men at Waterloo. He began the campaign with 85,000 men, lost 5000 on the 16th, and had a corps of 20,000 at Hal under Prince Frederick. He said that it was remarkable that nobody who had ever spoken of these operations had ever made mention of that corps, and Bonaparte was certainly ignorant of it. In this corps were the best of the Dutch troops; it had been placed there because the Duke expected the attack to be made on that side." There are 10,000 men missing in this calculation.

try support, and he was forced to withdraw before a counter-charge of English cavalry. Four charges, in which the heavy squadrons of the Guard, together with other French cavalry, hacked away at the constantly dwindling squares of Hanoverian and English infantry, were forced back within an hour.

It was already six o'clock; the Prussians had overcome the ineffective resistance of the small French force opposing them and were rapidly coming to Wellington's assistance. A more vigorous effort of the Prussians to reach the main field of action might have put a quicker end to the battle. It was only after Blücher, who had suffered badly from his fall at Ligny, joined them that they made a serious effort to reach Wellington's army. It had been only at 4 P.M. that they had engaged in a three-to-one struggle with Lobau's French detachment and now at six o'clock they had broken through. Napoleon had to divert the Young Guard from the scene of the most critical action to aid Lobau's masterly resistance. But by that time more Prussians had begun to arrive. Ney now launched an infantry attack at La Haye Sainte, and at 6.30 Drouet d'Erlon's corps carried the farmhouse. Had Napoleon had enough reserves, he might have won the battle, but Ney's pleas for fresh infantry met only with gruff refusals. Napoleon was unwilling to sacrifice the Old and Middle Guard, who had to be conserved for a final effort.

If military considerations alone had influenced the Emperor at this juncture, he might have retreated with a good claim to victory. But a retreat would have meant his political downfall. He knew, better than any, that a usurper must cast into the shadow the performances that a legitimate ruler might consider a claim more enduring than bronze. He determined upon a last assault. Eight battalions of the Middle Guard and the Old Guard attacked the English line near the Château of Hougoumont. Heavy artillery fire and musketry met them as they advanced; and when they came through the smoke, Wellington gave his famous order to charge. The British Guards jumped "up and at them" with bayonets fixed.¹ Soon they were joined by the cavalry. The Old Guard recoiled. The whole French force retreated in panic. Only the squares of the Old Guard held on till nightfall, covering the retreat of the others, until the Emperor ordered them likewise to retreat. Lobau's forces at Planchenoit continued to fight even after the main battle had been lost and prevented the Prussians from cutting off the retreat of the main army toward Charleroi. For the next two days a shattered, routed army made its way across the Belgian border into France.

Grouchy in the mean time had fought capably against Prussian forces that he had encountered on the Dyle River near Wavre. His struggle was still unfinished when, on the morning of June 19, he learned of Napoleon's overwhelming defeat on the previous day. Fearing his retreat might be cut off, he withdrew in good order. His failure to appear at Planchenoit and to take his part in the battle of Waterloo has frequently, on Napoleon's testimony, been considered the reason for Wellington's victory. But it must be remembered that he carried out Napoleon's orders to the letter — perhaps too literally — as long as he was able. When he was informed of Blücher's presence near Waterloo and ordered to turn and crush him, he was himself too busily engaged to dare to obey. Ney's failure at Quatre Bras and Grouchy's losing touch with the main body of the Prussians were fearful blunders. But the fact is that Napoleon was responsible for his own defeat. Wellington was not a better general than Napoleon, but he was strategist enough to take advantage of Napoleon's errors and disadvantages. A Scipio had again conquered a Hannibal.

It is difficult to resist the glamour that has come to be associated with the battle of Waterloo and not to assign to it far more importance than it deserves. Even if Napoleon had been victorious at Waterloo, he could not have won the

¹ Becke: *Waterloo and Napoleon*, II, 122, makes Wellington's command, "Up, Guard, ready!"

war and have maintained himself upon his throne. Neither Austrians nor Russians had engaged in that battle, while Napoleon had suffered almost irreparable losses. A victory would have enabled him to hold out a little longer, but, unless he could have succeeded in destroying the Coalition or in gaining allies for himself — neither of which seemed probable — his career would, nevertheless, soon have come to a close. The result of Waterloo was that it brought matters to a climax at Paris sooner than they otherwise might have been. Napoleon returned post-haste to Paris on June 21. His plan was to demand a temporary dictatorship of the Chambers and to summon all the available manpower of France to the defense of the country. But the Legislature of the *Acte Additionnel* was not the meek tool of former days. The Chambers, on the motion of Lafayette, voted themselves *en permanence* and paid no heed to the demands he presented through his brother Lucien. To have resisted, with hostile armies pouring in from Spain, Belgium, the Rhine districts, the Alps, would have been suicidal. The crowds in the streets of Paris still shouted for their Emperor, but he was unwilling to dare a popular *coup*. He decided to surrender. On June 22, on the demand of the Chambers, he abdicated in favor of Napoleon II. On June 25, he retired to Malmaison. From the day Louis XVIII left Paris until the day that Napoleon withdrew to Malmaison, exactly ninety-eight days had elapsed. Within the so-called Hundred Days a kingdom had fallen, an empire had been established, an empire had fallen, and now it was to be decided whether the kingdom would be reëstablished.

Upon the abdication of Napoleon, the Chambers created a Provisional Government under an Executive Commission of five members of whom Fouché was President. Louis XVIII had crossed into France in the rear of the advancing armies of Blücher and Wellington. At Cateau-Cambrésis, on June 25, he proclaimed the resumption of his rights, his continued adherence to the Constitutional Charter, and his intention to reward his loyal subjects and to punish the disloyal. The last clause was subsequently softened at Cam-

brai (June 28). Within a few days, northern France had
rallied to the white flag again.   But at Paris the repugnance
to the Bourbons that had made necessary their retreat was
no more favorable to their return.   Some people spoke of
acclaiming Napoleon II; others turned toward the Duke of
Orléans.   On June 23, the Chambers had adopted a resolution accepting Napoleon II as Emperor, but a commission sent to discuss the terms of peace with the Duke of
Wellington was informed that peace was impossible until
Napoleon had been delivered up and a regular government
created; a change of dynasty would make necessary the
guaranteeing of peace by further concessions of French
territory.   Resistance was futile.   Napoleon, to be sure,
sent an offer from Malmaison to lead the armies of France
in the capacity of a simple general.   But the Prussians had
gained the heights commanding Paris on June 29, and the
English were not far distant.   Realizing that Napoleon
was still a source of danger and (since the Allies had announced they were fighting him rather than France) an
obstacle to peace, the Provisional Government gave him
the alternative of flight or arrest.   Two French frigates
having been put at his disposal to escort him to the United
States, he left for Rochefort on the coast, just a few hours
before a squadron of Prussians posted into Malmaison with
orders to capture him.

The Chambers now discreetly surrendered.   Despite
Marshal Davout's desire to fight on, the city capitulated on
July 3.   The allied army entered on July 7, and on July 8
Louis was again at the Tuileries.   There had been no conspicuous demonstrations either of joy or sorrow at the second
restoration of the Bourbons, though Castlereagh seemed to
think that the second welcome of Louis XVIII was "even
more animated than his former entrance."   On the same
day Napoleon boarded the French frigate, the Saale, little
more than a prisoner of the Provisional Government.   His
ride from Malmaison to Rochefort, filled as it must have
been with his own forlorn thoughts, was not without enthusiastic displays on the part of the soldiers and peasants.

An English squadron, however, now blocked the port of Rochefort; and Napoleon, having surrendered all hope of escape, began to think of spending the remainder of his life in England. His confidence that his "most powerful, most constant, and most generous enemy" would also be a most noble captor induced him to reject all the means of escape put at his disposal by devoted followers. On July 15, he surrendered to Captain Maitland on board the Bellerophon, one of the vessels that had figured bravely in the battle of the Nile.

In the mean time, the new Government hastened to make peace with the Allies. The new Ministry, of which Talleyrand was President and Fouché, who for several days had been practically dictator at Paris, Minister of Police, set about the task immediately after the monarchy was again organized. To make the conclusion of peace easier, the French army was dismissed and the art treasures, taken by Napoleon, were returned to their former owners. Because of the determination of the Allies not to be as lenient now as they had been in 1814 and Talleyrand's unwillingness to permit Louis XVIII's realm to be regarded as conquered territory, the negotiations dragged on for about five months. On November 20, after Louis' personal mendicancy had succeeded in softening the original severe terms, the Second Treaty of Paris was signed. The boundary of France was reduced to that of 1790; thus France was obliged to cede a number of districts on the borders, including the fortresses of Saarlouis and Landau. An indemnity of seven hundred million francs, a huge sum in days when people were not used to talking in billions, and joint military occupation for five years were likewise considered necessary as punitive and preventive measures. It had been wise for the Allies to pretend, while the war was still going on, that they were fighting not France but Napoleon. Now that the war was over, however, and France could no longer resist, it was considered unwise to forget that, after all, France had welcomed and supported Napoleon. It was Castlereagh and Wellington who again prevented the Prussian military faction from

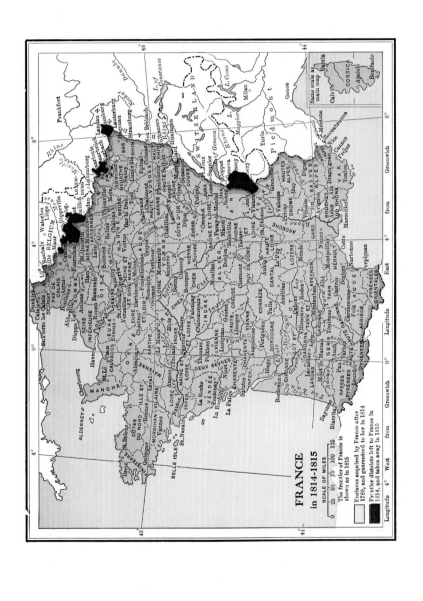

FRANCE
in 1814-1815

SCALE OF MILES

0   25   50   75   100 125

The frontier of France is
shown as in 1815

☐ Enclaves acquired by France after
1789, and guaranteed to her in 1814

■ Frontier districts left to France in
1814, and taken away in 1815

destroying France. "It is not our business," said Castle-reagh, "to collect trophies, but to bring back the world to peaceful habits." England, having already gotten her share of the spoils, could not afford, then as now, to see a potentially well-behaved neighbor and a good customer completely ruined.

Further guarantees of peace, however, were considered desirable. Alexander's eagerness for a confederation of Europe had been greatly enhanced by the strange influence exerted over him by a pietistic, mystic Baroness de Krüde-ner, who believed herself inspired by God. On the night of June 4, 1815, she had made her way to Alexander's tent at Schlüchtern, where he had fixed his quarters, and "for hours preached her strange gospel, while the Autocrat of All the Russians sat sobbing, with his face buried in his hands." From that day, the Baroness had accompanied the Emperor and was now living at Paris in a house connected by a secret door with the Élysée Palace, where Alexander lived. The Czar would come every evening to take part in the prayers that she conducted. On September 26, while the negotia-tions for the Second Treaty of Paris were still unfinished, he had persuaded the rulers of Austria and Prussia to form a Holy Alliance, to which the other Powers of Europe were asked to accede.

The Holy Alliance was obviously a sincere if impracti-cable scheme for the promotion of international understand-ing. The sovereigns who accepted the principle of the Holy Alliance pledged themselves to regard each other as Chris-tian brothers and their subjects as children. In that way there would be molded a republic of Christian states, which Alexander since 1804 had set up as his goal. "The sole principle of force, whether between the Governments or be-tween their subjects, shall be that of doing each other re-ciprocal service, and of testifying by unalterable good will the mutual affection with which they ought to be animated, to consider themselves all as members of one and the same Christian nation." Metternich called it "a high-sounding nothing," but neverthless Austria signed. Castlereagh called it a "piece of sublime mysticism and nonsense"; and taking advantage of the fact that the King of England was mad and the Prince Regent was not a sovereign, England did not sign. The Prince Regent, however, sent a letter to Alexander expressing his personal sympathies with the sentiment of the Holy Alliance. Every other ruler in Europe, except the Sultan, who was not asked, and the Pope, who refused to join any alliance, no matter how holy, under the hegemony of a heretic, signed the document.

But Castlereagh wanted an effective instrument to enforce peace. Alexander's wild scheme for a league of nations would have to give place to a hard-headed scheme for watching the chief disturber of the peace — France. Castlereagh saw in the renewal of the Treaty of Chaumont the possibilities of such a league of security. The Four Powers that had twice crushed Napoleon by concerted action must be kept together for similar exigencies in the future. Castlereagh succeeded to such an extent that on November 20, the same day as the signature of the Second Treaty of Paris, the four allies secretly affixed their sanction to a treaty reconfirming the engagements entered into at Chaumont and pledging the High Contracting Powers "to renew at fixed intervals, either under their own auspices or by their representative ministers, meetings consecrated to great common objects and the examination of such measures as at each one of these epochs shall be judged most salutary for the peace and prosperity of the nations and for the maintenance of the peace of Europe." Thus both the Holy Alliance and the Quadruple Alliance — both so frequently and mistakenly described by the first name alone — originated in an earnest desire to preserve the peace. It was not long before the Quadruple Alliance became the Quintuple Alliance (1818) by the admission of France and then broke up on the questions of the independence of the Spanish-American republics and of Greece (1829). During its brief duration, the Quadruple Alliance proved to be a most bitter disappointment to those that had expected the most of it. Peace was most endangered, after the second fall of Napoleon, by revolutions; and revolutions were caused primarily by the reactionary policy of the restored legitimate Governments. The Quadruple Alliance soon became, therefore, almost exclusively a means of supporting the reactionary policies of the Governments of Europe against England and their liberal minorities.

The peace and alliance (of which Frenchmen were not to learn until February, 1816) having been achieved, the French Government now turned its attention to the "White Terror" going on inside of France. Bonapartists and soldiers were no longer safe in the streets of the southern cities. Royal supporters massacred them at Marseilles in a manner that showed that reprisals can be as bloody when instigated by reactionaries as by revolutionists. Incendiaries were busy in Provence; bandits at work elsewhere. Marshal Brune was murdered at Avignon. Marshal Ney was arrested and brought to trial. Moncey, named president of the tribunal that was to try him, was sentenced to three months' imprisonment for refusing to serve. Ney had eventually to be tried by the Court of Peers. After a prolonged trial, he was found guilty of treason and executed on October 7. Louis XVIII was right in maintaining that, by allowing himself to be caught, Ney had done the royal cause more harm than by deserting to Napoleon on March 17. The execution of Ney was indeed a great error. It marked the beginning of a series of errors that the Bourbon Government, upon the instigation of the Count of Artois and an unmatchable royalist Chamber (*Chambre introuvable*), were to make. The reign of Louis XVIII was to pass without crisis, but the Count of Artois was to reign as Charles X for six years that were to end in revolution and deposition. An Orléanist monarchy, a liberal republic, an empire were to come and go, and in 1870, when the Third Republic was to be established, France was to be, in the words of Seignobos, what Napoleon had left it.

The Bourbons were to retard the progress of the revolution tremendously, but a comparison of any of the eastern European nations with any of the western European nations, both before and after the French Revolution and Napoleon, will suffice to show that the revolutions from 1789 to 1815 had not been in vain. Prussia and Russia, for example, had been very much the same in 1780. An en-lightened despot ruled over a vast territory in which there was a group of privileged classes and a group of suppressed classes. Serfdom still existed; the bourgeoisie had little political power; the nobility owned most of the land; the king was autocratic. Came the Revolution to Prussia and everything changed. But the Revolution, in the person of Napoleon, was fought out of Russia and never succeeded in taking root there. Russia in 1815, consequently, was much the same as she had been in 1780, except for an awakened sense of nationalism and liberalism, and continued to be the same until the 1860's. To claim that the tremendous differ-ence in the progress Prussia had made by the twentieth cen-tury as compared with that of Russia was entirely due to the influence of the French Revolution on the one hand and the lack of such influence on the other would be to disregard a myriad of other factors that have to be taken into considera-tion in such a comparison. That it was an important, even the most important factor, however, perhaps those who now, in the streets of Moscow and Leningrad, enact un-mistakable analogies to the French Revolution, are best equipped to state. Only in England, where there was little dissatisfaction with the political organization of the country and where the horror created by the excesses of the French Revolution caused a reaction and prevented the carrying out of a reform program that was already well on its way by 1789, can the French Revolution be said to have interfered with political progress. Even in England, the advances of the next generation were to be but echoes of the ferment on the Continent, which were themselves but reverberations of the French Revolution. The revolutionary tradition had been created.

And Napoleon? The Bellerophon [1] took him from Roche-

---

[1] There is a certain laconic fitness in the names of the ships with which Napoleon's career is associated. The tiny skiff on which he had fled from Egypt

fort to Plymouth, the nearest English port. On July 28, the English Government decided to send him captive to St. Helena. On August 2, the Four Great Powers agreed to regard him as their common prisoner. On August 7, he was taken from the Bellerophon to the Northumberland with a suite of twenty-five faithfuls. The little party of exiles reached St. Helena on October 17. There let us leave Napoleon, eating out his heart in sad recollection of the glory that he dictated, in apology and defiance, to a few followers, faithful even unto exile, but who found their faithfulness a burden; quarreling with an officious, meticulous, and unimaginative governor, Sir Hudson Lowe, whom he made miserable and who, nevertheless, would have liked to see him comfortable if it could have been done without violating any of many petty scruples; neglecting his health, because his last weapon against the combined powers of the earth was the scandal that he hoped his premature death would create. There would be a touch of redeeming pathos in his career if the story were true that, when in 1821 he died of cancer, his last words were a call for Josephine. But even that seems part of the legendary martyrology that he himself did the most to nourish in the memoirs dictated at St. Helena and which were eventually to make possible the Second Empire of Napoleon III. Whatever the defects of his plans — and they were many — or of his character — and they were more — no man ever had a greater influence upon the careers of his contemporaries and few more effect upon posterity. He was not a Man of Destiny, if by that moot phrase is meant that from the very first he had a clear-cut conception of what he wished to achieve, a plan into which he made his opportunities fit and toward which he bent every last effort. Once

to France in 1799 was named the Muiron. The vessel in which the triumphant British navy took him to Elba was called the Undaunted. That in which he sailed from Elba to his brief day of renewed glory in France was known as the Inconstant. And it was on the Bellerophon, christened after the Greek mythological hero who killed the Chimæra, rode Pegasus, and was doomed to spend his aging years in wandering over the earth, that he made the first lap of the trip to the little rock, lost somewhere between Africa and South America, and marked on the maps as St. Helena.

he had deserted his youthful allegiance to Corsica and Jacobinism, he became the opportunist *par excellence*.   But he was an opportunist with liberal ideals, urged on by a constant motivating force — the necessity of maintaining himself against England.   If he had any ideal at all, it was the ideal of efficiency, and this marriage of liberal opportunism with a passion for efficiency helped to create a Europe that was perhaps destined.

BIBLIOGRAPHY
CHRONOLOGICAL TABLE
INDEX

BIBLIOGRAPHY

PART I: DISSATISFACTION AND REFORM
BOOK I: THE ANCIENT RÉGIME
ORIGINAL SOURCES

THE best sources on the Ancient Régime are the *cahiers*. These have been collected, in part, in the *Collection de documents inédits sur l'histoire économique de la Révolution française*, and, in part, in the first six volumes of the *Archives Parlementaires*. There are also the splendid collections on local and charitable institutions entitled *Collection des inventaires sommaires des archives départementales (communales: hospitalières) antérieures (postérieures) à 1790* (about 300 volumes). There are literally hundreds of pamphlets printed in 1788 and 1789 that have survived. The collected works of the *philosophes* are all of great importance for the light they shed on this period. There are likewise a great number of memoirs on the reign of Louis XIV, XV, and XVI, including Saint-Simon, Retz, D'Argenson, Ségur, *The Travels of Arthur Young*, the *Souvenirs d'un Nonegénaire*, Mme. Campan, etc. For the most part, these are to be found in the collection of *Mémoires pour servir à l'histoire du commerce et de l'industrie de la France* (10 volumes, published by Hayem), and more especially in the *Collection des mémoires relatifs à la Révolution française*, by Berville and Barrière, and the *Bibliothèque des mémoires relatifs à l'histoire de France pendant la 18ᵉ siècle*. The *Mercure de France* was the leading French periodical of the time. In the *Almanach Royal*, there will be found yearly compendiums of statistical information, especially valuable for names and titles of office-holders. Isambert, *Dictionnaire de la Noblesse*, is a later undertaking of a similar nature. A great many translations of important letters, memoirs, writings, etc., are to be found in Brentano's *Broadway Library of Eighteenth Century French Literature*.

SECONDARY SOURCES

The following are the works covering the Ancient Régime in whole or for the most part:

Dedieu: *Histoire Politique des Protestants Français, 1715–1794*.
Kovalevsky: *La France économique et sociale à la vielle de la Révolution*.
H. Sée: *Economic and Social Conditions in France During the Eighteenth Century*.
A. Hassall: *The Balance of Power*.

M. Roustan: *Pioneers of the French Revolution.*
A. Aulard: *La Révolution Française et le Régime Féodal.*
S. Herbert: *The Fall of Feudalism in France.*
A. Wahl: *Vorgeschichte der französischen Revolution.*
H. Taine: *The Ancient Régime.*
Pizard: *La France en 1789.*
A. de Tocqueville: *The Ancient Régime.*
Broc: *La France sous l'ancien régime.*
E. J. Lowell: *Eve of the French Revolution.*
MacLehose: *Last Days of the French Monarchy.*
E. Lavisse: *Histoire de France,* vol. IX.
Cherest: *La Chute de l'ancien régime.*
Champion: *La France d'après les cahiers de 1789.*
Picard: *Les Cahiers de 1789 au point de vue industrial et commercial.*
Boiteau: *État de la France en 1789.*
A. H. Johnson: *Age of the Enlightened Despots.*
Philippson: *Age of the European Balance of Power* and *Age of Frederick the Great,* vols. XIV and XV of the *History of all Nations.*
Stryienski: *The Eighteenth Century.*
Lavisse et Rambaud: *Histoire Générale,* vol. VII.
Cambridge Modern History, vol. VI.

Marion, *Dictionnaire des institutions de la France aux XVIIe et XVIIIe siècles,* will be found particularly useful. Other dictionaries are Chéruel, *Dictionnaire des institutions, mœurs et coutumes de la France;* Boursin and Challamel, *Dictionnaire de la Révolution Française;* and Lalanne, *Dictionnaire Historique de la France.* The *Biographie Universelle* and the *Nouvelle Biographie Universelle* will be found the best dictionaries of biography. *Larousse* and the *Grande Encyclopédie* are also highly valuable. In addition to the general works mentioned above, consult: For Book I, Chapter I (Government under the Ancient Régime):

Brissaud: *A History of French Public Law.*
Babeau: *La Ville sous l'ancien régime.*
　　　　La Village sous l'ancien régime.
　　　　La Province sous l'ancien régime.
　　　　Paris en 1789.
Ardasceff: *Les Intendants en France sous le règne de Louis XVI.*
Esmein: *Cours élémentaire du droit français.*
Michon: *Adrien Duport.*
Gomel: *Les Causes financières de la Révolution française.*
Brette: *Atlas de Bailliages.*
Marion: *Histoire financière de la France.*

For Book I, Chapter II (Society under the Ancient Régime):

Levasseur: *Histoire de Commerce de la France.*
　　　　Histoire des classes ouvrières et de l'industrie en France avant 1789.

H. Sée: *L'Evolution commerciale et industrielle de la France sous l'ancien régime.*
Babeau: *Les Artisans et les domestiques d'autrefois.*
Mantoux: *La Révolution industrielle au XVIIIe Siècle.*
Knowles: *The Industrial and Commercial Revolutions in Great Britain in the Nineteenth Century.*
Babeau: *Les Bourgeois d'Autrefois.*
N. Webster: *Chevalier de Boufflers.*
Ferdinand-Dreyfus: *Un Gentilhomme d'Autrefois.*
Kareiew: *Les Paysans et la Question paysanne.*
Sicard: *L'ancien Clergé de France.*
Loutchisky: *La Propriété paysanne à la veille de la Révolution.*
   L'État des classes agricoles en France à la veille de la Révolution.
Babeau: *La vie rurale sous l'ancien régime.*
Bloch: *Études d'histoire économique de la France.*
F. M. Fling: *The Youth of Mirabeau.*
Chassin: *Les Cahiers des Curés.*
Marion: *La Vente des biens nationaux.*
De Goncourt: *La Société française pendant la Révolution française.*
H. Sée: *Recherches sur la misère, la mendicité et l'assistance en Bretagne à la fin de l'ancien régime.*
Funck-Brentano: *The Diamond Necklace.*
   Légendes et Archives de la Bastille
E. F. Henderson: *A Lady of the Old Régime.*
H. Sée: *La Vie économique et les classes sociales en France au XVIIIe siècle.*
Marion: *État des classes rurales dans la généralité de Bordeaux.*
Ducros: *French Society in the Eighteenth Century.*

For Book I, Chapter III (Political Philosophy of the Eighteenth Century):

Delbeke: *L'Action politique et sociale des Avocats.*
G. Brandes: *Voltaire.*
L. Stephen: *English Thought in the Eighteenth Century.*
Lecky: *History of England in the Eighteenth Century.*
C. Becker: *The Declaration of Independence.*
Buckle: *History of Civilization in England.*
W. A. Dunning: *Political Theories from Luther to Montesquieu.*
   Political Theories from Rousseau to Spencer.
Janet: *Histoire de la Science politique.*
H. Sée: *Les Idées politiques en France au XVIIIe siècle.*
Glumpowicz: *Geschichte der Staatstheorien.*
Redslob: *Staatstheorien der französischen Nationalsversammlung.*
T. Fowler: *John Locke.*
E. Faguet: *Le XVIIIe Siècle.*
Sorel: *Montesquieu.*
   Europe et la Révolution Française, vol. I.

Flint: *Historical Philosophy in France.*
Aldington: *Letters of Voltaire and Frederick the Great.*
    Voltaire.
G. Martin: *La Franc-Maçonnerie française.*
Cochin: *Les Sociétés de Pensée et la Révolution en Bretagne.*
Vaughan: *Political Philosophy before and after Rousseau.*
    Political Writings of Rousseau.
J. Morley: *Rousseau.*
    Voltaire.
    Diderot and the Encyclopedists
Amiel: *Rousseau.*
Ritchie: *Natural Rights.*
Selections from Voltaire's Philosophical Dictionary, edited by H. I. Woolf.
Desnoiresterres: *Voltaire et J. J. Rousseau.*
E. Faguet: *La politique comparée de Montesquieu, Rousseau et Voltaire.*
Esmein: *La Science politique des Physiocrates.*
Gide and Rist: *History of Economic Doctrines.*
Higgs: *The Physiocrats.*
H. Laski: *Political Thought from Locke to Bentham.*
Villeurse: *Les Physiocrates.*
Schinz: *Eighteenth Century French Readings.*

For Book I, Chapter IV (Staving off the Revolution):

Voltaire: *Siècle de Louis XIV.*
A. Hassall: *Louis XIV.*
J. B. Perkins: *France under the Regency.*
    France under Louis XV.
Rocquain: *The Revolutionary Spirit.*
    L'Esprit Revolutionnaire avant la Révolution.
Flammermont: *Remonstrances du Parlement de Paris au XVIIIᵉ Siècle.*
H. O. Wakeman: *Ascendancy of France.*
A. Hassall: *Balance of Power 1715-1789.*
Philippson: *Age of Louis XIV.*
E. Lavisse: *Histoire de France,* vol. VIII, part II.
H. Belloc: *Marie Antoinette.*
La Rocheterie: *Marie Antoinette.*
Imbert de Saint Amand: *Marie Antoinette.*
Droz: *Histoire du regne de Louis XVI.*
Say: *Turgot.*
A. D. White: *Seven Great Statesmen.*
Carré: *La Fin des Parlements.*
B. Fay: *Esprit Révolutionnaire en France et aux États-Unis à la fin du XVIIIᵉ Siècle* (also in English translation).
J. B. Perkins: *France during the American Revolution.*
Doniol: *Participation de la France à l'établissement des États-Unis.*
Rosenthal: *France and America.*
M. B. Garrett: *Convocation of the States General.*
    Beginning of the French Revolution.
    Controversy over the Composition of the States General, etc.

a series of articles in the *Howard College Bulletin*, 1923–26.
Lanzac de Labourie: *Mounier.*
Whitcomb: *Typical Cahiers of 1789.*
Brette: *Recueil de Documents relatifs à la Convocation des États généraux.*
Chassin: *Les Elections et les Cahiers de Paris.*
Tuttle: *History of Prussia.*
Reddaway: *Frederick the Great.*
Longmans: *Frederick the Great.*
Carlyle: *Frederick the Great.*
G. M. Priest: *Germany since 1740.*
Rambaud: *History of Russia.*
Bain: *Slavonic Europe.*
Anthony: *Catherine the Great.*
Waliszewski: *Catherine the Great.*
Hodgetts: *Catherine the Great.*
Larivière: *Cathérine le Grand.*
A. H. Johnson: *Age of Enlightened Despots.*
Bright: *Maria Theresa.*
      Joseph II.
Coxe: *History of the House of Austria.*

Book II: THE FALL OF THE MONARCHY

ORIGINAL SOURCES

The debates of the Revolutionary Assemblies are contained in the *Moniteur, Le Journal des Debats*, the *Procès verbaux* of the various assemblies, and the *Archives parlementaires*, in which, unfortunately, there is a gap between 1794 and 1799. The *Moniteur* was a daily newspaper (really begun in November, 1789, but earlier numbers later made up), which gave foreign and domestic news as well as the parliamentary debates. There are also a great number of other newspapers for the period — *Point du jour, Révolutions de Paris, Ami du peuple, Révolutions de France et de Brabant*, etc. The *Collection de documents relatifs à l'histoire de Paris pendant la Révolution française, publiée sous le patronage du Conseil municipal*, contains, among others, Aulard's *La Société des Jacobins* (6 volumes) giving the minutes of the leading revolutionary club and his *Paris pendant la réaction Thermidorien et sous le Directoire* (5 volumes), and Lacroix, *Actes de la Commune de Paris pendant la Révolution* (16 volumes). There are also over 300 volumes known as the *Collection de documents inédits sur l'histoire de France*, of which Aulard, *Recueil des Actes du Comité de Salut public* (19 volumes) is among the most useful for the French Revolution. The *Collection de Documents inédits sur l'histoire économique de la Révolution française* so far has emphasized the *cahiers* and the sale of public lands, though there are single volumes on a number of other important economic questions. They are put out by the *Commission de Recherche et de Publication des Documents relatifs à la Vie économique de la Révolution*, which also publishes a *Bulletin*. Buchez and Roux, *Histoire parlementaire de la Révolution française* is a collection of some very important sources with connecting comment; it is a good deal more than a parliamentary history. Duvergier, *Collection complète des lois, decrets, etc.*, devotes a large part of its 115 volumes to the French Revolutionary period. Cahen and Guyot, *L'Œuvre législatif de la Révolution française* is a splendid list with brief descriptions of the legislation of the Revolutionary Assemblies. Martens, *Recueil des traités . . . des puissances et états de l'Europe depuis 1761 jusqu'à présent* (97 volumes until 1920) will be found invaluable for a study of foreign affairs. This should be supplemented by the publications of the *Commission des Archives diplomatiques*, of which the most important volumes for us are the *Recueil des instructions données aux ambassadeurs et ministres de France*, a coöperative work by a committee including Sorel, Waddington, Hanotaux, etc., and Kaulek, *Les Papiers de Barthélemy*. The so-called *Dropmore Papers* (*The manuscripts of J. B. Fortescue*, edited by the Royal Commission on Historical Manuscripts) is invaluable for the correspondence of leading French and English diplomats. For economic and social conditions, the *Collection des inventaires sommaires des archives départementales* (*communales; hospitalières*) *antérieures* (*postérieures*) *à 1790*, already mentioned, is a veritable mine. There are a great many contemporary pamphlets and important contemporary accounts, of which the *Histoire de la Révolution par deux amis de la Liberté* (19 volumes 1792–1803) is the most often used. The memoirs for the period have been collected by Berville and Barrière, *Collection des mémoires relatifs à la Révolution française* (55 volumes), and in the *Bibliothèque des mémoires relatifs à l'histoire de France pendant la 18ᵉ siècle*. But some memoirs — such as those of Lafayette, Barère, Barras, Talleyrand, Carnot — appeared separately. Tuetey, *Répertoire général des sources manuscrits de l'histoire de Paris pendant la Révolution française* (11 volumes) quotes in full or gives summaries of a number of important manuscripts. An idea of the manuscripts in the *Bibliothèque nationale* at Paris can be got from *Notices et Extraits des Manuscrits de la Bibliothèque nationale* (*impériale, royale*) (38 volumes, 1787–1903). The best single guide to the study of the French Revolution is Caron, *Manuel pratique pour l'étude de la Révolution française*. The student can keep in touch with the new developments in the field through the current numbers of the *Annales historiques de la Révolution française*, edited by A. Mathiez and the

Société des Études Robespierristes (which is also publishing the complete works of Robespierre) and *La Révolution française,* edited by Aulard and the *Société de l'Histoire de la Révolution,* which is Dantonist. There were other historical periodicals on the French Revolution, which have since been discontinued.

CHIEF SECONDARY SOURCES

Every year the literature on the French Revolution grows larger. It would be futile to attempt to give a complete summary of it all. Some conception of the immensity of this literature can be received from Tourneaux, *Bibliographie de l'histoire de Paris pendant la Révolution française* (5 volumes) and Caron, *Bibliographie des travaux publiés de 1886 à 1897 sur l'histoire de France depuis 1789.* The most important general works are: A. Aulard, *Histoire politique de la Révolution française,* a history of the political developments of the Revolution by the Dean of students of the French Revolution, also obtainable in English translation (*The French Revolution,* 4 volumes); *Histoire socialiste,* edited by J. Jaurès, of which the volumes on the Revolution, by Jaurès himself, have been separately edited by Mathiez; Sorel, *Europe et la Révolution française,* the best study of international complications; E. Bourgeois, *Manuel pratique de politique étrangère,* briefer but very instructive; Chuquet, *Les Guerres de la Révolution,* the most careful study of the military history of the period; De la Gorce, *Histoire religieuse de la Révolution française,* among the best treatises on religious developments; Levasseur, *Histoire des classes ouvrières et de l'industrie en France de 1789 à 1870,* a splendid study of the economic phases of the Revolution; Espinas, *Philosophie sociale du XVIIIᵉ siècle et la Révolution,* a monograph on the political philosophy of the Revolution; E. Lavisse, *Histoire de France contemporaine,* which contains two volumes (I by Sagnac, II by Pariset) which have been described as the "best history of the French Revolution"; L. Madelin, *La Révolution,* which, in its English translation, is the most interesting one volume work in that language, despite a certain Catholic and conservative bias; H. M. Stephens, *French Revolution,* which is the best study by an English-speaking scholar, though inaccurate; J. H. McCarthy, *French Revolution,* which is also good; *The Cambridge Modern History* (vol. VIII, *The French Revolution*), a coöperative work of which it has been said that "the authors knew a great deal about the Revolution without being aware that there was a Revolution"; E. D. Bradby, *The French Revolution,* one of the most recent and sympathetic of the English summaries, carrying the story only to 1795; *La Révolution française* in Lavisse and Rambaud, *Histoire générale,* vol. VIII; Von Sybel, *Geschichte der Revolutionzeit von 1789*, an unfriendly German conservative estimate, obtainable also in English translation; Flathe, *The French Revolution* in *The History of all Nations* and Oncken, *Das Zeitalter der Revolution* in the *Allgemeine Geschichte in Einzeldarstellungen*, the fairest German expositions; Wahl, *Geschichte des europäischen Staatensystems im Zeitalter der französischen Revolution und der Freiheitskriege*, good for the history of countries outside of France; P. Kropotkin, *The Great French Revolution*, a study of the first years of the Revolution, favorable to the lower classes; A. Aulard, *Études et leçons de la Révolution française*, a collection of miscellaneous articles on important subjects; Aulard, *Les Orateurs de la Révolution*, an estimate of the leading figures of the Revolution; H. M. Stephens, *The Principal Speeches of the Statesmen and Orators of the French Revolution*, with short introductory remarks; Lord Acton, *Lectures on the French Revolution*, a valuable work of keen appreciation and insight; Mathiez, *La Révolution française* (the first three volumes also in English translation), now in the process of publication, four short volumes, carrying the story down to the end of the Convention, having already appeared; and Marion, *Histoire financière de la France*, a truly remarkable enterprise. A good many works, once considered valuable, are now no longer so considered. These are by Alison, Esquiros, Lamartine, Thiers, Blanc, Villiaumé, Carlyle, Von Holst, Michelet, and Quinet. Taine's *French Revolution* is still of great value, though severely criticized by Aulard. Small one volume works are numerous; among these are H. Belloc's, W Greer's, R. M. Johnston's, Mignet's (perhaps still the best, al though one of the oldest), S. Mathews' and W. O. Morris' There are also a large number of works on the year 1789-18·ʮ that are ostensibly meant for textbooks; these include volumes by C. D. Hazen, L. H. Holt and A. W. Chilton (good for military history), H. M. Stephens (good for the history of countries outside of France), J. H. Rose, and H. E. Bourne (perhaps the best of this group). Dictionaries for this period, in addition to those by Marion, and Chéruel, already mentioned, are Boursin and Challamel, *Dictionnaire de la Révolution française*; Lalanne, *Dictionnaire historique de la France*; Kuscinski, *Dictionnaire des Conventionnels*; and Robinet (and others), *Dictionnaire historique et biographique de la Révolution et de l'Empire*. For source materials conveniently arranged, students are urged to make frequent use of F. M. Anderson, *Constitutions and Select Documents Illustrative of French History*; L.G.W. Legg's *Select Documents Illustrative of the French Revolution*; G. G. Andrews, *The Constitution in the Early French Revolution*; and F. M. Fling, *Source Problems on the French Revolution*. In addition to these more general studies.

the following books will be found useful for the chapters indicated:

For Book II, Chapter I (The Estates General become the National Assembly):

A. Aulard: *Études et Leçons*, I, *Le Serment du jeu de Paume*.
J. H. Clapham: *Abbé Sieyès*.
P. F. Willert: *Mirabeau*.
Charavay: *Lafayette*.
Sedgwick: *Lafayette*.

For Book II, Chapter II (The People Prevent Counter-Revolution):

B. Fay: *L'Esprit révolutionnaire en France et aux États-Unis dans le XVIIIe Siècle* (also in English translation).
Flammermont: *La Journée du 14 juillet 1789*.
S. Herbert: *Fall of Feudalism in France*.
P. F. Willert: *Mirabeau*.
Lanzac de Laborie: *Mounier*.
E. D. Bradby: *Barnave*.
J. H. Clapham: *Sieyès*.
A. Aulard: *Études et Leçons*, VIII, *La Révolution Américaine et la Révolution française*.
C. E. Bourne in *American Historical Review*, VIII, *American Constitutional Precedents in the French National Assembly*.
Stoddard: *October 5–6, 1789* (Nebraska Studies).
Le Clerq: *Le 5–6 Octobre*.

For Book II, Chapter III (The Triumph of the Bourgeoisie):

S. A. Falkner: *Das Papiergeld der französischen Revolution*.
Stourm: *Les Finances de l'Ancien Régime et de la Révolution*.
Sagnac: *La Législation civile de la Révolution française*.
W. M. Sloane: *French Revolution and Religious Reform*.
A. Mathiez: *La Revolution et L'Église*.
A. Aulard: *Études et Leçons*, v, *Origines de la Séparation des églises et de l'état sous la Constituante, etc.*
Marion: *La Vente des biens nationaux*.
Gazier: *Études sur l'histoire religieuse de la Révolution*.
Redslob: *Die Staatstheorien der französischen Nationalsversammlung*.
L. Barthou: *Mirabeau*.
Debidour: *Histoire des rapports de l'église et de l'état*.
Sciout: *Histoire de la Constitution civile du Clergé*.
E. Faguet: *L'œuvre sociale de la Révolution*.
Lichtenberger: *Le Socialisme et la Révolution française*.
Stern: *Das Leben Mirabeaus*.
A. D. White: *Fiat Money Inflation during the French Revolution*.

For Book II, Chapter IV (The Counter-Revolution):

G. Lenôtre: *La Drame de Varennes*.
Paris in the French Revolution.

BIBLIOGRAPHY

H. Belloc: *High Lights of the French Revolution.*
Danton.

L. Madelin: *Danton.*

A. Mathiez: *Le Club des Cordeliers pendant la Crise de Varennes et la Massacre du Champ de Mars.*

Braesch: *Les pétitions du Champ de Mars,* in the *Revue Historique,* April 1923.

E. D. Bradby: *Life of Barnave.*

Mercy-Argenteau: *Correspondance secrète avec l'impératrice Marie Thérèse avec les lettres de Marie-Therèse et de Marie-Antoinette.*

Willert: *Mirabeau.*

For Book II, Chapter V (Constitutional Monarchy Fails):

Ellery: *Brissot de Warville.*

Daudet: *Histoire de l'émigration pendant la Révolution française.*

Blashfield: *Manon Phlipon Roland.*

Pope-Hennesy: *Madam Roland.*

Perroud: *Lettres de Madame Roland.*

Brissot: *Mémoires.*

W. Stephens: *Women of the French Revolution.*

Ferneron: *Histoire générale des Emigrés.*

L. Madelin: *Danton.*

H. Belloc: *Danton.*

Beesley: *Danton.*

Mortimer-Ternaux: *Histoire de la Terreur.*

Braesch: *La Commune du 10 Août, 1792.*

Pfeffer: *Insurrection of June 20, 1792* (Nebraska Studies).

La Rocheterie: *Marie Antoinette.*

H. Belloc: *Marie Antoinette.*

Droz: *Histoire du Règne de Louis XVI.*

Sagnac: *La Révolution du Août 10.*

A. Mathiez: *Autour de Danton.*

A. Aulard: *Études,* II, *Danton et les Massacres de Septembre.*

Book III: THE FIRST FRENCH REPUBLIC

ORIGINAL SOURCES

The original sources for Book III are the same as for Book II except that for Chapter IV (The Directory) the source materials are considerably rarer than for the earlier periods. The *Archives Parlementaires* are not available for 1794–99; the student must depend upon the *Moniteur,* the *Procès verbal,* and other contemporary newspapers, and Buchez and Roux, *Histoire Parlementaire de la Révolution française.* In the *Collection de documents inédits sur l'histoire de France,* the works that will be found of chief value for 1795–99 are *Correspondance de Carnot* by Charavay; *Recueil des actes du Directoire exécutif,* by Debidour; and the *Recueil de documents sur l'histoire de l'instruction publique pendant la période du Directoire.* In the *Collection de documents inédits sur l'histoire économique de la Révolution française,* several of the works on the sale of public lands in the separate departments carry the story beyond 1795, as do also the volumes on *Le commerce des cériales,* by Caron; *l'Agriculture,* by Bourgin; *L'Assistance publique,* by Bloch; *l'Industrie,* by Schmidt; *Le Papier-Monnaie et la Monnaie,* by Bloch. The *Papiers de Barthélemy* are available in the publications of the *Commission des archives diplomatiques.* Of the publications of the *Section historiques de l'État-major de l'armée* of the *Ministère de la Guerre* there are available about a dozen useful works on the military and naval history of the Directory. Of the *Collections de documents relatifs à l'histoire de Paris pendant la Révolution française,* Aulard's five volumes on *Paris pendant la réaction thermidorienne et sous le Directoire* are the most important, and there are also three volumes by Casanave on *Les tribunaux civils de Paris pendant la Révolution* (1791–1800); the four volumes by Tuetey on *Assistance publique à Paris pendant la Révolution* come down to 1796.

On the publications of the various societies for the study of the French Revolution, the following volumes contain some source materials on the history of the Directory: Mellié, *Les sections de Paris pendant la Révolution française;* Lacroix, *Le Departement de Paris et de la Seine pendant la Révolution;* Kuscinski, *Les députes au Corps Législatif ... de l'an IV à l'an VIII;* Ballot, *Le coup d'État du 18 fructidor an V;* Pierre, *Dix-huit fructidor;* Beauséjour, *Mémoires de famille de l'Abbé Lambert;* La Rocheterie, *Correspondance du Mis. et de la Mise. Raigecourt avec le Mis. et la Mise. de Bombelles pendant l'émigration, 1790–1800;* Pierre, *La déportation ecclésiastique sous le Directoire;* Broc, *Mémoires du Comte Ferrand;* Jerome, *Collectes à travers l'Europe pour les prêtres français déportés en Suisse pendant la Révolution* (1794–97); Rousseau, *Kléber et Menou en Égypte depuis le départ de Bonaparte.* Of the memoirs of the time relating to the history of the Directory the most valuable are those by Barras, Rémusat (*Mémoire sur ma détention au Temple*), Bouillé, Carnot, Talleyrand, Dumouriez, La Révellière-Lépaux, Gaëté, Thibaudeau, Roederer, Joseph Bonaparte, Lucien Bonaparte, and Napoleon Bonaparte. Duvergier's *Collection complète des lois,* etc., is complete from 1788 to 1824. For local history, there are several volumes of importance for this period among which are André, *Déliberation de l'administration départementales de la Lozère et de son directoire de 1790 à 1800;* Besançon, *Procès-verbaux des séances des administrations municipales de Villefranche-sur-Saône; Documents sur la Révolution française, Département de l'Yonne;* and *Documents pour servir à l'histoire de la Révolution française dans la ville d'Amiens.* On

Napoleon's early years, under the Directory, there are available his correspondence and numerous memoirs upon him, which will be mentioned again below.

SECONDARY SOURCES

The dictionaries and encyclopedias mentioned for Book II are likewise useful for Book III. Of the general histories mentioned in the earlier syllabus, those by Stephens, Mathiez, Bradby, Kropotkin, Acton, and Legg come to a close in or before 1795. The others are still useful, as indicated. Monographs of value are:

For Book III, Chapter I (The Girondin Supremacy in the Convention):

H. Belloc: *Robespierre.*
Hamel: *Robespierre.*
    Saint Just.
L. R. Gottschalk: *Marat*
Chevremont: *Marat.*
B. Bax: *Marat.*
Bougeart: *Marat.*
Mortimer-Ternaux: *Histoire de la Terreur.*
J. H. Rose: *William Pitt and the Great War.*
Rosebery: *William Pitt.*
Mahan: *Influence of Sea Power on the French Revolution and Empire.*
P. A. Brown: *The French Revolution in English History.*
G. P. Gooch: *The French Revolution and Germany.*
Lecky: *Ireland in the Eighteenth Century.*
Sagnac: *Le Rhin Français pendant la Révolution et l'Empire.*
C. D. Hazen: *American Opinion on the French Revolution.*
E. Faguet: *L'Œuvre Sociale de la Révolution* (on the army)
G. Lenôtre: *Tribunal de la Terreur.*
Schmidt: *Paris pendant la Révolution 1789–1800.*
Wallon: *La Terreur.*
    Les Représentans en mission.
    Histoire du Tribunal révolutionnaire.
Gros: *La Comité du Salut Publique.*
Perroud: *La Proscription des Girondins.*
Alengry: *Condorcet.*

For Book III, Chapter II (Jacobin Supremacy in the Convention):

Articles in the *Annales Révolutionnaires* from 1917 to 1924 on the *Enragés* by Mathiez.
Articles in the same publication on the *Terror*, 1924 to date.
C. Becker: *A Letter from Danton to Marie Antoinette*, in the *American Historical Review*, October, 1921.
A. Mathiez: *Autour de Danton.*
    Robespierre Terroriste.

La Compagnie des Indes.
The Fall of Robespierre.
Études Robespierristes.
La Vie Chère et le Mouvement social sous la Terreur.
Danton et la Paix.
La Révolution et les Étrangers.
Michon: *Correspondance de Maximilien et Augustin Robespierre.*
F. L. Nussbaum: *Commercial Policy in the French Revolution.*
W. B. Kerr: *The Reign of Terror.*
Aulard: *La Culte de la Raison et la Culte de L'Être Suprême.*
Robinet: *Mouvements religieux de Paris.*
J. H. Rose and A. M. Broadley: *Dumouriez and the Defence of England.*
Chassin: *La Préparation de la Guerre.*
Clarétie: *Camille Desmoulins.*
Chuquet: *Dumouriez.*
Gabory: *La Révolution et la Vendée.*
Gershoy: *Barère, Anacreon of the Guillotine* in *The South Atlantic Quarterly,* July, 1927.

For Book III, Chapter III (The Thermidorian Reaction):

H. W. Van Loon: *Rise of the Dutch Republic.*
E. Ludwig: *Napoleon.*
J. H. Rose: *Napoleon.*
Lenz: *Napoleon.*
W. M. Sloane: *Napoleon.*
H. A. L. Fisher: *Napoleon.*
F. M. Kircheisen: *Napoleon I: Sein Leben und seine Zeit.*
Napoleon I: ein Lebensbild.
De Goncourt: *Société pendant la Révolution française.*
Cambridge Modern History, vol. IX.
Lavisse et Rambaud: *Histoire Générale,* vol. IX.
Lavisse: *Histoire de France contemporanie,* vol. III.

For Book III, Chapter IV (The Directory):

J. McCabe: *Talleyrand.*
A. B. Dodd: *Talleyrand.*
B. Bax: *The Last Episode of the French Revolution.*
H. W. Van Loon: *Rise of the Dutch Kingdom.*
J. H. Clapham: *The Abbé Sieyès.*
Lecky: *History of Ireland during the Eighteenth Century.*
Guyot: *Le Directoire et la Paix de l'Europe.*
Guthrie: *Socialism during the French Revolution.*
Lichtenberger: *Socialisme et la Révolution française.*
Biographies and memoirs on Napoleon by F. M. Kircheisen, Lenz, A. Fournier, J. H. Rose, Driault, W. M. Sloane, O. Browning, A. Hassall, J. R. Seeley, J. C. Ropes, H. A. L. Fisher, Lévy, I. Tarbell, R. M. Johnston, E. Ludwig, Faure, P. Lanfrey, A. Thiers, Houssaye, Vandal, F. Masson, Bourrienne, Las Cases, Gourgaud, Montholon, and others.

Meynier: *Le Dix-Huit Fructidor An V.*
Luckwaldt: *Der Friede von Campo Formio.*
Montarlot et Pinquad: *Le Congress de Rastatt.*
R. B. Mowat: *Diplomacy of Napoleon.*
H. A. L. Fisher: *Napoleonic Statesmanship in Germany.*
G. P. Gooch: *The French Revolution and Germany.*
Gaffarel: *Bonaparte et les Républiques Italiennes.*
Southey: *Life of Nelson.*
Mahan: *Life of Nelson.*
            Influence of Sea Power on the French Revolution and Napoleon.
Cambridge History of British Foreign Policy.
Walizewski: *Paul I.*
J. H. Rose: *William Pitt and the Great War.*
De Goncourt: *La Société française pendant la Révolution et le Directoire.*
Stourm: *Les finances de l'ancien régime et de la Révolution.*
Atteridge: *Napoleon's Brothers.*
W. Geer: *Napoleon and His Family.*
F. Masson: *Napoléon et sa famille.*
G. Elton: *The Revolutionary Idea in France.*
A. L. Guérard: *Reflections on the Napoleonic Legend.*

Part II: STABILIZATION AND REACTION

ORIGINAL SOURCES

For the history of Napoleon (Books IV and V) the best sources are the *Moniteur*; the *Correspondance de Napoléon* (32 volumes, supplemented at various times by other additional publications); the memoirs of and on Napoleon (of which the more important are by Las Cases, Bourrienne, Talleyrand, Montholon, Rémusat, Thibaudeau, O'Meara, Mollien, Metternich, Ménéval, Miot de Melito, Ségur, Pasquier, Lucien Bonaparte, Joseph Bonaparte, among scores of others); Aulard's collection on *Paris sous le Consulat*; and the *Archives parlementaires*. There is a convenient arrangement of Napoleon's own words in diary form by R. M. Johnston (*The Corsican*). There is also a *Dictionary of Napoleon and His Times* by H. N. B. Richardson, and a review devoted to Napoleonic studies (*La Revue Napoléonienne*). The best bibliographies are F. M. Kircheisen (*Bibliographie des Napoleonischen Zeitalters*) and A. Lumbroso (*Bibliografia Ragionata dell' Epoca Napoleonica* — incomplete).

SECONDARY SOURCES

Of the larger studies on Napoleon, that by A. Thiers (*Histoire du consulat et de l'empire*) is very much pro-Napoleon. A good antidote is by P. Lanfrey (*Histoire de Napoléon I*). On Napoleon's military achievements F. L. Petrie (*Napoleon at Bay*, etc.); Vandal (*Napoléon et Alexander I*, etc.); Houssaye (*Jéna et la campagne de 1806*, etc.) are the chief authorities. For his **private** affairs, the works of Masson (*Napoléon et sa famille*; *Joséphine*; *Napoléon chez lui*, among others) are the best. For his public career, Driault (*La Politique extérieure du Premier Consul*; *Austerlitz*, etc.; *Le Grand Empire*; *La Chute de l'Empire*) and Kircheisen are probably the most important authorities. The better of the smaller biographies have been mentioned under Book III, Chapter IV (The Directory).

In addition, for the separate chapters, see:

For Book I, Chapter I (Napoleon Bonaparte becomes **Master** of France):

Atteridge: *Napoleon's Brothers*.
J. H. Clapham: *Sieyès*.
Chuquet: *La Jeunesse de Napoléon*.

For Book I, Chapter II (Napoleon Bonaparte becomes Monarch in France):

R. B. Mowat: *Diplomacy of Napoléon*.
W. Geer: *Napoleon and His Family*.
Cambridge History of British Foreign Policy.

For Book I, Chapter III (The Crystallization of the Revolution):

Esmein: *Cours élémentaire du droit français*.
Brissaud: *A History of French Public Law*.
Rose: *The Personality of Napoleon*.

For Book I, Chapter IV (Napoleon becomes Master in Europe):

H. A. L. Fisher: *Napoleonic Statesmanship in Germany*.
Rosebery: *Life of Pitt*.
J. H. Rose: *Life of William Pitt*.
　　William Pitt and the Great War.
　　William Pitt and Napoleon.
G. H. Priest: *Germany since 1740*.
Treitschke, *Germany in the Nineteenth Century*.
E. F. Henderson: *Short History of Germany*.
F. Schevill: *The Making of Modern Germany*.
Southey: *Life of Nelson*.
Mahan: *Influence of Sea Power on the French Revolution and Napoleon*.
　　Life of Nelson.

For Book II, Chapter I (The Continental System):

Heckscher: *The Continental System*.
H. Adams: *History of the United States*.
Melvin: *Napoleon's Navigation System*.
Tolstoi: *War and Peace*.

H. Belloc: *Napoleon's Campaign in 1812.*
E. Tarlé: *Le Blocus continental et le royaume d'Italie.*

For Book II, Chapter II (Liberation, Abdication, and Restoration):

E. F. Henderson: *Blücher and the Uprising of Prussia against Napoleon.*
G. S. Ford: *Stein and the Era of Reform in Prussia.*
J. R. Seeley: *The Life and Times of Stein.*
Oman: *The Peninsular War.*
Napier: *The Peninsular War.*
Meinecke: *Weltbürgertum und Nationalstaat.*
L. Madelin: *Fouché.*
Dubreton: *Louis XVIII.*

For Book II, Chapter III (Restoration and Reaction in Europe):

F. Freksa: *A Congress of Intrigue.*
W. A. Phillips: *The Confederation of Europe.*
Cresson: *Holy Alliance.*
Cambridge History of British Foreign Policy.
Webster: *British Diplomacy, 1813–1815.*
　　　　The Congress of Vienna 1814–1815.

For Book II, Chapter IV (The Hundred Davs):

Houssaye: *Waterloo.*
J. C. Ropes: *Waterloo.*
A. L. Guérard: *Reflections on the Napoleonic Legend.*
H. A. L. Fisher: *Bonapartism.*
P. Guedalla: *Second Empire.*
J. Park: *Napoleon in Captivity.*
N. Young: *Napoleon in Exile: St. Helena*
Houssaye: *1815.*
Becke: *Waterloo and Napoleon.*
Le Gallo: *Les Cent Jours.*

CHRONOLOGICAL TABLE

1713. Treaty of Utrecht.
The Bull *Unigenitus*.
1715. September. Death of Louis XIV. Accession of Louis XV.
The Regency.
1716. May. John Law's Royal Bank created.
1717. August. The Compagnie d'Occident founded.
1719-1721. War between France and Spain.
1720. Collapse of Law's schemes.
1723. Death of the Duke of Orleans.
Montesquieu's *Lettres persanes*.
1725. September. Marriage of Louis XV and Maria Leczinska.
1726. Voltaire exiled to England.
1730. Fleury tries to enforce the Bull *Unigenitus*.
1731. March. The Family Compact confirmed by Treaty of Vienna.
1733. War of the Polish Election begins.
Voltaire's *Lettres philosophiques sur les Anglais*.
1739. February-June. The Treaty of Vienna closes the Polish War.
1740. May. Death of Frederick William I of Prussia. Accession of Frederick II.
October. The War of the Austrian Succession begins.
1742-1745. Disorders and revolutionary crisis in France.
1745. Louis XV's illness at Metz.
May. Battle of Fontenoy.
1748. April-October. Treaty of Aix-la-Chapelle closes Austrian War.
Montesquieu's *Esprit des lois*.
1750. Rousseau's first Discourse (on the Arts and Sciences).
1751. Diderot's *Encyclopédie* begins to appear.
1752. May 8. Louis XV exiles the Parlement of Paris.
1752-1754. Disorders and revolutionary crisis in France.
1753. Rousseau's second Discourse (on the Origin of Inequality).
1755. Death of Montesquieu.
1756. January-May. The Diplomatic Revolution effected.
May. The Seven Years' War begins.
Voltaire's *Essais sur les Mœurs*.
December 13. Parlement obliged to accept the Bull *Unigenitus*.
1757. November. The Battle of Rossbach.
December. The Battle of Leuthen.
Helvétius's *De l'Esprit*.
1759. July. The Capture of Quebec.
August. The accession of Charles III of Spain.
Jesuits expelled from Portugal.
The *Encyclopédie* temporarily suppressed.
1760. Battles of Liegnitz and Torgau.
October. Death of George II of England. Accession of George III.

1762. June. Death of Peter III of Russia. **Accession of Catherine II.**
August 6. Parlement dissolves French Jesuits.
Rousseau's *Émile* and *Contrat social.*
1763. Treaties of Hubertusburg and Paris close Seven Years' War.
1764. Jesuits expelled from France with royal sanction.
Voltaire's *Dictionnaire philosophique.*
1765. Death of Francis I of Empire and Austria. **Accession of Joseph II.**
1766. Lorraine annexed to France.
The execution of La Barre.
1768 Corsica annexed by France.
1769. August 15. Napoleon Bonaparte born.
1770. April. Trial of the Duc d'Aiguillon.
May. Marriage of Louis and Marie Antoinette.
1771. January 19–21. Parlement of Paris exiled. **Maupeou Parlement** created.
Accession of Gustavus III of Sweden.
1772. August. First Partition of Poland.
1774. May 10. Death of Louis XV. **Accession of Louis XVI.**
July. Treaty of Kutchuk-Kainarji.
August. Turgot as Controller-General.
1776. Caisse d'Escompte created.
May 10. Turgot resigns. Clugny as Controller-General.
July 4. American Declaration of Independence.
1777. Necker appointed Director-General of Finances.
The Battle of Saratoga.
1778. February. French alliance with the United States.
July. War of the Bavarian Succession.
Death of Voltaire.
Death of Rousseau.
1779. Liberation of serfs on French royal domain.
1780. November. Death of Maria Theresa.
The *Encyclopédie* completed.
1781. Publication of Necker's *Compte Rendu.*
May. Necker resigns.
October. Cornwallis surrenders at Yorktown.
November. Joseph II abolishes serfdom in Austria.
1781–1783. Joly de Fleury and D'Ormesson as Controllers-General.
1783. September. Treaty of Paris closes the War of the American Revolution.
November. Calonne as Controller-General.
Pitt appointed Prime Minister.
1784. July. Death of Diderot.
1785. August. The Diamond Necklace Affair.
1786. August. Death of Frederick II of Prussia. **Accession of Frederick William II.**
Treaty of Eden.
1787. February 22. Assembly of Notables meets.
April. Calonne dismissed. Brienne as Controller-General.
May 25. Assembly of Notables adjourns.

June–October. Revolution in Holland.
August 6.   Exile of the Parlement of Paris.
August 15.   Austria and Russia declare **war on Turkey.**
September 24.   Parlement recalled.
Beginning of the Belgian Revolution.
Constitutional Convention at Philadelphia.
1788 May 8.   *Cour plenière* created.
July.   The Assembly of Vizelle.
August 8.   Estates General summoned.
August 25.   Necker summoned to Ministry.
November.   Second Assembly of Notables.
December.   Death of Charles III of Spain.   Accession of Charles IV.
December 27.   Third Estate given double representation.
1789. January 24.   Royal Lettres on the elections.
May 5.   Opening session of the Estates General.
June 17.   Third Estate declares itself the National Assembly.
June 20.   Tennis Court Oath.
June 23.   Third Estate defies King after Royal Session.
June 27.   Union of the three Orders.
July 11.   Dismissal of Necker.
July 14.   Capture of the Bastille.
July 17.   Louis XVI accepts Paris revolution.
August 4–13.   Privileges, serfdom, tithes, and dues revised or abolished.
August.   The Declaration of Rights accepted.
September 10.   Unicameral legislature created.
September 21.   Suspensive veto adopted.
October 5–6.   Popular uprising obliges King's removal to Paris.
October–November.   Division of France into active and passive citizens.
November 2.   Church property placed at disposal of the State.
December 19.   Assignats created.
December.   The Favras Affair.
1790. February.   Death of Emperor Joseph II.   Accession of Leopold II.
February–October.   The Nootka Sound Controversy.
March–May.   Redemption of feudal rents required.
April.   The Easter uprising in the Midi.
April 14.   The State assumes responsibility for the Church.
June 19.   Abolition of Nobility.
July 12.   The Civil Constitution of the Clergy adopted.
July 14.   The Fête of the Federation.
August.   The Nancy mutiny.
September 4.   Necker resigns.
September 6.   Naval mutiny at Brest.
September 29.   National Assembly authorizes 1,200,000,000 l. in assignats.
November 27.   Civil oath required of clergy.
December.   Leopold II suppresses the Belgian Revolution.

December 26. Louis XVI sanctions the civic oath of the clergy.
Burke's *Reflections on the French Revolution*.
1791. February. The *Chevaliers du poignard* affair.
March 2. Guilds abolished.
April 2. Death of Mirabeau.
May 7. Toleration of non-juring clergy granted.
June 14. The Chapelier Law against *compagnonages*.
June 21–25. Flight to Varennes and return to Paris.
July 5. The Padua Circular.
July. The Feuillant Club organized.
July 17. The Massacre of the Champ de Mars.
August 27. The Declaration of Pillnitz. Repeal of the *marc
d'argent*.
August 30. Peace between Austria and Turkey by the Treaty of
Sistova.
September 13. The union of Avignon with France.
September 14. The King accepts the Constitution of 1791.
September 30. The close of the National Assembly.
October 1. The Legislative Assembly meets.
November 16. Pétion defeats Lafayette for mayoralty of Paris.
November. King vetoes decrees against émigrés and non-juring
clergy.
December 24. Ultimatum on émigrés to Archbishop of Trier.
1792. January 9. Peace between Russia and Turkey by Treaty of Jassy.
February 7. Alliance of Prussia and Austria.
March 1. Death of Emperor Leopold II. Accession of Francis II.
March 10. Dismissal of Narbonne.
March 24. Roland ministry appointed.
March 29. Assassination of Gustavus III of Sweden.
April 20. France declares war upon Austria.
May. Louis XVI vetoes decrees on clergy and armed camp.
June 12. Dismissal of the Roland ministry.
June 20. Invasion of the Tuileries.
July 11. Declaration of *la patrie en danger*.
July 27. The Brunswick Manifesto.
August 10. Attack on Tuileries. Suspension of Louis XVI.
August 20. Desertion of Lafayette.
September 2–6. The prison massacres.
September 20. The Cannonade of Valmy. Last meeting of the
Legislative Assembly.
September 21–25. The creation of the French Republic.
October 21. Custine captures Mainz.
November 6. The Battle of Jemmapes.
November 19. The first "propaganda decree."
November 27 The annexation of Savoy.
December 11. The trial of Louis XVI begins.
December 15. The second "propaganda decree."
1793. January 4. Committee of General Defense created.
January 21. Execution of Louis XVI.

January 23. The Second Partition of Poland.
February 1. France declares war on England and Holland.
February. "Volunteer" army of 300,000 authorized.
March 7. War between France and Spain declared.
March 9–29. Revolutionary Tribunal established.
March 18. Dumouriez defeated at Neerwinden.
March 21. Local revolutionary committees created.
March 28. Property of émigrés confiscated.
March. The beginning of the Vendéan revolts.
April 3–7. The Committee of Public Safety created.
April 5. The desertion of Dumouriez.
April 23. Washington's declaration of neutrality. Deportation of non-juring clergy permitted. The "triumph" of Marat.
April 30. Representatives on Mission granted extraordinary powers.
May 4. The first law of the Maximum.
May 18. The Commission of Twelve created.
May 31–June 2. Expulsion and arrest of the Girondin leaders.
June 24. The Constitution of 1793 completed.
July 10. The Committee of Public Safety reorganized.
July 13. The assassination of Marat.
July 17. All feudal dues abolished.
July 27. Robespierre added to the Committee of Public Safety.
August 1. The metric system adopted.
August 10. Constitution of 1793 adopted but revolutionary government demanded.
August 14. Carnot and Prieur de la Côte d'Or added to Committee of Public Safety.
August 23. Levée en masse decreed.
August 28. Admiral Hood occupies Toulon.
September 5–6. Popular demonstration in Paris. Billaud–Varenne and Collot d'Herbois added to Committee of Public Safety. Revolutionary Army created. Law of forty sous. Division of Revolutionary Tribunal.
September 8. The Battle of Hondschoote.
September 17. The Law of Suspects.
October 10. Government declared "revolutionary until the peace."
October 14. Battle of Wattignies.
October 16. Execution of Marie Antoinette.
October 31. Execution of the Girondins.
November 10. The Worship of Reason inaugurated.
December 4. The "Constitution of the Terror" accepted.
December 19. Toulon surrenders to Republican Army.
The French East India Company scandal.
1794. February–March. The Ventôse decrees on property.
March 17–24. Trial and execution of the Hébertists.
April 3–6. Trial and execution of the Dantonists.
June 1. The sinking of Le Vengeur.
June 8. The inauguration of the Religion of the Supreme Being.

June 10.   The law of 22 Prairial.
June 25–26.   The Battle of Fleurus.
July 24.   Capture of Antwerp.
July 27–28.   Arrest and execution of the Robespierrists.
August 12.   Reorganization of the Revolutionary Tribunal.
August 24.   Reorganization of the Committee of Public Safety.
September 21.   Pantheonization of Marat.
November 11.   The Jacobin Club closed.
December 8.   The Girondins readmitted into the Convention.
December 16.   Carrier sentenced to death.
December 23.   The Maximum laws repealed.
December 27.   Pichegru invades Holland.
1795. January.   Depantheonization of Marat.
January 19.   Pichegru captures Amsterdam.
February 9.   Treaty of Peace with Tuscany.
February 15.   Treaty of La Jaunaie with Vendéans.
March.   The trial of Barère, Vadier, Billaud, and Collot.
March 21.   Uprising of 1 Germinal An III.
April 1.   Uprising of 12 Germinal An III.
April 5.   Treaty of Basel with Prussia.
May 7.   Fouquier-Tinville executed.
May 16.   Treaty of peace and alliance at The Hague with Holland.
May 20.   Uprising of 1 Prairial An III.
June 10.   Death of Louis XVII.
June 12.   Revolutionary government suppressed
June 22.   Treaty of Basel with Spain.
June 27–July 20.   The Quiberon Expedition fails.
July.   Jay's Treaty ratified by the Senate.
August 22.   The "two-thirds" decree.
October 1.   Belgium incorporated with France.
October 5.   Bonaparte suppresses Vendémiaire insurrection.
October 25.   Confirmation of laws against émigrés and non-juring clergy.
October 26.   Close of the Convention.
November 2.   The Directory inaugurated.
November 25.   The third partition of Poland.
December 31.   Pichegru grants Austrians an armistice.
The White Terror.
1796. February 27.   The Pantheon Club closed.
March 27.   Bonaparte takes command of the Army of Italy.
April 28.   The Armistice of Cherasco.
May 10.   Arrest of Babeuf.   Battle of Lodi.
May 15.   Treaty of Paris between France and Sardinia.
May.   Rebellion in Ireland.
August 2–4.   Battle of Castiglione.
August 19.   Treaty of San Ildefonso between France and Spain.
September 10.   Babeuvists attack Camp at Grenelle.
September.   Jourdan and Moreau retreat in Germany.
October 16.   Cispadine Republic created.

October 31. Directory's decree forbidding importation of English goods.

October. French recapture Corsica.

November 15–17. Battle of Arcola.

November 16. Death of Catherine II. Accession of Paul I.

December 16. Hoche starts for Ireland.

1797. January 1. Hoche returns without having reached Ireland.

January 14. Battle of Rivoli.

February 2. Mantua capitulates.

February 4. Assignats repudiated.

February 14. Battle of Cape St. Vincent.

February 19. Treaty of Tolentino between France and the Pope.

April 18. Preliminaries of peace at Leoben.

May 2. Mutiny of English sailors at Nore.

May 16. New Republic of Venice inaugurated.

May 27. Babeuf and Darthé condemned to death.

June 15. The Ligurian Republic established.

July 9. Cisalpine Republic created.

September 4. The coup d'état of 18 Fructidor An V.

September 19. Death of Hoche.

September 25. The "Consolidated Third" created.

October 11. Battle of Camperdown.

October 17. Treaty of Campo Formio.

October. Beginning of XYZ affair.

December 16. Opening of Congress of Rastatt.

Death of Frederick William II of Prussia. Accession of Frederick William III.

1798. February 15. The Roman Republic established.

March 9. The Congress of Rastatt yields the Left Bank of the Rhine.

March 29. The Helvetic Republic established.

May 11. The *Coup d'état* of 22 Floréal An VI.

May 28. Bonaparte sails for Egypt.

June 12. The Capture of Malta.

July 1. Alexandria occupied by the French.

July 21. The Battle of the Pyramids.

August 1–2. The Battle of Aboukir Bay (the Nile).

December 4. The French declare war on Naples.

1799. January 2. England, Russia and Turkey start the Second Coalition.

January 23. The Parthenopæan Republic established.

March 12. Austria declares war on France.

March 19–May 20. The siege of Acre.

April 28. French envoys to Congress of Rastatt attacked.

June 18. The Conciliar *coup d'état* of 30 Prairial An VII.

July 25. Bonaparte defeats Turks at Aboukir.

August 15. The Battle of Novi.

August 22–23. Bonaparte sails from Egypt.

September 16. The Battle of Zurich.

October 9–16. Bonaparte goes from Fréjus to Paris.
November 9–10. The *coup d'état* of Brumaire.
December 25. The Constitution of the year VIII inaugurated
1800. January 1. The new legislature meets.
February 17. Departmental prefectures created.
March 3. Lists of émigrés closed.
March 18. French court system reorganized.
March. Pius VII becomes Pope.
June 14. The Battle of Marengo.
September 30. Treaty of Mortefontaine between France and the
United States.
December 3. The Battle of Hohenlinden.
December 24. The 3 Nivôse plot to kill Bonaparte.
The League of Armed Neutrality of the North.
1801. February 9. Treaty of Lunéville between France and Austria.
March. Resignation of Pitt.
March 24. Murder of Paul of Russia. Accession of Alexander.
March 29. Peace between France and Naples.
April 2. First bombardment of Copenhagen.
July. Concordat of 1801 between Pius VII and Napoleon.
August 30. French Army of Egypt surrenders.
October. Peace between France and Russia.
1802. March 25. The Treaty of Amiens.
April 8. The Concordat of 1801 promulgated.
May. The Vendéan war ends.
May. Bonaparte made Life Consul.
June 7. Capture of Toussaint l'Ouverture by Leclerc.
August 2. Constitution of the Year X accepted.
French educational system revised.
1803. February. Act of Mediatization in Switzerland.
March–April. The *Reichsdeputationshauptschluss.*
April 30. Louisiana purchased by the United States.
May 18. War declared by England on France.
Emmet's rebellion in Ireland.
1804. February–March. The Cadoudal conspirators arrested.
March 21. The execution of the Duc d'Enghien. The Civil Code
promulgated.
April. Pitt becomes Prime Minister again.
May 18. The French Empire established by the Constitution of the
Year XII.
December 2. Coronation of Napoleon.
1805. March. Napoleon reorganizes the Batavian Republic.
May 26. Napoleon becomes King of Italy.
July 7. Austria joins the Third Coalition.
October 21. Battle of Trafalgar.
October 22. Capture of Mack's army at Ulm.
November 3. Treaty of Potsdam between Prussia and Russia.
November 13. Capture of Vienna
December 2. Battle of Austerlitz.

June 29.   Prussians occupy Montmartre.
July 8.   Louis XVIII reënters Paris.
July 15.   Napoleon surrenders to Captain Maitland.
September 26.   Foundation of the Holy Alliance.
October 7.   Execution of Marshal Ney.
October 17.   Napoleon reaches St. Helena.
November 20.   Second Peace of Paris.   The Quadruple Alliance.
November 27.   The Kingdom of Poland proclaimed.
1818. France admitted into Quadruple Alliance.
1821. May 5.   Death of Napoleon.
1824. Death of Louis XVIII.   Accession of Charles X.
1830. Overthrow of Charles X.   Accession of Louis Philippe.
1848. Overthrow of Louis Philippe.   Louis Napoleon President of the French Republic.
1852.   The establishment of the Second Empire under Napoleon III.
1870. Overthrow of Napoleon III.   The Third Republic established.

December 15.   The Treaty of Schönbrunn.
December 26.   Treaty of Pressburg between France and Austria.
1806. January 23.   Death of Pitt.
January.   The Ministry of All the Talents.
February–October.   Peace parleys between England and France.
March 30.   Joseph Bonaparte declared King of Naples.
May 16.   Order in Council blockading coast from the Elbe to Brest.
June 5.   Louis Bonaparte made King of Holland.
July 4.   Battle of Maida.
July 12.   Confederation of the Rhine established.
August 1.   End of the Holy Roman Empire.
August 25.   Execution of Palm.
September 13.   Death of Fox.
October 8.   War between France and Prussia.
October 14.   Battles of Jena and Auerstadt.
October 25.   Capture of Berlin.
November 21.   Berlin Decree.
Congress passes Non-Importation Act.
1807. January 7.   Order in Council prohibiting trade between French ports.
February 8.   Battle of Eylau.
April–June.   Convention of Bartenstein of Russia, Prussia, Sweden, and England.
June 14.   Battle of Friedland.
July 7–9.   Treaties of Tilsit.
September 2–5.   Bombardment of Copenhagen.
October 4.   Stein organizes new Prussian Ministry.
October 9.   Emancipation of Prussian serfs.
October–November.   French invasion of Portugal.
November 8.   Russia declares war on England.
November 11.   Order in Council permitting trade with France only through England.
December 17.   Milan Decree.
French Commercial Code.
Code of Civil Procedure.
Abolition of slavery in the British Empire.
Congress adopts the Embargo Act.
1808. March 1.   Jefferson signs the Non-Intercourse Act.
March 17.   Consistories for Jewish communities in France authorized.
March.   University of France organized.
April.   The Bayonne Decree.
May 2.   The *Dos de Mayo* at Madrid.
June 15.   Joseph accepted by Junta as King of Spain.
June.   The Tugendbund established.
July 22.   The Capitulation of Baylen by Dupont.
August 1.   Joseph withdraws from Madrid.
August 21.   Wellesley defeats Junot at Vimiero.
August 30.   French surrender Portugal by Convention of Cintra.

September 8.   Military treaty between France and Prussia.
September 27–October 14.   Congress of Erfurt.
November 19.   Local government in Prussia reformed.
December.   Napoleon in Spain.
French Criminal Code.

1809.   January 5.   Stein obliged to flee Prussia.
January 18.   Battle of Corunna.
April 6.   Archduke Charles proclaims First War of Liberation.
April.   English under Wellesley return to Portugal.
May 12.   Capture of Vienna.
May 17.   Annexation of Papal States by Napoleon.
May 21–22.   Battle of Aspern and Essling.
July 5–6.   Battle of Wagram.
July 28.   Battle of Talavera.
July–September.   The Walcheren Expedition fails.
October 14.   Treaty of Schönbrunn–Vienna.

1810.   March.   Napoleon divorces Josephine.
March 23.   The Rambouillet Decree.
April 1.   Napoleon marries Marie Louise.
May 1.   Congress passes the Macon Bill No. 2.
July.   Napoleon annexes Holland.
August.   Masséna invades Portugal.
August.   The Tariff of Trianon.
September 29.   The Battle of Busaco.
October–March, 1811.   Siege of the Torres Vedras Lines.
October.   The Fontainebleau Decree.
December.   Napoleon annexes Hamburg, Bremen, and Oldenburg.
December 31.   Alexander's tariff breaks with Continental System.
University of Berlin established.
French Penal Code.

1811.   March 20.   Birth of Napoleon II.
May 16.   Battle of Albuera.
University of Breslau established.
Prussian peasants granted two-thirds of their land.

1812.   January 19.   English capture Ciudad Rodrigo.
April 7.   Wellington takes Badajos.
April.   Alliance of Sweden and Russia.
May 3.   Coalition of England, Russia, and Sweden.
May 12.   Treaty of Bucharest between Russia and Turkey.
June 19.   The United States declares war on England.
June 24.   The invasion of Russia begins.
July 19.   Wellington captures Salamanca.
August 12.   Wellington captures Madrid.
September 7.   Battle of Borodino.
September 14–19.   Capture and Burning of Moscow.
October 19–December 14.   Retreat from Moscow.
November 18.   Allies forced back into Ciudad Rodrigo.
November 28–29.   Battle of the Beresina River.
December 30.   Convention of Tauroggen.

1813.   January 25.   Concordat of Fontainebleau.
February 5.   Marie Louise designated as Reg
February 26.   Treaty of Kalisch between Rus
May 2.   Battle of Lützen.
May 20–21.   Battle of Bautzen.
June–August.   Armistice of Pläswitz.   Congress
June 14–15.   Alliance of Prussia, Russia, and En
bach.
June 21.   Battle of Vittoria.
June 26.   French army retreats across Pyrenees.
June 30.   Napoleon refuses Austrian offer of mediat
August 12.   Austria declares war on France.
August 26–27.   Battle of Dresden.
September 9.   Treaty of Töplitz.
October 8.   Bavaria joins Coalition by Treaty of Ried
October 16–19.   Battle of Leipsic.
October 30.   Battle of Hanau.   French surrender last s
in Spain.
November.   The Allies issue the Frankfort Declaration.
December.   Allies announce intention to reduce size of F

1814.   January 14.   The Treaty of Kiel.
January.   Pius VII returns to Rome.
February 10–14.   Battle of Vauchamps.
February 14–15.   Wellington captures Bayonne.
February 27.   Battle of Orthez.
March 1.   Battle of Laon.
March 1–9.   Treaty of Chaumont.
March 31.   Allies enter Paris.
April 4.   Abdication of Napoleon.
April 12.   Artois enters Paris.   Soult surrenders Toulouse.
April 13.   Treaty of Fontainebleau.
April 18.   Armistice between Soult and Wellington.
April 20.   Napoleon's farewell to the Imperial Guard.
May 3.   Louis XVIII enters Paris.
May 4.   Napoleon arrives in Elba.
May 30–31.   The First Peace of Paris.
May 31.   Louis XVIII grants the Constitutional Charter.
September.   The Congress of Vienna begins.
December 24.   Treaty of Ghent between the United States and England.

1815.   January 3.   Secret Defensive Triple Alliance.
January 21.   Funeral of Louis XVI and Marie Antoinette.
March 1.   Napoleon lands in France.
March 20.   Napoleon enters Paris.
April 22.   The Additional Act to the Constitutions of the Empire
May 2–3.   Battle of Tolentino.
June 8.   Federal Act adopted at the Congress of Vienna.
June 16.   Battles of Quatre Bras and Ligny.
June 18.   Battle of Waterloo.

INDEX

INDEX

Berlin Decree, 374–75, 376, 377, 378
Bernadotte, Marshal Charles, 294, 301
323, 327, 368, 385, 396, 406, 412, 431
Berne, 77, 433
Berthier de Sauvigny, 136, 140
Bessarabia, 396
Billaud-Varenne, Jean-Nicolas, 242,
247, 248, 251, 257, 260, 261, 262,
267, 268, 269, 270
Bill of Rights, English, 71
Bishops, in Ancient Régime, 46–51;
against Jansenists, 93; on Civil
Constitution of the Clergy, 161, 174
Bismarck, Prince Otto von, 423
Black Forest, 287
Black Sea, 113 n.
Blücher, Field Marshal Gebhard
Leberecht von, 366, 393, 406, 409,
410, 444–47, 448
Bodin, Jean, 18, 68
Body Guard of the King, 148–50, 203
Bohemia, 394, 406
Boissy d'Anglas, François-Antoine,
270, 273
Bolingbroke, Lord Henry, 19, 62, 82,
114
Bolivia, 349
Bologna, 285
Bonaparte family, 238, 310, 379, 411;
Carlo, 310, 311, 313; Lucien, 238,
301 and n., 302–03, 442–43, 448;
Maria-Laetitia Romolino (Madame
Mère), 289, 310; Marianne, 313;
Pauline, 345. See also Jerome,
Joseph, Josephine, Louis, Napoleon.
Bordeaux, 40, 67, 140, 218, 237, 238,
246, 248, 405; Archbishop of, 143
Bordeaux et Bayonne, Intendency of,
10
Borghetto, battle of, 284
Borodino, battle of, 398, 407
Bosquet, 33
Bossuet, Jacques-Bénigne, Bishop, 18,
47
Bouche de Fer, by Fauchet, 153
Bouchotte, Jean-Baptiste-Noël, 255
Boudry, Monsieur de, 107
Bouillé, Marquis François-Claude de,
182, 186
Boulainvilliers, Comte Henri de, 106
Boulogne, 334, 358
Bourbon, House of, 7, 148, 308, 316,
321, 323, 334, 336, 337, 349, 353,
405; in Spain, 89, 177–78, 180, 279;
in Naples, 365, 382, 434; Restoration
of, 410, 411, 412–21, 429, 439, 441,
449, 453; Duke of, 90
Bourdon (de l'Oise), François-Louis,
255, 260
Bourgeoisie, as officials, 8, 9, 10, 52;
taxation of, 23; demands of, 28; at-

titude of, 42–44, 57; size of, 44; as
nobles, 52–53; Montesquieu on, 69,
71; among Physiocrats, 81; as citi-
zen guard, 132, 134; in National As-
sembly, 145, 147, 152–76; buy
church lands, 168; in Legislative As-
sembly, 196; in Convention, 217,
255; in Directory, 274, 276; in
Restoration, 414, 419
Bourse, 133, 147, 350
Brandenburg, 112
Braunau, 367
Brazil, 376, 422
Breisgau, 289, 324
Bremen, 376, 385 and n. 2.
Breslau, University of, 394; Treaty of,
401
Brest, 182, 295, 374
Breteuil, Baron Louis-Auguste de, 133
Breton Club, 140, 153. See Jacobins.
Brézé, Duc de, 126, 127, 128–29
Brienne, Napoleon at, 297, 311
Brienne, Archbishop Loménie de, 47,
100–02, 161
Brissot, Jacques-Pierre, before Revo-
lution, 83; as Mason, 85; on America,
86; as friend of negro, 153–54, 171 n.;
as Jacobin, 189, 190; in Legislative
Assembly, 195–96, 206, 211; in Con-
vention, 216
Brissotins. See Girondins.
Brittany, 8, 9, 15, 21, 26, 94, 140, 205,
284
Brody, 384
Brumaire, Coup d'état of 19th, 301–04,
315, 316
Brune, Marshal Guillaume, 300, 315,
316, 453
Brunswick, 371; Duke of, 367; Mani-
festo, 205–06, 234
Brunswick-Oels, Duke of, 395
Brussels, 133, 266
Bucharest, Treaty of, 396
Buchez and Roux, 141
Buckle, Henry Thomas, 70
Buffon, Georges Louis Leclerc de, 78
Bülow, General Friedrich Wilhelm
von, 445
Buonarroti, Philippe Michel, 283
Bureaux, 13
Burgundy, 7, 9
Burke, Edmund, 223
Busaco, battle of, 390
Buzot, François, 145
Byron, George Gordon, Lord, 78
Cadiz, 359, 360, 404
Cadoudal, Georges, 335, 336, 339
Caen, 10, 237, 238
Cahiers de doléances, 3, 34, 35, 37, 42,
50, 105, 117–20, 145, 156